The Victorian Woman

THE
VICTORIAN
WOMAN

by Duncan Crow

STEIN AND DAY/*Publishers*/New York

First published in the United States of America by
Stein and Day/*Publishers* 1972
Copyright © Duncan Crow 1971
Library of Congress Catalog Card No. 74-185885
Printed in the United States of America
Stein and Day/*Publishers*/7 East 48 Street, New York, N.Y.
ISBN 0-8128-1447-9

Contents

Contents

Illustrations

Illustrations

WHO WAS SHE?

Who was the Victorian woman?

To answer that question we must first answer another. Exactly what does the word 'Victorian' mean? When, to whom, and where does it apply?

Victorian is an ambiguous word. Its purely temporal meaning has been overlaid by an innuendo of denigration that was first given to it early in the twentieth century by a new generation antagonistic towards everything that Queen Victoria's reign seemed to represent. A reference point for this antagonism was provided by Samuel Butler's posthumous novel *The Way of All Flesh* which, although it had been written in the 1870s, was not published until 1903. Later this derogatory use of the word received powerful reinforcement from the fastidious mockeries of Lytton Strachey's *Eminent Victorians* published in 1918. 'Victorian' was confirmed in its panoply of disapproval. It carried with it overtones of stuffy complacency, moral certainty, priggery, resistance to change, dullness, lack of humour, over-ornateness, frowstiness, narrow-mindedness; to call someone Victorian in their outlook or behaviour was to accuse them of reaching the ultimate in reaction. Used in its temporal sense Victorian was generally qualified by early, mid, or late. But in its new colours the qualification disappeared and the denigration was allowed to sweep over the whole reign as if there were no distinction between one part of it and another.

Even if the denigration were justified the idea of a coherent whole certainly was not.

Victoria's reign lasted sixty-four years. 'It starts,' as Kitson Clark has so graphically epitomized it, 'with gentlemen fighting duels; it ends with gentlemen playing golf.'[1] To apply the

[1] Kitson Clark, *The Making of Victorian England* (Methuen, 1965).

adjective Victorian to both is correct, although to do so is to strip the word of the colours that later uses have painted over it. In this book Victorian is used to mean the whole period from 1837 to 1901. The word is restored to its unadorned, colourless, temporal sense and then a new colour is painted over it. This new colour need be neither praiseworthy nor derogatory; what one feels about it depends on one's own beliefs. The new colour is 'change' – 'Victorian' means 'from 1837 to 1901' and connotes a time of 'violently contrasted, rapidly changing life'.

To take some examples of this rapid change, consider first the revolution in transport. In 1837 the traveller, switching from stage to stage, could cover about 150 miles in twenty-four hours. This was hardly farther than he could travel in a day 5,000 years ago. Man had never been able to travel faster than a horse could carry him or the wind could blow his ship. Suddenly these limitations disappeared. The railway age, inaugurated in 1830 by the double track between Manchester and Liverpool, made it possible to travel 1,000 miles in twenty-four hours. In May 1869 when the first American trans-continental railroad was completed a journey of four months was cut to four days. And at sea when the *Sirius* and the *Great Western* in 1838 opened regular steam crossings of the Atlantic, the eastward voyage was cut from twenty-two to fifteen days and the westward from thirty-four to seventeen. The revolution in transport had a cataclysmic effect on the social, economic and political life of Victorian Britain and the United States.[1]

Nor was it only the transport revolution that had this effect. The commercial development of the telegraph was equally cataclysmic. By 1872 the first system of world-wide conveyance of thought without transportation was complete.

These contact techniques of steam and telegraphy which totally transformed the scale of human economic and social operations were evolved in the 1830s, a decade which for this reason, if for no other, marks the divide between the ancient

[1] And on personal happiness too. 'Oh, if you knew what joy this intelligence gave me,' wrote Fanny Kemble from Philadelphia on May 7, 1838, when she heard the news about the steamships. 'It seemed at once to bring me again within reach of England and all those whom I love there. And even though I should not therefore return thither the oftener, the speed and certainty with which letters will now pass between these two worlds, hitherto so far apart, is a thing to rejoice at exceedingly.' (Frances Anne Kemble, *Records of Later Life* (1882), Vol. I, pp. 145–6.)

and the modern. Thus Victoria came to the throne at the dawn of the modern world.

These developments affected people irrespective of their sex. But there were other technological changes which had a profound effect primarily on women. For example, the invention of the sewing-machine, the application of gas and electricity to the kitchen, municipal water systems, canning, refrigeration – all contributed to a domestic revolution, which no less than the revolution in contact techniques, effected a change in human ecology and thus altered the social climate.

These changes took place at a time when populations were beginning to expand enormously, and to agglomerate in towns. This increase in scale and social density created new problems as well as intensifying old ones. Factory regulations, credit systems, public health, education, local government, all called for an administrative expertise which had never existed before. Evolving techniques for the running of this new, growing and increasingly complex industrial society was as difficult and as skilled a task as inventing the new technology itself.

The next question to be answered is 'to whom does Victorian apply?' If the word were to be used only in its non-temporal colours the answer as far as women are concerned would be either a doll-like, bread-and-butter miss swooning on a sofa, or a sickly mother dying under the strain of a dozen births, or a strait-laced, thin-lipped, middle-class prude hidden in an over-ornamented pyramid of bombazine, who bullied her servants and looked down her nose at her neighbours. The accent, perhaps, would be on prudery.

But if that were the whole answer – and there were plenty of women like those examples – it would be ridiculously restrictive. What were the silent governess, the sweated seamstress, the nail-maker and the mill-girl if they were not Victorian? Florence Nightingale, Elizabeth Stanton, Barbara Bodichon, Laura Bell, Josephine Butler, Catherine Gladstone, Elizabeth Blackwell, Isabella Beeton, Theresa Yelverton, Victoria Woodhull, Elizabeth Haldane, Catherine Walters, George Eliot, Fanny Kemble, Mary Booth, Annie Besant, Beatrice Webb – none of these would have recognized herself in the bombazined battle-axe or the simpering miss with coy ringlets. Yet all were as much Victorian women as these popular conceptions. Agnes Wickfield was a Victorian no less than Dora Spenlow.

The Victorian Woman

As with 'when', 'Victorian' is stripped of its accustomed colours and a new one is applied. The answer to 'to whom' is: any or all women who lived in that time of violently contrasted, rapidly changing life between 1837 and 1901. By this definition the catchment-period includes a few women who were born as long ago as, say, 1770 and many who were alive when this book was published. If this seems over-extensive it should be remembered that everybody, to quote G. M. Young in his *Portrait of an Age*, 'is a little older or younger than somebody else' and that, therefore, if one is to comprehend all the generations which lived and influenced each other between 1837 and 1901 one must look to the outer limits of those generations, for 'the sequence of the generations is a continuous stream' and not a succession of time-segments. In practice it is true, the outer limits are of small significance – measuring significance by the crucial social yardstick of how much influence is wielded on other generations living at the time. Thus the very old in their chimney-corners at the beginning of the reign and the very young in their cots at the end are of little significance in the present instance.

But even with this slight contraction of the catchment-period a vast parliament of women is left. To consider it in any individual detail is clearly impossible. On the other hand to be overly synoptic in a search for ambitious generalizations would defeat the purpose of the book. As Aldous Huxley said in one of his later essays 'Generalizing about Woman is like indicting a Nation – an amusing pastime, but very unlikely to be productive either of truth or of utility'.[1]

The third question is 'Where?' To what areas does the word Victorian apply? Does it apply only to Britain, or does it apply as well to any other country?

In this book 'Victorian' is taken to apply primarily to Britain but also to refer extensively to the United States where there was a similarity in social attitudes until well on in the period. This similarity would have been hotly denied at the time. The antipathy between England and America was fierce and deep-rooted. There was little admiration for America in England, except among those who were trying to exist on sixpence a week and who saw it beckoning to them in their

[1] Aldous Huxley, 'Hyperion to a Satyr' in *Adonis and the Alphabet* (Chatto and Windus, 1956), p. 148.

14

dreams. For the Americans, hatred of England was part of their national heritage. The history of the United States began in battle against the English, and its pre-history was a warning of that battle. The single theme of its early literature, which was the literature of oratory, was the tyranny of England. Thirty years after the battle for independence England once again became the enemy in the war of 1812 and once again was defeated by the new American nation. Thereafter America turned its back on Europe which it considered corrupt, tyrannical, and oppressed by its aristocracies, and looked instead across the mountain wall behind its eastern states to the great hazy untouched West. But the influence of Europe, and especially of England, remained strong, at least until after the Civil War.

The Victorian woman, then, was any woman who lived at any time between 1837 and 1901, principally in Britain but also in the United States, and who had not reached the age of the chimney-corner before 1837. This book looks at the changing conditions under which half the population lived during those years.

1. *Top left:* Mrs Josephine Butler, *née* Grey, (*right*)
Mrs Mary Booth, *née* Macaulay, with her first child,
1873. *Bottom left:* Miss Florence Nightingale, aged 37,
after the Crimea, from a portrait, now in the National
Portrait Gallery, by Sir George Scharf, (*right*) Mrs
Thistlethwayte, *née* Laura Bell.

Part One
THE LOOKING-GLASS

'Women have served all these centuries as looking-glasses possessing the magic and delicious power of reflecting the figure of man at twice its natural size.'

Virginia Woolf, *A Room of One's Own*

2. Mrs Sallie Coles Stevenson in London, 1839, from a portrait by G. P. A. Healy.

Miss Adeline de Horsey about the time of her marriage in 1858 to the Earl of Cardigan who had led the Charge of the Light Brigade.

Chapter 1
ANATOMY OF PRUDERY

At the beginning of Queen Victoria's reign England was still predominantly an agricultural nation, a land of small towns and villages, of country seats and their surrounding estates, with only patches of industrial concentration to make, as George Eliot described it in *Felix Holt*, 'but crowded nests in the midst of the large-spaced, slow-moving life of homestead and far-away cottages and oak-sheltered parks'. The countryside was ruled by the local landowners who presided over their parishes in a state which often approached feudal splendour. Above them were the great nobles who lived with all the trappings of regality in great castles attended by hordes of servants. The power of the landed aristocracy in local affairs was all-embracing and was in no way lessened by the Reform Act of 1832 which loosened the ruling oligarchy's hold on the central political machine and reflected the rising strength of the middle classes. Until the end of the century – and beyond – the squires and lords of the manor ruled their local kingdoms with small interference from central authority. It was the local Justices of the Peace who were the focal point in each community and what they said and did was of more importance to the agricultural labourers in their hovels than the speeches in Parliament and the dictates of the Queen's Ministers.

The ladies of the manor were no less autocratic than their lords. One outstanding example to have been preserved in memoir is Augustus Hare's 'Grandma Leycester', a relation of the Stanleys of Alderley, who bullied the curates and made the village schoolgirls sing for her. She would see that there were no mumblers, 'dragging their mouths open by force and if they would not sing properly, putting her fingers so far down their throats that she made them sick'. But even centuries of autocratic landowners had not destroyed a spirit of independence. One day when Grandma Leycester was putting her fingers down little Margaret Beeston's throat Margaret bit her violently. When she was reprimanded for her wickedness she replied, 'What'n her put her fingers down my throat for. Oi'll boite her harder next time.'

There was nothing unusual in being knocked about by the Grandma Leycesters of the world. As Augustus Hare says, 'No servant would have thought of giving up a place which was essentially a good one, because they were a little roughly handled by their mistress. In those days servants were as liable to personal chastisement as the children of the house and would as little have thought of resenting it.'

Life, especially in the country, was ferocious, rugged and uncouth, with no refinements and few comforts to temper the barbaric conditions. It was a drinking age, and drink was the main alternative to work. When the men of Raveloe in George Eliot's *Silas Marner* were not working they were drinking in The Rainbow. With only one pub Raveloe was ill-served. In the remote, sparsely-populated Cumberland parish of Caldbeck, for example, there was no school, but for every eighteen of the three-hundred population there was a public-house or jerry-shop. 'The man who did not get drunk would have been the black swan which the white ones would have soon pecked to death,' wrote the fierce anti-feminist Mrs Lynn Linton,[1] whose father, James Lynn, was rector of the parish from 1814 to his death in 1855.

Vicar Lynn had small success in curbing the hard drinking of his parishioners or in changing their other customs, among them that pregnancy had to precede marriage. 'Not a man would have held himself justified in marrying before the woman had proved her capacity for becoming a mother.' The vicar's wife might have been a civilizing influence had she been able to hold mothers' meetings and Bible classes. But she was too busy being a mother herself to have time to spare for parishioners. In seventeen years of marriage Alicia Lynn bore twelve children, the last of them a few months before her death. The only

[1] Mrs Lynn Linton, *The Autobiography of Christopher Kirkland* which was, essentially, her own autobiography, though with names and sexes altered.

other lady 'of her own degree' in the parish was the squire's wife, Mrs Backhouse, and she bore child for child with Mrs Lynn.

Even if Mrs Lynn and Mrs Backhouse had had time to devote to parish work one may doubt whether it would have had much effect. Saturday nights in Caldbeck were spent in drinking and fighting, and to these orgies came a neighbouring parson who was more punctual at the fights, in which he took part, than he was at his own church next day. Sunday morning among the male parishioners was the occasion not for going to church but for a shave. Twenty was a good attendance at a Sunday morning service and 'in afternoons, when folks were late, the old clerk would ring the bell for a short three minutes, then shut the church door in a hurry – even if he saw someone coming in at the lych-gate – glad to be quit of his irksome duty for that day'.

James Lynn was also vicar of Crosthwaite, the parish in which the town of Keswick stands. Keswick was less uncouth than Caldbeck, though its moral standards were no different. It had a High School, a few resident gentry, and a coach to London three times a week, a journey which took three days and two nights.

Writing to her sister forty years later Mrs Linton recalled what their life in Keswick had been like: 'I should like to go over the old roads with you, and go back to the house where we were so young and so bored! We were not happy then, sweetheart. Life was frightfully dull to us, and wholly without colour or interest. Don't you remember how we flew to the Sunday School and Bible classes for interest?'

Mrs Lynn Linton's recollection of boredom can be matched by a host of other examples in the memoirs of the day. In the first volume of Augustus Hare's autobiography, for example, he refers frequently to the boredom and stagnation of country life and in one instance tells of a family in the Shires where there was so little to do out of the hunting and shooting season that the two uncles passed the time by trying to provoke each other and the young ones to yawn. Mrs Ellis, the writer of popular books on etiquette and social behaviour in the 1830s and '40s, has a passage in her *Women of England* in which she gives a picture of a family, bored with itself, antagonistic, trying to pass the evening: 'Looks are directed askance, books are opened and their leaves are methodically folded over; and yet the long dull evening will not wear away.' It is on such occasions, she told her readers, that a woman by her conversation should restore good-will, arouse interest, and make the evening pass happily. The women Mrs Ellis's books were written for had to spend a lot of time 'in the useful labour of the needle', or nursing, or just being 'at their humble, quiet houses where excitement from extraneous causes seldom comes' and where without conversation 'their days are indeed heavy, and their evenings worse than dull'. In *Cassandra* Florence Nightingale, before she began her nursing career, cried to God against the weariness and boredom of an empty life.

And Mrs Lynn Linton's description of the rough life at Caldbeck can also be matched a thousand times. At Hawarden, which lay on the main road between Chester and Holyhead, the main excitement for the 'Hardeners' was the passing of the mail coach four times a day, a passage that was much dreaded by the coachman and outside passengers because the villagers would gather in front of the many public-houses and pelt the coach with all the choicest muck from the middens. Mrs Lynn Linton's husband, W. J. Linton, the chartist and engraver, recalls in his *Memories* the yearly fairs at Bow and Camberwell and Smithfield, 'permitted gatherings these of unruly crowds, for whom was provided the roughest kind of amusement, theatrical and other, coarse, vulgar, and obscene, to suit the lowest tastes'. In the old days these fairs had met the conveniences of trade, but when Linton was a child they had become 'mere disorderly nuisances, a disgrace to even the rough "civilization" of the early part of the nineteenth century'. In 1837 that civilization was still rough. Britain was a land of violence, its coasts in the hands of smugglers, its roads under the rule of highwaymen, its towns subject to the mob.

Civilizing By Ignoring

Boredom and brutality were two outstanding characteristics of life in Early Victorian Britain. But they were not the only ones. They were accompanied by hypocrisy and prudery and snobbishness. And there are other valid epithets: energetic, ebullient, self-satisfied, earnestly exuberant – the first Victorians were all of these.

In *The Making of Victorian England* Dr Kitson Clark suggests the reasons for these outstanding Victorian characteristics: 'The concentrated industry of Victorians was the natural habit of men confronted by new and exciting opportunities. The uneasy Victorian snobbery was probably the result of the impact of new classes who wanted to secure their position in a traditional hierarchy, Victorian hypocrisy the result of the attempt to lay claim to new standards of conduct which proved to be too hard to maintain consistently, Victorian prudery the result of a struggle for order and decency on the part of people just emerging from the animalism and brutality of primitive society. These are probably signs of the pressures and strains in a community undergoing the process of growth and change.'[1]

That Victoria's reign was only a paper-width from the harsh centuries is a fact often forgotten. Because the Victorians had the appurtenances of modern life in unsophisticated form – railways, steamships, gas, summer holidays and, later in the century, electricity, telephones, refrigerated meat – they are often judged by later standards, standards which would not be adopted in passing judgement on, for instance, Boswell's London. Hypocrisy, prudery, and probably snobbery too, were the pawls that were used to prevent the ratchet-wheel of progress slipping back. If they are regarded in this light and not as characteristics that were unnecessarily adopted they assume a different significance. It is easy to despise Victorian hypocrisy, and the whole euphemistic approach that went with it, forgetting that this blinkered attitude was adopted to hide the proximity of the abyss in which seethed the primitive society the Victorians were struggling away from. It was a matter of whistling to keep up their courage. Possibly they felt that if they spoke the talisman words of hypocrisy and prudery often enough it would help to make those words come true – at least it would disguise the fact of how tenuous was their hold on this pleasanter life. To acknowledge the existence of a vice, was, they believed, to encourage it. Their only defence against slipping back into the slime was, it seemed, to ignore the immorality and horrifying cruelties that surrounded them, and to adopt the canons of ultra-propriety. Any concession to tolerance or laxer living would be to lift the pawl and start the slide back to total barbarity – or at any rate it would allow the still-surrounding darkness to encroach into the drawing-room. The family was

[1] Kitson Clark, op. cit., p. 64.

the only unit around which the defensive moat of respectability could be dug and guarded. The drawing-room was the citadel.

This attitude of 'civilizing by ignoring', the attitude which said, 'if you don't look at it, it will go away', had begun to gain acceptance by the 1820s. It was a reaction against the attitude current during the Napoleonic wars which had shown itself, as far as women were concerned, in the classical under-dressed form of fashion and in an inquiring outspoken mind with a tendency towards emancipation in thought and even, occasionally, emancipation in deed. In place of this classical outspokenness came the romantic attitude that disguised itself in periphrasis and euphemism – euphemism in thought, euphemism in speech, and euphemism in dress, which became ornately Gothic. A glorious example of the euphemistic approach that became the touchstone of Victorianism is this quotation from a book of minor morals written in the 1840s: 'The peculiar province of Woman is to tend with patient assiduity around the bed of sickness; to watch the feeble steps of infancy; to com-municate to the young the elements of knowledge, and bless with their smiles those of their friends who are declining in the vale of tears.' This is not only euphemistic in language, but even more euphemistic in thought, for it is euphemistically reminding woman that it is her place to be an unintelligent, subjected soother, that and nothing more. By the time of Victoria's accession romanticism, as the essence of this quotation shows, was degenerating into anaemic sentimentalism. Added to the wealth-imposed idleness of middle-class gentility it produced the image of the ideal Victorian lady.[1]

One notable consequence of making the drawing-room into the citadel of respectability was a fundamental change in the social attitude towards sex and its place in human relations.

[1] According to Virginia Woolf it was damp, 'the most insidious of all enemies', that was the root cause of the degeneration! The clear bracing climate of the eighteenth century gave way to damp, which crept into everything, altering the constitution of the English. 'Men felt the chill in their hearts; the damp in their minds. In a desperate effort to snuggle their feelings into some sort of warmth one subterfuge was tried after another. Love, birth, and death were all swaddled in a variety of fine phrases. The sexes drew farther and farther apart. No open conversation was tolerated. Evasions and concealments were sedulously practised on both sides.' (*Orlando* (Hogarth Press, 1928), p. 207.)

As part of the grand strategy for civilizing society so that it became safe for the rising middle classes it was deemed necessary to tame the savagery of sex so that it was no longer the gambolling cruel priapic anarchist that brought misrule through the carefully daubed dykes of propriety. The way to achieve this most effectively, it seemed to the collective subconscious of the 'civilizers', was to ban sex as far as possible from everyday life and to enlarge to its fullest extent the interpretation of the sixth commandment so that it brought social anathema and hell-fire not only on adultery but on all lewd thoughts and fumblings.

The first step was to drive sex out of the respectable household. Admittedly if this were to be done entirely and literally the procreation of children and with it the indisputable right of the head of the household to exercise his genital instincts would be stopped, a result that would defeat the main purpose if, as was sure to happen, the roughs continued to breed without restraint and in due course, by simple weight of numbers, forcibly inherited the earth. The solution was to apply the euphemistic approach and turn the begetting and bearing of children into an Eleusinian mystery. Ideally women would produce children by parthenogenesis; failing that, male impregnation should take place in a dark bedroom into which the husband would creep to create his offspring in silence while the wife endured the connection in a sort of coma, thereby precluding any stigma of depravity which would have been incurred by showing signs of life. Silence was important. If what went on in the dark bedroom was never mentioned, then, by a reversal of the psychological process which gives substance to a thought merely by the naming of it, sex could be dematerialized by ignoring it.

Having confined sex beneath the bedclothes by what is after all the acme of euphemism, that is by refusing to recognize its existence, another essential line of attack was to remove all other traces of it from the household. To ban it from conversation was easy enough: stern remonstrance and corporal punishment would keep the young in line. To ban it from the immediate sight was facilitated by the change in fashion which made women bell-shaped with skirts that concealed everything except the toe. Who could so much as imagine two female legs within that dome of drab material? Powerful aids as well as the

25

pulpit, were enlisted to keep the enemy in check. Anxiety-making doctors promised disease and disintegration to those who transgressed the ascetic rules against sex. Hideous instruments were sold to prevent masturbation. And lest any thoughts of sex should be encouraged through reading books an effective censorship was exerted on novel-writers by the economically all-important circulating libraries, like Mudie's, opened in 1842, which refused to stock a book unless it eschewed the faintest suspicion of sex. Above all the embargo on sex had its anchor in the new moral attitude of the young Queen's Court which totally rejected the farmyard frankness of earlier reigns.

'In the Covering. . . . Consists the Indecency'
In Aldous Huxley's *Crome Yellow* (set in the 1920s) one of the characters, Mr Scogan, quotes an anecdote about the French Court 'as an illustration of the customs, so genially frank, of the sixteenth century', and says he might have quoted other anecdotes to show that the customs of every other century were equally genial and frank – every other century bar the nineteenth. 'It was the astonishing exception,' he says. 'And yet, with what one must suppose was a deliberate disregard of history, it looked upon its horribly pregnant silence as normal and natural and right; the frankness of the previous fifteen or twenty thousand years was considered abnormal and perverse. It was a curious phenomenon.'[1]

Scogan's view is the generally accepted one. But it is not wholly correct. The Early Victorians did not invent prudery, nor did they invent 'the virgin in the drawing-room', which was what in fact, and despite her prolific offspring, they turned the Early Victorian lady into. Prudery was part of the puritan ascetic attitude to human existence and had existed since long before the nineteenth century, had existed in the Middle Ages, had existed at least since the early Christian Fathers and their Jewish predecessors. But not until economic conditions made 'gentility' possible did the social climate permit the long-nurtured plants of prudery and the other repressive aspects of puritanism to burst forth and flourish in the particular colours of the age. By the time Victoria came to the throne they were coming into full flower. Similarly the virgin in the drawing-room was the re-creation in a new setting of the beneficent

[1] Aldous Huxley, *Crome Yellow* (Chatto and Windus, 1922), p. 154.

great mother of antiquity. 'In the Middle Ages, when sex was frantically denied, the great mother image was saved by making her a virgin [i.e. the Virgin Mary]; her sexual processes did not exist. The Victorians after a lapse of some centuries brought her back as the bell-shaped angel who, to all intents and purposes, by means of a conspiracy of silence, also produced young by parthenogenesis.'[1] All this was not so much a deliberate disregard of history as Huxley's character suggests but rather the victory in an age-old struggle for those forces which in the past had usually, except for short periods, been overborne.

The United States provided especially fertile soil. Here the plant of prudery in the 1830s was sufficiently farther forward than across the Atlantic for English visitors to remark on its profusion with wonder. Harriet Martineau in a catalogue of 'the indulgent and chivalrous treatment' that was accorded to the American woman as a substitute for justice noted that 'especially, her morals are guarded by the strictest observance of propriety in her presence'.[2] Mrs Trollope, too, saw and heard many examples of over-affected modesty that aroused her scorn. She had a literary conversation in Cincinnati with a gentleman, professed to be a scholar, who regarded Shakespeare as obscene, inveighed against Byron, had never heard of Ford and Massinger, and held up his hands in horror at the very title of Pope's *Rape of the Lock*. A young German gentleman told her that he had once greatly offended an important local family by saying the word 'corset' in the presence of its ladies. A signpost representing a Swiss peasant girl with her ankles showing below her petticoat caused the ladies of Cincinnati to boycott the pleasure garden where it was displayed until the petticoat was painted longer. She was told that a picnic she proposed would never come off because it was considered 'very indelicate for ladies and gentlemen to sit down together on the grass'. Nude statues were regarded as obscene spectacles, and in Philadelphia at the nineteenth annual exhibition of the Pennsylvania academy of the fine arts she found that visitors had marked and defaced 'the casts in a most indecent and shameless manner'. Men and women visited this antique statue gallery in alternate groups. When Mrs Trollope arrived at the

[1] Hoffman R. Hays, *The Dangerous Sex: The Myth of Feminine Evil* (Methuen, 1966), p. 230.

[2] Harriet Martineau, *Society in America* (1837), Vol. II, p. 156.

door an old woman, evidently the guardian of the gallery, bustled up and told her, 'Now, ma'am, now: this is just the time for you – nobody can see you – make haste. The ladies like to go into that room by themselves, when there be no gentlemen watching them,' she added in explanation.

And yet despite this hyper-delicacy Mrs Trollope found herself shocked at some of the immodesty that went with it. To make her point she recounted an anecdote which 'is hardly fit to tell, but it explains what I mean too well to be omitted'. A young married lady, 'of high standing and most fastidious delicacy', told her that her house was opposite 'a mansion of worse than doubtful reputation'. One day the young lady and a lady friend were sitting at the window when they saw a young man they both knew ride up and go into the brothel. They went into the garden and watched for him at the gate. When he came out they stepped forward. 'Are you not ashamed to ride by my house and back again in that manner?' the young lady asked him. 'I never saw a man look so foolish,' she commented to Mrs Trollope.[1]

Another English visitor to the United States at this period was Captain Marryat, author of *Peter Simple* and *Mr Midshipman Easy*, who described his journeyings in *A Diary in America* published in 1839. Like Mrs Trollope he noticed that the Americans objected to everything nude in statuary.[2] This ridiculous sensitiveness applied also to language; there were certain words never used in America, but for which an awkward substitute was employed. Marryat gave an example of a young lady whom he was escorting at Niagara Falls and who slipped and grazed her skin. When he asked her if she had hurt her leg she turned away much offended. After some hesitation she told him that 'leg' was a word never mentioned before ladies; 'limb' should be used instead. 'Nay,' continued she, 'I am not so

---

[1] *Domestic Manners of the Americans*, 1832, passim. Mrs Frances Trollope, mother of Anthony Trollope and herself a prolific writer, went to America accompanied by three of her children at the end of 1827 to try to re-establish the family fortunes. She spent four years there, two of them in keeping an 'emporium' in Cincinnati. Instead of making a fortune the store lost money. The only thing left for her was to write a travel book, which she did with marked success.

[2] Similar manifestations of prudery were not unknown in England. Later in the century, for example, the Venus de Milo in the Leeds Art Gallery was concealed by aspidistras.

particular as some people are, for I know those who always say limb of a table, or limb of a piano-forte.'

Some months later Captain Marryat discovered that she was correct in her assertion that some people were more particular than even she. He escorted a lady to a seminary for young ladies. 'On being ushered into the reception room, conceive my astonishment at beholding a square piano-forte with four *limbs*. However, that the ladies who visited their daughters, might feel in its full force the extreme delicacy of the mistress of the establishment, and her care to preserve in their utmost purity the ideas of the young ladies under her charge, she had dressed all these four limbs in modest little trousers, with frills at the bottom of them!'

These piano legs in their modest little trousers became the symbol of prudery amongst its enemies. They may well have been the only ones of their kind – certainly there is no documentary evidence that anyone else ever actually saw piano legs similarly clothed, although there are plenty of reports of people who said they knew someone who had seen them. Nevertheless, unique or not, they gave rise to a whole tradition of trousered furniture and thirty years later when the great Girl of the Period controversy was raging a cartoonist who wanted to show his opinion of the anonymous author of that article depicted her as a hideous harridan painting at an easel which had its legs encased in drawers with frills at the bottom of them.[1]

The Americans, wrote Captain Marryat, 'forget that very often in the covering, and the covering only, consists the indecency, and that, to use the old aphorism – "Very nice people, are people with very nasty ideas"'.

Respectable Fears
If one were to judge simply from the novels of the day one might imagine that the banishment of sex had been achieved, that prudery was everywhere triumphant, and that this part at least of 'respectable' strategy had been totally successful. But apart from any other considerations such an artless judgement would ignore the important factor of man's perennial ambivalence to woman, his apprehensions about the dangerous nature of female sexuality and his hostility towards her, no less

[1] See Chapter 12.

than his pleasure in the cowed and doll-like 'looking-glass' that reflected him at twice his natural size.

Sex, of course, had not been banished from the land. Forbidden in the houses of the respectables it lost none of its strength elsewhere. If woman had been turned into the virgin in the drawing-room she had to compensate for this by being the prostitute elsewhere; and because of the extreme cosseting she received in the respectable home so the swing of ambivalence demanded that she be degraded and subject to physical brutality in her role as the hired instrument of man's pleasure outside the home. 'Thus,' says Hoffman Hays, 'the split concept, virgin and prostitute, was born.'[1]

It is difficult to be sure why this happened. Presumably the basis of it was that male apprehensions, which had gradually become quiescent over the centuries, were somehow re-activated through the discontents of industrial society producing unbearable tensions. While the Victorian age was economically expansive and forward-looking there were strong conflicts emotionally and intellectually. Religion became an arena of passionate belief and argument as against the calm, rationalist approach of the previous century. The Bible and the security which it offered were frighteningly challenged by Darwinism and the new sciences of anthropology and psychology. There was insecurity too in the memories of the Terror during the French Revolution and these memories were reinforced by the seething workers' riots that punctuated Victoria's reign, and by the Paris Commune in 1871. In coming to power themselves the middle classes had destroyed the feudal system which kept the masses in check. Their enjoyment of prosperity and economic expansion was shot through with the nightmares of the dark in which the appalling prospect of worker domination arose. 'All of these fears and tensions,' says Hays, 'were wound in and out of the relationship between the sexes.'[2]

All this suggests, correctly, that the 'Top Nation' Victorians felt their finger-hold on the new civilization to be so slight that it would take little to upset the whole affair and throw them back into the stews. The respectables were always conscious of the roughs lurking in the alleys. Sometimes, indeed, they emerged from the alleys into the main thoroughfares. Sir

[1] Hoffman R. Hays, op. cit., p. 231.
[2] ibid., p. 232.

William Hardman, a mid-Victorian chronicler, mentions several of these onslaughts which were done under cover of 'rough larking'. In July 1867 he writes of 'these wretches who are the great bane of London at present, who take occasion of all bands of music, processions, and suchlike, to defy the police, knock all respectable hats over their owners' eyes, and pick all respectable pockets'. That same summer at the great Volunteer Camp at Wimbledon, 'of course the roughs (damn them) had a fine time of it, and broke through all barriers, playing havoc with the respectables'. And in November the Lord Mayor's Show was marred, as it always was, by the violence of the roughs. 'I have said for many years,' wrote Hardman, 'that the mob of roughs which this annual spectacle brought into our streets was a sight hideous and most terrible.' What was true of mid-Victorian England was even truer of the beginning of the reign when the police forces were much more rudimentary.

Nothing is so conducive to a reactionary frame of mind as the fear that one's comforts may be snatched away. Believing that human beings were still fundamentally barbarous the respectables felt the imperative need to enforce rigid tenets of behaviour without which violence and the rule of the roughs would again become supreme. And by the beginning of Victoria's reign there were plenty of people who were anxious to avoid that catastrophe: the merchants and tradesmen, and the growing professional class which was itself largely called into being by the new society. Nor was it only because they were fearful of losing their physical possessions. It was also because they were unwilling to lose the opportunity to gain and use knowledge which this new society gave them. Primitive societies had no need of engineers, nor did they give opportunities to scientists. Primitive societies destroyed Priestley's instruments. New societies watched Faraday's experiments.

Chapter 2

THE GOLD LACE HATS

The Reform Act passed in 1832 was the first inroad the rising middle classes made into the political preserves of Britain's ruling oligarchy. Before the Act was passed the lower classes, encouraged by those who wanted to see the aristocracy's power curtailed, had had wild hopes that it would also give enormous benefits to themselves. In one of her numerous books of reminiscence Lady Dorothy Nevill, a descendant of Horace Walpole, tells of an elderly couple peacefully sleeping in their four-poster who were roughly aroused at an early hour by their excited maidservant bursting into the room and shouting 'It's passed! It's passed!' 'What's passed, you fool?' called the irritated old lady from inside the bed-curtains. 'The Reform Bill,' shouted the girl, 'and we're all equal now' – after which she marched out of the room leaving the door wide open to demonstrate her equality.[1]

But they were not all equal. The lower classes soon discovered that their hopes had been totally without foundation. In the bitter reaction that followed they began to form their own political organizations, and in 1836 the Chartist movement originated with the foundation of the London Working Men's Association. The People's Charter had six points. It demanded manhood suffrage, vote by ballot, equal electoral districts, annual Parliaments, no property qualification for M.P.s, and payment of M.P.s. The bitterness of the Chartists stemmed not only from the feeling that they had been duped by the Reform Act but also because of the terms of the hated Poor Law Act of 1834, which brought destitution to many of the agricultural

[1] Ralph Nevill (ed.), *Leaves from the Note-Books of Lady Dorothy Nevill* (Macmillan, 1907), p. 2.

districts. And there were other sources of discontent: trade unionists were resentful of the transportation of the Tolpuddle Martyrs in 1834, factory reformers were disappointed with the ineffectiveness of the 1833 Factory Act. For fourteen years, until it collapsed in the fiasco of its monster meeting on Kennington Common in April 1848, Chartism seethed through the mass of the working classes and haunted the respectables. Behind the ritual of Victorian respectability lurked the spectre of revolution

While this menace of the two nations was large in men's minds another struggle, less violent but no less deadly, was also going on. It was a struggle to decide who were to be the privileged. Was political control and the power that went with it to remain with the landowners despite the Reform Act, or was it to pass to the manufacturers whose riches, if perhaps not as great as those of the aristocrats, were nevertheless substantial? The struggle was epitomized in Disraeli's *Coningsby* published in 1844. Was power to stay with Lord Monmouth, Harry Coningsby's grandfather or was it to pass to Coningsby's father-in-law, Millbank, the Manchester manufacturer?

At the same time as this political struggle for supremacy was going on, the womenfolk of the middle-class attackers flattered their opponents by slavish imitation; in every respect possible they aped the ladies of the aristocracy. The closer their own status approached to the nobility the more ardently they worshipped. As George Meredith realized, snobbery is merely a form of egoism. 'I see now,' he wrote in *The Ordeal of Richard Feverel*, 'that the natural love of a lord is less subservience than a form of self-love; putting a gold-lace hat on one's image, as it were, to bow to it.' But though their dress and furnishings and social habits might follow closely in the shadow cast by the ladies of the Upper Ten Thousand, as Gladstone called them, the gulf between them was as great as that which stood between themselves and the poor.

To cross the gulf and be received in Society was an exercise that many attempted but few succeeded in. Wealth, as Mrs Sallie Coles Stevenson wife of the American Minister in London noted on her arrival in England from the United States in July 1836, was 'nothing as to the rank it gives, tho' all important as to the comforts. In vain rich bankers and merchants give feasts of which Lucullus might have been happy to have partaken; they are forced to keep within their own magic circle.'[1] Later in the century it was different. Wealth, whatever its origin, became a certain sesame into Society; but early in Victoria's reign Society was a closed and exclusive body, an assemblage of people who, according to Lady Dorothy Nevill's definition, 'either by birth, intellect, or aptitude, were ladies and gentlemen in the true sense of the word. For the most part fairly, though not extravagantly, dowered with the good things of the world, it had no ulterior object beyond intelligent, cultured, and dignified enjoyment, money-making being left to another class which, from time to time, supplied a selected recruit to this *corps d'élite*.'[2]

'Laborious beyond Anything'

The lives of the Upper Ten Thousand – the 'Gold Lace Hats' – were regulated by seasons as inexorable as the seasons of nature. From April to July and again from October to Christmas they congregated in London to dance and visit and dine, to go to the opera (where the nerves of one young visiting American dandy were 'affected terribly' by the décolletage),[3] to visit the Zoo on a Sunday when the animals were of secondary interest only, to drive in the Park, to exchange political gossip. Politics were inextricably entangled with Society; indeed the London season was timed to coincide with the session of Parliament, and political fortunes could be seriously affected by drawing-room gossip. 'I can give you no idea of London now,' Mrs Stevenson wrote to her Virginian sisters in May 1838. 'The streets and parks are crowded like the ballroom and I sometimes get jammed up in a fashionable street. Hyde Park is a spectacle to a foreigner, such splendid equipages, liveries etc. etc., so many beautiful women on horseback and dashing beaux. The routs are formidable. Mr Stevenson goes to them. I do not venture often. The dinner parties are pleasant if they did not last so long.'

'The life of a real woman of fashion here is laborious beyond anything,' she wrote in another letter that same month – 'to rise at eleven or twelve (but more frequently one or two), breakfast in her dressing-room, go out at three to a concert or to the

[1] Edward Boykin (ed.), *Victoria, Albert and Mrs Stevenson* (F. Muller, 1957), pp. 21–2.

[2] Ralph Nevill (ed.), *The Reminiscences of Lady Dorothy Nevill* (Arnold, 1906), p. 100.

[3] Henry Wikoff, *The Reminiscences of an Idler* (N.Y. and London, 1880).

Park to exhibit her languid graces, dine at eight – and go to the opera and three and four parties besides until five in the morning! Most horrible! To go to bed when the glorious sun is rising – and that too, in a country where there is so little sunshine.' On the only occasion on which Mrs Stevenson came near to being out all night at parties it made her so nervous that she couldn't sleep and felt as if she 'had been doing something very wicked'.[1]

The customs of fashionable London did not all transplant successfully to the republican air of America. In 1839 Mrs Stevenson's 23-year-old niece Angelica came to London with her husband, President Van Buren's eldest son Abram, on their wedding trip. Through the Stevensons the young couple had an entrée everywhere and were introduced to the splendours of life at Court. On their return to Washington, where Major Van Buren was private secretary to his father, they repaid this kindness, firstly by carrying tales to the President of the gay aristocratic life Angelica's aunt and uncle were leading in London, and secondly by introducing British Court customs at the White House. Angelica, installed as hostess for the President, dressed herself in Court fashion with a long train and a headdress of feathers, seated herself on a daïs, had her guests announced by footmen, and returned their curtseys with formal bows. The opposition to this quasi-regality was explosive and political. The President, already suspected of cosmopolitan tastes by the fiercely nationalist American voters, was blamed for his daughter-in-law's aristocratic pretensions and his defeat in the 1840 presidential election was largely the result of this un-American activity.

When the London season ended some people went abroad to the German spas or else travelled ponderously about the Continent. Fanny Kemble wrote to her friend Mrs Jameson on August 1, 1837 that 'after a riotous London season' her family had 'broken itself into small pieces and dispersed. My mother is at her cottage in Surrey . . . ; my father and sister are gone to Carlsbad – is not that spirited? – though indeed they journey in search of health rather than pleasure.' Lady Dorothy Nevill recalled that when her family travelled on the Continent at that period the party consisted of eleven: six of themselves, two maids, a footman, a French cook, and an inefficient courier. Their

[1] Edward Boykin (ed.), op. cit., pp. 137–8.

transport consisted of the family coach, a barouche, six saddle-horses with two attendant grooms, and two fourgons to hold the *batterie de cuisine* and the family's six beds, which had to be unpacked and made up every night 'for in those days there were hardly any real hotels in the country through which we travelled'.[1]

For those who preferred to remain in England in August and September the fashionable scene moved to Cowes, on the Isle of Wight, for the yachting. Thereafter, before the London season began again and after it had finished, the Upper Ten Thousand would visit each other in their country houses. It was the understood thing for people to go to certain houses at certain times each year, an annual event that was only disturbed by marriages or deaths. 'We did not expect the constant change which seems so essential now,' said Lady Cardigan in 1909 when she published her *Recollections*. 'We made and kept our friends in those conservative Early Victorian days; we enjoyed ourselves in a quiet way; husbands did not go North and wives South; we used our bed pillows to sleep on and not to fight with – in short, if the modern debutante had to stay in the country house as it was sixty years ago, she would probably think Society was about on a level with a maiden aunt's views.'[2]

Lady Cardigan (before her marriage to the general commanding the charge of the Light Brigade at Balaclava she was Miss Adeline de Horsey) was born into the Upper Ten Thousand in 1824. In February 1842 she was presented at Court and shortly afterwards went with her parents to the first fancy-dress ball given by Queen Victoria. 'Our dresses were lovely. My father wore the uniform of a Garde Française, and my mother was dressed as a Court lady of the same period. I went as a Louis XV shepherdess. Mamma took endless pains in seeing that my costume was perfectly designed and carried out, and the result amply repaid her ... My hair was exquisitely *poudré*, and my beautiful pink and white brocade gown, garlanded with roses, looked as though it had actually belonged to my prototype at Versailles.'[3] She wore her dress again at Stafford House in July when the Royal Ball was reproduced there.

[1] Ralph Nevill (ed.), op. cit., p. 20.

[2] The Countess of Cardigan and Lancastre, *My Recollections* (Eveleigh Nash, 1909), pp. 52–3.

[3] ibid., pp. 34–5.

After a gay season of innumerable balls, parties, dinners and breakfasts the de Horseys went to Cowes for the month of August. Adeline's mamma gave a ball for her at the King's House, a former residence of George IV, which they had taken that year.

From Cowes the de Horseys went to Savernake to stay with the Ailesburys who had been at Cowes with them and from there to Badminton where the Duke and Duchess of Beaufort had a large family party. And from Badminton they went to visit Lord Forester at Willey Park, Shropshire, where Adeline met Lady Jersey and her daughter, Lady Clementina Villiers. Lady Jersey was the greatest *grande dame* in London Society, and her house in Berkeley Square was the centre of the Tory Party. After Willey Park they went to Belvoir Castle, the seat of the Duke of Rutland. The fifth Duke's son, the Marquis of Granby, was a man 'of consummate tact and presence of mind', according to Lady Cardigan. At one house party he was greatly smitten by a pretty young married lady. She showed him that his interest was returned and he paid a visit to her room after she had gone to bed: 'The lady was asleep, and just as the Marquis was about to rouse her, the door opened and the husband, whom he supposed to be otherwise engaged, appeared unexpectedly on the scene. It was an embarrassing moment, but the Marquis, who was equal to the occasion, held up a warning finger and exclaimed in an anxious whisper, "Hush! Don't disturb her, she is fast asleep; I was passing, and I thought I smelt fire – but all's well." The husband thanked him with honest gratitude, and doubtless felt all the happier for being under the roof of such a solicitous host.'[1]

The de Horseys usually spent Christmas at Beaudesert, Lord Anglesey's place. 'We were always a merry party and we dined in the large hall which is one of the chief features of the house . . . There was no hunting or shooting at Beaudesert and our amusements were very simple ones. After lunch we walked over Cannock Chase, and those ladies who did not care for walking rode sturdy little ponies. We returned to tea, and after dinner there was music, cards or dancing. We thoroughly enjoyed ourselves and nobody was bored although,' as Lady Cardigan added with the sneer that the older generation never seems able to keep out of its comments on its successors, 'we did not smoke

[1] ibid., p. 60.

cigarettes, lose money at bridge, or scour the country in motor cars to kill time.'[1] Another popular way of passing the time at country houses was amateur theatricals. On a visit to the Earl of Chesterfield's seat at Bretby in the autumn of 1844 Adeline and her friends acted de Musset's *Le Caprice*.

'*Nor is it . . . lady-like to be . . . in Love*'

Aristocratic young ladies were no different from the girls in the cotton mills or the listless young ladies on their middle-class sofas – in one respect at least. They were all anxious to know their romantic future. One day, disguised in a borrowed cloak, bonnet and veil, Adeline visited a fortune-teller in Bridge Street, Westminster, 'which was not at all a nice neighbourhood'. 'Ah, my pretty young lady,' she was told. 'Fate holds a great deal in store for you. You'll not marry for several years, but when you do it will be to a widower – a man in a high position. You will suffer much unkindness before you experience real happiness, you will obtain much and lose much, you will marry again after your husband's death, and you will live to a great age.'[2]

Adeline was quite impressed, but also a little disappointed, for after her romantic daydreams the prospect of a widower was rather depressing. But the prediction came true – or else the prediction was tailored later to suit the events! Lord Cardigan was a widower and so, too, were nearly all the men who proposed to her. Lord Sherborne asked her – he was a widower with ten children. The Duke of Leeds asked her – he was a widower with eleven children. And among the other widowers who proposed to her were the Duke of St Albans, Prince Soltykoff, Disraeli, Christopher Talbot, M.P., and Harry Halfteck. As well as these proposals which she refused, she received one which she accepted from the Count of Montemolin, pretender to the Spanish throne. In the event she did not marry him because the marriage would not have been considered valid under Spanish law.

Although young ladies might dream of love it was not considered to be a necessary prerequisite of marriage. Quite the contrary. When, in the early 1830s, Catherine Gladstone's sister Mary Glynne, who later married Lord Lyttelton, persisted

[1] ibid., p. 59.
[2] ibid., pp. 37-8.

in refusing an eligible lord because she would not and could not love him, her aunt, Lady Charlotte Neville-Grenville, told her 'Women are not like men, they cannot chuse, nor is it creditable or lady-like to be what is called in love; I believe that few, very few, well-regulated minds ever have been and that romantic attachment is confined to novels and novel-readers, ye silly and numerous class of young persons ill-educated at home or brought up in boarding-schools.'

Aunt Neville's code of decorum matched her views on the undesirability of romance. When her nieces were interested in a charity bazaar she wrote to Catherine that she hoped, 'nothing may turn you and Mary into shopwomen. I declare I do not know which I should dislike most, to hear of your waltzing or your selling, those who practise the one would shine at the other.' Nor did she approve of young ladies riding to hounds: 'it lowers women in ye eyes of all and renders them what I am sorry to know many young ladies are – cheap'. Young ladies, she said, should be neither 'missy nor pushing'.[1]

Great care was needed not to make oneself 'cheap'. Adeline de Horsey damaged her reputation as a young lady by riding in the Park without a groom. Later she ruined it completely by being seen in the Row with Lord Cardigan, who was a married man. He was also an exceedingly rich one. He had seven sisters. All of them married men of title and each received a dowry of £100,000 on her wedding day. When he was young, Lord Cardigan, who was the seventh Earl, fell in love with a married woman who was divorced by her husband on his account. During the two years that elapsed before the decree was made absolute Cardigan discovered that she had an ungovernable temper. This no doubt accounted for the answer he is said to have got from her husband, when he told him of his willingness to give him satisfaction: 'Satisfaction, my dear sir,' answered the aggrieved husband. 'I look on you as my greatest friend. You have already given me the greatest possible satisfaction by taking off that bloody bitch of a wife of mine.' Nevertheless Cardigan married the ex-Mrs Johnson and lived unhappily with her for thirty-two years. In July 1858 she died, and a few weeks later he married Adeline. In 1868 he himself died after a fall from a horse and five years later Adeline became the Countess de Lancastre.

[1] Georgina Battiscombe, *Mrs Gladstone* (Constable, 1956), pp. 16 and 18.

Lady Cardigan's disregard for the conventions resulted in her being snubbed by Society. But she got her own back when she published her *Recollections* containing many stories of the aristocracy which they would rather had been left unwritten. These *Recollections* were ghost-written for her by Maude ffoulkes, who did a similar job for the ex-Crown Princess of Saxony and for that Countess Marie Larisch who was deeply involved in the Mayerling scandal.[1] That all three books of reminiscence owe much to the imaginations of the author and her subjects is undoubted. Nevertheless, Lady Cardigan's fairy tales were woven into a sufficient warp of truth to receive praise and damnation from either hand. Queen Mary, who was an expert on the habits of the aristocracy, is said to have been much diverted by the book. First published in 1909, Lady Cardigan's *Recollections* went into fourteen editions in twenty months.

'Women Have No Passion'

The lives of the Upper Ten Thousand were not all as unconventional as Lady Cardigan's, or as some of those described by her. But there were other rebellious spirits, although they were not unconventional in the sense of flouting the strict conventions of the day as far as their morals were concerned. There were a number of highly individual women who refused to limit their activities to the drawing-room accomplishments of their sisters. Some of them indeed became the yeast that started the movement for women's emancipation. The curious thing is that in several of these cases the ladies concerned were very much opposed to what came to be called Women's Rights. They were content to regard their own individual efforts as a freak of nature and not see them as the expression of a new social movement.

Queen Victoria herself was one of these. In her own daily life she combined the duties of wife and mother with those of an active Sovereign, but she did not draw any conclusion from this about the capabilities of the sex as a whole. She abhorred the idea of Women's Rights and tried to keep the professions closed to women. She was especially opposed to women doctors. She herself was always squeamish about anatomical descriptions and the idea 'of allowing young girls and young men to enter the

[1] See Violet Powell, *A Substantial Ghost* (Heinemann, 1967).

dissecting-room together' was, she wrote to Gladstone, *'awful'*. Indeed she was less upset at the cry of Votes for Women than she was at the horrifying thought of women studying things in the dissecting-room 'which could not be named before them'.[1] To her daughter Princess Alice, however, it was not a horrifying thought; in defiance of her mother she studied anatomy and marvelled at the way in which the human body was made.

Not that Queen Victoria was a woman-hater. She had her own brand of feminism, which was a chronic rage at the exploitation of 'us poor women' by insatiable husbands. 'The animal side of our nature is to me – too dreadful,' she wrote to the Princess Royal; and in another letter to her daughter, after the birth of the future Kaiser, she referred to 'that despising of our poor degraded sex (for what else is it, as we poor creatures are born for Man's pleasure and amusement)' which 'is a little in all clever men's natures. Papa even is not quite exempt though he would not admit it.'[2]

Another professed anti-feminist who had a profound effect on the position of women was Caroline Norton. It was her personal struggle to get the custody of her children from her husband that provided the spur for the Infants' Custody Act of 1839. Up to that time if a woman and her husband were living apart the wife had no rights whatsoever over her children. The new Act laid down that a judge in equity might make an order allowing mothers against whom adultery was not proved to have the custody of their children under seven, with right of access to their elder children at stated times.

There were some women who reacted against their cosseted existence by striving to break the clutching bonds of family. One of the bitterest cries against the inanity of an upper-class lady's existence was made by Florence Nightingale, whom many consider to have been the most outstanding woman of the nineteenth century. Florence was the younger daughter of a rich, upper-class family. Her mother was the grand-daughter of Samuel Smith, a rich merchant. Her father had taken the name of Nightingale when he inherited a fortune on his twenty-first birthday. Florence was born in 1820 and grew up in an atmosphere of luxury, culture and idleness. There were large country

[1] Elizabeth Longford, *Victoria R.I.* (Pan, 1965), pp. 496–7.
[2] ibid., pp. 355 and 473

houses to live in, formal gardens to walk in, foreign countries to visit, the London Season, friends, literature and all the paraphernalia of pleasant living. But for Florence this was not enough. In 1842, a year of starvation, misery and riot, she was deeply affected by the horrors she saw around her in the English countryside. She felt that she had a call from God to devote her life to some useful purpose – but what it was to be was not revealed to her until some years later when she became obsessed with the desire to nurse. But it was 'as if I had wanted to be a kitchenmaid', she said afterwards. Indeed it was worse than that for the nurses of those days were such slatterns that no properly brought up kitchenmaid would dream of associating with them.

For many years Florence's passion to do something useful with her life was so thwarted that she many times wished for death as the only release from her tortured boredom. 'What have I done this last fortnight?' she asked in her diary in 1846. 'I have read the *Daughter at Home* to father, and two chapters of *Mackintosh*; a volume of *Sybil* to Mama. Learnt seven tunes by heart, written various letters. Ridden with Papa. Paid eight visits. Done company. And that is all.' Weary neutral days and endless evenings. 'For how many years I have watched that drawing-room clock and thought it would never reach the ten! And for twenty or thirty years more to do thus!'

Marriage seemed a poor alternative. To spend her life arranging domestic things would simply be 'to be nailed to a continuation and an exaggeration of my present life' – and that would be intolerable. 'Very few people,' she wrote, 'lead such an impoverishing and confusing and weakening life as the women of the richer classes.' 'We do the best we can to train our women to an idle, superficial life; we teach them music and drawing, languages and poor peopling – "resources" as they're called, and we hope if they don't marry they will at least be quiet.'

Florence refused to be quiet. In the depths of her despair she wrote a long rambling repetitious book called *Suggestions for Thought to Searchers after Religious Truth*. Included in it is an essay called *Cassandra* which is a bitter and scornful indictment of upper-class society as it bore on women.

'Why have women passion, intellect, moral activity – these three – and a place in society where no one of the three can be exercised?' Women, she said, 'go about maudling to each other and teaching to their daughters that "women have no passion". In the conventional society, which men have made for women, and women have accepted, they *must* have none, they *must* act the farce of hypocrisy, the lie that they are without passion – and therefore what else can they say to their daughters, without giving the lie to themselves?'

The worst of all was that 'women never have a half-hour in all their lives (excepting before or after anybody is up in the house) that they can call their own, without fear of offending or of hurting someone'. There were even married women in society who had been heard to say that they wished they could break an arm or leg so that they could have a little time to themselves. Many indeed took advantage of the fear of 'infection' to get some time. 'Women have no means given them whereby they can resist the "claims of social life". They are taught from their infancy upwards that it is a wrong, ill-tempered action and a misunderstanding of "woman's mission" (with a great M) if they do not allow themselves *willingly* to be interrupted at all hours.'

It was the family which was the all-important Juggernaut crushing individual lives beneath it. 'The family uses people, *not* for what they are, nor for what they are intended to be, but for what it wants them for – its own uses. It thinks of them not as what God has made them for, but as the something which it has arranged that they shall be. If it wants someone to sit in the drawing-room, *that* someone is supplied by the family, though that member may be destined for science, or for education or for active superintendence by God, i.e. by the gifts within. This system dooms some minds to incurable infancy, others to silent misery.'

*

But while some sat in silent misery others were envying them their position. To belong to the upper class removed a woman from the thousand accidents of commercial and professional life that brought penury to middle-class homes and resulted in 'educated destitution' for the women of the household. Even if it were not on the scale of Lord Cardigan's sisters' some financial provision could always be made for the daughters of the aristocracy, and if they did not marry they became 'maiden aunts' who played a crucial part in family life – many of them indeed, like Florence Nightingale herself, played an important part on an even larger stage and throughout Victoria's reign one can trace much of the social philanthropy of the time to the actions of these women.

Chapter 3
THE MIDDLE THREE

In the first forty years of the nineteenth century the population of Britain (that is, of England, Scotland and Wales) almost doubled, rising from 10·5 millions in 1801 to 18·1 millions in 1841. As the economic activity of the country grew and became more sophisticated there was a disproportionate increase in that part of the population connected with trade and manufacture and with the professions. Theirs was an equivocal position, uneasily poised between the pull of the gold lace hats above and the clutching fingers of poverty below. When the men had achieved this middle class by their financial or professional status, the responsibility for demonstrating that they had achieved it and for maintaining them socially in this slippery position was the women's. To do this they adopted certain rules, rituals and symbols to distinguish them from the lower part of the population. Naturally the rules and rituals they adopted were copied from the upper class, but in copying them they discarded the more free and easy rough human ways of the upper class, for these, in a middle-class context, could be mis-interpreted as coarseness which would have made the middle class indistinguishable from the lower classes. The special characteristic the middle class adopted was gentility, a term that may be taken to include most of those attributes (hypocrisy, prudery, and snobbery) which are erroneously thought of as peculiarly Victorian. Naturally there was a great demand to learn how to keep oneself safe in the new 'middle' area. And it was the women's duty to learn this lesson – a duty which they eagerly accepted.

The process had begun in the latter part of the previous century. From 1760 onwards there occurred the economic and

45

technological changes which produced a new pattern of society. It began with the agrarian revolution. Engrossment of farms and widespread enclosure of common land were the two instruments that destroyed the centuries-old rural organization and substituted a new capitalist one. It was the growth of the towns, itself the result of industrial organization and growing population, that called the capitalist agriculture into being.

It is outside the scope of this book to pursue the fascinating inquiry into why the population began rapidly to increase in the eighteenth century. But the increase was fundamental, for it was on it and the demand it created for goods as well as food that the rest all hinged – the inventions, their technological feasibility, the new factories, and thus the gamut of the industrial revolution. It is often said that the agrarian revolution preceded the industrial revolution. In fact they were broadly contemporary, the one called into being with the other through demand.

What we are concerned with here is not what caused the increase in population, but what resulted from it, so far as those results affected women. Engrossment and enclosure produced the landless labourer and the landless labourer's wife at one end of the social spectrum; and at the other they produced the 'lady' in the farmhouse. There were, it is true, a number of women at this select end of the spectrum who were actively interested in the new 'scientific' agriculture; but there were many more who began to withdraw from an active participation in affairs, and towards the end of the century it was becoming rare for a gentlewoman to have any personal responsibility for her household or her dairy, which had previously been the most important and productive part of women's work in agriculture. It now became the ambition of the wealthier farmers' wives to ape the upper classes and achieve 'gentility' by doing nothing. This had a deleterious effect. 'The market and the many-sided activities of the household had provided excellent opportunities for the development and exercise of practical skill and business acumen which had no counterpart in the leisured life now adopted. The training in financial affairs and the knowledge that the family income consisted of the joint earnings of the farmer and his wife not only added interest to women's lives, but also tended to a development of independence and initiative.'[1]

[1] Ivy Pinchbeck, *Women Workers and the Industrial Revolution* (Routledge, 1930), p. 35. This is the classic study of the subject.

The desire to 'live better' brought first the separate dining-table; then the separate dining-room. Arthur Young was one of those who were severely critical of the 'foolish farmers' – or, more particularly, of the 'foolish farmers' wives', for the changes that came with a rising standard of comfort he blamed on the new attitude of the women. 'I see sometimes, for instance, a piano-forte in a farmer's parlour, which I always wish was burnt; a livery servant is sometimes found, and a post-chaise to carry their daughters to assemblies; these ladies are sometimes educated at expensive boarding-schools, and the sons at the University, to be made parsons: but all these things imply a departure from the line which separates these different orders of beings.' Young was strongly opposed to any such departure. 'Let these things, and all the folly, foppery, expense, and anxiety that belongs to them, remain among gentlemen. A wise farmer will not envy them.'[1] Perhaps not, but his wife and daughters would.

The effect of educating the daughters as 'boarding-school misses' was to make the changes more pronounced. The conventions they learnt at school were brought back to the farmhouse – and to the town houses of the merchants and the manufacturers, for their daughters too were at the same schools. It was the standardizing effect of the schools that spread the new fashions in behaviour and accentuated them. The daughters were taught to turn up their noses at the domestic chores of home, and their mothers had to keep pace with them. Had this escape from drudgery been satisfyingly used as the result of any real education it would have been all to the good. But it wasn't. The girls were taught to pass their time elegantly with the sort of drawing-room accomplishments that the ladies of the manor had stamped with gentility. Work was shunned and any gentle-woman who was obliged to earn her own living was an object of pity to her friends, as, for example, was Jane Fairfax in Jane Austen's *Emma*. The role of the archetypal Victorian lady was in fact created by her grandmother.

The women learnt their social lessons by copying others and by reading books of etiquette, of which a great many were published in the 1830s and '40s, on both sides of the Atlantic. Some were practical instruction manuals, like *Etiquette for the Ladies*, sub-titled *Eighty Maxims in Dress, Manners and Accomplishments*,

[1] *Annals of Agriculture*, Vol. XVII, pp. 156–7.

the fourth edition of which was published in 1838. *Etiquette for the Ladies* told its readers how to carve, not to eat with their knife, when to wear gloves, when to pay calls ('the proper hours for morning visits are from two to five'), what ornaments to have, and what clothes to wear ('coloured shoes are not considered consistent with good taste, though delicate pink and faint blue have each their advocates').

Other books concentrated more on attitudes. One of the most prolific authors of this type was Mrs Ellis. Among her many books found in middle-class households were *Women of England* (first published in 1839), *Daughters of England* (1843), *Wives of England*, dedicated 'by permission' to the Queen (1843), and *Mothers of England* (1845). Her *Women of England* went through sixteen editions in its first two years and was re-published again in 1843, 1844 and 1846.

In its first pages Mrs Ellis defined the readership her book was aimed at. It was those women 'who belong to that great mass of the population of England which is connected with trade and manufacture, as well as the wives and daughters of professional men of limited incomes; or, in order to make the application more direct, to that portion of it who are restricted to the services of from one to four domestics – who, on the one hand, enjoy the advantages of a liberal education, and, on the other, have no pretension to family rank'.

A calculation made some years later suggests that this potential readership might have included up to one quarter of the female population. In a book of *Essays on Women's Work* published in 1865, Bessie Rayner Parkes wrote: 'It has been roughly calculated that the middle ranks are about three times as numerous as the upper ranks; or in other words, of thirteen units, *one* would represent the aristocracy, *three* the middle ranks, and the remaining *nine* stand for the "masses".'[1]

The advice Mrs Ellis gives to the 'Middle Three' is always to steer a course between observing gentility and giving oneself false airs. She warns her Women of England against having ideas above their station whether in dress or in manners. They were gentlewomen yes, but ladies no, and they should not run the risk of the ridicule that would attend them if they aped the ladies who had nothing more to do than give orders. On the other hand they must be very careful not to indulge in looseness

[1] Bessie Rayner Parker, *Essays on Women's Work* (Strahan, 1865), p. 74.

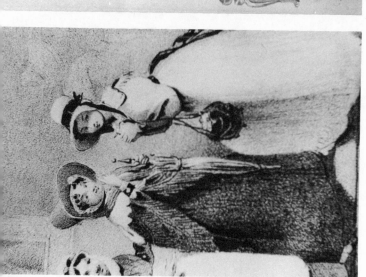

3. *Left*: Philadelphia lady on her way to church c. 1830. 'I never saw, or read, of any country where religion had so strong a hold upon the women' – Mrs Trollope *Domestic Manners of the Americans*, (*centre*) Antique Statue Gallery, 'Now, ma'am, now this is just the time for you – nobody can see you' – Mrs Trollope *Domestic Manners of the Americans*, (*right*) Young lady in concert dress, 1835.

4. *Top:* 'No mere human hands
... could have wrought such a
miracle'. The Crystal Palace in
Hyde Park, London, 1851. The
Ladies Mile (*right*) in Hyde Park
as depicted by Gustave Doré. It
was here that all the fashionable
world sauntered on foot, on horseback, and in carriages, seeing and
being seen.

of minor morals which might destroy their status as gentle-women. It was minor morals which would help to keep the dark beast of coarseness and brutality out of their homes.

These minor morals were a more intimate line of defence than religion which was, in theory at least, the great protective ethic of the time. And indeed, Mrs Ellis hinted, minor morals might be more effective than religion when one considered how men disregarded the message of Christianity even though they were regular church attenders.

Is There a Servant in the House?

The main distinguishing mark between the middle-class woman and those who were considered socially inferior was the attitude of mind which demanded that she should have at least one servant to wait on her. Nor was this aspiration unknown to later generations, and certainly until World War II brought an end to domestic service as a large-scale occupation in Britain, there were many housewives whose symbol of having 'arrived' was when they could employ a maid.

Given the all-important single servant who was the passport into the middle classes, one's exact position within the ranks of the Top Nation was indicated by the number of servants one had. To be complete a household needed three servants: a cook, a parlourmaid, and a housemaid; or, when there were children (and the first baby usually arrived before a man was fairly out of his honeymoon, 'for the honey-moon of your "happy man"', said an article on the *Ethics of Early and Frugal Marriages* in Tait's *Edinburgh Magazine* of February 1858, 'lasts at least a twelve-month'), a nursemaid instead of a parlourmaid would be employed. The single general servant would be paid about £9 or £10 a year, the housemaid and the nursemaid £1 or £2 more, and the cook's wages would be anything from £15 to £19.

With new recruits always struggling tight-lipped into the middle class it was to be expected that one of the first things they had to learn from the books of etiquette they so eagerly bought was how to treat their servants. The cardinal point to remember was that having acquired a servant one should not do her work for her. In *Wives of England* Mrs Ellis warned her new middle-class readers against this fault: 'It can never be said that the atmosphere of the kitchen is an element in which a refined and intellectual woman ought to live; though the department itself is one which no sensible woman would think it a degradation to overlook. But instead of maintaining a general oversight and arrangement of such affairs, some well-intentioned women plunge head, heart, and hand, into the vortex of culinary operations, thinking, feeling, and doing what would be more appropriately left to their servants.' This was not, however, a very prevalent fault in the 1840s. Rather was it 'the fault of our grandmothers, and we are endeavouring to improve upon their habits by falling into the opposite extreme ... in our eagerness to secure ourselves personal ease and indulgence'.[1]

Wives of England included a long chapter on the treatment of servants and dependents. Treat them like human beings, Mrs Ellis said firmly, human beings with hope and feelings, and for whom you have some responsibility. Clearly the run of middle-class housewives had the upstart corporal's attitude. Nor were their daughters any better. 'Servants are generally looked upon by thoughtless young ladies as a sort of household machinery,' Mrs Ellis says in *Women of England*. These young ladies should behave towards their servants with kindness 'blended with dignity'; and they should be considerate – not only to the servants but to their brothers and sisters too.

Mrs Ellis and the Queen

Mrs Ellis, the middle-class housewife's mentor, was born Sarah Stickney. She was brought up in the Society of Friends but later found herself unable to accept all the Quakers' tenets and became a Congregationalist. In 1837, two years after the death of his first wife, Sarah married the Reverend William Ellis, a well-known missionary.

As well as her famous *Women, Wives, Daughters* and *Mothers of England* series she wrote some two dozen books with such titles as *Summer and Winter in the Pyrenees, The Royal 'Favourite': Fisher's Drawing Room Scrapbook, The Juvenile Scrapbook, The Sons of the Soil* and *Family Secrets, or Hints to Make Home Happy.* She had strong views about girls' education and to carry them out in practice ran a school for girls called Rawdon House.

The guidance offered by Mrs Ellis's books of behaviour was in complete accord with the aspirations of her readers. Following the Queen's marriage to Prince Albert in February 1840 the

[1] Mrs Ellis, *Wives of England* (1843), pp. 261 and 262.

family home became the fulcrum of English middle-class life. The Queen and her husband were models of marital propriety and parental strictness. After the excesses and barbarities of the Regency the family life of Victoria and Albert probably saved the Crown. In Victoria's own view after twenty-two years as Sovereign, her success as a queen depended on three aspects of her family life: a moral Court, domestic harmony, and the good education of her children.[1] And in a letter to her uncle, King Leopold of the Belgians, on October 20, 1844 she wrote: 'They say no Sovereign was ever more loved than I am (I am bold enough to say) and this because of our domestic home, the good example it presents.'[2] The example was certainly of great moral importance to many of the Queen's subjects and provided an ideal for the middle classes.

The Queen was very much a woman of her time. She was moulded by the attitudes of the day, and conversely, because of her position, she helped to mould them. She was a model Lady – as the 1840s required a model Lady to be. Although she was head of the State and attended punctiliously to her duties, nevertheless she conformed to the popular acceptance that woman is a relative creature, and in her personal relationship with Albert she was in every respect a dutiful wife. She bore him nine children. One advantage at least accrued to her female subjects from this extensive motherhood. To help her during the birth of her eighth child on April 7, 1853 she allowed Dr John Snow to give her chloroform. This mark of royal approval helped Snow to popularize the use of anaesthetics. 'It might well be claimed,' says Elizabeth Longford in her superb biography, 'that Queen Victoria's greatest gift to her people was a refusal to accept pain in childbirth as woman's divinely appointed destiny.'[3]

As Mrs Ellis noted in *Women of England* the Victorian attitude inherited from previous centuries, was that women were 'from their own constitution, and from the station they occupy in the world, strictly speaking, relative creatures'. 'In her intercourse with man, it is impossible but that woman should feel her own inferiority; and it is right that it should be so', for a woman's part 'is to make sacrifices in order that his enjoyment may be

[1] See Elizabeth Longford, op. cit., p. 348.
[2] Quoted on p. 230 of E. Longford, op. cit.
[3] ibid., p. 292.

enhanced'.[1] The word enjoyment was interpreted in its widest sense to include the satisfaction of every appetite, mental and physical. It was a woman's duty perpetually to humour the male whom she had sworn to love, honour, and obey. But while it was her duty as a wife to love her husband, it was her duty as a lady to do so without passion. For a lady to derive pleasure from copulation was unthinkable; indeed medical books told her categorically that to do so showed a disturbing abnormality. A lady's duty was to shut her eyes, grit her teeth, and, as Queen Victoria is reputed to have told one of her daughters who married abroad, 'think of England', or, on a more practical level, prepare for yet another pregnancy.

Women's inferior position, said Mrs Ellis, was in accordance with the nature of things because 'the great leading defect in woman's character', was that she did not have 'a just estimate of the relative importance of things in general'. She was apt, for instance, 'to attach as much importance for the time to the failure of her musical performance, as to the failure of a bank; and she appears to care little for the invasion of a foreign country when injury is threatened to her best attire'.[2]

A woman's object in domestic life should be 'the promotion of the happiness of others', especially, of course, the happiness of her husband. It was her duty to provide a place of refuge, a sanctuary from the remorseless skin game outside. She was the guardian angel of the citadel of respectability. In John Ruskin's phrase she was the queen in 'a walled garden', who must refine man's baser instincts by giving him an all-encompassing desexualized womb into which he could retreat – 'home is always around her'. Mrs Ellis foreshadowed this Ruskinian attitude. 'To men belongs the potent ... consideration of worldly aggrandisement; and it is constantly misleading their steps, closing their ears against the voice of conscience, and beguiling them with the promise of peace, where peace was never found.' While they are still boys they have learnt to invest 'with supreme importance all consideration relating to the acquisition of wealth'. On Sundays the boy hears 'of a God to be worshipped, a Saviour to be trusted in, and a holy law to be observed: but he sees before him, every day and every hour, a strife, which is nothing less than deadly to the highest impulses

[1] Mrs Ellis, *Women of England* (1839), pp. 155 and 223.
[2] ibid., pp. 351–2.

of the soul, after another God – the mammon of unrighteous-
ness – the moloch of the world; and believing rather what men
do, than what they preach' he follows suit. It is a woman's duty
to remind the grown man that there are higher things in life
and 'to win him away from this warfare'. Her duty is to act as
his second and peripatetic conscience and to prevent him from
falling into the snares and temptations of the world. When the
tired Victorian businessman returns home 'jaded and speech-
less 'with a mind confused by the many voices which ... have
addressed themselves to his inborn selfishness or worldly pride'
it is her duty to correct him as he stands 'before the clear eye of
woman, as it looks directly to the naked truth, and detects the
lurking evil of the specious act he is about to commit'.[1]

'An Englishman in a State of Adultery Is Miserable'

For a woman the dangers of dalliance were great. If she was
found out she was ruined. Unlike a man a woman got no second
chance – 'of a man's love it must be remembered that if once
destroyed it is destroyed for ever'.[2] Mrs Ellis stressed the need for
decorum. Prudery was the only safe attitude for gentlewomen
to adopt.

'It is an unspeakable privilege enjoyed by the women of
England,' she wrote in *Wives of England*, 'that in the middle
ranks of life a married woman, however youthful and attractive,
if her own manners are unexceptionable, is seldom or never
exposed to the attentions of men so as to lead her affections out
of the proper channel. How much is gained in domestic and
social happiness by this exemption from customs which prevail
on the Continent, it is here unnecessary to attempt to describe,
for I cannot imagine there is any right-minded woman, still less
any Christian wife, who does not number it amongst the peculiar
blessings of her country and her sex. Yet,' she warned her readers, 'even in our privileged land, where the established rules of
society are so much more favourable than in others to the
purity of social morals and the sanctity of home enjoyments,
there may occasionally occur an attempted deviation from these
rules on the part of ignorant or unprincipled men.' But these
deviations, she said reassuringly, could readily be choked off
by a 'discountenancing look', and by talking happily and rapidly

[1] ibid., pp. 51–3.
[2] Mrs Ellis, *Wives of England*, p. 164.

about one's husband! Then she wagged an admonishing finger. Nothing, she wrote, would do more to invite deviations than 'speaking in complaining terms either of a husband, or of his behaviour towards yourself'. The safest defence against temptation, she told the wives of England, was a 'sincere and faithful love for the companion of your choice'. Those who wished, 'as all must do, to ward off insulting familiarity and court respectful consideration' must cultivate 'a lady-like manner'.[1]

These 'attempted deviations' were not so occasional as Mrs Ellis suggested. Certainly any woman who walked along a street in London and other large towns was liable to be pestered by pavement Romeos. In May 1869, a quarter of a century after *Wives of England* was published, the weekly London periodical *Echoes* was recording the great annoyance caused to ladies even in fashionable Piccadilly and St James's Street by street satyrs who addressed them with 'complimentary insolence'. And in January of that same year *Echoes* had attacked the *Daily News* because the newspaper contended that young ladies who were insulted by men in the street brought at least half the insults on themselves by the way they 'walked the world unmistakably self-conscious of their attractiveness'. Presumably they had not quite judged the correct amount of 'lady-like manner' to counter their natural desire to be noticed. It is a thrilling problem that every generation of young ladies has to face anew.

Public manners did not deteriorate between 1843 and 1869 – if anything they improved slightly – nor were young ladies any less conscious of their attractiveness at the beginning of the reign. Furthermore, if the deviations were only occasional in the 1840s then, before Hippolyte Taine came to England in the 1860s, there must have been a marked change in the unexceptionable morals of Mrs Ellis's readership, for Taine found that 'although marriage is regarded with profound respect and public opinion concerning it is rigid', and that 'in the great body of the nation, among well brought-up people, wives are almost invariably faithful,' nevertheless there were 'some hitches in the regard for this rule ... among the class of "tradesman", and among certain of the nobility of the second order, people of fashion, who travel and whose *moeurs* are modelled on those of the continent'. These hitches among 'the well-to-do shopkeepers' occurred 'because their women are idle. Not having, as in

[1] ibid., p. 146.

France, the recourse of the theatre and visiting, nor like the wives of gentlemen, that of patronage and the care of the poor, above the need to work, never having to cook or to sew, they wither in idleness; the great emptiness of boredom is a wide open door to seduction.' As a rule their lover was 'a man of the world, a rich gentleman who deals at their shop'. But the English character was so rooted in puritanism that it was incapable of relishing a pleasure gladly. Even for the lover, said Taine sadly, 'excepting in the case of a few profligates the situation is disagreeable. An Englishman in a state of adultery is miserable; even at the supreme moment his conscience torments him.'[1]

But it was not necessary for a deviation to go to the supreme moment before a woman lost her reputation. A waver was enough. Indeed it was enough if a waver was suspected even when none had occurred. Mrs Ellis conceded that there were many 'sufferings and inconveniences incident to women from their slavery to the opinion of the world'. But she was against any relaxation. Vigilance was essential at all times in the continual struggle against the animalism of men which would take advantage of the slightest encouragement.

Righteousness Makes Riches
To avoid the temptations and accidie of idleness women could turn to religion. This at least was a province in which they could shine and one where, according to Mrs Sandford in *Woman in Her Social and Domestic Character* (6th Edition, 1839) men would 'not infrequently defer to their judgement'. Religion was indeed a dominant interest of the middle classes and because of the importance that these 'middle three' came to have in the affairs of the nation during Victoria's reign, religion consequently became a dominant national interest.

The puritan attitude which characterized the so-called 'non-conformist conscience' of Victorian times was a facet of middle-class life that had persisted through earlier centuries. After its brief rule during the Commonwealth, in the middle of the seventeenth century, it had had to wait for the true dawn of middle-class ascendancy under Queen Victoria before it could flourish throughout the land. Institutionally it found expression in the Society for Promoting the Due Observance of the Lord's

[1] *Taine's Notes on England*, translated by Edward Hyams (Thames and Hudson, 1957), pp. 80 and 96–7.

Day which was founded in 1831, chiefly by Church of England clergymen and laymen. But it did not need to rely on a Society for its acceptance. Religion permeated the whole of middle-class life, affecting thought and conduct, and determining ethical ideals. This is not to suggest that all the 'respectables' were religious in the sense of being spiritualized. Religion connoted a standard of moral behaviour rather than a canon of theology. Conduct, not belief, was the all-important point. For many Victorians religion was not an expression of real spiritual faith. It was a tribalistic ritual insisted upon by those puritanical middle classes who were now influencing the tribe; and it was a ritual apparently sealed with Royal approval, for the public behaviour of the Queen and her Consort was as sanctimonious and sabbatarian as that of any of their prissiest subjects. To ignore the ritual was to court disaster. Promotion in one's profession and the good-will of one's customers depended materially on whether or not one went to church on Sunday. A census of churchgoing throughout Britain one Sunday in March 1851 showed that out of a total population of 20·8 million, 7·3 million (about one-third) attended a place of religious worship that day, half of them at Anglican churches, the rest at nonconformist churches and chapels.

Actually going to church on Sundays was only a part of the ritual. The respectable middle-class family subscribed equally assiduously to its Bible-reading in the home, organized prayers, listening to and reading sermons, and especially, the strict Sabbatarianism that could turn Sundays into a purgatory of boredom and frustration. No amusements, no games, no laughing, no whistling, not even a walk – except to church. Nor was this stagnation peculiar to England. In Philadelphia chains were put across the streets on Sundays to prevent traffic passing. The Sabbatarian purgatory was long enduring and is not wholly extinct today.

By some respectables religion was seen as a method of keeping the lower classes where they belonged, by instilling discipline into them through the necessary stimulus of fear – in this case fear of damnation. The church, they believed, would have a civilizing influence and was thus part of the move away from the abyss of barbarity. The 'civilizers' felt that provided they could get the evangelical principles of moral conduct accepted as what *ought* to govern men's behaviour, then even if only lip service, or

56

less, was paid to these principles this would nevertheless be an improvement on allowing the amorality of barbarism to go unchallenged. For centuries the church had kept up the struggle with hardly any perceptible success, but it had been in no hurry and appreciated the worth of constant pressure. Now, however, the evangelicalism of the 'non-conformist conscience' – which, incidentally was also powerful among conformists – stabbed its way through these Fabian tactics and used every means in its power, including social blackmail, to inflict wounds on its enemies.

Perhaps the religious characteristic that most revolts the ordinary easy-going human being is sanctimoniousness. Those awful improving clergymen! Hooray for Sam Weller's father, one shouts, when he kicks the red-nosed Stiggins out of The Marquis of Granby and half drowns him in the horse-trough. But to the respectable Victorians themselves this sanctimoniousness was not at all unacceptable. On the contrary it showed that people were afraid to ignore the ritual and that the puritanical ethic of the evangelicals was gaining ground. That there is a close connection between the prevalence of a system of puritan morals and the growth of capitalism seems undoubted. Capitalism, even when it masquerades as state socialism or communism, has no interest in social justice, which in any case is an impossible ideal in human affairs, but it depends for its successful functioning on the rigid adherence by its practitioners to a sacrosanct, if often inequitable, code of behaviour that must always be interpreted in the strictest manner without question. Clemency is itself a crime, because 'once you start that sort of thing', as the saying goes, 'you never know where it will end!' And in any case clemency is non-negotiable, whereas capitalism depends on negotiable confidence among its initiates, even if the confidence is only that the other man is trying to get the better of you. To the Victorian 'middle three' it was clear that God approved of both puritan morals and capitalism. It was equally clear, therefore, that if you were poor it was your own damn fault. Poverty was the result of sin – indeed it was a sin. Nevertheless, there were some who tried to improve themselves and these, in the revealing phrase of the time, were called the Deserving Poor.

Another use of religion, especially for women, was to furnish an outlet for what might be called moral insobriety. This was especially so in the United States where Harriet Martineau got

The Victorian Woman

the impression that religion 'appears to abound, but is not usually of a healthy character'. Revivals conducted by itinerant preachers, swept the country at irregular intervals and produced spiritual orgasms that for many developed into physical orgies. Religion was also a way of relieving boredom. We have already seen Mrs Lynn Linton reminding her sister how they used to go to Sunday school in Keswick simply for something to do; and Mrs Ellis was disturbed at the reflection that the interest of many young ladies in philanthropy and the dissemination of religious knowledge was occasioned 'more by the excitement it produced and the exemption it afforded from domestic duties than from a true spirit of religious goodness'.[1] In the United States religion was a full-time occupation with many women. 'I never saw, or read, of any country where religion had so strong a hold upon the women, or a slighter hold upon the men,' wrote Mrs Trollope.

But when all this depreciatory analysis has been concluded the fact remains that many women, then as now, had a genuine and wholesome love of their God whom they worshipped with simple honesty and disinterested devotion. There must have been many who, like Mrs Gladstone, derived an active pleasure from churchgoing and for whom absence from church was a real sadness. And many, too, like Charlotte Yonge the novelist, whose life was bounded by religion and who found it by far the most exciting of all subjects. Born in 1823, her most impressionable years coincided with the new enthusiasm in the Church of England and this enthusiasm was lastingly communicated to her by her friend John Keble who, in 1835, became vicar of Hursley, next door to Otterbourne where she lived. As a novelist – which she became despite the disapproval of her grandmother who considered that it was extremely low to profit by the fruits of one's labours – she viewed herself, she said, 'as a sort of instrument for popularizing Church views', and her object in all her books was to make goodness attractive. Her first success, *The Heir of Redclyffe* published in 1853, did just that. She took the prevailing literary fashion of romanticism and turned it into a respectable churchgoing creed, retaining the attractiveness of the Byronic hero but replacing his disreputable attributes and behaviour by honourable actions and religious motives. This reformation of the romantic was precisely suited to the new

[1] *Women of England*, p. 246.

ethos of the day and *The Heir of Redclyffe* appealed strongly to the novel-reading public despite its many failings as a book. In her other successes – including *Heartsease* (1854) and *The Daisy Chain* (1856) – Charlotte Yonge continued to celebrate the cult of the family and the importance of religion in the family's life.[1]

The predominance of religion in Victorian times can hardly be over-stressed. From the new enthusiasm in the Church of England which began just before the reign started, the revival of religion in England burgeoned and reached its full flowering after the Crimean War and the Indian Mutiny in the 1850s. Religion supplied so much – not only an object of reverence and affection, but it gave a sense of purpose and the answer to unanswerable questions. Together with filial obedience and patriotism it gave a reason for death and suffering, for ambition and success, for life itself. It provided excitement and the comfort of belonging to a tribe. It allowed intensive, intoxicating obsessive gossip. Its curates, vicars, archdeacons and bishops were sublimated sex symbols – a man in church-black was exciting and subtly libidinous without being dangerous. In a pre-cinema age – and the cinematograph had begun before the reign was over – it provided women with the equivalent of film stars.

[1] 'Religion', as Georgina Battiscombe pointed out in her biography of Charlotte Yonge (Constable, 1943), p. 17, 'is none the less genuine because it lacks any element of mysticism and a certain type of piety finds its best expression in family prayers round the breakfast-table rather than in the ordered ceremonial of a Church service or the secret outpourings of the individual soul.'

Chapter 4

YOUNG LADIES

Both Mrs Sandford and Mrs Ellis were highly critical of the ladies of their day whose faults, they agreed, stemmed from the system of education which taught girls the wrong subjects and gave them the wrong standards. It concentrated exclusively on accomplishments. What was the point of proficiency in the use of globes or in Latin, Italian or even French when the girls would never have the need to use such knowledge? What a girl needed to know was how to care for the sick and how to sew and how to cook, and these things she did not learn at school. Furthermore, the competitive spirit which prevailed at school gave them the wrong ideas. When they came home there would be no question of competing; it was their duty to submit to the will of their elders, especially their male elders.

Girls were taught at their boarding-schools to think of themselves as young ladies to such an extent that when they came home the butcher's daughter could not stand the sight of raw meat, and the draper's daughter eloped with a merchant's clerk rather than have to assist in her father's shop. The cult of idleness gave young women airs which made them want to flop about listlessly on sofas all day and to complain of their nerves when it was suggested they should do anything useful. 'I do not know how it may affect others,' wrote Mrs Ellis, 'but the number of languid, listless and inert young ladies who now recline upon our sofas murmuring and repining at every claim upon their personal exertions, is to me a truly melancholy spectacle.'[1] And this studied idleness was not only disgraceful but dangerous as well, because the 'falling away of pecuniary means' was

[1] *Women of England*, p. 83. The scene of this attitudinized inactivity was the drawing-room.

always a threat in most middle-class homes. When Thackeray described the disaster that befell the Sedleys in *Vanity Fair* he was not exaggerating what could happen to a merchant and his over-spiritualized daughter.

One wealthy middle-class drawing-room was unsparingly described by Wilkie Collins in his early novel *Basil*:[1] 'Never was a richly furnished room more thoroughly comfortless than this – the eye ached at looking round it. There was no repose anywhere. The print of the Queen, hanging lonely on the wall, in its heavy gilt frame, with a large crown at the top, glared at you: the books, the wax flowers in glass cases, the chairs in flaring chintz-covers, the china plates on the door, the blue and pink glass vases and cups ranged on the chimney-piece, the over-ornamented chiffoniers with Tonbridge toys and long-necked smelling bottles on their upper shelves – all glared at you. There was no look of shadow, shelter, secrecy, or retirement in any one nook or corner of those four gaudy walls. All surrounding objects seemed startlingly near to the eye; much nearer than they really were.' A Victorian drawing-room with its clutter of furniture, ornaments and knick-knacks was hell for the claustrophobic. The social psychologist might discern in its plethoric decoration a symbol of the womb complex which assailed the Victorians as a result of their struggle with incompatibles, just as their insistence on domestic virtues and domesticity for women was part of the same complex.

Morning calls, light reading, and fancy work, varied with a little sketching and singing and the collection of shells or the making of shell boxes, seaweed albums, and wax flowers were some of the ways in which the early Victorian young lady was brought up to spend her time.

One particularly popular form of needlecraft was Berlin woolwork, so called after a Berlin printseller who, at the beginning of the century, conceived the idea of publishing coloured needlework designs drawn on squared paper in imitation of canvas. Each square represented a stitch and the system was so foolproof that even the inept could produce reasonable results. Berlin woolwork was first taken up in England in the 1830s and

[1] Published in 1852, this was a new departure in English novel-writing because it dealt with love and passion in the middle class as opposed to high society which convention had hitherto made the only possible setting for a novel.

remained a craze for thirty years among women of every class. By about 1840 it had become almost as widespread in the United States where needlework pictures, done in tent stitch and usually of American heroes, had been popular since the Revolution. This type of subject was ousted by the romantic and biblical scenes of the Berlin patterns which remained in fashion well into the 1880s, much longer than in England.

Another way of passing the time was by writing letters to friends and relatives. From January 10, 1840 there was a radical change in British postal organization which gave a tremendous fillip to letter-writing. Until then postage had been charged by distance: 9d to send a letter the 110 miles from London to Birmingham; 11d for the 184 miles from London to Manchester; 1s 1d for 373 miles to Edinburgh. There was a 2d post for places within three miles of the General Post Office in London, and for a distance not exceeding fifteen miles the rate was 4d. For all these rates only a single sheet of paper was carried; a second sheet automatically doubled the amount. It was for this reason that letters were written 'cross' – that is, having filled the sheet from top to bottom the writer turned it at right angles and covered the page again with lines going across the others. The charges were collected by the postman when he delivered the letter – and if the addressee could not or would not pay, then the letter had to be returned to the sender. In 1827 Harriet Martineau was bewailing that she was so hard up she 'dreaded the arrival of a thirteen penny letter'. To avoid payment, code-marks were often used on the outside of letters so that messages could be passed without delivery being accepted.

Under the new system, chiefly invented by Rowland Hill, a letter not exceeding half an ounce in weight could now be sent 'from any part of the United Kingdom, to any other part, for One Penny'. Writing to an American friend in December 1839, Harriet Martineau joyfully welcomed the new system: 'Our greatest achievement of late has been the obtaining of the penny postage ... It will do more for the circulation of ideas, for the fostering of domestic affections, for the humanizing of the mass generally than any other single measure that our national wit can devise.'

Young ladies might also spend some of their time in philanthropy. 'Poor-peopling', as Florence Nightingale called it. There were strict rules attending it. For ladies to feel and express sympathy was permissible; for them to take action beyond parlour charity was not. Thus in the United States it was permissible for ladies (other than Southern ladies) to hold anti-slavery opinions, but it was considered an affront to their modesty for them to act on those opinions by attending meetings. Those who did were denounced as having cast off the refinement and delicacy of their sex.

Not all young ladies were as over-refined or as delicate as they affected to be. For one thing the conditions of life did not allow it. Nor did intrinsic human nature. On December 10, 1841 Emily Hall, aged twenty-two and her elder sister Louisa drove from Hemel Hempstead to Fulham 'in pouring rain and through floods of water which at times rose to the floor of the carriage'. They passed the time by 'reading the Breach of Promise action that fills the papers at present'.[1]

The affectation of refinement was an indication of the taste of the times. To be above domestic duties and to be skilled in elaborate feminine delicacy – to be a Dora Spenlow in fact – was considered the necessary foundation for a young lady's chief purpose in life: to find a husband. This was her sole aim. She was brought up, educated and trained for the marriage market. Marriage was the goal, the romantic denouement at which all the novels ended.

In the United States it was the same. Girls' education was much what it was in England. They were taught subjects which were supposed to be necessary simply because all the other girls learnt them – time-filling accomplishments which would enable a woman to occupy her attention harmlessly, would improve her conversation, make her something like a companion to her husband (when she got one), and in due course enable her to give her children rudimentary lessons. As Harriet Martineau put it, 'the sum and substance of female education in America, as in England, is training women to consider marriage as the sole object in life, and to pretend that they do not think so'.[2]

No 'Warning Whisper' in America

The social conventions which governed young ladies differed in one important respect between England and America. Mrs

[1] O. A. Sherrard, *Two Victorian Girls*: with extracts from the Hall Diaries edited by A. R. Mills (Muller, 1966), p. 47.
[2] Harriet Martineau, op. cit., Vol. II, p. 157.

Stevenson remarked on this difference in a letter from London to her niece Sally Rutherford in Virginia. 'With us, as soon as a woman marries, no matter how young, she retires from the great theatre of the world and buries herself in obscurity and retirement ... Here it is very different, young ladies are not permitted to appear in public without being accompanied by their mothers, or a chaperon, who is required to watch her with Spanish vigilance. The presence of sensible and dignified matrons gives a higher tone to Society, and also has the effect of making married women more solicitous both in adorning their minds and persons and of cultivating all those graces which embellish life.'[1]

In the United States there were no chaperons. English visitors, especially lady visitors, were amazed at the degree of freedom thus allowed to American young ladies. Mrs Houstoun, whose *Hesperos: or Travels in the West* was published in 1850, was particularly struck by the free and easy way in which they made arrangements for their dances. 'When a ball is to be given, it is the young ladies of the house, not the mammas and papas, who invite the guests. *They* are not supposed to be any judges of *who*, and are only necessary as supplying the means for the entertainment of the society. . . . A chaperon within the limits of a dancing-room would not be allowed on any consideration and very few single ladies after they have passed the age of twenty-five are considered eligible for admission.'

These young ladies who asked whomever they wanted to their dances and who banned chaperons from the dancing-room were just as tenacious of their freeborn American rights in the matter of going out alone with any young gentleman who happened to be their favoured admirer of the moment. A popular amusement was to drive out on a Sunday in a gig, the lady wearing her best bonnet and feathers and the gentleman smoking his cigar. Such a disregard for convention would have been a social crime in England. Nor did the freedom of young American ladies stop with choosing their partner for a ball or a Sunday drive. It was also their habit to choose their husbands for themselves. This privilege was seldom disputed, or so Mrs Houstoun heard.

It was all this freedom of young ladies that caused the

[1] Edward Boykin (ed.), op. cit., p. 272.

absence of that retiring modesty in the countenances and deportments of most of the pretty pedestrians who were to be seen on Broadway. 'What other result can be expected when young ladies are thus prematurely launched into an independent career?' asked Mrs Houstoun. 'What but hardihood of demeanour and unfeminine ease of manner? No warning whisper from an anxious mother is heard, hinting to them that it is time to *stop*, when gay and girlish spirits may have led them perchance to overstep the bounds of strict decorum – what wonder then that the "laugh without any control" should be so much too often heard and that romping giddy girls should become dressy, uncompanionable wives and negligent and careless mothers.'

Nevertheless there were two characteristics which offset any laxity of behaviour. The first was that a young and pretty girl could travel alone 'with perfect safety, from Maine to Missouri, and will meet with nothing but respect and attention the whole way'. Of how many other countries could such a remark be made, Mrs Houstoun wondered. It was her firm conviction that if ever chivalry and courtesy to women were entirely banished from one side of the Atlantic they would take refuge on the other.

The second characteristic which more than offset any shortcomings in behaviour was the strength of mind and energy of purpose which informed American ladies and to which Mrs Houstoun paid a warm tribute. 'The very character I have been describing will, if necessary, throw aside her silks and satins and accompany her husband into the half-formed settlements of the far West. There she will endure without a murmur or word of repining the toils and dangers and often sickness attending their new mode of life; and when (as too frequently happens) their husbands are reduced by one unfortunate speculation from wealth and ease to poverty and privation then it is that *their* fortitude smooths the path of misfortune and *their* courageous exertions lessen the force of the blow.' What husband could ask for more?

Mrs Houstoun, like every other English chronicler of the idiosyncrasies of American manners, ended her analysis of American ladies by remembering her own friends – 'gentle, feminine friends, and refined and accomplished women' – who did not have the failings and follies she had been discussing and who almost made her regret her criticisms. All in all, however, she felt that these were just and that her friends were the exception rather than the rule.

Either A Governess Or . . .

Even for those millions of young ladies in England and America who were never called upon to endure the hardships of the far West, the realities of married life were harshly different from the enchantments they had dreamed of on their drawing-room sofas. Perhaps it was as well for some that the novels they read did end with church bells and orange blossom!

'What is it you are expecting?' Mrs Ellis asked her engaged or newly-wed readers in *Wives of England*. 'To be always flattered? Depend upon it, if your faults were never brought to light before, they will be so now. Are you expecting to be always indulged? Depend upon it, if your temper was never tried before, it will be so now. Are you expecting to be always admired? Depend upon it, if you were never humble and insignificant before, you will have to be so now. Yes, you had better make up your mind at once to be uninteresting as long as you live to all except the companion of your home; and well will it be for you if you can always be interesting to him.'[1] So choose wisely, she told the young ladies, for if you choose ill your life will be a ghastly misery.

But to find a paragon was not easy. Indeed to find a husband at all was not always easy. Sometimes there was no marriage for a young lady. Even had every marriageable man chosen a wife, there would still have been spinsters, for there were about half-a-million surplus women in Britain at this period. It was a superfluity which worried the Victorians considerably, and emigration societies were started in order to encourage un-married women to go to the Colonies where they were in short supply. Emily Hall's other sister, Ellen, wrote in her diary on May 22, 1860 that after dinner she had been joined by Miss Elizabeth Stewart and they 'fell to talking about love and marriage. We agreed that people – ladies at least – ought to be educated to do without it and then they would be less inclined to marry unless the very best were offered to them.'[2] Most ladies, however, seemed glad to get anything, though they had plenty

[1] Mrs Ellis, *Wives of England*, pp. 16–17.
[2] O. A. Sherrard, op. cit., p. 255.

of time to repent later during the 'mass of trifles' which formed a middle-class woman's married life.

Not all young ladies were content with the restricted drawing-room life that convention forced upon them. Like Florence Nightingale they resented the fact that they had 'passion, intellect, moral activity' but occupied a place in society which prevented them from exercising any of the three. Charlotte Brontë was tortured by the inanity that was forced on woman. In *Jane Eyre*, published in 1847, she wrote: 'Women are supposed to be very calm generally: but women feel just as men feel; they need exercise for their faculties and a field for their efforts as much as their brothers do. They suffer from too rigid a restraint, too absolute a stagnation, precisely as men would suffer; and it is narrow-minded of their more privileged fellow-creatures to say that they ought to confine themselves to making puddings and knitting stockings, to playing on the piano and embroidering bands. It is thoughtless to condemn them, or laugh at them, if they seek to do more or learn more than custom has pronounced necessary for their sex.'

Jane Eyre's situation was one that many middle-class girls came to. The country's economy was expanding fast but its credit system was not sophisticated enough to cope with the surge of business. The result was that bank failures were common and bankruptcies among tradesmen and merchants an everyday occurrence. Nor was it only bankruptcy that brought disaster. For some unhappy homes there would come 'a day of weeping and mourning, a day when the master lies cold and still in his upstairs room; when the hearse carries him away, and the mother assumes her widow's cap. Then,' wrote Bessie Rayner Parkes, 'the two servants have to be dismissed. Then the young brothers seek for situations as best they may, and the daughters likewise. But the youths succeed, and the girls fail.'[1]

They failed because they were totally untrained for any kind of work. 'Deep into the heart of English society eats the cankering notion that women of the middle class lose caste by household activity. It is a notion rather than a reality, as those who attempt to brave it soon discover. But there it is, enthroned in endless rows and terraces, and crescents and squares – wherever the poor but genteel merchant and the second-rate professional

[1] Bessie Rayner Parkes, op. cit., p. 82.

men reside; men with from three hundred to four hundred per annum and a growing-up family; men who *might* save a little, men who *might* insure, but who keep two servants and do neither. If indeed the girls had been withdrawn from household work in order that they might be fitted for some remunerative employment there would be no cause for complaint; but ... there *never will* be remunerative employment for the majority of middle-class women.'[1] Thrown on their own, non-existent resources by the bankruptcy or death of the head of their family there was only one thing for these untrained girls to do apart from casual sewing – or rather, there were two things. As the *Saturday Review* wrote in an article on the hardships of a governess's life 'a woman, driven to choose a profession at all, has, if she be well disposed, a mere Hobson's choice. She must either be a governesss, *aut id quod dicere nolo*', that is, a prostitute.

The article in the *Saturday Review* was discussing a typical advertisement for a governess which had appeared in *The Times*. To this advertisement there were 140 replies. 'One is sorry to hear of so much virtue in distress,' wrote the *Saturday*. 'On the other hand one is glad to find that in so large a mass of distress there is still so much virtue.'[2]

The amount of distress was unquestionable. It was charted by the Governesses Benevolent Institution, which had its beginning in 1841 but did not start active work until two years later. As a result of a public meeting held in May 1843 a ladies' committee was formed for 'affording assistance privately and delicately to ladies in temporary distress'. The committee was 'appalled' at the cases that came to their attention. In nine months to March 1844 they received and examined 102 requests of which they assisted fifty-six. The greater part of the remainder were 'reluctantly declined for want of sufficient funds'.

One of the terrible penalties of the profession was destitution in old age. A governess would work for perhaps twenty-five years at the most, at a salary which would perhaps start at £25 a year and seldom rise beyond £80. If, as was often the case, she had some relative to support or if she became ill it was impossible for her to set aside anything for her old age. The G.B.I.

[2] ibid.
'Wanted A Governess' in the *Saturday Review*, September 3, 1859.

founded annuities for aged governesses. In the first year £500 was invested to create a perpetual annuity of £15 'and for this small yearly sum there at once appeared about thirty candidates, *many of them entirely destitute*'. In succeeding years the number of annuities increased, some of the money contributed by the eventual beneficiaries themselves. Two other forms of assistance started by the G.B.I. were a home to lodge governesses who were out of work and an asylum for those who were too old to work.

'We suppose nobody becomes a governess from choice,' wrote the *Saturday Review*. Taine would have agreed with this. 'The lot of a governess in England,' he said, 'is not a pleasant one; see for example the novels of Charlotte Brontë. Most of those I have met have turned their faces into wooden masks, and nothing could be more startling when the face in question is young. Manner, bearing, everything is artificial and made to order, composed and maintained in such a manner as never to lay the subject open for a moment. Even after several days of familiarity and away from the house in which they are employed they remain on the defensive. The habit of keeping a sharp watch and firm control over themselves is too strong; one might take them for soldiers on parade.'[1]

This is the usual image of the governess, but there were those who did not agree that it was at all true. Lady Cardigan pooh-poohed the idea of the downtrodden governess: 'The prevailing idea seems to be that the early Victorian novelists presented an accurate picture of the troubles that beset the paths of young ladies who were obliged to earn their own living. I have no patience with what I consider is entirely false, and the Brontës are largely responsible for the fancied woes of the governess. . . . All I can say is, I never had a governess of this description and I don't think any of my friends had. The ladies who taught us were clever, sensible women who were treated as ladies, but who were tactful enough not to become too familiar with their employers and their friends. The governesses in aristocratic families moved in quite a world of their own; they visited among themselves; they had their own "set", and they formed a sort of society in society. They took their pupils whenever they visited each other, and I can recall many delightful after-noons and evenings spent with cheerful smiling young women

[1] Taine, op. cit., pp. 89–90.

who seemed thoroughly to enjoy themselves, and who did not long for a small, smothered life in the shape of marriage with a parson.'[1]

The burden of evidence, however, is against Lady Cardigan.

[1] The Countess of Cardigan and Lancastre, op. cit., pp. 21–2.

Chapter 5

'THE NEWLY DISCOVERED REGIONS'

Young ladies did not work; women did. The convention which kept a middle-class miss idle in the drawing-room did not apply to the lower classes; economic necessity was too strong. In 1841, when the first census of the new reign was taken, the percentage of women and girls in employment in Great Britain was 22·9 – just over two million out of a total female population of nine-and-a-half million (9,514,800). They were employed in more than 300 trades. But almost all of these accounted for only about one quarter of the women employed. The three categories of domestic service, textiles and dress manufacture, and agriculture together employed 1,604,000 women and girls – almost three-quarters of the total female working population of 2,176,500. The chief occupation for an employed woman in Britain was to be a domestic servant, an extension, in fact, of the daily life that most of the 7,338,300 non-employed women in the country led. One in every ten of the total female population was a domestic servant.

In Ireland the incidence was slightly different. The number of women and girls in employment was over one million (1,157,700) out of a total female population of 4,155,500. Domestic service was not the chief occupation. It took second place to textile manufacture. Domestic service, textiles and dress manufacture, and agriculture employed 1,095,400 women and girls, almost 95 per cent of the 1,157,700 in employment. Textiles alone employed almost one half.

In 1851, when the second census of the reign was taken, the number of women and girls in employment in Great Britain had increased to almost three million (2,988,600) out of a total female population of 10,659,600. The percentage of females employed had also increased substantially to 28·9. Domestic service, textile and dress manufacture, and agriculture were still the main occupations. They now employed 2,460,400 – over four-fifths (82·3 per cent) of the total female working population as against 58·8 per cent in 1841. However, there had been changes in their order of importance. Manufacturing as a whole came first, its numbers having more than doubled in ten years; indeed the number employed in textiles and dyeing alone was larger than 'all manufacturing' in 1841. A significant increase was in the number of female metal-workers. This reflected the increase in the metal-working trades as a whole, which showed the growing sophistication of British industry. Another sign of a more complex economy was that new employments began to make their appearance. For example, in 1854 women clerks, suitably chaperoned, were employed by the Electric Telegraph Company in Manchester.

In Ireland it was another story. Here there was no sophistication of the economy, no expanding population. Starvation and emigration during the horrors of the Hungry Forties reduced the population from 8,175,100 in 1841 to 6,552,400 in 1851. Of this, females decreased from 4,155,500 to 3,361,700 and the female working population to 919,600. The percentage of females employed fell slightly from 27·8 to 27·4.

Decline of Domestic Industries
Before the large-scale extension of the factory system resulting from the inventions of the latter part of the eighteenth century there were numerous home industries which had provided employment for women and children for generations. Chief among these were the textile industries, which indeed were Britain's chief industries. Spinning, carding, weaving and the many other processes involved in clothmaking were carried on in the home. Other important domestic industries for women were lacemaking (which employed at least three-quarters of the female population in Bedfordshire), straw-plaiting for hats, glovemaking, buttonmaking ('buttony' as it was called in Dorset), knitting, and needlework of all kinds. Another domestic industry which gave employment to women was the small metal trade, the 'toy trade' as it was called, which was chiefly located

in the Birmingham, Wolverhampton, and South Staffordshire region.

As a result of changing trade conditions and the greater economic efficiency of the new machines, the domestic industries failed one after another. But this failure was gradual, and varied greatly over the country. In some districts indeed the domestic system survived throughout most of the nineteenth century.

The cotton spinners had been the first to be affected by the new inventions, and by 1837 the cleaning, carding, roving, and spinning of cotton was wholly a factory operation. A large amount of weaving, however, was still carried on domestically. Hand-looms still out-numbered power-looms, though the hand-loom weavers were by now in the depths of poverty and were soon to sink to the lower depths. In the woollen industry domestic work, usually weaving but sometimes spinning as well, continued for another decade or more. In the towns the weavers worked in appalling conditions of dirt and disease. This was especially so of the cotton and worsted weavers who were in considerably worse distress than the woollen weavers. But to a weaver anything was better than a factory. The loss of independence – even if it was independence to starve and rot of disease – and the disintegration of the family working unit, which factory work entailed, was against all the instincts and traditions of the weavers.

The Children's Employment Commission reported in 1843 that pillow lacemaking 'still finds occupation for many thousands of women and children in the dispersed population of Northamptonshire, Oxfordshire, Bedfordshire and Buckinghamshire and likewise in Devonshire'. Machine lacemaking also gave outwork to domestic lacemakers. There were 180,000 women and children employed thus in their homes in the early 1830s, their work consisting of embroidering, mending, drawing and pearling the fabric made by the machines. It was work that could be ruinous to the eyesight. One girl lacerunner told the 1833 Factory Commission that her work had made her eyesight so bad that when she went 'a long way to see a man hanged t'other day she couldn't see him a bit after all' even when she got right up close to the gallows. Despite the strain on their eyes, however, she and the other girls preferred domestic work to a factory, she said, because at home they had their liberty and their meals 'comfortable, such as they are'.

Straw-plaiting for hats was another domestic industry that became important from the turn of the century. A writer in the *Essex Review* noted that in the lanes of Essex around 1840 'you scarcely met a woman, or child over five years old, whose fingers were not busily plaiting'. In 1860 a skilful plaiter could still make five shillings or seven and sixpence a week.

Domestic glovemaking, however, was in a parlous state, and was almost extinct in its old centres of Worcester, Woodstock and Yeovil. In this case it was not the factory system that destroyed the trade but the removal of import restrictions and the change in fashion from leather to cotton and silk gloves. Hand knitting for market had virtually died out except in Westmorland and in the remote dales of Yorkshire and Lancashire where there was no other possible employment for married women apart from a few weeks' haymaking. The wages were wretched: two shillings to two and sixpence a week for women, and sixpence to one and threepence for children. But poverty kept them at work. With the introduction of power machinery in the 1870s knitting became a factory industry.

Buttonmaking as a domestic industry continued in Dorset until 1851 when the introduction of the patent machine-made linen button brought it to an end. Wages were tiny, but the wage of the agricultural labourer was itself so low that it was imperative for the women and children to make some contribution, however small.

There was one occupation that did not figure in the Census Returns, but which employed a large number of women and girls – many of them very young girls. For some it was a whole-time occupation, for others a part-time way of earning a little extra. How many prostitutes there were in Britain at the beginning of Victoria's reign is not known, but there were certainly many thousands. According to the Children's Employment Commission the immorality of dressmakers and domestic servants was proverbial. Chastity among the straw-plaiters was 'at a sad discount, while prostitution was at a high premium'. The morals of the lacemakers were said to be nearly as low; prostitution was 'rife among them from the same causes – scanty earnings, love of finery, and the almost total absence of early moral culture'. Similar evidence can be found for every domestic industry in turn. The early Victorians themselves were convinced that the girls in the cotton mills were more immoral than anyone else, but later research has shown that this belief had no evidence to back it.

As the domestic industries failed there were three options open to the women. Firstly, they could follow the work to the factories which were the outcome of the technological and industrial changes. To begin with, however, it was not out-of-work domestic glovemakers and unemployed domestic spinners who became the new factory population, for the antipathy of domestic workers towards machinery was so strong that they shunned the factories in the early days, and the 'hands' came largely from agricultural workers displaced by the agrarian revolution, from domestic servants, from the unskilled and from parish paupers.

Secondly, they could endeavour to find other employment. For example, in those districts where the type of crop was suitable there came into existence women day-labourers. Hand-hoeing, weeding, planting crops, digging potatoes, pulling turnips, gathering stones and dressing meadows were all part of a woman day-labourer's work. They were also extensively employed in the huge market gardens on the south-west outskirts of London. To the farmer, women day-labourers had two advantages: their rates of pay, being based on the accepted principle that their wage was only supplementary, were lower than a man's; furthermore, the women need only be employed seasonally or casually.

Thirdly, if neither factory work nor alternative employment was available the women reluctantly gave up work altogether – reluctantly, not because the leisure was unwelcome but because of the financial hardship that resulted. When women, and their children, were working at home either in husbandry or domestic industry it was only necessary to pay a man sufficient for his own support; the rest of the family supported itself. The onset of the agrarian and industrial revolutions destroyed the basis of the family wage by depriving the landless labourers' women and children of work they could do at home. The men's wages were slightly increased to help him maintain his family, but the gap was not filled, even when an allowance was made from the poor rate. This financial hardship that was a consequence of the factory system was one of the bitterest complaints made against it by the working men. Furthermore, when machine labour did away with the wholesale necessity for women's labour, 'even the

75

increased wages earned by men did not reconcile them to the economic dependence of their women and children who remained unemployed at home. So accustomed were they to the idea of a family wage . . . that the substitution of the individual wage and the responsibility of the father for the entire support of his family were changes which at first were neither welcomed nor understood.[1'] The new economic dependence of a woman on her husband had powerful psychological effects.

In the United States where the factory system arrived a generation later than it did in England the effect of mechanization on domestic industries was the same. But there was an important difference in the source of female labour for the new factories. Unlike England, this new factory population did not include displaced women agricultural workers. Such women did not exist. In America there had long been an unshakeable prejudice against women – except, of course, slave women – working in the fields. Nor did the new factory workers include many who had been domestic servants for the simple reason that white domestic servants were few and far between. The reality of slavery and the 'fable of equality', as it was called in 1832 by Mrs Trollope in her *Domestic Manners of the Americans*, had jointly created such a horror of domestic service that girls believed abject poverty was preferable.[2] From the beginning, therefore, it was the women who had already been employed in domestic manufacture, farm girls and seamen's daughters, who formed the bulk of female labour for the New England factories, and this labour, as in Old England, outnumbered the men employed. For instance, in 1832 out of 5,000 operatives in the famous mills at Lowell on the Merrimack 3,800 were women and girls.

Unlike the near-sighted lacerunner whose eyes were so bad that she could not see the man being hanged, the girls of New England welcomed the chance of working in a factory. Opportunities for women's employment were even more limited in the United States than in England. Not only did the same prejudices

[1] Ivy Pinchbeck, op. cit., p. 122.

[2] Fanny Kemble had a lady's maid in Philadelphia in 1834 who had ruined her health as a seamstress and whom she employed at £25 a year. She had little to do, with 'two holidays a week, all my discarded wardrobe and every kindness and attention.' She gave in her notice, the reason being, as she finally confessed, because 'she could not bear being a servant'. (Frances A. Kemble, op. cit., Vol. III, p. 15.)

prevail but there was an additional one in that the Americans prided themselves on their chivalry towards women and as Harriet Martineau who visited the States from 1834 to 1836, pointed out, one consequence of the 'chivalrous taste and temper of a country with regard to its women is that it is difficult, when it is not impossible, for women to earn their bread. When it is a boast that women do not labour, the encouragement and rewards of labour are not provided. It is so in America.'[1]

The girls may have regarded domestic service with horror, but in avoiding it, so limited were the other opportunities for women's employment, they became instead domestic slaves in their own homes. The drudgery of the mill was less irksome than the drudgery within their farm homes. Certainly they worked thirteen hours a day at their machines, but when the thirteen hours were up they were their own mistresses and not subject to parents or brothers, who could make the drudgery endless. Furthermore, they had companions who were not solely members of the family or near neighbours; they had some choice in friendship. And above all, of tremendous psychological importance, they could for the first time in their lives, and for the first time in the lives of countless millions of women, earn money and spend it as they pleased. Harriet Robinson, a Lowell mill-girl who later became an active feminist, described the freedom of the spirit that their meagre wages gave to the unmarried women in the early factories. 'They could gratify their tastes and desires without restraint and without rendering an account to anybody. At last they had found a place in the universe, and were no longer obliged to finish out their faded lives a burden to their male relatives.'[2]

To begin with, the factories needed as many women as they could get. Because of the demands of agriculture and the constant migration of young men, who left home to follow the advancing frontier in the West, there was a shortage of male labour in the eastern States. Indeed, ever since Western migration had started there were more women than men in Massachusetts and in some of the other older states. But in due course advances in mechanization overtook the numbers of women wanting work, especially when these were greatly

[1] Harriet Martineau, op. cit., Vol. II, p. 177.
[2] Harriet Robinson, *Early Factory Labour in New England* (Boston, 1889), pp. 11–12.

augmented by Irish immigration in the Hungry Forties. When this happened the brief golden age of the American factory was over. Exploitation of labour, especially female labour, took its place. Those who had had to earn their own living were forced to fall back on women's chief employment, sewing, that last refuge of starving morality. This in turn forced wages even lower in an occupation that was always overcrowded and underpaid.

'Quite Naked to the Waist'

Changes in traditional jobs for women were caused almost entirely by economic pressure and industrial development. In one important instance, however, the change was the result of social pressure. Just as spinning and other domestic industries had been traditional for generations, so too had the employment of women as mineworkers. But the mining communities were so closed and isolated that no one knew or cared that women were working under appalling conditions underground. In 1833, when Tufnell was investigating conditions in the Lancashire textile mills for the Factory Commission which reported that year, he also looked at some of the mines in the neighbourhood. He was horrified to find that women and children were employed underground. He reported that 'it must appear to every impartial judge of the two occupations that the hardest labour in the worst room in the worst-conducted factory is less hard, less cruel, and less demoralizing than the labour in the best of coal-mines'. Tufnell's disclosures had no immediate result, but seven years later Lord Ashley (afterwards Lord Shaftesbury) used them as a plank in his demand for the setting-up of a Commission to examine the employment of children in mines and factories. Shortly after it had started work the Commission, which consisted of Thomas Tooke the economist, Dr Southwood Smith (both of whom had been on the 1833 Factory Commission), the Factory Inspectors Leonard Horner and Robert J. Saunders, and some twenty sub-commissioners, decided on its own initiative to include in its remit all women working in mines.

In May 1842 the Children's Employment Commission published the first two volumes of its famous Report. These dealt with the barbaric working conditions in the mines. The following year two further volumes were published dealing with employment in trades and manufactures. It was the Mines

Report that first stirred the public conscience to demand the mitigation of some of the horrors of industrial employment. R. H. Horne, one of the sub-commissioners, wrote that the full description of the mines furnished by this report might be entitled 'Travels Into Newly Discovered Regions', so little was previously known of them. The report told of children and young women employed as hurriers, or putters, to push the corves of coal along underground roadways too low and too narrow for animals to work in. It told of trappers who opened the doors to let the corves pass through and in so doing pushed air along the fetid dripping galleries to ventilate the pit – little boys and girls, almost always under eight years of age, often five or six, sitting all day long in places where there was no day.

But it was not the barbarity disclosed in these calmly told horror stories that sparked public indignation. The Report included a number of sketches showing the type of work that women and children did in the mines. One or two of the sketches made on the spot also showed miners at work in their habitual naked state. It was these sketches that did it. 'The sight of them,' wrote R. H. Horne, 'caused great commiseration among all those who could feel for poor people; and great annoyance and disgust to the fine senses of all those who could not, or would not. Lord Londonderry declared that the sketches were offensive – made him quite sick – and were "calculated to inflame the passions". *The* passions – what passions? The passions of pity and indignation. True, the sketches were often "disgusting"; but for that very reason the cause, not the explanatory sketches should be removed.' Lord Londonderry inveighed in Parliament against the 'humanity mania' that had bitten people like Lord Ashley.

What upset the respectables in such cases as young Patience Kershaw's, for example, was not that she hurried three cwt. corves a mile or more underground for eleven hours a day on her hands and knees, wearing a belt and chain that passed between her legs, but that she worked among getters who were naked except for their caps. The respectables were appalled to learn that in the West Riding of Yorkshire where girls were almost universally employed as trappers and hurriers in common with boys, the girls employed as hurriers, who were of all ages from seven to twenty-one, 'commonly work quite naked down to the waist. The boys of similar ages who work with them are also naked down to the waist and both (for the garment is pretty much the same in both) are dressed, as far as they are dressed at all, in a loose pair of trousers, seldom whole in either sex. In many of the collieries as has been already stated the adult colliers whom these girls serve work perfectly naked.' The Queen's Top Nation was horrified at the thought of naked men and half-naked women consorting together in the mines. The fact that actual nakedness was hardly the straw to break the camel's back in such hell-holes, especially when one remembered the total lack of privacy in the hovels in which the miners lived, was not something that respectable readers of the Report were in a position to evaluate.

There is little doubt that the Commissioners, determined to get some action taken on their Report and well understanding the state of respectable opinion, were astute enough to realize the effect that the 'naked' sketches would have. Opinion, indeed, became so worked up that no one really bothered about the numerical extent of the slavery: in fact it applied to about 2,500 women and girls of all ages in the East of Scotland, and possibly about the same number in other localized parts of Britain. And something did happen. A Bill was introduced in June 1842, passed into law in August, and came into effect on March 1, 1843.

But women and children did not disappear immediately from the pits as the Act said they must. In some places the Act was only enforced when the inspector called. Many of the women, with no other wage-work to turn to, disguised themselves as men. It was not callousness that made Dr Mitchell, one of the sub-commissioners, hesitate to condemn heavy pit-bank work for women in Staffordshire: 'when we consider how many employments men have engrossed to themselves, and how few ways there are for women to gain their living, we must be cautious not to attempt to narrow what is already so limited'.[1]

The problem might have been overcome by compensation, but even though speakers in the House of Lords foretold the destitution that would result from excluding women from the pits the question of compensation, as Dr Pinchbeck says, 'was so far beyond their horizon as never to be suggested or discussed'.[2] This is a point which it is easy to forget. A criticism is

[1] *Parliamentary Papers, Mines*, 1842, xvi, p. 12.
[2] Ivy Pinchbeck, op. cit., p. 268.

5. *Above:* Crinoline, 1855, and 1860.

Above left: The end of crinoline, 1865, *The Era of the Photograph,* (*right*) A Bloomer of the 1850s.

6. Fashions for little girls, 1873, as drawn by George du Maurier for *Punch*.

Taking Time by the Forelock.
Gwendoline: 'Uncle George says every woman ought to have a Profession, and I think he's quite right'.
Mamma: 'Indeed! And what Profession do you mean to choose?'
Gwendoline: 'I mean to be a Professional Beauty!' (du Maurier in *Punch*, 1880).

TAKING TIME BY THE FORELOCK.

sometimes made of the Victorians that their various Commissions and Reports uncovered one disgrace and abuse after another and yet they did nothing effectual to stop them. But it should be remembered that in most cases they had no machinery to amend the abuses. And not only did they lack the administrative machinery, they lacked the mental furniture. The question of compensation or a maintenance allowance for displaced women mineworkers was a case in point. Such an answer to the problem was an idea far beyond them. They did not know about it, they could not consider it, any more than they could have considered nuclear energy as a way of supplying electricity. The more State action that is taken, the easier it becomes to take more. But in Victorian times reform again and again seemed impossible because it demanded the social equivalent of the invention of the wheel – it demanded machinery which did not exist and which mental attitudes and outlook made it impossible to create. For instance, until the work of Charles Booth in the 1880s there was no adequate interpretation of even the few statistics that were available.

Within a few weeks of the Act coming into effect petitions were flooding into Parliament 'praying', as R. H. Horne said, 'to have all the good undone before its natural effect has had time to operate'. Horne, who was famous to the public as the author of a long narrative poem called *Orion* and famous among his friends for his swimming prowess and his webbed toes, investigated the metal trades in the Wolverhampton district for the Children's Employment Commission. In order to lend his weight against any campaign aimed at repealing the Act he wrote a long article on the Commission in the first issue of the *Illuminated Magazine*, a periodical edited by Douglas Jerrold that ran for a few years from 1843. 'It is an unalterable decree of nature,' he wrote, 'that man to maintain a healthy condition of body or mind must *work*; but there is no decree in nature that man should be a slave. . . . To labour hard is honourable . . . but when the honest working man is treated like a beast and his wife and children like the commonest cattle, then, indeed, it is time for his countrymen to bethink them of their boasted freedom, their excellent institutions, and the Christianity of the owners of the soil.'

Although the exclusion of women from the pits caused penury among many to begin with, ultimately, humanitarian

81

considerations apart, it did good. Even before the Act there had been many mining districts in which women and girls were not employed in the pits. In these there could be no doubt that the miners' homes were better tended than in districts where the women worked underground. It was the women's influence which largely determined the state of society. As the Mines Report declared, 'Give to the collier the comforts of a clean and cheerful home, and the companionship of a sober and decently educated female, not degraded to brute labour by working in the pits; let her attend to a mother's and housewife's duties; and you will soon change the moral condition of the collier.'

'Let her attend to a mother's and housewife's duties' . . . that, in Victorian opinion, was the proper job for a woman. All women were regarded as potential and actual mothers. A woman who worked was, in Wanda Neff's phrase, 'an affront against nature and the protective instincts of man'.[1] She was also an economic competitor.

'Death and The Drawing Room'

The Act of 1842 affected comparatively few women. There were many others who continued to work in conditions that were almost as brutalizing as those that obtained in the mines. And there were others whose work, if less gruesome, was no less pernicious. The conditions under which dressmakers had to work were appalling. The title of an article which appeared in the June 1843 issue of the *Illuminated Magazine* put the situation in a nutshell: 'Death and the Drawing Room or The Young Dressmakers of England.'

But while the thought of half-naked women in the mines was something that upset the Victorian respectables, there was no such feeling of disgust at the thought of young girls being worked to death in dusty sewing-rooms. As the anonymous writer of the article said, the people who luxuriate in others' misfortune 'will only read the description of the young dressmakers which we are about to give, to hug themselves in their own comfortable state, and to look round their own blooming daughters and say "thank God".'

There was no exaggeration in the 'melancholy truths', nor was it the first time they had been brought before the public. An

[1] Wanda F. Neff, *Victorian Working Women* (Allen and Unwin, 1929), p. 37.

article by James Grant in the *Females Advocate* for January 1841 had stated them 'with earnest distinctness' though they had carried little conviction. Now, however, the evidence collected by R. D. Grainger, 'one of the gentlemen employed by government in the Children's Employment Commission' had furnished a fund of information on the subject which could no longer be questioned.

Grainger's Report stated that 'besides journeywomen working at their own homes there are in London 15,000 females who are employed by dressmakers and milliners, of whom the very great majority are between the ages of sixteen and twenty-five'. Their hours of work were inordinately long. 'In London there are two busy seasons: the principal one begins in April and ends in July or the commencement of August; the second lasts from October to Christmas. During these seasons, but especially the former, the young persons are, on the average, required to work eighteen hours a day, including the time allowed for meals. These are the hours in all the principal houses in town. Long as these hours are, they are very often exceeded. It is not uncommon to begin at six and even five a.m. and go on until two and three in the morning; sometimes from four a.m. till twelve at night. Some witnesses who were in a position freely to state the facts mention that they have for three months successively worked twenty hours out of the twenty-four.'

The rate of sickness, blindness and death from this slavery was so high that, according to one witness, 'if a constant accession of fresh hands from the country were not provided, the business could not be carried on'.

One of the most noticeable social habits of the Victorians was excessive mourning – excessive, that is, by the standards of a later age. The rules were rigid. What with full, half, and quarter mourning, and the range of relatives and public figures for whose death each degree of mourning was ordained, many women in the Top Nation were never out of mourning from one year's end to another. This was excellent for the owners of dress-shops and mourning emporia, but it was another nail in the coffins of the young dressmakers. 'Perhaps it would not be impossible,' the *Illuminated Magazine* article suggested, 'to form some rough estimate of how many early graves are filled by each wedding order, by each drawing-room, and how many humble homes are filled with real sorrow by the conventional assumption of the trappings and suits of woe in every court mourning, for on all these occasions the toil of the young dressmaker is redoubled.'

On the occasion of the general mourning for William IV in 1837, one witness told Grainger she had worked without going to bed from four o'clock on Thursday morning till half-past-ten on Sunday morning, during which time she had had no sleep at all. 'In order to keep awake she stood nearly the whole of Friday night, Saturday, and Sunday morning, only sitting down for half-an-hour for rest. Two other young persons worked at the same house for the same time; these two dozed occasionally in a chair.' This witness, who was then nineteen, was made very ill by this great exertion and when she finally went to bed on Sunday she could not sleep. Her feet and legs were hideously swollen and her feet seemed to overhang her shoes.

The result of these privations was a foregone conclusion. 'Many of these young women owing to the hard treatment they receive lose their virtue; they would do anything rather than return to such labour. As a great number of them come from the country and have no immediate friends in London they are exposed in a peculiar degree to the temptations of the metropolis. Their employers, who ought to supply the place of their natural protectors, are in general indifferent to the moral evils to which they are exposed; religion is never thought of. In the season it is not uncommon to work on some part of the Sunday.' One doctor who gave evidence was convinced that 'in no trade or manufacture whatever is the labour to be compared to that of the young dressmakers; no men work so long. It would be impossible for any animal to work so continuously with so little rest.'

All Grainger's witnesses were agreed that this iniquitous system was totally unnecessary. There was an abundance of unemployed dressmakers who could have been brought in during any temporary pressure of work; and there were also large numbers of needlewomen to whom the plainer parts of the work could at all times have been farmed out cheaply. But while no restriction of hours was enforced employers could go on working their apprentices and other 'hands' until they dropped, in order to save any additional cost. There were a few honourable exceptions among the employers, who had shortened the hours of work. Some of these told Grainger that they had found 'their pecuniary interest and their sense of right were identical; the amount of work done having been actually greater in a fewer hours, because the young persons were able to work with energy.'

It was the thoughtless habits of the rich and fashionable customers as much as anything which were responsible for the misery of the dressmakers' apprentices. For one thing there were 'unreasonable requisitions for large orders to be finished in the shortest possible time'; for another there was 'the long delay in paying their bills by ladies of fashion', which made the employers cut staff and wages to the bone. This, said the *Illuminated Magazine* article, was 'the cause of the failure of dressmakers and milliners; and, were their difficulties for ready money lightened by prompt attention to their just remuneration, one cause of the toil and suffering we have described would be removed'.

Even worse off than the dressmakers – if abject misery is susceptible of comparison – were the slopworkers who did plain sewing, usually making shirts, in the squalor of their lodgings, 'sewing at once, with a double thread, a shroud as well as a shirt'. William Shaw, an army clother, wrote a report of a meeting of slopworkers held on December 3, 1849 in Shadwell, in the East End of London. The purpose of the gathering was to investigate the sufferings of the women. About 1,200 turned up, and by asking them to hold up their hands rough statistics were gathered. Only three or four of them had underclothing; 508 had borrowed clothes to come; 151 had never had beds; 464 had asked for parish assistance in the past week; and 238 had been forced to leave their lodgings because they could not pay the rent. In the whole 1,200 only five had earned six shillings during the last week. Earnings commonly ranged from half-a-crown to under one shilling.

It was the slopworkers whose miseries Tom Hood lamented in the 'Song of the Shirt' which appeared in the 1843 Christmas number of *Punch*:

> 'O! men with sisters dear,
> O! men with mothers and wives!
> It is not linen you're wearing out,
> But human creatures lives!'

It is hardly surprising that among slopworkers and dressmakers those who had sufficient attractions left after the desolating effect of filth and starvation went on the streets part-time to try to bring their earnings up to a subsistence level. When Hippolyte Taine went to Cremorne Gardens one Derby Night in the 1860s, he and his friends sat down near three young women who, like all the others there, had gone to Cremorne to be picked up. 'One of them,' wrote Taine, 'was very gay and wild: I have never seen such overflowing animal spirits. Another, modest, quite pretty, rather subdued, was a milliner by trade, entirely dependent on herself. She has a friend, or lover, who spends her Sundays with her.' Taine looked at her carefully. 'It was clear that she had the makings of an amiable and respectable girl. What had been the turning point?' he wondered.[1] It was an artless question. Poverty was the answer, as it was for so many thousands of others.

A first step towards trying to alleviate the sweated conditions of dressmakers was taken in 1843 with the formation of an 'Association for the Relief and Protection of Young Persons Employed in the Dressmaking and Millinery Departments in London'. The Association had an impressive list of influential ladies of rank supporting it, but its achievements could only be nugatory without legislative help. 'The principle has now been recognized that childhood and youth are in need of, and are entitled to, legal protection,' said the anonymous writer in the *Illuminated Magazine*, 'but there is, amongst the youngest class, one which claims an especial protection. This class consists of the apprentices. Apprenticeship has become in many trades a grievous slavery.'

The slave conditions under which the apprentices worked meant that it was harder for the journeywomen to find employment, or at least to find employment that was adequately paid. The labour market was overstocked and the conditions of the workers were in consequence deplorable. 'That the case would be greatly ameliorated if the apprentices and young "improvers" were protected by law is evident; and the public will look to Lord Ashley to continue the good work he has begun and to force the consideration of their case on the attention of the legislature.'

Legislative help did not come for another quarter of a century and even then it was ineffective. In July 1869, two years after the passing of the Workshops Act which was intended to improve conditions, the London weekly *Echoes* published a

[1] Taine, op. cit., p. 37.

comment on 'Milliners and Their Slaves': 'We want a new Hood to sing the song of the dressmaker; we want someone to stir the hearts of English ladies so that their patronage may be withheld from those milliners who employ their workgirls beyond the legal hours. The favourite *locale* of these malpractices is the West End parish of St George's, Hanover Square and on several occasions since the passing of the Act dressmakers in that neighbourhood have been taken before the amiable Mr Tyrwhitt and fined forty shillings – a paltry forty shillings! Why, so small a fine is a mere bagatelle when we remember the enormous profits made by these vampires to whom a week or two in gaol, with a strictly prison diet, would do a great deal of good. We have not the honour of belonging to the gentle sex; but if we did, we know several milliners' shops which we would *not* patronize; and if the ladies of Mayfair and Belgravia did their duty by their poorer sisters, these female slave-drivers would soon put up the shutters.'

The 'Song of the Shirt' was as topical in 1864, when Mrs Gladstone wrote to *The Times* about the misery of needle-women who received sevenpence a gross for stitching collar-bands and who, after paying for their own cotton, were left with 2¾d a day, as it was when it was published twenty years earlier. Indeed it was still valid in 1884 when the young Beatrice Potter, later to become Beatrice Webb, worked as a button-holer in a sweat-shop in the East End of London as part of her self-imposed training for her career as a social investigator. The sink of sweated labour was as noisome as ever right to the end of Victoria's reign.

The Field Gangs

Conditions for women workers in the towns were bad; they were not much better in the country whence so many had come with the fond hope that they would be exchanging a dreary stagnating life for the lights and excitements of a city. The proportion of rural women engaged in agriculture in the early years of Victoria's reign varied according to the district and season. In the south-western counties of England there were few families where either the wife or the children were not employed in farm labour, though in those districts of Dorset and Devon where the domestic industries of buttonmaking or lace-making were still comparatively thriving the women usually stayed at home and the children worked in the fields. But in places where domestic industries had disappeared, in East Anglia for instance, farm labour was the only available occupation. In the Woodbridge area of Suffolk about half the women were said to be employed in agriculture. As to the season: at hay- and harvest-times, whatever the district, there were usually as many women and girls working in the fields as men and boys.

The 1843 Government Inquiry into the Employment of Women and Children in Agriculture found that women were working at the chief tasks in agriculture in all counties. For example, a Dorset farmer called Burgess told the Commissioners that he employed six to eight women all the year round – 'in winter, in threshing and hacking turnips for sheep, at other times, in hoeing turnips and keeping the land clean, in hay-harvest and corn-harvest. In winter they work whilst it is light, and in spring from eight till six, with an hour and a half for dinner: at hay-time and harvest hours are not so regular. Women reap, I have employed forty women at a time in reaping. Generally they get eightpence a day; at harvest one shilling with two quarts of ale or cider; sometimes if they work at task work at harvest they earn one and sixpence a day besides drink; they also get one and sixpence a day at turnip-hoeing, which is task work, but with that there is no liquor.'

Married women were preferred as day-labourers, and as younger women were often prevented by their families from constant and regular work in the fields, many of those engaged full-time were between the ages of forty and sixty – some indeed were still to be found working in the fields at seventy.

The large number of women and children working outdoors during the first decades of Victoria's reign was the direct result of the 1834 Poor Law, which began a new unhappy era for the agricultural labourer. For nearly forty years, since the Speenhamland Act of 1795, his wage in many districts had been supplemented from the rates, and this allowance took the place, partially at least, of the earnings from domestic industry by which his wife and children had formerly supported themselves; agricultural wages had been based on the assumption that they were not the complete family wage. The 1834 Act abolished allowances, and the agricultural depression, together with the over-stocked labour market, prevented the expected rise in wages which would have off-set this abolition. 'The married man's wage, therefore, remained at a minimum and had in some way or other to be supplemented for the support of the family. The farmer on his side was still compelled to economize and could not afford to pay a higher price for the same labour. But by providing extra work for women and children he could receive a further profit on his outlay and could also ease conditions for the labourer. This, therefore, was the solution adopted,' and women and children increasingly worked in the fields.[1]

In certain districts, especially in the eastern counties where the system originated, this increased labour was organized on the Gang System. A farmer in need of labour would apply to a local gang-master who would contract to do the work for an agreed sum. He then selected from the people in his employment as many men, women and children as he thought necessary and sent them to the farm under an overseer. The Gang System imposed great physical hardship on the labourers because of the distances the gangs had to walk to and from their work in all seasons and all weathers. They might have to walk seven or eight miles each way and work from 8.30 a.m. to 5.30 p.m. For the adults this was hardship enough; for the little children of seven or less the suffering was indescribable.

The Gang System arose because of the lack of labour in closed parishes. A closed parish was one in which cottages had been pulled down and no new ones built in order to reduce the landowner's liability to pay poor rates. The labourers who were thus prevented from living in closed parishes had to go some miles away to the open parishes in which there were no restrictions on settlement. Thus there was an imbalance between labour centres and labour needs, and it was to correct this that the gangs grew up in the open villages.

When the 1843 Commissioners examined the Gang System they found that its economic advantages for the farmers were far outweighed by its injurious influences, both physical and moral. The moral influences may be imagined, when one remembers that the employment of a woman and her payment for work depended on the pleasure of the gang-master and his overseer. The brutality and licence of some gang-masters was atrocious. Sometimes a court case resulted.

One case, one of many, heard at the Downham Market
_____
[1] Pinchbeck, op. cit., p. 85.

Sessions in Norfolk concerned a girl of thirteen who complained in court that the gang-master had pulled her down and pulled her clothes up to the waist. It was dinner-time and the other boys and girls in the gang were around. When she called for help the others laughed. 'Open your legs more,' the gang-master said to her. When she tried to sit up he hurt her hand. 'He was on me and I could not get up because he was laying on me flat,' she told the court. 'I was on my back on the ground.' A witness, another girl of thirteen, said the plaintiff had taken the gang-master's stick away from him; that he got on her and rubbed her face, but did not pull up her clothes. The gang-master, who was seventy-two years old, got two months hard labour.

The 1843 Report condemned the Gang System; nevertheless, it gathered strength for another twenty-five years until at last public opinion was sufficiently aroused by its worst features to demand an inquiry which resulted in the regulation of the gangs. By the Gangs Act of 1867 no child under eight years of age could be employed, all gang-masters had to be licensed, women were not allowed to work in the same gangs as men, any woman working under a gang-master had to be accompanied by a woman also licensed to act as a gang-master, and Justices of the Peace were empowered to regulate the distances which children were allowed to travel on foot. The final blow to the gangs came from the Education Act of 1870 which made it illegal to employ children under ten in agricultural work. When child labour could no longer be exploited the Gang System perished.

The First Step to the Haymarket
According to the Dorset farmer, Burgess, one could always pick out the women agricultural workers at church on Sundays 'by their size and ruddy looks'. In his opinion this showed that working out of doors was 'a good thing for women'. It was an opinion airily shared by the medical profession; apart from the rheumatism that came from insufficient clothing and hard weather conditions agricultural work was deemed to be healthy. But this was to ignore the sort of home life these agricultural workers had. They lived in filthy, damp, ill-ventilated and over-crowded cottages. There were no baths and scant hot water for washing either themselves or their clothes. The general standard of health was, in fact, low because of insufficient food and the

necessity of putting wet clothes on again next morning because there was insufficient means of drying them properly overnight. It is not surprising that if there was a domestic industry in the neighbourhood it was preferred to field labour.

An article in the *Saturday Review* of April 3, 1858 stated bluntly that the cottage bedroom was the first step to the Haymarket. The state of rural labourers' cottages was such that girls between school and going into service lived in conditions where incest was forced on them without them even knowing what the word meant. 'The promiscuous herding of children in their immature years' is a 'not infrequent prelude to a life of harlotry.' Cottage reform was a subject, said the *Saturday*, which people did not usually talk about, but it was, 'to speak plainly, one of the great necessities of the day' and one which must be faced unless people wanted 'to live forever in a fool's paradise of self-illusion'.

The abysmal condition of rural housing was borne out a decade earlier in the Report of the 1843 Commissioners. Mr Henry Phelps told the Commissioners that at Studley in Warwickshire 'it is not at all uncommon for a whole family to sleep in the same room. The number of bastards in that place is very great.' This he attributed not to the women working in the fields, 'but more to the want of proper accommodation in the cottages'. In one case at Studley there were twenty-nine people living under one roof. And at Stourpaine in Dorset one of the Commissioners found that the ordinary accommodation of a labouring family in that district was typified by 'a room 10 ft square, roof with open thatch, and only 7 ft high in the middle, with one window of about 15 ins square' in which a family of eleven slept in three beds – the mother and father and two young children in one, two grown-up daughters and a younger girl in the second, and four sons in the third.

Nor did these conditions improve for many years. Augustus Hare, in the first volume of his autobiography, describes the state in which a family called Gudgen lived at Southgate north of London. 'Two dirty, shaggy children never washed or combed since their mother was taken ill. The eldest daughter in tattered clothes with dishevelled hair was washing some rags, the fumes of which filled the room, while the floor was deep in dirt.' When Hare asked about the sleeping arrangements the mother replied: 'We have but two beds and I sleep in the middle of one with Martha on one side and Polly on the other, and Lisa has her head out at the bottom and sleeps at our feet; and father sleeps in the little bed with Emma on one side and Tom on the other and Georgey, he lies at their feet, and Lu, she lies with her grandmother.' This was in 1853.

When Taine visited England a few years later he was appalled at what he found. 'Some of the cottages are very poor, built of wattle and daub, with thatched roofs, the rooms too low and too small, the windows also too small, the interior walls too thin. Think of a large family crowded into two such rooms in winter, with clothes drying on them, baby linen hung up to air, and a roaring fire: during the long periods of rain and snow they must live in an unwholesome atmosphere breathing their own bodily emanations. Many of the mothers have haggard faces blotchily red, and a wasted exhausted look; they have too many children and are all overtired. The tenant of one of these cottages was a day-labourer, married, father of six children, and earning twelve shillings a week.'[1]

Nor did bad housing escape the bitter humour of *Punch*. One cartoon published in 1861 showed a landowner pointing out the virtues of his stables to Mr Punch – 'handsome, clean stall, well aired, plenty of light, drainage, perfect ventilation, the best water and the best feed possible, and good treatment, that's my plan'. From the stables they move on to a cottage. The squalor in the single room is horrible. 'Your stable arrangements are excellent,' says Mr Punch to the landlord. 'Suppose you try something of the sort here! Eh?'

Nails, Chains, and Phossy-Jaw
A domestic industry which gave employment to women was the 'toy trade'. This was the collective name given to the small metal trades which were chiefly located in the Birmingham, Wolverhampton, and South Staffordshire areas. It was these areas to which R. H. Horne specifically referred as the 'newly-discovered regions', so little was known of them by the general public.

The small metal trades made nails, chains, nuts, bolts, screws, bits, buckles, stirrups, files, and locks. All, except lockmaking, employed women and children extensively. They worked in squalid domestic workshops hidden 'like bird-nests' up filthy courts and alleys, their half-naked bodies filthy and misshapen

[1] Taine, op. cit., pp. 128–9.

from the posture they had to work in. In some of the trades more sophisticated machinery was introduced and the domestic workshops gave place to factories. But until well after the middle of the century domestic employment was far greater than factory employment in the metal trades. In many cases a single factory would be divided up into numerous separate workshops each run by a small master whose labour was organized domestically, so that the transition from one type of organization to the other was often imperceptible and equivocal.

In fact domestic organization in the small metal trades persisted throughout the whole of Victoria's reign. So too did the conditions described by Horne. 'The workshops of the small masters,' he wrote in the *Illuminated Magazine*, 'are usually of the dirtiest, most dilapidated, and confined description, and situated in the most filthy and undrained localities at the back of their wretched abodes.' Some of the masters were 'respectable and humane men, who do not suffer any degree of poverty to render them brutal', but there were many more who behaved towards their employees, 'not so much with neglect and harshness, as with ferocious violence, the result of unbridled passions, excited often by ardent spirits, acting on bodies exhausted by overwork, and on minds which have never received the slightest moral or religious culture, and which, therefore, never exercise the smallest moral or religious restraint'.

Nearly fifty years later the Reverend Harold Rylett wrote an article about this same region for the December 1889 issue of the *English Illustrated Magazine*. Although he was not prepared to say 'that the dwellings of the people are any worse than the dwellings of the labouring poor in most of our large towns' he found that the sanitary arrangements throughout the nail and chain districts were 'simply disgusting'. Indeed he was puzzled that the general health of the people should be so good (apart from an abnormally high death-rate among children) while the sanitary arrangements were so bad. 'It is quite a common thing to find an overflowing midden adjoining a nail or chain shop or within two yards of it; and open drains flowing for hundreds of yards past the houses and the shops in which the people live and work are of frequent occurrence.' It was 'without exception the filthiest district I ever saw, and I have seen all the large towns of Great Britain and Ireland'. And apart from the stench and the ordure there was a depressing pall of squalor. 'Most of the houses in which the nailers and chainmakers live are small, and many are in a most dilapidated condition. Indeed, the entire district covered by the nail and chain trades presents a most melancholy appearance. Here you have a whole street in ruins; there you have another street where the houses appear to be on the very verge of toppling over.' And the workshops were worse than the houses. 'It is not uncommon for the people to be compelled to "quit working" whenever there is a fall of rain.'

Nevertheless, despite these conditions and the harshness of the work, many of the women themselves were strongly opposed to any legislative interference with their employment. In 1887 when a new Factory Act was under discussion, a deputation from the Cradley Heath Nail and Chain-Makers went to see the Home Secretary in order to dissuade him from any restrictions on their working. When he told them that it was wrong for women to be made to do such hard work they looked at each other wonderingly because it was clear that the poor man did not know what he was talking about. Nail and chainmaking was their life; they could look after themselves and wanted no misplaced help from a paternal government.

Coal-mining and the 'toy trade' were brutalizing occupations for women. So, too, was some of the work in the pottery industry where women were increasingly employed from 1845 on after the introduction of machinery. But there were others where the nature of the work was literally deadly. Match factories gave girl workers the hideous agony of phossy-jaw, in which the lower jaw was slowly eaten away by fumes from the phosphorus used for the match-heads. Ventilation and washing would have lessened the danger, but no one thought of washing or of blowing the fumes away. When the girls took off their clothes at night the material glowed from the phosphorus that had impregnated it – and where the girls' skin was not protected by clothing it glowed too!

Chapter 6
ALL THE FAULT OF THE FACTORIES

As the reformers had intended, respectable opinion was aghast at the disclosures in the reports of the Employment Commissioners, but the shock was not equally spread. Women in the mines was a horrifying revelation; but women in the brutal agricultural gangs was something to get less worked up about (no doubt because rural employment was so commonplace and of such long-standing that its conditions were considered part of the natural order), and the women in Horne's other 'newly-discovered regions' were allowed to go on working under the conditions he described for even longer. What did take root in the minds of the respectables, however, was the conviction that the cause of all the trouble was the factory system. It was the factory system which had made women work. It was the factory system which had produced the appalling conditions.

In fact neither the work nor the conditions, at least in their squalor, were new. Women had been spinning and weaving since time immemorial; they had been working in the mines since coal was first hewed. And the work they did under the domestic system was neither as pleasant nor as satisfying as the myth would have us believe. Even today, when there is a wealth of published research to show that the myth misrepresented the truth, the popular conception of the industrial revolution is of a Moloch that overwhelmed the peasants' golden days.

Why, then, did the myth arise? The answer is 'ignorance'. There had been reformers who investigated industrial conditions before the 1830s and 1840s, and there had been official reports

95

on the subject earlier in the nineteenth century. But these had been ignored and forgotten, partly because the climate of the times was not conducive to social sympathy and to a desire to improve conditions, partly because such reforming zeal as there was had been concentrated on the long struggle to abolish slavery. Thus, when the new investigators and reformers began to examine the conditions of the poor in the 1830s and 1840s, they found what to them was a new and unbelievable state of squalor and misery. Their researches, as Horne wrote, were 'Travels into Newly-discovered Regions'. They found women and children working in the black dark of the mines, they found them in the Dantesque hell of Wolverhampton and Willenhall, they found them in the unhealthy conditions of the cotton-mills. Undoubtedly the reformers and those respectables whom they influenced were upset by the brutality in the mines and the metal-shops, where drunken masters grievously assaulted their apprentices; but what upset many of them even more and sent them into paroxysms of disapproval were the 'grave moral dangers' attendant on the unrestricted mingling of the sexes which occurred in the mines and in the mills. Their assumption was that if the sexes were allowed to mix freely immorality would automatically follow. It was this that really agitated the respectables, and their disapproval was just as strong half-a-century later when, for example, the Reverend Harold Rylett paid his visit to the Black Country and reported in the December 1889 *English Illustrated Magazine* that the use of the oliver in the making of spike nails was 'nothing short of a scandal', because to use this treadle-operated sledge-hammer a young girl had to grasp a man round the waist.

According to Ivy Pinchbeck's researches, criticism of the factory system that persisted throughout at least the rest of the century was based largely on the evidence given to the Sadler Committee in 1832, and a great deal of this evidence was suspect because of 'the extraordinary manner' in which the questions were frequently put to the witnesses. 'Extraordinary manner' was the phrase used by a sub-commissioner of the 1833 Factory Commission who re-examined some of the principal witnesses the year after the Sadler Committee.

On the basis of the Sadler Committee's report it was assumed that the conditions were the result of the factory system instead of its being realized that they were simply an exaggerated continuation in an urban setting of the conditions that had obtained rurally. Coming from their comfortable, well-ordered homes most of the Top Nation were unaware that to the Lower Nation these conditions were standard. Furthermore, when they questioned the 'hands' about conditions as they were in the factories and as they had been in the cottages under the domestic system, it is to be expected that they would be told they were better in the old days. This was not only because it is a general human characteristic to refer back nostalgically to the 'good old days' but because despite the long hours, wretched pay, and disgusting working conditions in the cottages, factory work imposed a much stricter regularity and discipline in hours and overseeing, and was therefore more irksome for that reason. Liberty, if only to starve, was what the 'hands' missed most. Also, if one is living in a stinking Manchester cellar with the court full of ordure and offal and the walls dripping sewage, one is unlikely to reply that these conditions, if not better, are certainly no worse than one was accustomed to in a daub cottage in the country. Present distress effaces past misery.

There were those who tried to point out the facts that were being forgotten. R. W. Cooke Taylor in his *Factories and the Factory System* published in 1844 said that visitors to Manchester made 'the double blunder of believing that all its working classes belong to the factory population, and that all the ill-health and misconduct they witness among females of the lower ranks in that town may be ascribed to the factory system'.[1] Only in rural districts, he said, could the factory system 'fairly be tested by its own merits'. The rookeries of Manchester were in existence before the turn of the century, before the factories came to the town. It was the overcrowding that resulted from the growing population, including a large Irish element with abysmally low living standards, that exacerbated the evils of the lower depths.

But opponents of the factory system included the rookeries and the factories in a single sweep of the hand. They did not want to be told that there was not necessarily a causal relationship. They paid heed only to those who told them that domestic-system conditions were better because they disapproved of the new system for reasons of morality.

As well as the opportunities they thought it gave for

[1] R. W. Cooke Taylor, *Factories and the Factory System* (1844), p. 39.

97

immorality, the factory system was deplored by the respectables because they considered that it encouraged early and improvident marriages and undermined the sanctity of family life. By employing women in cotton-mills, Lord Ashley apostrophized in a House of Commons debate, 'you are poisoning the very sources of order and happiness and virtue; you are tearing up root and branch all relations of families to one another, you are annulling, as it were, the institution of domestic life decreed by Providence Himself, the wisest and kindest of all earthly ordinances, the mainstay of peace and virtue . . . and therein our national security'.

A woman's place was in the home; if she went out to work as an unmarried daughter that was bad enough – if she went out as a married woman that was dreadful. The upper and middle classes believed that working wives made idle husbands. They believed, too, that the widespread employment of married women was disintegrating the home-life of the industrious poor. The assumption behind this was that under the domestic system the woman at home had time to be a good mother, whereas away all day in a factory she had the almost impossible task of reconciling the demands of her work with those of her home.

This belief rested on an exaggerated idea of the extent to which married women were employed in the factories. The spread of the factory system had certainly provided many more jobs for women – for instance in 1818 there were 57,323 of both sexes employed in cotton-mills; by 1839 the number of women and girls alone had increased to 146,331. But this increase was not confined to married women. Broadly speaking, married women formed between a quarter and a third of all women working in factories. Nevertheless, the declamations of those who deplored the employment of married women overbore the available statistics and the myth was created that the factory system swept married women into its maw and created appalling domestic conditions in the mill towns. 'With greater justice,' as Ivy Pinchbeck says, 'an outcry might have been raised that women's agricultural work was ruining the home life of the countryside.'[1]

The majority of women in English factories were unmarried and under twenty-six years of age. They were anathema to

[1] Ivy Pinchbeck, op. cit., p. 199.

respectable Victorian thought. In Disraeli's *Sybil* they are represented by Harriet, who has left home to work in a factory and spends her short leisure hours drinking in The Temple. Girls who supported themselves, and what is worse, did not help to support their parents, girls who were independently-minded, who swore and smoked and drank and had their sexual adventures, were real Trojan mares. They were not at all to respectable taste, because the new middle-class ladies in their civilizing crusade did not want the example of these emancipated women to gain wide currency.

When Mrs Houstoun visited the New England factories at Newburyport on the Merrimack in 1849 she and her party 'were filled with admiration'. Everything was so clean and well-ordered. But what struck her most in comparison with an English mill was 'the air of respectability (I might almost coin the word, and call it *ladylikeness*) observable in the female operatives. There were several hundred women and girls employed in this factory, and I was assured that the moral character of each was subjected to the strictest investigation before they were engaged. The dress, appearance, and manners of these females are very much on a par with those of the "young ladies" in a milliner's shop in London. But we were told, that so high was the standard of character among the factory girls, and so elevated their tone of feeling, that anyone among them who was suspected of lightness of conduct was shunned by the rest, and was, in most cases, expelled from the factory. I have seldom seen so many pretty girls collected together as at the Newburyport Mills, and they all looked *as* healthy as Americans usually do – which perhaps is not saying much.'

The high moral character of these model New England factory girls, whether genuine or not – and there is evidence to suggest that lapses from grace were not as rare as Mrs Houstoun's eulogy implies[1] – must have seemed to the English visitors in remarkable contrast to the generally-held opinion about English factory girls that they had neither virtue nor a sense of shame. But the truth was that factory morality was no worse than working-class morality generally. The immorality of agricultural gangs was established – though Lord Ashley for one

[1] See for example E. J. Dingwall, *The American Woman* (Duckworth, 1956), p. 69.

never referred to it. Morality was no better among the female nailers of Birmingham, or the domestic lacemakers of Nottinghamshire and Bedfordshire, or the women employed in the North Staffordshire potteries, or domestic servants in London and elsewhere. The Top Nation detractors of the factory system were saddling it with responsibility for a state of affairs that existed independently of it. The causes were common to all large towns and were not peculiar to factory life at all. It was the dreadful housing conditions and filthy lodging-houses in which both sexes were huddled indiscriminately together that provided the environment for degradation. As a witness to the 1904 Interdepartmental Committee on Physical Deterioration concluded: 'The standard of morals in a factory very largely reflects the standard outside it.'

Dodging the Tax on Love

There were two other major questions concerning the employment of mothers in Victorian industry. First, did employment of married women in cotton-mills diminish their fertility? And second, how did it affect the infant mortality rate?

The evidence on the first point shows that employment in cotton-mills undoubtedly resulted in smaller families, but whether this was the result of 'moral restraint' or contraceptive measures is not certain. Information about birth control had been circulating in England since the early 1820s. Francis Place, the reformer and breeches-maker of Charing Cross, started to distribute the first of what his enemies called his three 'diabolical handbills' in 1823. This first leaflet was headed 'To the Married of Both Sexes' and described in the simplest language how conception could be prevented. The method suggested consisted in 'a piece of sponge, about an inch square, being placed in the vagina previous to coition, and afterwards withdrawn by means of a double twisted thread, or bobbin, attached to it'. Because this method depended on the female it seemed most likely to be successful, and there were no injurious consequences from its use, 'neither does it diminish the enjoyment of either party. The sponge should, as a matter of preference, be used rather damp, and when convenient a little warm.'

This first leaflet circulated by the thousand in the industrial North, despite the fact that there was strong opposition to it among many working-class organizers. Its successors were equally popular. These were addressed 'To the Married of Both Sexes in Genteel Life' and 'To the Married of Both Sexes of the Working People'. The latter was in even simpler language than the first handbill and included a statement of the purpose behind this first systematic attempt to teach birth control. Large families, it said, led to poverty. Smaller families would ultimately result in a shortage of labour and hence higher wages and shorter working hours. 'You will have some time for recreation, some means of enjoying yourselves rationally, some means as well as some time for your own and your children's moral and religious instruction.' Nor should anyone be put off by the thought that this was some deep-laid plot of the upper classes: 'You cannot fail to see that this address is intended solely for your good. It is quite impossible that those who address you can receive any benefit from it, beyond the satisfaction which every benevolent person, every true Christian, must feel at seeing you comfortable, healthy and happy.'

Parcels of the handbills were sent to the editors of working-class newspapers, copies were used as wrappers for cheap tallow candles and as coverings for penny boxes of snuff, others were distributed to the wives and daughters of mechanics and tradesmen at markets, others again were dropped down areas to the servant girls scrubbing the steps. It was for distributing handbills in this fashion that the seventeen-year-old John Stuart Mill was arrested and sent to prison for a few days. The handbills were also reprinted in Richard Carlile's *Republican* and publicized, though strongly opposed, in T. J. Wooler's *Black Dwarf*.

In May 1825 Carlile himself published a long article 'What is Love' in the *Republican*. It was written, he said, in response to a flood of letters 'asking, begging, praying for, offering to pay for, more information upon this important subject', to which he had made passing reference in an article a few months earlier. The evils of too large families, Carlile wrote, were 'a tax upon love'. He drew attention to the evils that arose from 'bastard children, from deserted children, from half-starved and diseased children' and from overcrowding and bad housing. Abortion and infanticide were common. Better prevention than cure. He quoted in full 'To the Married of Both Sexes of the Working People'. The importance of the 'preventive check' was, he said, that no married couple need have more children than they wanted and could maintain; no woman need endanger her life; there need be no illegitimate children where they were not wanted by the mother; and sexual intercourse might be made independent of the dread of conception. This last point was particularly upsetting to moralists.

In February 1826 'What is Love' was reprinted as a pamphlet. It had a frontispiece showing a naked Adam and Eve, and a new title. It was now called *Every Woman's Book; or, What is Love*. The reader was told of a prudent but not surprisingly unnamed English duchess 'who never goes out to dinner without being prepared with the sponge'; and of a gentleman who 'has made an experiment of using the sponge unknown to the female, of which she was ignorant until it was shown to her'. Although the text of the handbill was now deleted the various preventive methods were briefly explained. 'One is to wear the skin, or what in France is called the *baudruche*, in England, commonly, *the glove*. These are sold in London at brothels, by waiters at taverns, and by some women and girls in the neighbourhood of places of public resort such as Westminster Hall etc.' Another method suggested was partial or complete withdrawal at the moment of emission. And a third means was to emit the semen in the cavity below the womb by 'lying in a parallel line on the female, leg on leg, at the time of emission' – a suggestion that was amended in a later edition to read 'by mutual withdrawing or elevation of the body at the time of emission'.

Carlile's book went quickly through several editions and by the beginning of 1828 ten thousand copies had been sold. There may have been a somewhat wider circulation of contraceptive methods than some purchasers of the book expected. Another publication called *Every Woman's Book* came out at this time. Its subject, however, was cooking, which was not, as Carlile pointed out, every woman's business!

In 1832, a year after it had first been published in the United States, the first English edition of Robert Dale Owen's *Moral Physiology* appeared. Although most of it was devoted to the social and eugenic arguments for family limitation it also described three preventive checks: *coitus interruptus*, the vaginal sponge, and thirdly, 'a covering made of very fine, smooth, and delicately prepared skin', whose efficacy was certain but which was disagreeable on the score of cleanliness, 'a baudruche being fit for use once only and costing about a dollar'. In later editions the vaginal sponge and condom methods were omitted. *Moral Physiology* sold on average a thousand copies a year for the next forty years.

Early in 1832 the American doctor Charles Knowlton published his *Fruits of Philosophy, or the Private Companion of Young Married People*. Knowlton was the first to recommend chemical methods and douching and, according to Peter Fryer, has 'every right to be called the founder of American contraceptive medicine'.[1] *Fruits of Philosophy* was published in Britain as a sixpenny pamphlet in 1834. For the next forty years it contributed to the quiet spread of knowledge about contraception, and then in 1877–9 it became the means by which contraceptive methods spread like a flood at the time of the Bradlaugh-Besant trials which are described in a later chapter.

The extent to which this information was read and talked about can only be inferred from occasional statistics and from an understanding of human nature. Most historians of population and contraception are agreed that before the Bradlaugh-Besant trials there was only a 'limited percolation downwards' of birth control information. Perhaps, however, it would be truer to refer to it as a limited percolation sideways and upwards. The information was, and had been for centuries, the stock-in-trade of the prostitute and the courtesan. Surely it is more likely that knowledge of it should spread first in the classes from which the prostitutes came and in which the cruelties of life were such as to put 'moral refinement' at a premium? As Margaret Hewitt says in *Wives and Mothers in Victorian Industry*, 'given the conflict between motherhood and money-earning, it would be highly unlikely that the operatives had not acquainted themselves with the information contained in these handbills and articles. This supposition gained support from the wide circulation enjoyed by Place's handbill in the manufacturing districts of the North, and from the results of a survey by the Manchester Statistical Society in 1835 *On Immoral and Irreligious Works Sold in Manchester*,' which showed that during the previous year six hundred copies of *The Bridal Gem*, *Fruits of Philosophy* and *Moral Physiology* had been sold.[2] This may not seem many, but

[1] Peter Fryer, *The Birth Controllers* (Secker & Warburg, 1965), p. 103.
[2] Margaret Hewitt, *Wives and Mothers in Victorian Industry* (Rockliff, 1958), p. 95.

illiteracy was so prevalent that the spread of information cannot be equated with the number of copies sold. One copy of the *Fruits of Philosophy* sold to a literate factory girl would mean that the information was shared with all her friends. Any worker in a modern office will know that such information passes as much by word of mouth as it does on the printed page. Indeed, at the same time that immorality in the factory districts 'was being computed according to offspring born out of wedlock', says Wanda Neff on the authority of the Sadler Committee Report, 'the charge was made that the fact that no more unlawful children could be produced for the records was attributable to the wide circulation of books on birth control by Richard Carlile'.[1]

Nor need one imagine that the reading of Carlile was confined to prostitutes, actual and potential. One witness told the Sadler Committee: 'Where individuals are congregated, as in factories, I conceive that means preventive of impregnation are more likely to be generally known and practised by young persons.' On the other hand, the year after the Sadler Committee, the Factories Inquiry Commission heard from a prominent Leeds medical practitioner, Dr Hunter, that in his opinion although books and pamphlets ('the disgrace of the age', the Sadler Committee had called them) were on sale in the district very few came into the hands of the working classes, and, he added, 'I firmly believe they are never acted upon.'

Despite Dr Hunter the impression remains that working women, married and unmarried, were using birth control.

Infant Mortality
On the second major question, the infant mortality rate, the conclusion is inescapable that substantial employment of women away from home, whether in field or factory, did inevitably lead to a high infant death rate. For example, the mortality of infants under a year old in England and Wales as a whole in 1855 was 153 per 1,000 births. Whereas in Lancashire it was 186 per 1,000, in the East Anglian counties of Essex, Suffolk and Norfolk it was 155, and in Westmorland it was only 105. The fact that the death rate of infants was so high in East Anglia shows that it was not simply the slum conditions of town life which caused infant mortality. The employment of the

[1] Wanda Neff, op. cit., pp. 54-5.

mothers was also an important factor. It was in East Anglia that the Gang System flourished and it was the daily absence of mothers working in the gangs that caused the high death rate. The children would be left in the care of some old woman or young girl who was either unfit or unwilling to look after and feed them properly. In one of her *Essays on Woman's Work* published in 1865, Bessie Rayner Parkes wrote of 'the frightful mortality among children who are left to the care of youthful inefficient nurses, the accidents by fire and water and dangerous falls'.[1] 'There can, in fact, be no doubt,' says Margaret Hewitt, 'that throughout Victoria's reign, in so far as babies had to be artificially fed because of their mothers' absence at work their lives were imperilled.' To such a pass did this come that in 1871 a Select Committee was set up to consider the Best Measures of Protecting Infants put out to Nurse.

Nor was it only unsuitable artificial feeding that killed off the infants of working women. Many of them were drugged to death. Bessie Parkes was told 'of an abominable practice occasionally pursued by ignorant mothers when leaving their children for the day; namely, tying a bit of sponge which had been previously dipped in some narcotic into an infant's mouth for it to suck! A very certain method of keeping the poor little thing quiet during its hours of loneliness.'[2] The widespread use of 'sleepy stuff' and 'Quietness', which were preparations of laudanum, was responsible for many deaths. The vicious circle was this: the mother wanted to get back to work as soon as she physically could after the birth of a child. She put the infant out to nurse with some old woman or young girl. The nurse fed the infant on bread and water pap. This gave it violent indigestion and when it woke screaming it was given 'sleepy stuff' to quieten it. As the misfeeding became chronic the doses had to be increased until the child died of 'teething' or 'convulsions', that is to say it died of violent indigestion or an overdose of laudanum. To break the circle the mother had to be kept off work until she had weaned the child. This in turn produced hardship and interference with 'the sanctity of the domestic hearth'. Not until 1891 was a clause included in the Factory and Workshops Bill of that year to make it illegal for any employer of labour at such premises 'knowingly' to employ a woman within four weeks of

[1] Bessie Rayner Parkes, op. cit., p. 151.
[2] ibid, p. 152.

her confinement. This clause, for a variety of reasons, was strongly opposed by the Women's Rights party.

The Early Factory Acts
From the outset, opposition to factory legislation was hydra-headed. 'The greed of the manufacturers,' wrote Wanda Neff in *Victorian Working Women*, 'was a formidable foe.' 'Greed' is an emotive word and if one is to be as judicial as possible one should perhaps substitute 'desire for profit'. As John Bright said, he was in business for no other reason than to procure for himself and his family 'a comfortable income'.[1] The manufacturers argued that any statutory reduction of hours would result in loss. They were backed in their argument by political economists and factory inspectors who maintained that fixed capital could only show a profitable return if it was worked over long hours – an argument that still has currency but has been met in some industries by shift-working. Nassau Senior advanced his famous theory that all the profit was derived from the last hour of work. Nor was it only on the grounds of applied economics that the economists, those professors of the 'dismal science', were opposed to regulations. Any Government regulation of industry was regarded as a fundamental interference with the liberty of

[1] There is an interesting example of what one might call the 'Eminent Victorians attitude' in C. W. Cunnington's *Feminine Attitudes in the Nineteenth Century* when he is discussing John Bright's opposition to the reduction of working hours for women and children. Bright, he says, opposed the reform because he felt strongly that it would give more time for vice. 'That it might also mean diminished profits for himself as a mill-owner,' Cunnington adds cuttingly, 'was a thought which certainly never passed beyond the threshold of his unconscious mind.' But in fact Bright made no bones about the economic basis of his opposition to all interference by the State in trade, nor about the purpose for which he carried on his trade. He had never professed, he said, 'to keep on my manufactory for the benefit of my workpeople, or for the sake of clothing my customers. My object is, by the expenditure of capital, and by giving labour to a business, to procure for myself and family a comfortable income, with a hope of realizing something like a competency at a late period of my life.' He may have believed that shorter hours would encourage vice, but he also believed, consciously and openly, that it would be bad for his business.
This example provides a glimpse of the paradox: the Victorians left the impression of adopting certain attitudes that they never, in fact, pretended to adopt in their own time. They created and left an image of themselves that the Eminent Victorians school knocked down and kicked to pieces – but what they were in fact knocking down was the image, not the truth.

the subject, although paradoxically none of the early Victorian economists opposed intervention by the Government for the bettering of social conditions. Even Harriet Martineau regarded legislation to enforce the boxing-in of machinery as iniquitous, although no one could accuse her of wanting to see women and children mangled.

There were others, like John Stuart Mill, whose reasoning led them, surprisingly it might seem, to a similar conclusion from different premises; Mill feared that legislation to protect women would retard their emancipation. There were fears of foreign competition. There was inter-party bitterness. And there was the unrelieved gloom of Ashley and others which made people suspect that he was over-blackening the picture. All these hostile agencies combined to hinder factory legislation – as well, that is, as public apathy.

It was also maintained that the whole movement for factory legislation was a plot on the part of cotton-spinners to benefit themselves by getting a ten-hour working day for which they would be able to get twelve hours' pay. They were accused of inventing tales of cruelty to children and making investigators believe them.

The first of these investigators was Michael Sadler, M.P., and his Committee which, in August 1832, reported on conditions in the factories. The following year a Royal Commission reported on the same subject. Arising out of these Reports came the Factory Act of 1833. This forbade the employment of children under nine (as an earlier Act in 1819 had done) and restricted the hours of children under thirteen to eight hours daily, and those from thirteen to eighteen to twelve hours. The new Act contained an important innovation in that it appointed four inspectors to see that its regulations were obeyed. In 1833, too, the first appropriation for education was made by the Government and children in the factories were supposed to have two hours' schooling daily – but this was a mockery.

As with earlier Factory Acts – for there had been Acts in 1802, 1819, 1826 and 1830 which were on the whole ineffective because there was no system of inspection – the Factory Act of 1833 applied only to textile-mills, specifically excepting silk-mills. This was because legislation was so unpopular that it could neither be passed nor applied over a wider field; also because it was in these textile-mills only that there was a sufficient aggregation of people to make the problem appear significant.

The 1833 Act did not benefit the men. Its effect was to bring more women into the mills to replace the children. The women worked for less wages than the men; they were more amenable; they could stand up to the gruelling stretch of hours better; and, unlike the men, they were not organized – although even the men's unions were not particularly effective at this period. For all these reasons the women were preferred by the employers, and for the same reasons they aroused the antagonism of the men.

Francis Place told the men that they should refuse to work with women and girls. This would make the mill-owners sack the females. They would then go home and have time to attend to domestic duties, men's wages would rise, and there would be the dual benefit of the man earning a family-supporting wage and the woman keeping a comfortable house. But this desirable reform ignored the position of the single woman or the wife whose husband could not, or would not, get work. The theory of the reform may have been excellent, the practice was much less so.

In 1835 the total number of women of all ages in factories – and one should remember that in the 1830s and 1840s the word 'factory' was synonymous with 'mill' – was 196,383. In 1839 the number had risen to 242,296, of which a little more than a half (130,104) were over eighteen. This increase was partly the result of the introduction of new and improved machinery, as for instance the substitution of power-looms for hand-looms, but it was mainly the effect of the 1833 Act. The percentage of women workers was fifty-six in cotton, and about seventy in worsted, silk, and flax.

In 1847 the numbers had risen still further:

	Males over 18	Females over 18
Cotton	85,533	117,667
Woollen	27,610	16,215
Worsted	7,366	22,133
Flax	10,430	25,978
Silk	7,359	16,238
	138,298	198,231

The total of 198,231 women is comparable with 130,104 in 1839. There was a preponderance of adult women everywhere except in the woollen-mills where the power-loom was still little used. In the cotton factories women worked in almost every department, though the men were mule-spinners. So too in silk factories, but in the woollen and worsted factories they were spinners as well as weavers.

Influenced by the 1842 Act which, in removing women and children from the mines, had established a crucial precedent against the free play of *laissez-faire*, the next Factory Act, in 1844, restricted the hours of work of *women* as well as of children over thirteen in the textile-mills (including silk-mills) to twelve hours a day, to be worked between 5.30 a.m. and 8.30 p.m. This had the indirect result of restricting the hours of men too, as the processes could not be carried on without the women and children. Other details of this Act strengthened the law by increasing the power given to the inspectors, by excluding protected persons from the workroom during meal-time, by appointing fixed periods for meals, and by timing the hours of work and meals on a public clock approved by the inspectors. Conditions for women were also improved by the fencing of machinery.

Further progress was made with the Factory Act of 1847, which limited the hours of work for women and young persons over thirteen to fifty-eight a week. When the Act was passed there was rejoicing in the North of England – but the rejoicing of the 'Lancashire Witches' was premature. No times were fixed by the Act, so double-shifts were introduced, even though there was a trade depression in 1847. A good trade year in 1849 exacerbated the evil, and the following year its legality was upheld by a judgement of Lord Parke.

The Factory Act of 1850 fixed the hours for protected persons within the limits of 6 a.m. to 6 p.m., or 7 a.m. to 7 p.m., allowing an hour-and-a-half for meals, with work ending at 2 p.m. on Saturdays. The total time to be worked was two hours longer than before, but Lord Ashley was among those who supported the new Bill, suffering the vituperation of his former adulators in consequence. The 1850 Act established a normal working day for women and young persons for the first time. And it removed uncertainties by its directness.

The disasters that had been foretold as a result of parliamentary interference did not happen. Not only were the restrictions beneficial to the individual worker but they were in the long run advantageous to the textile industries as well. 'What was accomplished in other kinds of women's labour only after years of delay in legislation or by the slower force of public opinion was quickly brought about for factory women by the Law of 1850. They were the favoured class of women workers by the middle of the century, protected by law, and earning the same wages as men, where their work was equal in quantity and quality. Although in small part they shared the benefits of various philanthropic measures designed to assist working women, they were in less need, and consequently made little use of such relief.'[1]

When Beatrice Webb, or Beatrice Potter as she then was, visited a Bacup cotton-mill with one of her cotton operative cousins in October 1886, the new era was readily apparent. The hands, she wrote to her father, 'are a happy lot of people – quiet workers and very sociable – men and women mixing together in a free-and-easy manner – but without any coarseness that I can see; the masculine sentiment about marriage being that a man's got no friend until he's got a woman of his own! Parties of young men and women go off together for a week to Blackpool, sometimes on cheap trips to London – and as women earn as much or nearly as much as the men (except the skilled work) there is no assumption of masculine superiority. Certainly this regular mechanical work, with all the invigorating brightness of machines, and plenty of fellow-workers of both sexes, seems about the happiest lot for a human being – so long as the hours are not too long.'[2]

It was in the factories that the country's future lay.

[1] Wanda Neff, op. cit., p. 83.
[2] Beatrice Webb, *My Apprenticeship* (Longmans, 1926), p. 168.

Chapter 7

THE EXHIBITION YEAR

Britain in 1851 was a nation bursting at the seams. It was expanding in all directions – in population, in trade, in industrial output, and indeed in territory, for emigration and annexation were creating an Empire which was to last until the middle of the twentieth century.

The population of Britain grew from 18·1 million in 1841 to 20·8 million in 1851, 23·1 million in 1861, and 26·1 million in 1871 – a decennial rate of increase of 12·3 per cent, 11·0 per cent and 12·7 per cent. Indeed, during the whole of the nineteenth century the decennial increase was never lower than 11 per cent and between 1811 and 1821 it went as high as 17·9 per cent. The average over the whole century was 13·5 per cent. The birth rate reached its highest point between 1871 and 1875 and then fell off, a decrease which is discussed in a later chapter. But even then it continued at a high rate until the decade from 1911 to 1921 when, from 10·3 per cent in the previous decade, the decennial rate of increase fell to 4·7 per cent. The population of Great Britain doubled between 1801 and 1851, and then doubled again in the next sixty years.

A similar story of enormous increase is to be found in the country's trade figures. Imports in 1831 were worth £48 million; in 1841 they had increased by 30 per cent to £63 million; in 1851 they had gone up another 60 per cent to £100 million and by 1874, when a great slump hit the country, they had reached £370 million. Exports increased at an even faster rate. From £60 million in 1831 they increased by 70 per cent to £102 million in 1841 and then almost doubled to £197 million in 1851. In 1874 they had reached £297 million.

Economic growth was on such a scale that it altered the social ecology, creating new problems as well as intensifying old ones.

Britain in the 1850s was in fact an emergent nation, emerging from its rural and small town past into an industrial urban economy. By 1860 the new wealth was beginning to have a positive effect on wages. From then on real wages began to increase, first in Britain, then in Europe and North America – and this process continued until the early 1900s. Psychologically the country's richness gave the Top Nation a feeling of superiority and exhilaration. As C. W. Cunnington says in his *Feminine Attitudes in the 19th Century*, it was the firm conviction of the upper classes 'that British ideas, British customs, British goods and British religion were immeasurably the best in the world, and that it was our moral duty to export them to less fortunate nations'.[1] This enormous self-complacency found its perfect symbol in the Great Exhibition.

The Crystal Palace
London in 1851 was a city of excitement. The whole population was agog, for this was 'the Exhibition year'. It is difficult now to imagine the extraordinary enthusiasm that the Great Exhibition created. It was not just an exhibition as one thinks of an exhibition today – although in the material sense that is all it was: a vast collection of exhibits ranged for mile upon mile in a building specially erected for the purpose in Hyde Park. Its promoters, it is true, had visions beyond the mere display of 'the Works of Industry of All Nations'. Under the active chairmanship of the young Prince Consort they planned an exhibition which they hoped would stimulate a much-needed improvement in industrial design, would further encourage those bounding exports, and – an aim dear to the Prince's earnest heart – would give a great fillip to technical education, which was virtually non-existent.

None of these worthy objects, it need hardly be said, had any appeal for the public. Indeed when the project first began it was the laughing-stock of London. There was nothing then to suggest that even before it was opened the Great Exhibition would have been transmogrified from a formidable clutter of

[1] C. W. Cunnington, *Feminine Attitudes in the 19th Century* (Heinemann, 1935), p. 151.

7. Mrs Beeton (*left*), without whose book no household could be properly run. The Hon. Mrs Caroline Norton (*above*), R. B. Sheridan's grand-daughter and one of the first woman journalists.

A Victorian Bedroom. The lady is the Hon. Mrs Gerald Wellesley whose husband was the Dean of Windsor. In her youth she was nicknamed 'The Measles' because she was so lovely that all the young men who met her inevitably fell in love with her. *Susan Lady Tweedsmuir.*

8. A Victorian Family. The Curtis family of Alton, Hampshire, 1865, and (*below*) their 'domestics'. The father, Dr Curtis (seated on the right), was a local doctor. His grandfather was Jane Austen's doctor when she lived at nearby Chawton. *Curtis Museum.*

bits and pieces into an array of glory. The worthy aims failed, but the exhibition was a fantastic success.

Without doubt it was the special building that was largely responsible for the magic. Designed by Joseph Paxton, it was a gigantic glasshouse of fairy-tale fame. 'When I first saw it glittering in the morning sun,' recalled one visitor many years later, 'I felt as if Aladdin and the Jin who was the slave of the lamp must have been at work upon it – no mere human hands and hammers and builders' tools could have wrought such a miracle.' While it was being built Paxton's friend, Douglas Jerrold, christened it in *Punch*. He called it the Crystal Palace. The name gave a new image to the whole exhibition. Scorn changed to excitement. No longer dull and earnest and uplifting, it promised to be an occasion of gaiety and light.

On May 1 the Queen opened the Great Exhibition in the presence of 25,000 invited guests and season-ticket holders. From the outset people crowded to see it. Excursion trains poured them into the main-line stations. Hundreds of omnibuses and thousands of cabs jammed the streets. Each day an average of 43,000 people came to stare in wonder. One day as many as 93,000 people crowded into the building. To meet the needs of the thousands of visitors from abroad there were twenty-six interpreters – and several dozen foreign policemen whose job it was to keep an eye open for known bad characters from their own countries.

There was a great deal to catch the interest of the visitors, so much indeed that like all exhibitions it was just a nightmarish blur to some visitors. 'I find I'm used up by the Exhibition,' Charles Dickens wrote to a friend. 'I don't say there is nothing in it: there is too much. I have only been twice, so many things bewilder me. I'm not sure that I have seen anything but the Crystal Fountain and the Amazon statue from Berlin.' Everyone saw the Crystal Fountain. It stood in the centre of the transept and was the meeting-point for all the lovers in London that year.

The Exhibition was divided into four sections – raw materials; machinery; manufactures; and fine arts. In the western half of the building were the exhibits from Britain and the dependencies, more than 7,000 separate exhibits arranged in thirty classes. The eastern part was filled with almost as many exhibits from foreign countries. These were arranged according to their latitudes, the countries lying nearest to the equator being placed nearest the central transept.

When the Exhibition opened some of the foreign exhibits had not yet arrived, especially those from the United States, and to begin with the huge American eagle presided over a vast emptiness. To Hepworth Dixon, who two years later became editor of *The Athenaeum*, this initial emptiness was apposite; space, he said, was America's greatest resource.

With its 14,000 exhibits the Crystal Palace was the rendezvous for all the rubbish, skill and beauty of the age. There were chintz patterns from Paris, church plate from Coventry, Chinese vases in jade stone, a pendant lamp from France, a stove and fender from Sheffield elaborately ornamented and decorated until its true purpose was hidden under the superabundant convolutions. 'The present is the age of shams'; said an article on 'Recent Decorative Art' in Chambers's *Papers for the People* No. 65 in 1850. 'Works of art are *tacked on* to works of utility. One idea is lost amid a host of conflicting ones . . . there prevails indiscriminate addition of ornament everywhere.' This sort of folderol was all very fine in a country which had over one million domestic servants to do the black-leading and dusting. Domestic servants indeed were second only to agricultural workers as the most numerous occupational group.

One of the most attractive classes in the machinery section was the array of carriages beside the west Entrance – carriages with names that expressed their elegance and enshrined their origins: barouches, coburgs, cabriolets, landaus, dog-carts, jaunting-cars, victorias, amemptons, traps, britzkas, phaetons, buggies, berlins, broughams, gigs, sociables, curricles, clarences, chariots. . . . There were as many makes of carriage as there were of cars in a later age. The carriage was the all-important symbol of a higher middle-class income, that is to say from £550 to £600 a year and over.

Around the carriage court were the other machines, including two classes of machinery in motion, most of it from Britain and the United States. An American sewing-machine, a brand-new invention, attracted much attention. Cotton machinery from Lancashire was much in evidence, as well it might be for cotton was the greatest single industry in Britain, employing half a million people. And there were many examples of locomotive construction in which Britain excelled.

In his address at the first meeting of the Royal Commissioners who organized the Exhibition, Prince Albert had said that its purpose was 'to give a true test and a living picture of the point of development at which the whole of mankind had arrived in the great task to conquer nature; to give a new starting point from which all nations will direct their further exertions'. With the exception of the transport and mining industries, this point was barely advanced enough to justify Britain's proud title of the Workshop of the World. Steel was little used and the great inventions of metal manufacture were yet to come. Petty craftsmanship rather than mass production was the order of industry. It is curious indeed to realize that all this great British manufacturing industry that was the pride of 1851 hardly employed more people than were working in domestic service.

In some mysterious way the Great Exhibition in its Crystal Palace precipitated a new image of Britain from the murky solution of the nation's life with its miasma of confused motives. And what was remarkable to most people was that the image which revealed itself was not the one they had feared might emerge. Instead of finding anarchy they were reminded of the nationalism they had felt in the Napoleonic wars and saw a bright, intoxicating image that had within it the flash of distant lights to lead the imagination forward.

For one thing London was not given over to pillage and rape as many had confidently prophesied. The spectre of unrest had persuaded the pessimists that when the roughs and the respectables met in Hyde Park red revolution would result. Their anxiety was renewed when, after a few weeks, there were reductions in the admission prices. Originally season tickets cost three guineas for gentlemen and two guineas for ladies, subsequently they were reduced to thirty shillings and a pound. Until May 26 the price of daily admission was five shillings, but on that day a daring innovation was made. The price of admission on Mondays, Tuesdays, Wednesdays and Thursdays was reduced to one shilling. The first day there was little sign that the reduction would make any great difference. But by the first Thursday the daily admission rate had topped 50,000 and there were few shilling days thereafter when it fell below that figure.

The prophets of revolution watched the first of the shilling days with 'told-you-so's' ready on their lips. Eight inspectors, thirty-eight sergeants, and 609 constables were on duty inside the building. But nothing happened – just the shoving, barging and struggling of 50,000 people out to enjoy themselves. Within a few weeks it was plain that something totally unexpected had happened. Although there was some justification for the prophets of doom in that one million people, 7 per cent of the population, were on relief, nevertheless when the Pounds and the Shillings, as *Punch* called them, did actually meet under the one roof there was no rioting, no disorder of any sort – or very little! As the official report was to put it when the Exhibition closed: 'An uninterrupted succession of arrivals of large numbers of all classes, both from the provinces and from abroad, the absence of experience as regards their conduct under circumstances so new and unprecedented, and the impossibility of conjecturing the course which might be taken by unscrupulous agitators, led many most intelligent persons to anticipate these arrivals with anxiety and even with alarm. But the experience of a few weeks dissipated these apprehensions.'

It was incredible. So great was the pride and thankfulness that strangers shook hands, people wept openly in public places. The realization that there could be one nation, added to the pride in the thundering machines, stirred the strains of imperialism in the stoppered English heart.

The surge of national pride shared a place, incongruously it might seem, with the dreams of universal peace that hovered among the exhibits. These dreams were conjured up by the apostles of Free Trade. Their optimism, reinforced by the repeal of the protectionist Corn Laws in 1846, was extravagant. Free Trade, they said, would destroy the barriers between nations, the rivalry of trade would supersede the rivalry of war; Free Trade would herald perpetual peace, a Brotherhood of Nations. Indeed it was of these hopes that the Great Exhibition had been born. Paxton himself, who was knighted for his achievement, said 'No means are so beneficial to the human race as those which bring men in contact with each other, thus rubbing off the rust of prejudice and ill-will. If that is good between man and man, how infinitely greater the benefit as between nation and nation. Fancy a Brotherhood of Nations!' It was a fancy indeed which received a severe jolt less than two months after the Exhibition closed when Louis Napoleon staged his successful *coup d'état*; it was blown to bits three years later in the slaughter of the Crimea.

'The Dear Drunken People'

The absence of riot in Hyde Park did not mean that the social temper of the age had undergone an abrupt change and that the country had suddenly become de-barbarized. Far from it. Cruelty, squalor and brutality still spread a careless horror throughout the land. Excursion trains took people to watch public executions as well as bringing them to London for the Great Exhibition. Drunkenness was rife. When Ralph Waldo Emerson visited England in 1847 he was horrified by the number of drunken women he saw in the streets of Manchester and Liverpool; and while a lady might, with reasonable safety to her person and decorum, walk round the Crystal Palace in 1851, it was impossible for her, even though accompanied by a gentleman, to walk down Tottenham Court Road in the evening because of the drunks lying in the gutter. Nor was there any improvement a decade later. When Wilkie Collins visited the Isle of Man in 1863 to get local colour for *Armadale* he found that the Douglas hotels were 'crammed with thousands of rough-and-ready visitors' from the manufacturing districts and every third shop was 'a spirit-shop and every second inhabitant drunk'. The temperance movement, begun in the 1830s and strengthened in the 1850s by the formation of the U.K. Alliance (1853) and the Band of Hope Union (1855), had so far made little impression on the vast wastelands of drunkenness.

Sometimes, however, the sight of drunks did not cause distress. Lady Lytton, wife of the first Earl of Lytton, was so happy to be in England again after four years in India where her husband had been Viceroy that as she came ashore at Portsmouth in August 1880, she exclaimed, 'Oh, the dear drunken people in the streets! How I love them.'

Nevertheless the absence of riot in 1851 was significant. The coarse habits of the past, though still deep-rooted, were being attacked, and powerfully attacked, by the ladies of England. Their aim, subtly directed from their drawing-rooms, was to have the impurities of life restrained and lessened before the inequalities were tackled.

The First Ladies

At length the time came when the Great Exhibition had to close. The last day was October 11, 1851. By that time it had been open for 141 days and had been visited by over six million people. The receipts from admission totalled £424,322 2s, of which £529 17s 5d had to be deducted for loss on light gold, defaced, spurious, and foreign coins. Messrs. Schweppe's, who had the catering contract, sold over £75,000 worth of refreshments, including thirty-three tons of ham, 28,000 sausage rolls, 870,000 plain buns, 935,000 bath buns, and a million bottles of their soda water, lemonade, and ginger beer – no alcohol was allowed.

Fortunately for the visitors – and for the first time in Britain's history – public conveniences had been provided by the thoughtful Commissioners. Noting in their report that 827,820 people had spent £2,441 15s 9d on these during the course of the Exhibition they added that no apology was needed for recording these facts 'which, throughout the whole time of the Exhibition, strongly impressed all concerned in the management with the necessity of making similar provisions for the public wherever large numbers are congregated and with the sufferings which must be endured by all, but more especially by females, on account of the want of them'.

Chapter 8

CRINOLINE
AND BLOOMERS

One of the more obvious ways in which the new wealth was apparent was the richness of dress and finery to be seen in the streets. The 1850s was a decade when 'extravagance in dress is one of the prevailing vices of the age', said a contemporary periodical, and the *Saturday Review* in an article on 'Milliners' Bills' in its issue of October 31, 1857, commented that this extravagance in dress was only one form of a general extravagance that permeated a large section of the country.

From the revealing fashions of the early years of the century, when women's dresses were simple in line and diaphanous in material, the trend had been towards hiding more and more. This trend was a symptom of the changing social temper and of the different relationship between the sexes. After a period of frank display women began to hide their charms so that they would re-awaken the interest of men who were presumably considered to be satiated. The change to the Gothic fashion in dress was part of the change to Gothic attitudes in manners.

By the early 1830s women's dresses were almost theatrical in their exuberance. *The Maids, Wives and Widows Penny Magazine*, for instance, which began weekly publication in October 1832, was one of the many magazines whose engravings and beautifully coloured plates show the enchanting fashions of the time. The day dresses are in gay colours and are worn with broad pelerines. They have enormous upper-arm sleeves and are covered with intricate frogging and embroidery. Their skirts reach to mid-calf. The huge deep poke-bonnets are bright with ribbons and embroidery. The whole effect is of a gorgeous scintillating hour-glass. In the evening the elaboration is even greater: richly embroidered dresses of white moiré, trains of crimson velvet, bare necks and arms, feathers and flowers in turbans of tissue.

Throughout the 1830s the social temper towards women continued to change and the exuberance of dress disappeared. The basic shape remained, with the skirt lengthening from mid-calf right down to the foot, but the angularity and aggressiveness disappeared and was replaced by soft lines indicating the sweet prettiness of a Sunday doll, the image of the 1840 woman. As the 1840s went by, the changing fashion accurately reflected the rejection of all forms of work by any woman who considered herself to be a lady. Thus the sleeve openings grew larger and larger, making the hand appear even smaller as a symbol of the helplessness and gentility of its owner. Skirts went on expanding and expanding until they became a huge, heavy dome supported by half a dozen petticoats and a bustle. They reached right to the ground and concealed everything except the toe so that walking became like a perpetual struggle through shallow water. Tight lacing became fashionable, the tighter the more fashionable. A jacket was worn, and a mantle and shawl out-of-doors. The shawl was immense and to be able to manipulate it correctly was the sure mark of a lady. Bonnets were still the fashion, and indeed the bonnet was the keynote of the time, for it was a perfect symbol of meekness and modesty.

Ground-length clothes brought a new problem for women – what were they to do when walking in the muddy streets of London, or in the equally clogging lanes of the country? Dr Edward John Tilt in his *Elements of Health and Principles of Female Hygiene* published in 1852, the first book dealing comprehensively with the subject of women's hygiene, divided ladies, 'in respect to walking', into three classes:

'I. Those who never raise the dress, but walk through thick and thin, with real or affected indifference to mud. These are generally country ladies, who have never been abroad and but little in town.

'II. Those who raise the dress, but allow the mass of under-clothes, like the mud-carts in Regent Street, to collect the mud and beat it up to the middle of the leg. This class is the most common.

'III. Those chosen few, who, without offending the rules of modesty, which of course must take precedence of all others, know how to raise both dress and petticoats, so as to protect both.'

Was there anything indecent in showing a neatly-dressed ankle? Dr Tilt asked. Or to view it in another light, was economy no object? Was it immaterial whether a dress was spoiled or not, whenever it was worn out walking? 'But supposing economy be no object, what are we to say of health? How many of our fair readers have caught colds or serious disorders of the monthly function from remaining for hours with a mass of wet clothes wrapped round the feet and legs, eventually leading them to the determination never to walk out unless there be no chance of soiling their boots – thus again undermining health by close confinement; and by following an absurd species of false delicacy, fostered by a mother, who, while condemning the appearance of a narrow line of white above the boot in the morning, will take her daughter at night to the Opera and teach her to admire the grace, the poetry, and the display of a set of semi-naked women.'[1]

'A Social Invention'

As the domes of skirt grew more and more massive it became increasingly difficult to sustain them. By 1856 a silk dress required about twenty yards of material and it was obvious that some new sub-structure must be introduced if women were not to collapse in immovable heaps on the ground. Already the answer had been found. Petticoats, especially those worn under evening dress, became stiff and some ladies evolved the famous artificial crinoline which was at first a hooped, skeleton skirt, then a wired petticoat and then finally, the perfected article, the watch-spring crinoline which cost from fifteen to thirty shillings.

Exactly when the first crinolines were worn is a matter of dispute. One view is that the Empress Eugenie brought the first crinoline to England when she came on a state visit with her husband, Napoleon III, in April 1855. Her dress was grey with black lace and pink bows. Another view, which also credits the

[1] Dr Edward John Tilt, *Elements of Health and Principles of Female Hygiene* (1852), pp. 193–4.

Empress with being the crinoline's innovator, claims that she adopted it to disguise her pregnancy later in 1855 when she was carrying the Prince Imperial.[1]

Henry Mayhew, on the other hand, says that the practice of wearing crinoline started to become fashionable soon after the Great Exhibition. Possibly the fashion went from England to France rather than the other way round, and Eugenie gave it the royal blessing when she re-imported it during the state visit. The perfected article was on sale in 1857 and remained in fashion for a decade, although from 1863 it began to shrink and became flatter in front, while the skirt was gored so that most of it hung at the back. This gathering of material soon developed into an enormous bustle and 'crinoline' changed into 'crinolette', with the hitched-up skirt becoming a short overskirt or tunic like an apron.

The name 'crinoline' came from the French *crin*, the horse-hair-stiffened fabric used for petticoats, designed to distend the dress into the massive dome of fashion. The artificial crinoline kept this distention but gave freedom to the legs and reduced by several pounds the weight to be carried. No longer did women have to struggle against the hampering burden of a heap of petticoats. One lady talking to her niece at the end of the century recalled the days when crinoline first came into fashion. She told her that the freedom was unbelievably marvellous after all the clutter that had preceded it – never in her lifetime had a woman's body been so free.

The blessing of freedom was marred for some by the involuntary displays they gave. On June 3, 1859, *The Times* published a letter from 'E.S.': 'Lycurgus,' he wrote, 'excused the Spartan scantiness of female attire by saying that public decency served as a veil to them. That may have been the case in Sparta, but we have only to watch the curious and inquisitive glances of the crowd, who immediately stop to see a fashionable lady descend from her carriage or cross a muddy street to feel that safeguard

[1] It was part of a Victorian lady's duty to disguise her pregnancy. Virginia Woolf makes this point in *Orlando*, pp. 211–12: 'Were they not all of them weak women? Wearing crinolines the better to conceal the fact; the only fact; but, nevertheless, the deplorable fact; which every modest woman did her best to deny until denial was impossible; the fact that she was about to bear a child? to bear fifteen or twenty children indeed, so that most of a modest woman's life was spent, after all, in denying what on one day at least every year was made obvious.'

does not exist in London. No man of ordinary feelings of delicacy can pass an hour in the streets without seeing much to startle, if not to shock him.' These displays, he concluded, were becoming a great social evil.

The following day J.B.E. countered this suggestion in a letter which *The Times* published on the 7th. J.B.E. said he had originally been against crinoline, but now he liked the fashion, provided it was not extreme. 'God forbid that the mind of Christian men should be so ill-regulated as to see immodesty or indecency where they simply and innocently admire.'

The *Saturday Review* agreed with J.B.E. It also opposed E.S.'s opinion that Balmoral boots were indecent. 'Indecent they are not, except to those who are naturally indecent. As to short petticoats and dainty boots, they are a vast and positive improvement, both as regards health and cleanliness, on thin slippers and draggle-tailed trains.' Balmoral boots had brass eyelet holes and elaborate leather embroidery; some of them had high heels. The Queen herself, when the occasion warranted, wore Balmoral boots.

There was no doubt, however, that crinoline made it an interesting time for *voyeurs*. A conundrum of 1863 asked: 'Why may crinoline be justly regarded as a social invention?' and the answer was: 'Because it enables us to see more of our friends than we used to.' In a letter to his friend Holroyd, in Australia, William Hardman remarked in March 1862 apropos the futility of a meeting called to abolish crinoline that 'the girls of our time like to show their legs . . . [The excision is Hardman's editor's] I don't see why they should be interfered with; it pleases them, and does no harm to us: I speak for married, not single men'. Hardman was uxorious in the extreme.

In another letter Hardman had a further and much quoted comment on the same subject. Had crinoline reached its climax, he wondered. 'Women getting into omnibuses, servant-girls cleaning doorsteps, all show their —— on occasion.' [The excision in this case was Hardman's own.] Just what they showed may perhaps be metrically surmised from the first verse of a little ditty which Hardman's friend George Meredith, to whom women were the first of wonders, wrote to him from Ryde where he was about to set sail for a yachting trip along the South Coast:

'To-morrow I am going,
I cannot tell you where;
The wind is stoutly blowing
The ladies' ——— bare.'

It is interesting to note from Hardman's letters that even at the height of the fashion for crinoline there were occasions when it was not worn. Hardman took the wife of a friend to see the illuminations for Princess Alexandra's wedding to the Prince of Wales in March 1863. For this excursion into the crowded streets the lady went 'to attire herself befittingly, with a total absence of precious metals and crinoline'. The lady, incidentally, was about fifty, an age which Hardman, then aged thirty-five, described as 'advanced in life' and one which put her among 'the old folks'.

George Meredith himself included his own sweeping criticism of crinoline in an article on Princess Alexandra in the *Ipswich Journal*. Its effects, he wrote, had been 'morally worse than a *coup d'état*. It has sacrificed more lives; it has utterly destroyed more tempers; it has put an immense division between the sexes. It has obscured us, smothered us, stabbed us.'

As Meredith's polemic shows, it was not only on grounds of decency that crinoline had its opponents. Like other fashions crinoline went to the extreme and had many inconveniences. 'Crinolines seem to have been a great trouble, particularly in tours abroad', the young Beatrix Potter noted in her journal after talking to her Grandma Leech, who found it impossible to ride a mule while wearing one until at last she discovered a way 'of tying one side of the crinoline top to her waist, when she managed very nicely'. The Marchioness of Londonderry was another lady who discovered the inconvenience of crinoline when she sent for an apothecary to remove a fishbone from her throat and he, on being ordered imperiously to begin, had to tell her ladyship that he could not get within yards of her throat because of the crinoline being so enormous and solid!

An article in *The Alexandra Magazine* of August 1864 on 'Women's Dress in Relation to Health' wrote of 'the ridiculously large hoops which are now in fashion and which make it necessary to put so extravagant a quantity of material into skirts and everything else worn over them. There is not a single thing to be said in favour of hoops of this absurd size. They are very ugly, and they take up so much space as to be very inconvenient, both to the wearers and everyone around them. Leaving good taste out of the question, kind feeling alone ought to put an end to this stupid fashion which makes our dress a nuisance in every railway carriage, omnibus, and pew, and all other places where the sitting room is small.' Another great disadvantage was the risk of accident. 'Since hoops came again into fashion cases of injury and death from the burning of clothes have been more common and much attention has been lately directed to them.'

Lady Dorothy Nevill was once showing a lady an engraving of her friend Richard Cobden which hung near the drawing-room fireplace in her Hampshire home when her crinoline caught fire and was instantly in a blaze. She only saved herself from being burnt to death by keeping her presence of mind and rolling in the hearthrug. The gentlemen had not yet joined them after dinner and the other ladies were powerless to help because their own enormous crinolines would have blazed up had they come too close.

Despite the danger and the inconvenience crinoline was worn in the mills; fashion, understandably, was more important to the girls than function.

But though coroners warned against crinoline, and *Punch* made fun of it, and both Florence Nightingale and the Queen were against its excesses, nevertheless the vogue for the crinoline lasted a long time.

'Drawers Are of Incalculable Advantage'

To wear crinoline with ease and manage it with decorum was a skilled art. The problems involved may be better imagined than described, especially if one remembers 'all other places where the sitting room is small'. One particular effect it had was to hasten the slowly-growing fashion among Top Nation women of wearing drawers. The feeling that to wear them was immodest was almost atavistic. It arose from the fact that they were a form of trousers, which was a masculine article of attire. In 1841 *The Handbook of the Toilet* drew attention to the advantage of wearing flannel next to the skin 'all the year, over the whole body and arms as low as the middle of the thighs: but alas! very few ladies will do so. Ladies should not be sparing of flannel petticoats, and drawers are of incalculable advantage to women, preventing many of the disorders and indispositions to which British females are subject. The drawers may be made of flannel, calico or cotton, and should reach as far down the leg as possible without their being seen.' But 1841 was early days for the habit and the *Handbook's* advice was heeded by few. One vicar's wife wrote in high dudgeon to a ladies' magazine which had suggested that wearing drawers was good for the health. She and her daughters, she wrote, would never dream of doing anything so unladylike.

Another strong advocate of the 'utility of drawers' was Dr Tilt. In his *Elements of Health and Principles of Female Hygiene*, written before crinoline, he referred to an earlier work of his on menstrual diseases in which he had laid great stress on the fact that girls were clothed in short frocks and 'trowsers until they are about to become women, and then trowsers, drawers – all are thrown aside, and the body is exposed to our piercing easterly winds, and an ever-varying climate . . . or to cutting draughts when waiting for the carriage in hall or passage after continued exercise in a hot crowded room. Should fashion command, the loins will be constantly kept in a state of undue warmth by two or three inches of padding, petticoat, and dress; why, then, should the slenderest covering be denied to a part of the body hitherto carefully protected? Evidently the use of drawers would preserve women from numberless infirmities – sometimes even from death.' He quoted the sad case of a young lady who went to a ball – 'though the period of the month was inconvenient to her' – got hot, caught cold, and died of acute inflammation of the womb. Drawers would have saved her, as they would benefit others. 'Unless the constitution, however, be peculiarly weak, we should not recommend the drawers to be made of flannel, but of fine calico, and they need not descend much below the knees. Thus understood, the adoption of drawers will doubtless become more general in this country, as, being worn without the knowledge of the general observer, they will be robbed of the prejudice usually attached to an appendage deemed masculine. From drawers to trowsers the distance was never great; so, perhaps, some of our readers may ask, "should not, then, the costume worn in childhood be retained?" To this we at once reply in the negative. The usual dress of English-women requires no such modification, either for health or grace. As it is, it imparts warmth, comfort, and elegance. But besides imparting warmth to the body, dress has its undoubted effect over the imagination and conduct of the wearer; and in assuming our costume, there would be a great likelihood of women assuming our masculine manners, which would not enhance their charms. It is, therefore, important that there should be a different costume for the girl and the woman, in order that on quitting one for the other, girls should feel that they were promoted in Society and that therefore more is expected of them.'[1]

The trowsers or long drawers worn by little girls had legs that could be taken off and changed in the same way that in earlier decades sleeves could be taken off dresses and changed for evening wear. The fastenings of the drawer-legs did not always remain secure and the accident that befell Beatrix Potter's mother one summer day in 1845 was the accident that often befell other little girls in gardens and streets all over the country. 'Mamma was once walking in the garden when a little girl, when one of the gardeners called after her that she had lost something, and presented her with an elegant embroidered drawer-leg.'

The advent of crinoline created a situation in which it became increasingly clear to everyone that it was unladylike not to wear something under the dress now that the obscuring folds of petticoats had been removed. In the 1850s Top Nation ladies began to overcome their repugnance at wearing something that had an affinity with men's attire. But it was many years before the habit spread to women of the poorer classes. They did indeed 'all show their —— on occasion'.

The Bloomers

The 1850s also saw another development in women's dress, although this one, unlike crinoline, was short-lived and limited in its appeal. An additional attraction at the Great Exhibition one Friday in September 1851 had been a party of 'Bloomers' – that is, ladies dressed in Bloomer attire. This was their first appearance. The Bloomers came to England from the United States where the costume they wore was developed in 1850 from a mountain-climbing costume of Fanny Kemble's and named after Mrs Amelia Bloomer, publisher and editor of *The Lily*, the first paper devoted to the rights of women. A contemporary described it as consisting of 'something between a gipsy hat and a "wide awake" of straw; a white collar turned down upon a velvet coatee of Lincoln Green, buttoning tight round the waist

[1] Dr Tilt, op. cit., p. 192.

but open, and showing a frilled shirt at the bosom, the sleeves fitting the arms closely and skirts descending to the knee; the "bloomers" are exceedingly full to the knee but tight from there to the ankle, where they are drawn close.'

The appearance of Bloomers at the Great Exhibition was the first of many promenades undertaken by courageous reforming ladies to popularize the new freedom of dress. Public meetings were held. There was one, for example, at the Royal Soho Theatre on October 6 with the London Bloomer Committee on the platform. There was also a Grand Bloomer Ball at the Hanover Square Rooms. This proved disastrous to the good name of the Bloomers. Only ladies dressed in correct Bloomer attire were admitted – unfortunately these, in the main, turned out to be ladies of the town, and a fantastic orgiastic brawl brought the evening to an end.

Punch immediately took over 'Bloomerism' as its latest *bête noire* and despite public meetings and other attempts to popularize the costume, the taunts and protests directed against the Bloomers eventually drove them out of London. Nevertheless the fashion, if fashion it may be called, did not entirely disappear and in November 1866 we find William Hardman writing to his friend in Australia about Dr Mary Walker, an American lady who obtained her M.D. degree in New York, in 1855, and was later appointed a surgeon to the United States Army. She then became a public lecturer on temperance, equal rights for women, and dress reform. It was as a lecturer that she visited England in 1866 and aroused both interest and scorn by her attire, which consisted of a long frock-coat and black trousers. *The Spectator* based an article about female dress on Dr Walker's appearance. It was very ugly, the article said, dwarfing the figure and furthermore it was 'false to the ethical theory of women's dress, which should be faintly enticing or fascinating'. Commenting on this article Hardman wrote that what the writer was driving at 'is pretty plainly evident when he goes on to remark that women's first function is to be mothers, and that the dress of the Second Empire with all its faults is preferable to the Bloomer costume although it passes the narrow line between enticement and allurement. The writer evidently . . . would fain see everything . . . [Hardman's editor's excisions]. Nay more, he thinks that, subject to certain police principles perfectly well understood and not worth describing, the wider the licence assigned to human caprice in dress the better for civilization. I wonder what limits he would assign to the shortness of petticoats. He further asks, why should women not ride astride? I confess I don't know, except that conventionality requires that women should, as far as lies in their power, keep their legs together.'

Even as late as 1881 there was a report in a weekly paper about two ladies 'of acknowledged position' who had been seen in Bond Street wearing at least the essential part of the Bloomer costume. One of the two was Lady Harberton, inventor of the divided skirt and a determined advocate of 'rational dress' during the 1880s and 1890s, whose 'Rational Dress Society' achieved no more immediate success than the Bloomers had done thirty years earlier.

Perhaps the greatest drawback to the acceptance of Bloomerism was that it came from New York instead of Paris. In the eyes of the British, ladies no less than gentlemen, nothing good could possibly come from across the Atlantic. From across the Channel was a totally different matter – as crinoline bore witness. If only the Empress Eugenie had worn a Bloomer costume . . . !

The Bloomers did not disappear without trace. They found their way into the literature of the day. One of the best known of them is Constantia Mendlove, the daughter of the Turtle Doves Hotel at Handley Cross. Constantia reclined 'afternoonly' on a rose-coloured sofa commanding a view of the letter-cage and the hall which formed a sort of centre of attraction for visitors to Handley Cross. High Change was about noon and for this Constantia would dress in the full-blown costume of a Bloomer. The great gun was Major General Sir Thomas Trout who was wheeled into the hall in his garden chair. Sir Thomas's appearance brought forth 'the fair lady, in her silver-buttoned light-blue silk vest, with a flowing jacket of a darker blue above a lavender-coloured tunic and white trousers, fingering her cambric collarette and crimson silk necktie above her richly-figured shirt, with mock-diamond buttons scattered freely down the front'. According to Mrs Flummocks, otherwise known as the Crusher, on account of the way she dealt with ineligible young men who approached her daughters, Constantia's was a 'ridiculous costume'. But it gave considerable satisfaction to the great Sir Thomas.

Surtees's classic is one of a number of literary reminders that the mid-Victorian age was not entirely prudish and euphemistic. The blunt bluff world of the Shires took no notice of the mealy-mouthed approach that the circulating libraries imposed. *Handley Cross* indeed contains at least one unashamed reference to the facts of life, which is not the sort of thing mid-Victorian novels are generally renowned for! Mr Jorrocks on his way back from hunting with his coat all muddy from a fall is mocked by the locals as he enters Handley Cross.

'A-a-a! ar say Fanny!' exclaims Mrs Gallon, the landlady of the Barley Mow, to Mrs Blash, the pretty but rather wordy wife of the barber, across the street, 'Ar say! Old Fatty's had a fall!'

To which Mrs Blash, with a scornful toss of her head at Mr Jorrocks who is admiring her, replies. '*Hut!* He's always on his back, that old feller.'

'Not 'alf so often as you are, old gal!' retorts the now-indignant Jorrocks, as he spurs on out of hearing.

Chapter 9
HELP FROM THE
BEETONS

An important aid to home dressmaking was the introduction of scale diagrams which could be made into paper patterns. These first appeared in No. 1 of *The Englishwoman's Domestic Magazine* in May 1852 and were continued in a regular feature called 'The Fashions and Practical Dress Instructor'. The new magazine was originated and edited by a talented twenty-one-year-old publisher called Samuel Orchart Beeton whose firm of Clarke, Beeton and Co. had that same month brought off a great *coup* by being the first to publish *Uncle Tom's Cabin* in England.

Published monthly at twopence the cap octavo-sized *E.D.M.* was one of the first magazines devoted exclusively to women and their interests. It was 'an illustrated journal, combining practical information, instruction and amusement' and contained articles on household management, surgeon's advice to mothers, cookery, the toilette, dressmaking, and things worth knowing (such as how to remove stains from the hands, clean ermine victorines, kill flies, and make noyeau equal to martinique). It also had fiction and miscellaneous articles including, for example in Volume VII (1858-9), 'Religions of the World', 'Dangerous Ornaments', 'Can We Live on £300 A Year?' and 'The Economy of Dress'. The editor's object, as stated in the first number, was 'to produce a work which should tend to the improvement of the intellect, the cultivation of the morals, and the cherishing of domestic virtues'. But he carried out this ponderous-sounding object with a light and entertaining touch. The circulation increased steadily until by 1860 it had reached 50,000.

'The Practical Dress Instructor' was one great attraction. Another was the 'Prize Composition'. The subjects for this started with such themes as 'The Duke of Wellington's Funeral' and 'On the Influence of a Mother's Teaching in After-Life'. Later, before the feature was dropped, the subjects became more intimate: 'The Unselfish Love of Woman contrasted with the Exacting Selfishness of Man', and 'Do Married Rakes make the Best Husbands?' There was also, initially, a personal column called 'Cupid's Letter Bag' where readers' romantic problems were answered by the editor himself.

From 1856 onwards the cookery and household management notes in the *E.D.M.* were writen by the editor's wife. Samuel Beeton and Isabella Mayson were married on July 10, 1856 when Sam was twenty-five and Isabella twenty. Isabella had already had considerable experience of household management on a large scale before her marriage. Her father died when she was five leaving her mother with little money and four children, of whom Isabella was the eldest. Two years later Mrs Mayson married a well-to-do widower in Epsom, who had four children of his own. Their marriage produced another twelve children so that Isabella was one of a family of twenty. Her stepfather, Henry Dorling, was a printer who printed the racecards for the Epsom meetings. He had inherited this business from his father, William Dorling, who was in close contact with the racing world and had invested in the Epsom Grand Stand Association which was formed to provide more comfortable accommodation for the public at the Epsom meetings. The Grand Stand, a large stone building with dining-rooms and living-rooms, could accommodate five thousand spectators. Henry Dorling carried on his father's interests and became clerk of the course at Epsom. When his family grew too large to be accommodated in the house in Epsom the younger children were sent to live in the Grand Stand between race meetings. Here they were looked after by Isabella. Small wonder that she had plenty of experience of family catering on a large scale.

Mrs Beeton's Book

The cookery notes which Isabella Beeton wrote for the *E.D.M.* were based on recipes which the readers were invited to send in. There was an overwhelming response. As well as these she got other from the leading chefs to whom she was introduced. Lord

Wilton's cook was one from whom useful recipes were obtained, the Duke of Rutland's cook another. These cookery notes were the basis for her famous book.

In November 1859, *The Book of Household Management* began to appear in monthly parts at threepence each part. In October 1861, after the appearance of the twenty-fourth part, it was published complete at seven and sixpence. This *Book of Household Management* soon became popularly known as 'Mrs Beeton' a name by which it is still known today. In 1863 those parts of it dealing with the kitchen and the recipes were published separately as *The Englishwoman's Cookery Book.*

'Mrs Beeton' was not the first Victorian domestic 'bible' written by a woman. In the 1830s *the* English cookery-book was Mrs Rundell's *New System of Domestic Cookery, formed upon Principles of Economy and adapted to the Use of Private Families* which had been published about 1820. Margaret Dodd's *Cookery Book* published in 1830 was the next to become the fashion. Then in 1845 came Eliza Acton's *Modern Cookery for Private Families.* Miss Acton was a poet, but her poetry failed to sell. With a wisdom denied to most authors she went to the publisher and said: 'Give me the subject of a book for which the world has a need and I will write it for you. I am a poet but I shall write no more poems. The world does not want poems.' 'What we want,' the publisher told her, 'is a really good cookery book.' She took years over the task and succeeded brilliantly.

The first edition of 'Mrs Beeton' gave valuable guidance on how to run a household as well as how to cook all the meals the household required. It covered the whole field of domestic science. As its sub-title said, it was a work 'comprising information for the mistress, housekeeper, cook, kitchen-maid, butler, footman, coachman, valet, upper and under housemaids, lady's maid, maid of all work, laundry maid, nurse and nursemaid, monthly, wet, and sick nurses, etc. etc., also sanitary, medical and legal memoranda; with a history of the origin, properties and uses of all things connected with home life and comfort'.

With her detailed description of how the mistress of a household should comport herself Mrs Beeton was following in the tradition of the books of etiquette and minor morals which had been so popular a decade or two earlier. But she went into much greater detail than Mrs Ellis's *Wives, Mothers, Daughters and Women of England.* In those it was necessary for the reader to disentangle the exact practice of daily life from the general moralistic wadding. In Mrs Beeton's *Book of Household Management* the precise details were specified as if in army orders.

The comparison with the army was made by Mrs Beeton herself. 'As with the commander of an army or the leader of any enterprise,' she wrote, 'so it is with the mistress of a house.' On her depended the whole success of the operation. If she was lazy or careless, so would her servants be lazy and careless. On her, too, depended the happiness, comfort and well-being of her family. Mrs Beeton had herself too often seen the discomfort and suffering brought about by household mismanagement not to realize how important it was that a household should be properly run and well fed. 'I have always thought,' she said, 'that there is no more fruitful source of family discontent than a housewife's badly cooked dinners and untidy ways. Men are now so well served out of doors – at their clubs, well-ordered taverns and dining houses – that, in order to compete with the attractions of these places, a mistress must be thoroughly acquainted with the theory and practice of cookery, as well as being perfectly conversant with all the other arts of making and keeping a comfortable home.'

The chief domestic virtue which the mistress required for the proper management of her household was early rising. And as well as being an early riser, the model mistress of the Victorian household should also be clean, frugal, hospitable, good-tempered and discriminating in her choice of friends.

The great event of the day was dinner. Careful preparations for this must be made, especially if there were to be guests. The half-hour before dinner was the most trying time for the hostess. However, she must display no kind of agitation at all the possible disasters that were running through her mind, but must 'show her tact in suggesting light and cheerful subjects of conversation, which will be much aided by the introduction of any particular new book, curiosity of art, or article of vertu, which may presently engage the attention of the company. Photograph albums, crest albums, new music, will aid to pass a few moments pleasantly.' It was the hostess's duty to make her guests feel happy, comfortable, and entirely at their ease. And the guests, Mrs Beeton added, should also remember that having accepted the invitation they had come to the house to be happy.

At the dinner-table the guests were enjoined to observe certain well-established rules. They should not ask for a soup or fish twice 'as in doing so part of the company may be kept waiting too long for the second course, when perhaps a little revenge is taken by looking at the awkward consumer of a second portion.' When the finger-bowls were put on the table, ladies were warned that they should only wet the tips of their fingers. 'The French and other continentals have a habit of gargling the mouth; but it is a custom which no English gentlewoman should in the slightest degree imitate.'

A revealing comment on the changing attitude of men towards women and on male habits was included in Mrs Beeton's remarks about a properly conducted dinner. 'In former times when the bottle circulated freely among the guests, it was necessary for the ladies to retire earlier than they do at present, for the gentlemen of the company soon became unfit to conduct themselves with that decorum which is essential in the presence of ladies. Thanks, however, to the improvements in modern society and the high example shown to the nation by its most illustrious personages, temperance is in these happy days a striking feature in the character of a gentleman. Delicacy of conduct towards the female sex has increased with the esteem in which they are now universally held, and thus the very early withdrawing of the ladies from the dining-room is to be deprecated.'

It was the duty of the hostess to introduce all the guests to each other. To rely simply on the servant calling out the names was not sufficient as they were frequently mispronounced. In Mrs Beeton's opinion this calling out of names was 'a cheerless and depressing custom, although in thus speaking we do not allude to the large assemblies of the aristocracy, but to the smaller parties of the middle classes'. A lady at a private ball should not refuse an invitation to dance unless she was previously engaged because she must presume that her hostess had invited only people whom she knew to be perfectly respectable and 'of unblemished character, as well as pretty equal in position, and thus, to decline the offer of any gentleman present, would be a tacit reflection on the master and mistress of the house'. Mrs Beeton added, for the benefit of young people who might read her book, that 'introductions at balls and evening parties cease with the occasion that calls them forth, no

introduction at these times giving a gentleman a right to
address afterwards a lady. She is consequently free next morning
to pass her partner at a ball of the previous evening without the
slightest recognition'.

On those occasions when the family dined alone, the mistress
should still insist on the same cleanliness, neatness and scrupu-
lous exactness as she would if company were present. Only in
this way would the servants be properly trained to cope with
the 'difficult occasions'.

Mrs Beeton described in meticulous detail the duties of all
the servants in the household. In doing so she adopted an
attitude that was atypical of the time, in that she wrote about
servants as if they were human, whereas most references to them
at this time made them creatures of no importance.[1]

The first edition of *The Book of Household Management* consisted of 1,172 pages of small, closely-spaced print. It was an
immediate success. In the first year over 60,000 copies were
sold. A second edition was published in 1863. And successive
editions have gone on appearing ever since. The book's American equivalent was, perhaps, Catherine Beecher's *The American
Woman's Home* which contained information ranging from
recipes to sewing instructions, from the planning of a house so
that it was easy to run, to the best ways of maintaining the
niceties of harmonious family living.

When Mrs Beeton's book first appeared there were no
household management or cookery columns in the daily press
and the publication of women's magazines was in its infancy.
Mrs Beeton provided knowledge which was not readily obtainable elsewhere and tens of thousands of housewives relied on her
book to lead them in the ways of home comfort and good cooking. The domestic arts in Britain were in the doldrums in early
Victorian days. It was thanks to Mrs Beeton and her book that
they improved in the later part of the reign, although even then
there was a long way to go. The two things which struck Clara

[1] Another writer of the time who took the same humanitarian attitude
towards servants was Wilkie Collins, and in some of his novels the servants
are carefully drawn and play an important part in the story. This respect
for servants caused criticism to be levelled against him, as, for instance, by
Percy Fitzgerald who complained in his *Memoirs of an Author* (1894) that
'such things are below the dignity of official narrative for it is notorious
that the opinions and judgments of servants are not only valueless, but
are often actual distortions of the truth'.

Collet most when she was doing social work in the East End of London in the 1880s were the amount of wasted intelligence and talent among the girls and the wretchedness of the married women. 'A secondary education in cooking, cleaning, baby management, laws of health, and English literature should follow that of the Board School, and the minimum age at which full time may be worked should be gradually raised,' she wrote in April 1892 in an essay on *Prospects of Marriage for Women*. 'Bad cooking, dirty habits, overcrowding, and empty-headedness are the sources of the drunkenness, inefficiency, immorality, and brutality which obstruct progress among so many of the poor.' Three years later, in the 1895 edition of *The Handbook for Women*, Helen Blackburn commented on the novelty of domestic science classes which even then were only just becoming available even for better class women.

Mrs Beeton did not have long to enjoy the success of her book. She had four children, all boys, the first two of whom died in infancy. In giving birth to the fourth on January 29, 1865 Isabella developed puerperal fever and on February 6 she died, a few weeks before her twenty-ninth birthday. Her husband outlived her by twelve years. His publishing business was ruined in the Overend, Gurney crash in May 1866 and he sold his copyrights with his own services to Ward Lock who continued to publish *The Englishwoman's Domestic Magazine* and *The Young Englishwoman* (which he had launched in October 1864) as well as new editions of *The Book of Household Management*.

A Warm Bath Every Week

Like the extravagance of dress and finery to be seen in the streets, the enormous success of Mrs Beeton's book was a sign of the prosperous times. Between 1851 and 1871 the British nation grew richer and richer. Especially was this true of 'the middle three' as can be seen from an analysis of income tax returns. Although these returns do not afford an exact standard because the middle classes extended below the minimum assessment limit of £150 a year, nevertheless they give a clear indication of what was happening. While the population increased by one quarter during the twenty years and the number of occupied males over twenty increased by almost the same percentage, incomes of over £150 a year increased by four-fifths and the number of Schedule E assessments (for employed

persons) of £200 a year and over almost doubled, going up from
19,044 to 37,192. Most of this was an increase in real incomes
because prices rose by only about 5 per cent during the period.[1]

Mrs Beeton's book reflected some of the ways in which these
increased incomes were being spent. The references to dinners,
wine-taking, servants' duties, coachmen, carriages – all show
that these had become accepted as an essential part of the
'paraphernalia of gentility'. The standard of living, regarded
both as a norm to which the middle classes aspired and as a
level which they attained, rose rapidly during the 1850s and
1860s. Indeed to keep in the same social position, let alone
improve on it, during these twenty years required an additional
expenditure of 50 per cent. For those who led the field in the
rise of incomes this presented no problems, but for those who
were trying to keep up with the Joneses and whose incomes were
not increasing proportionately it created agonizing dilemmas.
Hence the stream of references to and complaints about the
cost of living in contemporary magazines and books.[2]

Analysing middle-class expenditure in *Prosperity and Parenthood* J. A. Banks has shown that the smaller the family income
the greater the proportion spent on food, and that when there
was a rise in income it was immediately followed by a dis-
proportionately large increase in expenditure on washing and
mangling. The census of 1851 showed that in Great Britain
there were 145,000 washerwomen, slightly more than the
number of merchant seamen and pilots.

But although cleanliness, and the wearing of frequently
washed linen, was part of the middle-class pattern, it was an
aspect of gentility that needed frequent stressing in an epoch
when the population as a whole gave off what Disraeli, one
summer's day in 1860 when Queen Victoria was surrounded
by members of the new Volunteer Movement, described to her
as a 'high *esprit de corps*'. In his *Elements of Hygiene* Dr Tilt
deplored the fact that when children reached the age of seven or
so 'the use of the bath' was 'too often, in this country, completely

[1] The analysis is made in J. A. Banks, *Prosperity and Parenthood: A Study
of Family Planning among the Victorian Middle classes* (Routledge & Kegan
Paul, 1954).

[2] See for example on p. 131 reference to the article in *The Englishwoman's Domestic Magazine* for April 1859 asking 'Can we Live on £300
A Year?' by 'we' meaning its middle-class readers, and by 'live' meaning
'in the fashion which our status demands'.

abandoned. A tepid bath every week could not fail of being beneficial, and those who cannot afford such a luxury in their own homes, may nevertheless still let their children enjoy the benefit of those admirable institutions abounding in several parts of the metropolis, where an excellent bath may be had for sixpence.'[1] The Greeks and Romans, he reminded his readers, considered bathing so important for health that they built 'palaces of gorgeous proportions' for the practice. 'Why have we, then,' he asked, 'allowed our better knowledge of the laws of the human frame, and of the two pounds of saline fluid daily permeating through our clothes in the shape of perspiration, to be hitherto almost useless? Looking around us, it would seem to be the popular belief that, except for little children, it was not judicious to bathe the whole body. It is true that by the institution of baths and wash-houses the poor can have a bath for twopence, but some similar institution is wanted for the middle classes; for though a better kind of bath can be obtained at these institutions for sixpence, of which many gentlemen avail themselves, most ladies, while they are afraid of seeking cleanliness at a building constructed for the benefit of the poor, are not sufficiently well-off to take baths at the old expensive establishments. We trust, however, that before long England will, in this respect be as well provided as her continental neighbours.'[2] He strongly advised adults to have a warm bath every week.

An important element in the increased domestic expenditure of the middle class was servants' wages. The census of 1871 pointed out that wives and daughters at home 'do now less domestic work than their predecessors; hence the excessive demand for female servants and the consequent rise of wages'. This rise amounted to about 30 per cent over the twenty years from 1851, but even so of itself it added only about 3 per cent of the total income to the proportion spent on servants.[3] It was the 'excessive demand' (which came not only from the increased domestic idleness of middle-class women resulting from their menfolk's growing wealth, but also, as the census omitted to point out, from an increase in their numbers because of the growing size of the middle class as a whole) and especially the greater employment of the most expensive types of domestic

[1] Dr Tilt, op. cit., p. 146.
[2] ibid, pp. 384-5.
[3] Banks, op. cit., p. 85.

labour – nursemaids, cooks, housemaids, and housekeepers, that was the main cause of the increased expenditure. Between 1851 and 1871 while the population of England and Wales increased by just over a quarter and the number of separate families went up by 36 per cent, female domestic servants increased by 57 per cent. Of these the number of general servants went up by just over a third, but the employment of cooks, housemaids and nursemaids more than doubled, while the number of house-keepers doubled and then doubled again. Another indication of the rising standard of middle-class living is to be found in the number of coachmen employed. Over the twenty years they increased at three times the rate at which households increased. More and more families now flaunted that higher middle-class status symbol – a carriage and horses.

The increasing leisure of middle-class women that was made possible by the capacity to pay for more and more servants had one unlooked-for result. By freeing certain women from the all-consuming labour of domesticity it enabled them to devote their time to forging a revolution in the status of women and to join with those other middle-class women whom misfortune and circumstance had thrown on their own resources. Together they formed the nucleus of the 'women's movement' which was to gather strength throughout the remainder of Victoria's reign.

Part Two

THE PRINCESS, SIX FEET HIGH

'Take Lilia then for heroine . . .
And make her some great Princess, six feet high'
Tennyson *The Princess*

Chapter 10

'ONE OF THE CHIEF SOCIAL MOVEMENTS OF THE DAY'

The Rights of Man by Tom Paine was published in 1791 as an answer to Burke's antagonistic *Reflections on the Revolution in France*. It was not the first answer. In 1790 the talented and beautiful Mary Wollstonecraft produced her *Vindication of the Rights of Man* and two years later she followed it with *A Vindication of the Rights of Woman*. In the ferment of ideas at the end of the eighteenth century the position of women was not a subject to be ignored.

The main argument of the *Vindication* was that women are human beings and should be recognized and treated as such. Because of their servility and ignorance they were acting as a drag on the wheel of progress. The book was not so much an attack on men for keeping women in this servile state as an attack on women for remaining in it. Mary Wollstonecraft's plea was that sex should be abolished as a radical dividing line in society and its distinctions should be only a minor matter. It was the 'privileges' of women which were their chief disability. They were not privileges at all, but a code of prison rules; and the women were not queens, but prisoners. 'I lament,' she wrote, 'that women are systematically degraded by receiving the trivial attentions which men think it manly to pay to the sex when in fact they are insultingly supporting their own superiority.' It was all right if love animated such behaviour, otherwise how awful it was to see a man anxiously picking up a handkerchief or shutting a door for a lady when she was perfectly able to do such a thing for herself. Instead of this mass of courtesies Mary Wollstonecraft wanted to substitute the rights of a human being. The first step towards achieving this was through the education of women. The second important step was to give women economic independence. As long as they continued to be ignorant and economically dependent on the whims or wiles of some man, be he husband or father, or under the rule of an employer who paid them the miserable pittance which passed for a woman's wage, they could never hope to realize their own true selves or to assist in human progress.

Mary Wollstonecraft's *Vindication of the Rights of Woman*, the first feminist bible, was considered a heretical and blasphemous book by all those whom her husband, the philosopher William Godwin, described as 'the pretty soft creatures that are so often to be found in the female sex, and that class of men who believe they could not exist without such pretty, soft creatures to resort to'. The philanthropist and bluestocking Hannah More, who was a pioneer of the Sunday School movement, voiced the opinion of the majority when she wrote to Horace Walpole, 'I am sure I have as much liberty as I can make use of now I am an old maid; and when I was a young one, I had, I dare say, more than was good for me. . . . There is, perhaps, no animal so much indebted to subordination for its good behaviour as woman.'

Mary Wollstonecraft's plea was that of a prophet crying in the wilderness, for she was expressing sentiments that were far, far ahead of the time when the social climate would make it possible even to entertain their realization. Why should not unmarried women become doctors, farmers, and shopkeepers? she asked. 'Business of various kinds they might likewise pursue, which might save many from common and legal prostitution' – by legal prostitution she meant marriage, which was entered into primarily or even solely as a means of subsistence. And she claimed the Parliamentary vote for women.

Mary Wollstonecraft died in 1797, a few days after giving birth to a daughter who later became Shelley's second wife. It was Mary's posthumous son-in-law who was the first poet to raise the question of woman and her relation to modern life. Shelley himself died in 1822, and ten years later the woman question began to occupy a noticeable place in the new poetry that was being published. Although the rationalist and agitator

9. *Top:* Jobs for the girls – the London Telegraph Office in 1871, from *The Graphic.* *Bottom:* the New World re-dressing the (bank) balance of the Old! (New York Millionairesses about to start for Europe. They are studying – not Murray and Baedeker – oh dear no! – but Burke and Debrett and taking note of all the unmarried Peers). Clara Van Deppenbeck: 'What a pity they don't publish their photographs as well as their ages and titles!' du Maurier in *Punch* 1881.

10. *Left to right:* Fashions of 1869. 'Crinoline changed into crinolette with an enormous bustle at the back and the hitched up skirt becoming a short over-skirt'. *Crow Collection.* Hazards of Foreign Travel. Customs search at Bellegarde. *La Vie Parisienne.*

G. J. Holyoake wrote that in 1840 women had no civil rights and there was no demand for them, yet it was at this very time that the rights of women were being discussed by the poets.

In *Locksley Hall*, published in 1842, Tennyson showed that he had begun to consider the question: 'Weakness to be wroth with weakness!' his angry hero exclaims, 'woman's pleasure, woman's pain – Nature made them blinder motions bounded in a shallower brain: Woman is the lesser man.'

Five years later he returned to the theme in *The Princess* which is a comprehensive discussion of the whole philosophy of womanhood and the position of women in the world and contains all the common prejudices of men about women and their work. The prologue describes how the poet and his friends wander in the grounds of the large house where they are staying. One of the party is their host's daughter Lilia. They all listen to a story of a feudal heroine of Lilia's family who, rather than yield to the will of a king, took arms against him and conquered him. When the story is done someone asks 'Where lives there such a woman now?' and Lilia replies: 'There are thousands now such women, but convention beats them down; It is but bringing up; no more than that; You men have done it: how I hate you all.'

'Ah, were I something great,' she continues, 'I would shame you then,

> That love to keep us children. O I wish
> That I were some great princess, I would build
> Far off from men a college like a man's,
> And I would teach them all that men are taught;
> We are twice as quick!'

In her college, Lilia says, angrily shaking off a male hand that 'played the patron with her curls' she would make it 'death for any male thing but to peep at us'.

One of the poet's friends says to him,

> 'Take Lilia, then, for heroine. . . .
> And make her some great Princess, six feet high.'

Thus out of Lilia's wish is created the fable which forms the poem. It is a mock-heroic story of a Prince of the North who has been betrothed to a Princess in the South and made her his ideal. When the time comes for the marriage to take place

Princess Ida refuses to marry. Enthralled by the idea of rescuing women from the slavery of men she has established a college where girls will be trained to become human beings as knowledgeable as men. Until the work is complete men must be kept away, because their presence might make the girls fall in love with them and this would be fatal for, as the Princess says, '*there lies our weakness – in our leaning to tenderness, in our personal cry for love*'. It is for this reason that no man may enter the college except on pain of death. But in the end the Princess herself falls in love with her Prince and dissolves the college.

Tennyson's heroine was based on Lady Lucie Duff-Gordon, only child of John Austin, the jurist, and the bluestocking Sarah Austin. Although Mrs Austin could easily have produced original work she confined herself to translating, and was the first to introduce German literature to the English public. The reason for thus limiting herself was that, as she often told her friend Barthelemy St. Hilaire, she feared that by publishing anything of her own she might 'expose herself to criticism and she always considered it improper in a woman to provoke a possible polemic'.

Despite the evidence to the contrary given by Mrs Austin and a host of others from time immemorial, it was argued that as a woman's brain was smaller in cubic content it was therefore inevitable that she was unable to reason or to generalize or to pursue a connected line of thought as well as a man could. It was the accepted belief that she was both mentally and physically inferior to man; that she was, in fact, a relative creature, as Mrs Ellis and others were continually reminding her. Even the brilliant Lady Mary Wortley Montagu did not argue that the sexes were equal when she complained angrily of the contempt in which women's intellectual capacity was held, and pleaded for women to be allowed better opportunities to develop their minds. 'We are a lower part of creation. We owe obedience and submission to the superior sex and any woman who suffers her vanity and folly to deny this, rebels against the laws of the Creator and the indisputable order of nature.'[1]

The legal status of women confirmed this condition of relativity. Laws and customs were nominally to protect a woman, but in fact they put her at a severe disadvantage.

[1] Quoted in Georgiana Hill, *Women in English Life* (Bentley, 1896), Vol. II, p. 43.

According to Sir William Blackstone, whose *Commentaries on the English Law* published in 1765–9 were for well over a century the lawyers' authority on both sides of the Atlantic, wives were classed with minors and idiots and had no responsibility under the law. Even before marriage, when a woman became engaged she could not dispose of any of her possessions without her fiancé's approval. On marriage her legal existence was suspended and became incorporated into that of her husband. She was, in the legal phrase, a *feme covert* – 'my wife and I are one and I am he'. She was, in fact, civilly dead.

Property, liberty, earnings, even a wife's conscience, all belonged to her husband, as did the children she might bear. She could sign no contract, make no will, cast no vote – a disability which she shared with unmarried women. The marriage service emphasized her lowly station and her obligation to 'obey'. Until 1857 no divorce was obtainable by a woman in Britain, except in extremely rare cases through special Act of Parliament, which meant that it was available only to aristocratic wealth; for the others death was the only release. And until 1884 a woman could be imprisoned for denying her spouse his conjugal rights. Even the right of a man to prevent his wife by force from leaving him was not successfully challenged until 1891. Murder and high treason were the only crimes that a woman was considered 'able' to commit *on her own* in her husband's presence, a presumption not abolished until 1925.

In the United States, although the letter of the law was on the whole no less strict than in England, the different conditions gave rise to different precedents which varied from state to state. Like so much else when it crossed the Atlantic, the law was modified by the circumstance of the American forest and American distance. The shortage of women and the need for everyone to work their utmost in developing the virgin continent meant that a married woman's legal non-existence was sometimes overlooked by the courts when necessity demanded. Divorce too, though not easy, was far less impossible than in England. Nevertheless the rulings of equity were a charity, whereas the 'civil death' of married women was fundamental law.

The Christian religion, too, was a powerful force in proclaiming and maintaining women's inferior position. On its Judaic inheritance it had erected the myth that woman's subordinate place was a punishment for the original sin of Eve. It worshipped the words of Paul that 'man is not of the woman but the woman of the man'. It took as gospel John Knox's personal rage against Mary Tudor and Mary Queen of Scots, and believed that 'after her fall and rebellion committed against God', there was put upon woman 'a new necessity, and she was made subject to man by the irrevocable sentence of God'.

It was this assertion of inferiority reiterated over the centuries that rankled in women's hearts and caused the bitterness some of them now began so vehemently to express.

The 'Separate Exertions' –

Writing in 1860 of the profound change in the ideas of women that had gradually developed after the year 1780, and of the more rapid development that had happened within the past forty years, Bessie Rayner Parkes (afterwards Madame Belloc), one of the early leaders of the women's movement, thought that while the great social theories of the eighteenth century might have provided a philosophical base for the onset of the movement, its immediate cause was economic. 'The emigration of men, the creation of the factory system, the disruption from numerous causes of the simple old life – simple, kindly, and in many instances coarse,' all this, she wrote, 'threw numbers of women on their own resources. Then began the cry for equal advantages, equal education. The slow process of natural development was too tardy for the pressing need.' Admittedly there would in any case have been 'a few vigorous intellects exerting themselves on the problems of social life and even pushing the claim of equality to an extreme. But except for the material need which exerted a constant pressure over a large and educated class, the "women's movement",' she maintained, 'could never have become in England a subject of popular comment and, to a certain extent, of popular sympathy'.[1]

Such organization as there was in the women's movement in 1860 was of recent origin. Even ten years before, Bessie Parkes recalled, although there had been active groups of people deeply interested in improving female education and employment opportunities and in reforming the law about married women's property, 'there was no centre of meeting, nor any one work

[1] Bessie Rayner Parkes, *Essays on Woman's Work*, 1865, pp. 54-5.

which could be said to draw together the names of the ladies so actively employed. But the separate exertions carried on were surely and solidly laying the foundations of what has now taken its place as one of the chief social "movements" of the day.'[1]

– Education

The first of these separate exertions was in education. Both Mary Wollstonecraft and Tennyson's Princess had declared that if woman was to escape from her servile dependence on man she must first be educated. Lack of instruction rather than lack of capacity was the limiting factor. It was a woman's part to be negative and to accept whatever was laid down by men. A solid education would make women pedants who would 'embarrass men by displaying talent and learning' and 'worry them with theories and opinions'.[2] It would also withdraw them from household duties and, even more reprehensible, it would make them free-thinkers and therefore less moral.

In the Lower Nation girls' education, such as it was, was little different from boys', except that even fewer girls than boys went to school and that sewing was included in their lessons. In the agricultural districts these lessons were given in dame-schools; in the towns and thickly-populated districts they were given in Sunday Schools or charity schools or in the schools of the nonconformist Bible and Foreign Schools Society and the Church of England National Society,[3] which since 1833 had had a grant of £20,000 a year from the Government 'for the erection of schoolhouses for the education of the poorer classes', the first grudging acknowledgement that the State had some responsibility for the education of its citizens. In so far as no distinction was made in the sex of the children who might attend the voluntary societies' schools, and derive what benefits they could from the Government's money, it may be said, as Alicia Percival has pointed out, 'that the girls of "the poorer classes" were allowed a place in the State, as Mary Wollstonecraft

[1] ibid., p. 55.
[2] Georgiana Hill, op. cit., p. 45.
[3] Whose full name was the National Society for Promoting the Education of the Poor in the Principles of the Established Church throughout England and Wales. £30,000 a year was also granted to the voluntary societies for educational work in the West Indies.

would have wished, and this some time before their wealthier sisters'.[1]

The education of these 'wealthier sisters' in the Top Nation was either in the hands of the girls' parents, or it was left to governesses, who might or might not have any competence, or it was entrusted to small boarding-schools chosen for their ladylike qualities rather than for the educational opportunities they provided. In Dr Tilt's opinion 'domestic education' was undoubtedly preferable to a boarding-school because 'the vigilant eye of a mother' was 'able to correct any deviation from right principles'. Instead of boarding-school at home, some parents, because it was so much cheaper than in England, sent their daughters to schools abroad, a practice which did not meet with Tilt's approval because, he wrote enigmatically, 'it has often interfered with the future prospects of our country women, unless parents wish their children to settle on the Continent'.[2] Theresa Longworth, who was to become internationally famous in the 1860s when she dared to stand up for her rights in the great Yelverton Marriage Case, was one such example – certainly of a girl educated on the Continent, and possibly too of one whose future prospects were thus interfered with! The daughter of a wealthy but parsimonious Manchester silk manufacturer, Theresa was educated in the Ursuline Convent at Boulogne where she was taught a range of subjects including music, drawing, history, science, grammar, sewing, and arithmetic.

In English boarding-schools, girls' education was, in the words of the Schools Inquiry Commission 1864–8, 'fragmentary, multifarious, disconnected; taught not scientifically as a subject, but merely as so much information, and hence, like a wall of stones without mortar, it fell to pieces'. The form this mortarless education took was to make the girls learn interminable catechisms. A standard book was *Mangnall's Questions*, first published in 1800 and still in use in half the girls' schools in England sixty years later, when another famous volume of the same type was published called the *Child's Guide to Knowledge*. Miss Richmal Mangnall is said to have been the original of Thackeray's Miss Pinkerton whose most celebrated pupil, if not her best student, was Becky Sharpe. The sort of

[1] Alicia Percival, *The English Miss* (Harrap, 1939), p. 259.
[2] Dr Tilt, op. cit., pp. 278–9.

unsystematic catechism that passed for education went like this:

Q. What is a whalebone?

A. A sort of gristle found inside the whale in long, flat pieces three or four yards long; it supplies the place of teeth.

Q. Are there not four hundred or five hundred of them in one whale?

A. Yes; they stick to the upper jaw and form a kind of strainer to keep in the sea-snails and other small creatures upon which whales live.

Q. What is whalebone used for?

A. To stiffen stays, umbrellas, and whips.

Q. Are not umbrellas of great antiquity?

A. Yes; the Greeks, Romans, and all Eastern nations used them to keep off the sun; *ombrello*, in Italian, signifies 'a little shade'.

Q. Did not the use of this article travel from Italy into the other countries of Europe?

A. Yes; but very slowly, for they have scarcely been used in England above eighty years.

Using this 'noxious brood of catechisms' a girl could be hurried through the Roman use of maple, Queen Elizabeth's opinion of silk stockings, a description of the jewel Queen Victoria gave to Florence Nightingale, the sort of cat Dick Whittington sold to make his fortune ('A. Yes, but it was not the *whiskered mouse-killing* cat, but the coasting, coal-carrying cat that realized his fortune') – all this and much more without having one principle made intelligible to her. Indeed when Lewis Carroll made his Walrus tell the Oysters that the time had come

'To talk of many things,
Of shoes – and ships – and sealing wax –
Of cabbages – and kings'

he was being as systematic as any schoolmistress with her class, or governess with her charges. This was 'the torture of women's education' that Elizabeth Barrett Browning's Aurora Leigh had to suffer from her aunt.

The first step in the development of education arose out of the Governesses' Benevolent Institution. It seemed to Frederick

Maurice and his fellow Christian Socialists, including Charles
Kingsley, Charles Mansfield and J. M. Ludlow, that the only
way to improve the economic position of governesses was for
them to be taught to be better teachers. If they were more
proficient at their jobs they might be better able to demand
higher salaries. With this object of instructing governesses, a
series of Lectures for Ladies was organized in 1847 by Maurice,
who had been professor of English history and literature at
King's College, London, and who was now its professor of
theology. The lectures were given by King's professors and
attracted so much interest, taking in other pupils as well as
governesses, that the following year Maurice and his friends
founded Queen's College for Women in Harley Street, London,
where it still functions to this day. The fees were 9 guineas a
term or £26 5s od a year, and the course lasted four years.
Permission for its name was given by Queen Victoria, whose
interest in the College was aroused by one of her ladies-in-
waiting, Miss Murray. The name was some protection against
the charges of the respectables, who considered that a College
for women was 'unladylike behaviour' and a threat to the social
proprieties.

The specific connection with governesses and would-be
teachers was soon lost in the demand for education that came
from other young women who wanted to learn more than the
rudimentary knowledge they had got from governesses or
parents or from some ladies' seminary. In 1852 Queen's
College was incorporated with an identity quite separate from
the Governesses' Benevolent Institution.

The year after Queen's College was founded a second ladies'
college came into existence. This was Bedford College, now part
of London University, and it differed from Queen's in that the
latter was entirely governed by men and the only share that
women had in the management was that of attending the
lectures as 'lady visitors' or chaperons. Bedford College on the
other hand, had a mixed board of management.

The two colleges provided a cadre of women who were
capable of running schools for girls that could provide an
education comparable with the public schools at which their
brothers were taught. Among those who attended Queen's
College in its first year was Frances Mary Buss. She was twenty-
one and for three years had been running a school which her

mother had founded. Two years later this private school was re-organized as the North London Collegiate School and Miss Buss became its headmistress. The second of the two most famous names in nineteenth-century English girls' education, Dorothea Beale, also attended Queen's College, first as a pupil and then as a tutor in mathematics. In 1858 she became head-mistress of Cheltenham College which had been founded four years earlier. Through Bedford and Queen's 'the whole standard of female education in regard to history, the dead and living languages, mathematics, and musical science, was changed', wrote Bessie Parkes.

Queen's was not the first college to which women were admitted. They were entitled to study at the two London colleges of University College and King's. But they did not do so for two reasons. In the first place the standard was immeasur-ably too high for them because of their inadequate secondary education; and in the second place to share lectures with men students would have been unladylike – a hazard that may seem laughable today but one which was of crucial importance in the middle of the nineteenth century. To be considered unladylike was to court the outer darkness – and often to reach it! Addition-ally University College was undenominational – it had been founded in 1826 by Bentham, Grote, Brougham and other Liberals and dissenters to break the Church of England monopoly on higher education – and as such was morally suspect by respectable parents. King's was founded in 1829 as an episcopalian counterweight to University College, an honourable rivalry which is still perpetuated though not on account of the original religious reasons.

– Philanthropy

Most of the women who were active in trying to improve the position of their sex were young. There were two, however, Mrs Mary Howitt and Mrs Anna Jameson, who belonged to the older generation and who played an important part in encour-aging the younger ones and also in restraining them from actions which would be considered unladylike and would therefore do the cause more harm than good. Both were well-known women writers. Because of her literary reputation, which had all the hallmarks of respectability, Mrs Jameson's lectures on 'Sisters of Charity' and 'The Community of Labour', delivered in the

drawing-rooms of two lady friends in 1855 and 1856 and afterwards published, had a powerful influence in crystallizing the
thoughts of those who wanted to use the growing philanthropic
work of women as a wedge for securing women's rights.

Even more important for the future was the example of
Florence Nightingale. In 1853, holding a steady course through
the hysterics of her mother and her sister Parthenope, she
became Superintendent of the Institution for the care of Sick
Gentlewomen in Distressed Circumstances which opened new
premises in Harley Street, London. Her outstanding contribution was to demonstrate that organized duties were more
valuable than unorganized devotion, which was often only
self-indulgent. Providing patients 'with clean beds and good
food' was 'more effectual than to sit through the watches of the
night cheering the dying moments of the patient expiring from
scurvy and bed sores. But it was not so picturesque.'[1]

It was this practical, unemotional approach that she brought
to Scutari in 1854 and which she applied to nursing the Crimean
casualties. As it turned out, gratitude supplied the picturesque,
so that she became a national heroine, especially among the
Lower Nation. In a letter to Parthenope written on January 18,
1856 Mrs Gaskell, the novelist, told how the Manchester
work-people had come to a meeting 'ready to cheer and applaud
their heroine – for they feel her as theirs, their brother's nurse,
their dead friend's friend – in a way which they don't know how
to express. "*You* benevolent ladies! Why you women all play at
benevolence – look at Florence Nightingale – there's a woman
for you." That was a speech made to me not long ago.'

– *Married Women's Property*

In 1855 Barbara Leigh Smith, then aged twenty-eight, was
seized with the idea that she must campaign for the law to be
amended so that married women might retain their earnings
for their own use.

The lead in giving married women some rights over property
had already been taken in the United States. In 1848 New York
State had passed a Married Women's Property Act, which other
states were beginning to copy. The New York Act, however,
applied only to property brought into the marriage, not property

[1] Cecil Woodham-Smith, *Florence Nightingale* (Reprint Society edition,
1952), p. 87.

earned afterwards – indeed earning was hardly considered because, in the words of an American feminist 'all society was built on the theory that men, not women, earned money and that men alone supported the family'.

Barbara Leigh Smith, later to become Madame Bodichon, was a cousin of Florence Nightingale and was brought up in a wealthy, well-connected radical household. Her father, Benjamin Smith, was Radical Member for Norwich. It is noticeable indeed how the pioneers of the women's movement in England came almost exclusively from families with a long tradition of philanthropy and reform. Many of these families had taken an active part in the campaign for abolishing slavery. When that campaign achieved success in 1833 the energies that had been devoted to it were now released for other reforms. It was from the social conscience of this evangelical and nonconformist 'cousinhood' that the impetus came for much of the social legislation of Victoria's reign. Inevitably, with its background of social reform and religious nonconformity or evangelicalism, the domestic atmosphere in which the girls of these families grew up made them unwilling to accept the conventional status of women as a chattel. Unitarianism and the other nonconformist beliefs had the liberating effect of making those young women with any spark of initiative more ready to struggle for a measure of independence.

Another, most important, influence in the lives of most of these young women was an older man. Sometimes this was a father, brother, husband, or other relative. But not always; there was, for instance, the Queen's 'dear Lord M'. In the case of Barbara Leigh Smith, who was left motherless at an early age, it was her father's enlightened attitude which allowed her to develop her talents. He gave each of his children an income of £300 a year as soon as they came of age. Elizabeth Barrett too owed much to her father, and although his views on his daughter's marriage to Robert Browning at the age of forty made him into a dramatic monster, nevertheless her love for him and her gratitude for all he taught her is shown in the dedication to her collected poems, published two years before her marriage. And Beatrice Potter, later Beatrice Webb, one of the famous nine Miss Potters, had a father who always talked to his daughters as equals. Even when they were young girls he would discuss with them 'not only his business affairs, but also religion, politics, and the problems of sex, with frankness and freedom',[1] and he would take them with him on his travels about the world, especially to the United States and Canada where he had railroad interests. Florence Nightingale, it is true, was an exception as far as fatherly help was concerned. Her father, no less than her mother, was religiously opposed to her attempt to make what she considered a worthwhile life for herself in nursing. On balance, however, one can say that the attitude of the father or dominant male relative was the determining factor in the sort of life a girl was permitted to live. If the father was possessive and jealous, as the Victorian cult of family tended to make him, and wanted to keep his daughters in a kind of private harem for virgins, it was virtually impossible for a girl to break out of the trivial round of family duties. But if she had her father on her side, then however restricted others' attitudes were, she had a chance of escaping into a fuller life.

Barbara Leigh Smith began her task by publishing a *Brief Summary in Plain Language of the Most Important Laws Concerning Women*. In this she was following the literary footsteps of Mrs Caroline Norton who, in 1852, had written *English Law for Women in the 19th Century* which she circulated privately.

The *Brief Summary* was brought to the attention of the Law Amendment Society by Barbara Leigh Smith's friend Davenport Hill, Recorder of Birmingham. The Society received a report on it from one of its members, Sir Erskine Perry, and decided to back the reform it suggested. In order to raise support public meetings were held and petitions drawn up. These were organized by a committee formed by Barbara Leigh Smith. It was the first feminist committee in Britain. Among those who signed the original petition were Mrs Jameson, Mrs Howitt and Elizabeth Barrett Browning. Even names such as these, however, were not sufficient to allay the genuine fears of those who believed that such a reform would disrupt society, destroy homes, and make women into grasping Shylocks. The public meetings arranged by Barbara Leigh Smith and her friends were countered by others held to drown the reform in obloquy. But the petitions had their effect and a Bill was introduced in May 1857. It was presented in the House of Lords by Lord Brougham and in the House of Commons by Sir Erskine

[1] Beatrice Webb, *My Apprenticeship* (Longmans Green, 1926), p. 10.

Perry. To the joy of its adherents it passed its second reading without much opposition. In the event, however, it was lost.

– *Divorce*

The reason for the failure of the Married Women's Property Bill which proposed that property rights and the power to make wills should be extended to married women, was the introduction of another Bill, brought in by Lord Cranworth. The purpose of this Bill was to abolish the jurisdiction of ecclesiastical courts and make divorce accessible otherwise than through act of Parliament. This proposal was even more iconoclastic than the suggestion that married women should have property rights. The opposers of this second Bill had no doubt that it threatened the sanctity of the home. They were violent and interminable in their opposition to it. Gladstone, for example, made twenty-nine speeches against a single clause in the Bill, many of them of substantial length.

One of those who took a vehement part was Caroline Norton. She was not interested in the broader claim for women's rights but only, because of her own experience, in the particular right of a woman who had to leave her husband. She proposed certain amendments to the Bill. These were: (1) that a deserted wife should be protected from her husband's claims to her earnings, (2) that a separate maintenance for a deserted wife could be paid into the hands of a trustee, (3) that a separated or divorced wife should be given the power to inherit or bequeath property as if she were single, though without resuming possession of property owned before or inherited or earned during the marriage, and (4) that a separated or divorced wife should be given the power to sue and be sued, and to enter into contracts in her own right. In fact, the basis of her amendments was that a deserted, separated, or divorced wife should have all the powers of a single woman.

These amendments were incorporated in the Bill. At once they destroyed the gravamen of the other reform. After all, if injured wives were protected, why on earth should uninjured wives want any rights over their property? The result was that Barbara Leigh Smith's Bill for married women's property rights was defeated. The Marriage and Divorce Bill on the other hand, was passed in 1857 and with later amendments in 1858,

1884 and 1896 it remained the basis of the marriage law for a long time. Its thesis accurately reflected the opinion of the time as regards women. In effect, it stated that any man might divorce his wife for adultery, but that adultery alone was not a sufficient ground for a woman to obtain a divorce. There are echoes of Mrs Ellis in its contention that it was 'natural' for a man to be unfaithful and that a woman must expect to put up with it. But if the husband added cruelty or desertion or the crimes of sodomy, bestiality, or rape to his adultery then the wife had grounds for divorce. The Act also made it legal for divorced people to remarry, and there was a provision for legal separation which, if the courts allowed, could give to the injured wife the custody of the children, protection from her husband, and the payment of a maintenance, as well as allowing her to retain possession of any future earnings or inheritance. By this Act, says Cunnington, 'woman obtained the privilege of physical decency'.

– Employment

Thwarted in their desire to achieve property rights for married women, Barbara Leigh Smith and her friends began to concentrate on another major difficulty. This was the question of employment.

In 1861 the number of women and girls in employment in Great Britain was 3,386,800 out of a total female population of 11,449,600. The percentage of females employed was now 29·5, compared with 28·9 in 1851. Domestic service, and textiles and dress manufacture were the main occupations, employing 2,629,400, or 77·6 per cent of the total female working population, while manufacturing as a whole was still first in importance. In Ireland the total population was now down to 5,798,900, of which females were down to 2,961,500 and the female working population to 848,500. Even here the percentage of females employed was up: 28·6 compared with 27·4 ten years earlier.

But these national figures included few middle-class women. The opportunities for employment open to them were very limited. Educated destitution, to use Bessie Rayner Parkes's phrase, was an evil that she and her colleagues considered was not receiving the attention it deserved. It was indeed very much a problem of the middle class, and these ladies who wanted to relieve this destitution were, on the whole, middle-class ladies. Their first move was to start a journal in which the problems and suggested cures could be discussed. In October 1856, while she was in Edinburgh, Bessie Parkes came upon a stray number of a periodical which she thought could be turned into the journal they wanted. Mrs Jameson provided technical advice and Barbara Leigh Smith provided the money. But after negotiations it was decided that, rather than alter an existing periodical, it would be better to start afresh. In March 1858 the first number of the *English Woman's Journal* appeared. Seven years and seventy-eight numbers later the *Journal* was amalgamated with the *Alexandra Magazine*.

Around the active shuttle of the *Journal* which threaded the 'separate exertions' even if it did not draw them together, other practical steps were taken to improve the position of women. In June 1859 Jessie Boucherett came to London to organize the Society for Promoting the Employment of Women with the object of developing and extending 'the hitherto restricted field of female labour by the establishment of industrial schools and workshops where girls may be taught those trades and occupations which are at present exclusively monopolized by men'. Those thus trained, it was claimed, would be capable of becoming 'clerks, cashiers, railway ticket-sellers, printers, etc.'. The *Journal* had already started a small register, and this was now incorporated in the new Society and the two offices were brought together at 19 Langham Place, London. The Society started a law-copying office. Its manager was Maria Rye who had first come in contact with the other 'women's rightists' at the time of the Married Women's Property Bill when she had been engaged to look after the large amount of correspondence which the Bill entailed. Before long the law-copying office gave rise to an organized movement for emigration. So many women applied for employment to whom it was impossible to give jobs that Maria Rye tried to assist some of them to emigrate. Soon the arrangement of emigration began to take precedence over the law-copying business, which was delegated to a forewoman. Miss Rye went on an emigration ship herself, in order to find out the condition of the labour market and the best means of providing help. In due course the Middle-class Emigration Society was established at 12 Portugal Street, London.

Another small development in the field of employment was

the establishment by Miss Emily Faithfull of the Victoria Press which printed the *English Woman's Journal*. Miss Faithfull herself, who might be considered the very epitome of respectable spinsterhood – apart, that is, from her 'strong-minded' establishment of a printing press run by women – a few years later became the bizarre performer in a scurrilous divorce case in which she was cited as a co-respondent by Lady Codrington.

As well as the yeast that was provided by the *Journal* and its associated enterprises, there was another forum in which women's rights were discussed. The National Association for the Promotion of Social Science was formed in 1857, with Lord Brougham as its President. As its name suggests its purpose was to discuss all those aspects of social reform which were most pressing. This in itself, in an age when the principles of association were barely understood, was a novel departure. But even more revolutionary was the fact that from the outset women were not only admitted to meetings but were positively encouraged to come. Naturally their presence meant that the aims and desires of a woman's movement were brought to the attention of the Association's members. As if to nail the flag of revolution to the mast a young woman, Miss Isa Craig from Edinburgh was appointed assistant secretary.

It was in the offices at 19 Langham Place that the Woman's Movement which was to be the centre of so much controversy for the rest of Victoria's reign and beyond, really began to function. To begin with the organization may have been rudimentary and the successes small, but what the new movement lacked in power it made up for in vitality and enthusiasm. 'Why should not women be hairdressers, hotel managers, wood engravers, dispensers, house decorators, watchmakers, telegraphists? Out! Out! Let us see if we can make them do it! Why does the school of design threaten to exclude them? We must have a petition at once; and the Royal Academy, why does it not admit women students? We must knock politely on its doors. And then there were the swimming baths in Marylebone, why were they not open to women? Did the manager say that women did not want to use them? Nonsense, of course they did. If thirty women came would they be opened? Very well, thirty women should come; and every Wednesday afternoon the young ladies trooped away from the office to help to stir the face of the waters. Nothing must be let slip, be it small or great, in the campaign they had begun to wage.'[1]

The eager young ladies from Langham Place who went knocking on the doors of the Royal Academy and plunging into the Marylebone swimming baths on Wednesdays were continuing the tradition of earlier agitations. Though their targets were different, their methods were similar. Both the campaign for the abolition of slavery and the Anti-Corn Law League, which had achieved its success with the repeal of the Corn Laws in 1846, had used their own variations of swimming on Wednesdays. They had drawn up petitions, called public meetings, flooded the country with articles, run their own periodicals. In the years to come the women were to become just as polemic.

[1] Ray Strachey, *The Cause* (1928), p. 96.

Chapter 11

'THIS WILD DISTURBANCE
OF THE FEMALE MIND'

Hepworth Dixon, editor of the influential London literary
weekly *The Athenaeum* and whose *New America* was published in
1867, considered that the most outstanding characteristic
about the United States next to its huge size was 'the dis-
proportion almost everywhere apparent between the sexes'.
Although the older states like Maryland, Massachusetts and
New Hampshire had roughly as many women as men, the
newer states and the territories in the West had very few women.
California in 1860, for example, had three men to every woman,
Washington four, Nevada eight, and in Colorado they were
as many as twenty to one. The census compiled in 1860 revealed that there were 730,000 more white males than
white females in the United States. No country in Europe
(except the Papal States, where circumstances were somewhat
unusual) could show a similar situation. Indeed, in France,
England, Germany and Spain, females were in large excess of
males.

The shortage of women was extremely noticeable in the
Western territories and Hepworth Dixon, who visited the
United States particularly to study the position of women in
American society, found it strange at first to be waited on at
table by a lady with whom he had recently been discussing
Keats, or whom he had just heard playing Gounod. But with so
few women, every girl was a lady and almost every woman a
wife. There were no servants, certainly no white servants, for
'what girl of spirit would let herself out for hire when the Church
door is open and the bridal bells are ready? Who would accept

the position of a woman's help when she has only to say the word and become a man's help-mate?'[1]

Even in the Eastern states where the balance between the male and female population was more equal, the effect of living in a country where there were more men than women showed itself in many ways. Dixon called them 'a variety of plagues'. These fads and fancies drove women 'into a thousand restless agitations about their rights and powers; into debating woman's era in history, woman's place in creation, woman's mission in the family; into public hysteria, into table-rapping, into anti-wedlock societies, into theories about free-love, natural marriage and artistic maternity; into anti-offspring resolutions, into sectarian polygamy, into free trade of the affections, into community of wives. Some part of this wild disturbance of the female mind, it may be urged, is due to the freedom and prosperity which women find in America as compared against what they enjoy in Europe; but this freedom, this prosperity, are in some degree at least the consequences of that disparity in numbers which makes the hand of every young girl in the United States a positive prize.'[2]

Among foreign observers of women's place in society there was generally a tendency to regard their own countrywomen as having less freedom than the women in the country they were visiting. Thus Mrs Houstoun and Hepworth Dixon both thought women were less restricted in the United States than in Europe; Taine thought women in England had more freedom than women in his native France; and Samuel Goodrich, author of the enormously popular American *Peter Parley* stories, reported that American women were even more secluded and more domestic than women in England. Harriet Martineau on the other hand had been horrified at the downtrodden condition of American women. Among these women there were many who agreed with her rather than with Dixon and Mrs Houstoun, and who felt bitterly that they had neither freedom nor prosperity.

Seneca Falls

It was in the United States that the organized movement for woman's rights began. On July 19 and 20, 1848, the year of revolutions in Europe, 'a convention to discuss the social, civil

[1] *New America* (Hurst and Blackett), Vol. II, p. 22.
[2] *ibid*, pp. 30-1.

and religious rights of woman' was held in the Wesleyan Chapel at Seneca Falls, a small industrial town in the Finger Lakes region of New York State, south of Lake Ontario. The convention was called by five women: Mrs Elizabeth Cady Stanton, the thirty-three-year-old daughter of a judge and wife of an abolitionist leader, who lived in the town; Mrs Lucretia Coffin Mott, a founder of the first Female Anti-Slavery Society, who was on a visit with her husband to Waterloo near Seneca Falls; Mrs Jane Hunt, the Motts' hostess; Mrs Martha C. Wright, Mrs Mott's sister; and Mary Ann McClintock. All five were Quakers. The two main instigators were Elizabeth Stanton and Lucretia Mott.

For her honeymoon trip in 1840 Mrs Stanton had accompanied her husband to a World Anti-Slavery Convention in London. Despite protests, the Convention had decided that only the men delegates should sit in the main hall and that the women must sit in the gallery, taking no part in the deliberations. This excommunication was seminal, for among the women delegates excluded with Elizabeth Stanton was Lucretia Mott, whom she thus met for the first time and who greatly influenced her.

Born in 1793 on Nantucket Island Lucretia Coffin had been brought up in a Quaker sea-faring community where women had to play a dominant part while the men were away at sea. Her father was for a time a whaling-ship captain before going into business in Philadelphia, and her mother at one time kept a store. In her teens she became a schoolteacher and had early experience of unequal pay for equal work. When she was eighteen she married James Mott, who went into business with his father-in-law in Philadelphia. Here at the age of twenty-eight Lucretia was ordained a minister by her Quaker meeting, which gave her invaluable training as a public speaker. The Motts were active abolitionists, their home a busy station on the Underground Railroad that brought escaped slaves to freedom.

After their frustrating, humiliating hours in the gallery at the World Anti-Slavery Convention Lucretia Mott and Elizabeth Stanton walked and talked, discussing, in Mrs Stanton's words, 'the crucifixion of their pride and self-respect'. Action for reform was imperative, but how and when could it be taken?

'This Wild Disturbance of the Female Mind'

On returning to the United States Mrs Stanton became friendly with the Grimké sisters, Sarah and Angelina, the daughters of a South Carolina slave-owning family who were public speakers in the abolition cause, and whose anti-slavery speeches were also speeches for woman's rights. She also maintained a correspondence with Mrs Mott. The need for action remained strongly in her mind. She joined with Paulina Wright Davis and Ernestine Rose in campaigning for the passage of the Married Women's Property Bill which was before the New York State legislature. The Bill, which was backed by wealthy citizens anxious to protect their daughters' marriage portions, eventually became state law in 1848 after twelve years in committee. By this time the Stantons had moved to Seneca Falls and Elizabeth was the mother of seven children. In this small community she felt isolated, bored, beset by the drudgery of domestic life. Her frustration brought the need for organized action to flash-point. The spark was provided by the passage of the Married Women's Property Act and by the presence of Lucretia Mott in nearby Waterloo.

Although the organizers feared a flop, the Seneca Falls meeting was a success. Three hundred of both sexes turned up and crowded into the little chapel, including forty men on the first day which was supposed to have been for women only. Elizabeth Stanton made her maiden speech in which she said that the time had come for 'the question of woman's wrongs to be laid before the public'. All the resolutions were carried unanimously, except one calling for women to be given the vote in accordance with the Declaration of Independence, a reform dear to Mrs Stanton.

Other local conventions were held in New York State and in Ohio, and in 1850 the first national Woman's Rights Convention, called by Lucy Stone, was held in Worcester, Massachusetts, with Paulina Wright Davis of Rhode Island presiding. The Convention passed the following resolutions: 'That every human being of full age, who has to obey the law and who is taxed to support the Government, should have a vote; that political rights have nothing to do with sex, and the word "male" should be struck out of all our state constitutions; that the laws of property as affecting married persons should be revised so as to make all the laws equal – the wife to have during life an equal control over the property gained by their mutual toil and sacrifices, to be heir of her husband to the extent that he is her heir, and to be entitled at her death to dispose at will of the same share of the joint property as he is.' The Convention also voted other resolutions declaring that women had a right to a far better education that they then had, that they should be allowed a fair partnership with men in trade and adventure, and that they should have a share in the administration of justice.

National woman's rights conventions also organized by Lucy Stone were held annually until the Civil War, and as well as these national gatherings there were many local meetings in towns from Indiana to Massachusetts. These meetings and conventions attracted ribald comments in the press – and not only in the American press. On February 7, 1857 the London *Saturday Review* pilloried the latest national convention. 'Let them form a Grand United Female Railway Association to be stoked and engineered by women of experience in Bloomer costume,' it jeered.

As well as at the conventions and meetings, the problems women had to face in a man's world were discussed in periodicals devoted to the cause: Paulina Wright Davis's *The Una*, Jane Swisshelm's *Pittsburgh Visiter*, the *Woman's Advocate* edited by Anna McDowell, and Amelia Bloomer's *The Lily*, which was published in her home-town of Seneca Falls. When Elizabeth Stanton came to Seneca Falls, Mrs Bloomer's paper was concerned only with advancing the temperance cause, but under the powerful influence of Mrs Stanton it soon became exclusively interested in woman's rights while its owner joined her persuader in adopting the costume which was to bear her name.

The last woman's rights convention before the Civil War was held in Albany in February 1861. Thereafter all activity for the cause of women's emancipation came to a standstill while many of the women themselves worked for the Sanitary Commission, which was a widespread voluntary organization for the welfare of the troops and their families. This experience gave the Sanitary women 'the opportunity to learn how to organize the multitude of women's clubs that were to spring up after the war and bring an extraordinary cohesiveness and a smattering of culture to millions of American women in the small towns'.[1]

[1] Andrew Sinclair, *The Better Half* (Cape, 1966), p. 180.

More Than the Mechanism of a Pudding

The Seneca Falls Convention is traditionally regarded as the birth of the woman's rights movement, but as Eleanor Flexner has pointed out in this context, 'we are on solid ground only if we remember that birth is a stage in the process of growth'.[1] In this particular case the gestation period stretched back to the previous century. Even before the publication of Mary Wollstonecraft's *Vindication*, which became as much a bible for American as for English feminists, the new United States had produced its own feminist philosopher. Under the pen-name of Constantia, Mrs Judith Sargent Murray, the daughter of a Massachusetts sea-captain and merchant, wrote, during the years of revolution, an essay on woman's rights which she published in 1790. Her thoughts were in parallel with Mary Wollstonecraft's and echoed those of Lady Wortley Montagu. Chief of woman's rights, she claimed, was the right to education. It was the difference in education and the continued advantages thereafter that was the source of man's mental superiority, not any immutable natural law.

Judith Murray was not alone at the time in calling for improvement in educational opportunities for women. 'Is it reasonable,' asked Dr Benjamin Rush in a speech in Philadelphia in 1787, 'that a candidate for immortality ... should at present be so degraded as to be allowed no other ideas than those which are suggested by the mechanism of a pudding or the sewing of the seams of a garment?'

In fact, a quarter of a century had to pass before any 'other ideas' were publicly allowed. Then, when the westward movement was drawing the men from the Eastern states, and the industrial revolution had begun to disrupt the old social climate, the dormant demands were re-stated and the springs of action began to operate.

In 1818 Hannah Mather Crocker published her *Observations on the Real Rights of Women* in which she acknowledged her debt to Mary Wollstonecraft, but disagreed with her demand for 'the total independence of the female sex'. God had been right to deprive woman of equality with man in the Garden of Eden, but now the teaching of Christianity was

[1] Eleanor Flexner, *A Century of Struggle* (The Belknap Press of the Harvard University Press, 1959), p. 77.

167

removing God's curse, and it was right that women should now be educated.

The following year Emma Willard, whose best-known contribution to literature is the poem 'Rocked in the Cradle of the Deep', published *An Address to the Public; Particularly to the Members of the Legislature of New York; Proposing a Plan for Improving Female Education.* Mrs Willard, who had had an unusually liberal education from her free-thinking father, started a seminary for girls at her house in Middlebury when her husband's bank failed. The *Address* had no practical effect in Albany, but a little farther up the Hudson at Troy, the town council were persuaded by it into putting up the money for Mrs Willard to build a girls' school. The Troy Female Seminary, now known as the Emma Willard School, was opened in 1821 and run by its founder until she retired from teaching in 1838. It was a conservative institution for the daughters of the middle class, and its emphasis was on religious and moral instruction. Nevertheless, its curriculum went as far as discretion would allow. Girls were taught history, geography, arithmetic, and innocuous physiology, as well as the becoming graces for a lady. Elizabeth Stanton went to Troy Seminary.

Another seminary which advanced the course of girls' education was one run by Catharine Beecher at Hartford, Connecticut, from 1824 to 1832. It was she who wrote *The American Woman's Home*, the book that may be called the American *Mrs Beeton*. Catharine Beecher's greatest contribution to education, shared with Emma Willard, was in the training of teachers.

The next landmark was the foundation of Oberlin College in 1833. Oberlin may be compared in its original educational status with Queen's College in London which, as we have seen, was not started until 1848. The interval between broadly similar events in the early history of the woman's rights movement on both sides of the Atlantic was usually of this order, with the Americans leading in action if not in philosophy. Oberlin began as a seminary and developed into a college. Its importance to educational advance in the United States was that it was open to all comers regardless of race, colour, or sex.

The single most significant step for female education, however, was taken in 1837 when Mount Holyoke was founded. Although it did not achieve collegiate status until 1893, after

Vassar, Wellesley, Smith, and Bryn Mawr, yet it prepared the way for them all. Mount Holyoke was founded by Mary Lyon whose creed was that her students must be prepared for more than just home-making and teaching.

The advance of education for white American girls was difficult enough. For coloured girls, despite the example of Oberlin, it was well-nigh impossible.

In 1845 the incipient feminists were encouraged by a new 'bible' arguing the case for woman's rights, the first since Mary Wollstonecraft's *Vindication*. Called *Woman in the Nineteenth Century*, it was written by Margaret Fuller, a transcendentalist who was born in Cambridgeport, Massachusetts, in 1810. Despite its obscuring mysticism and other defects which came from it being 'a showcase for Miss Fuller's immense erudition'[1] it had an important and lasting effect. Unlike the *Vindication* it did not preach the actual equality of the sexes, but maintained that woman must fulfil herself, in her own way, as an individual. 'What Woman needs is not as a woman to act or rule, but as a nature to grow, as an intellect to discern, as a soul to live freely and unimpeded.'[2] Margaret Fuller's active work for the emancipation of women never reached its full development because, returning from Italy with her Italian husband and her child in 1850, when she was forty, she was drowned in a shipwreck within sight of the New York shore. But her book was of great consequence and in the view of Elizabeth Cady Stanton and Susan B. Anthony she 'possessed more influence upon the thought of American women than any woman previous to her time'.

Another early feminist to whom Stanton and Anthony might have given this palm had her memory not become something of an embarrassment to the woman's movement at the time they were writing was Frances Wright. Frances was born in Dundee, Scotland, in 1795 and was left an heiress by the death of her parents when she was still only a young girl. During a strict upbringing in England she developed a passionate enthusiasm for the United States, where she believed it would be possible for a woman to have liberty and not be a relative creature. With her sister she toured the States from 1818 to 1820 and then wrote a successful book about her travels called *Views of Society*

[1] Eleanor Flexner, op. cit., p. 67.
[2] Quoted in Andrew Sinclair, op. cit., p. 51.

and Manners in America. She became the friend of Mary Shelley, the poet's wife and the daughter of Mary Wollstonecraft. In 1824 Frances returned to the United States in company with Lafayette, whose mistress she was reputed to be. She was also reputed to be the mistress of Robert Dale Owen, who arrived in America with his socialist father, Robert Owen, in 1825 and who six year later wrote *Moral Physiology*, the first book on contraception to be published in the States.

Frances Wright was one of that small band of rich women whose fortune gave them the power to live by their own rules; and these rules were not at all in accord with convention. She started a plantation at Nashoba, Tennessee, where slaves were to be allowed to buy their freedom through the earnings from their labour. The rigid customs of the South were abandoned at the Nashoba plantation, for Frances thought that the answer to black slavery was the free mulatto. She proclaimed the right of woman to sexual freedom outside marriage. 'No woman can forfeit her individual rights or independent existence, and no man can assert over her any rights or power whatsoever beyond what he may exercise over her free and voluntary affection,' she wrote of Nashoba. And she went further in her attack on sexual mores. 'Let us not attach ideas of purity to monastic chastity, impossible to man or woman without consequences fraught with evil, nor ideas of vice to connections formed under the auspices of kind feeling.'[1]

At Nashoba she was joined by her friend Mrs Trollope at the beginning of 1828. A few months later the experiment, carried out in a bleak clearing in the forest, failed. Frances Wright settled in New York and began to make public speeches in support of the Workingman's Party in the election of 1828. From this she went on to give public lectures in various cities, creating a great stir by her fiery and brilliant advocacy of women's educational rights and her attacks on religion and women's sexual bondage. Frances Wright was the first woman to speak regularly in public, 'but although wonderful', as one modern American social historian has written,[2] 'she was not respectable' because of her heretical views on sex and other rights for women. She was condemned as a loose woman, and

[1] Quoted in Andrew Sinclair, op. cit., p. 36.
[2] William L. O'Neill, *The Woman Movement* (Allen and Unwin, London, and Barnes and Noble Inc., New York, 1969), footnote to p. 19.

her views were rejected with horror by polite society. Nevertheless, although this understandable rejection put a stopper on
the discussion of woman's status among respectable circles for
years to come, when the woman's rights movement did begin in
the United States at the end of the 1840s it included most, if not
all, of the theories that Frances Wright had advanced. Only
later, after 1870, did the feminists feel bound to repudiate the
more radical speculations they had been entertaining in order
that by respectability and propriety they might gain the vote.
In England, on the other hand, decorum was the rule from the
start and Frances Wright would have been spurned by all
English woman's rightists.

The Priorities of Reform

While educational opportunities were slowly being improved
there arose the demand for reform in other directions, which had
its first practical expression at Seneca Falls in July 1848. As the
backgrounds of Elizabeth Stanton and Lucretia Mott suggest,
it was through the abolition movement that this demand was
evolved. The American Anti-Slavery Society was founded in
Philadelphia in 1833 – two years after the slave Nat Turner had
led an unsuccessful slave revolt in Virginia and the same year in
which the abolitionists in England had achieved their aim. It
was in the anti-slavery societies that American women 'first
learned to organize, to hold public meetings, to conduct
petition campaigns. As abolitionists they first won the right to
speak in public, and began to evolve a philosophy of their place
in society and of their basic rights.'[1]

There was some difference of opinion about the priority
these rights should have. Elizabeth Stanton and her new friend
Susan Anthony, whom she had persuaded away from temperance reform work, felt that the struggle for the vote was para-
mount. But in its early days the movement as a whole was less
concerned with the vote than with the control of property and
earnings, with the guardianship of children, with divorce laws,
with opportunities for education and employment, with civil
death, and with the whole concept of inferiority perpetuated by
established religion. It was not until after the slaves were freed
(if in name only) that general interest turned first to temperance and then at last to the vote.

[1] Eleanor Flexner, op. cit., p. 41.

Another important reform topic in the early days was dress. It was discussed at the first national convention in Worcester. Commenting on this in *New America* Hepworth Dixon said that 'it would hardly be outstripping facts to say that the husk and shell, so to speak, of every question now being raised for debate in America as between sex and sex belongs to the domain of the milliner and the tailor. What are the proper kinds of clothes for a free woman to fold about her limbs? Is the gown a final form of dress? Is the petticoat a badge of shame? Does a man owe nothing to his hat, his coat, his pantaloons, his boots? In short, can a female be considered as equal to a male until she has won the right to wear his garb?'[1] Dixon conceded that queries like this had a serious as well as a comic side, but there was no doubt that it was the comic side that prevailed in public fancy and in the press.

One of the first women to wear coat and trousers was Helene Marie Waber who besides being a writer on reform, on female education, and on dress, was a practical farmer, ploughing land, sowing corn, rearing pigs and going to market, dressed like a man in boots and breeches. Another lady who adopted male attire was Mary Walker, one of the first woman doctors, who later appeared on the lecture platform in London, and whose coat and trousers caused much merriment to William Hardman among others. And it was from the desire for dress reform that the Bloomer costume arose. In an age when even the freedom of crinoline had not entirely removed the feeling of clutter about the legs, it was understandable that the more daring of women should want to adopt the comfort of men's wear.

Dress was a serious question to the reformers if not to their critics, but there was another topic which most people conceded to be of some seriousness. This was the position of women in marriage. The reformers maintained that the whole theory of the common law in relation to the married woman was unjust and degrading. What, they asked, were the natural relations of one sex to the other? Was marriage the highest and purest form of these relations? What were the moral effects of marriage on man and wife? Was marriage indeed a holy state?

It was notable that the different sects of social reformers – Mormons, Tunkers, Perfectionists, Shakers – all started their efforts towards a better life by discarding the conventional

[1] *New America*, Vol. II, p. 179.

marriage laws and ceremonies and substituting their own. The Mormons, initially at any rate, allowed each man to have several wives. The Tunkers endeavoured to do without carnal relations. The Perfectionists had 'complex marriage' in which a whole community belonged to one large family. The Shakers were celibates who repudiated marriage altogether as being one of those temporal institutions which had no place in the life of the elected children of grace. This celibacy provided a refuge for at least one woman whose legal husband, so Lucy Stone told Elizabeth Stanton, 'gave her no peace either during menstruation, pregnancy, or nursing'.

Eliza's Truth of Woman

There were many who objected to the low status of women but fewer who regarded her as a superior being. The chief prophetess of those who did was Eliza Farnham of Rensselaerville, N.Y., who in 1842, the same year in which Joseph Smith, the founder of Mormonism, received a command from God to restore plurality of wives, received by intuition the Truth of Woman. When this truth came to her she had recently written a book about her travels in the great Western prairies. But before sharing her revelation with others she spent four years as matron of the women's wing at Sing Sing prison, wrote another book about the prairies, was widowed and re-married. Then she began to announce her principles and attract converts.

Woman, Eliza Farnham maintained, was in every respect a superior being to man. She based this on a host of evidence. To start with a woman proved her mental superiority by her inability to reason constructively – the very criticism that was often levelled against woman Eliza now turned to woman's advantage. Woman, she said, had no need to reason (which was only a lower form of arriving at knowledge) because she had the ability to arrive at an understanding of everything by intuition. Intellect, that stronghold of man, was nothing more than a coarse bungler dealing with Nature in a slow, material way, gathering up a few dates and facts, catching through harmonies at law. What was this gift compared with a woman's grace? That which man with his logic, observation and procedure, toils up to in a generation, she perceives at once. And as the ultimate proof of this had not man, she asked, been using his reason for ages past without having fallen on the central truth of life, the natural sovereignty of the female sex? The reign of science was over, the reign of spiritualism had begun. Science was the offspring of man, spiritualism of woman. The first was gross and sensual, a thing of the past; the second was pure and holy, a thing of the future.

Eliza Farnham had no special theology to teach. She rejected Peter and Paul, Luther and Cranmer – especially Peter and Paul who had put women under men. But she did have some faith in Swedenborg. Her evidence for the Truth of Woman lay in the syllogism that life is exalted in proportion to its organic and functional complexity, woman's organism is more complex and her totality of functions larger than those of any other being inhabiting the earth, therefore, her position in the scale of life was the most exalted. It was the same, she said, through all the animal grades. The females have more organs than the male, and organs are the representatives of power. All females have the same organs as males, with two magnificent sets of structure which males do not have, structures which concern the nourishing of life. The uninitiated might imagine that Mrs Farnham, a wife and mother, had made a mistake in counting the organs of male and female. Had she not forgotten something? Something that might upset the list? She had not. At one stage in her career she had studied medicine in New York. She could therefore point out that woman was also provided with this structure although it was not immediately apparent and was 'treated in the books as rudimentary'. Its purpose in the female was clear. It was for 'the wider diffusion of nerves, whose more concentrated presence would scarce consist with the functional economics and health of adjacent parts'. Exactly what this meant she did not further explain, but she was satisfied that it proved her point.

Mrs Farnham admitted that the male was often physically larger than the female 'in so far as size can be measured by bulk of body, by length of arm and by width of chest'; but against any argument that might be urged from this in favour of the male she held that the male was bigger only in the grosser parts (in bones and sinews), not in nerves and brains. Where the higher functions came into play, woman was in advance of man. Her bust had a nobler contour, her bosom a finer swell. The upper half of her skull was more expansive. All the tissues of her body were softer and more delicate. Her voice was sweeter, her ear quicker, her veins were of brighter blue, her skin of purer white, her lips of deeper red. More than all else, her brain was of higher quality and of quicker growth.

These ingenious views on the superiority of woman were published in a two-volume book, *Woman and Her Era*, in 1864, the year of Eliza Farnham's death. In it she carried her argument to the farthest limit and did not shirk any possible question which might be raised by those who doubted the Truth of Woman. For example, she maintained that menstruation was an example of a 'law of order' in the economy of female life which replaced 'the licence of mere waste in the masculine'. She also expounded her original views on the purpose of copulation and consequent conception. These views, incidentally, caused great mirth to William Hardman, who drew the attention of his Australian friend Holroyd to them. According to Mrs Farnham it was the female who had in her ovum the entire living germ of any future offspring. Man had nothing to do with it. All he gave to the sovereign female creator was 'the food which the germ requires to start it into life'.

Thirty years later another Eliza, Eliza B. Gamble, published in New York a book on *The Evolution of Woman* in which she followed the same line of reasoning in even more detail. Woman's superiority over man was demonstrated in a number of ways that Mrs Farnham had neglected. For example, the hair on the male body showed that man was a less developed creature. Furthermore, more men than women were colour-blind, they lacked physical endurance, they had structural defects, and above all they had those 'abnormal appetites which are constantly demanding for their gratification those things which are injurious to his mental and physical constitution'. These abnormal appetites – by which she meant men's sexual desires – were the bane of woman's existence and must be brought under control. How was this to be done? According to Eliza Gamble by 'the cultivation of the higher faculties developed in and transmitted through females'.

Eliza Gamble's views, while they are clearly extravagant by any rational standard, nevertheless are interesting from the emphasis they give to firmly held Victorian beliefs, as firmly held in Britain as in the United States. The first of these is contained in her remark that the gratification of a man's 'abnormal appetite' is injurious to his mental and physical constitution. The Victorian belief was that ejaculation, more especially when it was self-administered or indeed involuntary, was wasting a man's substance. Instead of the current expression 'to come' the Victorians more often said 'to spend', and this points the direction of their thought. Masturbation or excessive copulation – and excess was easily reached if one accepted the doctors' view that once every ten days, or perhaps once a week, was a 'normal' frequency – led infallibly, it was believed, to gibbering lunacy. As one of Lucy Stone's brothers wrote to her, 'Nine-tenths of all the half-grown men and of all the invalids, and men of half-minds have become what they are by their own or their fathers' indulgence in the Beastlike use of their generative organs.' This belief was strongly upheld by the medical profession who were, in Dr Alex Comfort's phrase, 'the anxiety makers of the age'. The guilt that the Victorians spread broadcast over our sexual functions is with us still, and has its roots in social beliefs much more than in medical evidence.

The second belief was that women were without passion and were therefore entirely subject to male brutality without deriving any pleasure from copulation themselves. This belief, it was true, came up against awkward exceptions: there was no doubt that numerous women enjoyed being both the lovers and the friends of men. This ardour, however, was considered to be bestial and no properly brought-up lady should admit to it, even to herself. From this frustration arose much havoc in the minds of Victorian ladies on both sides of the Atlantic.

The Perfect Marriage

There were some who did not eschew the pleasures of sex. At another extreme of thought from Eliza Gamble and the celibate Shakers was the body of reformers who called themselves as far as their dogma was concerned, Perfectionists, and in the social aspects of their beliefs, Bible Communists. They professed to base their theory of family life on the New Testament, especially on the teachings of Paul. They claimed to have restored the divine government of the world. They put the two sexes on an equal footing. They declared marriage to be a fraud and property a theft. They abolished all human laws as it affected themselves and formally renounced their allegiance to the United States.

11. *Above, left to right*: Mary Wollstonecraft, 'talented and beautiful'. Mrs Lynn Linton wrote the most famous article *The Saturday Review* ever published. Barbara Leigh Smith, later Madame Bodichon, helped by an enlightened father, Annie Besant, *(far right)* 'Martyr of Science'. This photograph appeared in the frontispiece of the report of her trial with Charles Bradlaugh for publishing *The Fruits of Philosophy*.

12. *Top left:* Frances Wright lived by her own rules, *(right)* Lucy Stone of the American Woman Suffrage Association, called the first national Woman's Rights Convention in 1850. *Bottom left:* Susan B. Anthony of the National Woman Suffrage Association, hated 'Boss-town', *(right)* Elizabeth Cady Stanton, leader of the National with Anthony, was one of the five who organized the famous meeting at Seneca Falls in 1848.

The founder of this sect, which related free love to religious practice and therefore undoubtedly attracted many women who were thus given the opportunity of enjoying sexual relations without guilt feelings, was John Humphrey Noyes. Noyes was a tall, pale man, with sandy hair and beard, grey dreamy eyes, an appealing mouth, and high forehead. To look at he was said to be a little like Thomas Carlyle, a comparison which pleased him. Before he founded the Bible Communists, who had their main community at Oneida Creek in New York State, he had in turn been a graduate of Dartmouth College in Connecticut, a law clerk at Putney, Vermont, a theological student in Andover, Massachusetts, a preacher at Yale, a seceder from the Congregational Church, an outcast, a heretic, an agitator and a dreamer. With the foundation of his community at Oneida Creek in 1848 he at once became, for some people at any rate, a prophet who enjoyed light from heaven and personal intimacy with God.

The 300-strong Oneida Creek community, which earned a profitable living from agriculture and various domestic industries, was one of three which Noyes established, the other two being at Wallingford and Brooklyn. The core of their domestic system was the relation of the sexes to each other, which the Perfectionists called 'a complex marriage'. A community of goods, they said, implied a community of wives. Noyes maintained that it was wrong to say either that a man could love only once in his life, or that he could love only one object at one time. 'Men and women,' he said, 'find universally that their susceptibility to love is not burnt out by one honeymoon or satisfied by one lover. On the contrary, the secret history of the human heart will bear out the assertion that it is capable of loving any number of times and any number of persons; and that the more it loves, the more it can love. This is the law of nature.' Hence at Oneida Creek the central domestic fact of the household was the complex marriage of its members, to all the others of the opposite sex, a rite which was reckoned to have taken place on the entrance of every new member, male or female, into the Family.

Contrary to the theory of sentimental novelists and others Noyes believed that the affections could be controlled and guided, and that they would produce far better results when rightly controlled and rightly guided than if left to take care of themselves.[1] Certain general principles were adopted to achieve this end – nominally at any rate. One such was termed 'the principle of the ascending fellowship'. It was regarded as 'better for the young of both sexes to associate in love with persons older than themselves, and, if possible, with those who are spiritual and have been some time in the school of self-control'.

Another general principle was that it was not desirable for two persons to become exclusively attached to each other. A third was that no person should be obliged to receive 'at any time, or under any circumstances, the attention of those whom they do not like. The Communities are pledged to protect all their members from disagreeable social approaches. Every woman is free to refuse every man's attentions.'

The free love of the Oneida Community aroused much local antagonism when the Family first settled there. Noyes's enemies, said that it was adopted not for Perfectionist religious motives, but out of a low taste for orgiastic promiscuity. But Noyes maintained that the sexual principle was the helpmate of the religious principle. 'Religion is the first interest, and sexual morality the second in the great enterprise of establishing the Kingdom of God on earth.' In linking religion with sex he showed a deep understanding of female psychology. To all attacks from outsiders he answered, 'Look at our happy circle; we work, we rest, we study, we enjoy; peace reigns in our household; our young men are healthy, our young women bright; we live well and we do not multiply beyond our wishes.'

The system of living at Oneida Creek gave a great deal of power to women, certainly much more than they enjoyed under ordinary law, and all those whom Hepworth Dixon saw when he visited Oneida seemed busy, brisk and content – except for one whose complaint he chose not to reproduce. Perhaps it was because the Community did not multiply beyond its wishes that the women were so content. How it did this was something else that Dixon did not describe to readers of *New America*. In fact it employed the unusual sexual practice of *coitus reservatus* by which the male members of the Community trained themselves never to reach the point of orgasm. It was on this rare refinement of the sexual impulse that Noyes's philosophy was based.

[1] How Mary Glynne's aunt would have approved of this tenet! (see p. 39).

Noyes explained his theories of sex and described the method he and his Community used for civilizing 'the lion of the tribe of human passions' in his *Bible Argument* published in 1844 and, more fully, in *Male Continence* written about the time of Dixon's visit. 'It is held in the world,' he wrote, 'that the sexual organs have two distinct functions, viz., the urinary and the propagative. We affirm that they have three – the urinary, the propagative, and the amative, i.e. they are conductors, first of the urine, secondly of the semen and thirdly of the social magnetism.'

After his wife had suffered repeated miscarriages which nearly killed her, Noyes decided that in future their sexual relationship should be amative not propagative. How to make it so? Unlike Robert Dale Owen he rejected *coitus interruptus,* having no wish to follow Onan. And he disapproved of contraceptives, 'Those tricks of the French voluptuaries'. Instead he decided on male continence, which was later called *karezza* by the American Doctor Alice Bunker Stockham in a book of that name published in Chicago in 1896. Starting in 1844 he had experimented and 'found that the self-control it required is not difficult; also that my enjoyment was increased; also that my wife's experience was very satisfactory, which it had never been before; also that we had escaped the horrors and the fear of involuntary propagation'.[1]

---

[1] As Aldous Huxley pointed out (see Appendix to 'Ozymandias' in *Adonis and the Alphabet*) Noyes was not the first to discover the benefits and pleasures of *coitus reservatus*. There had been earlier sects who also practised what the Hindus called Tantra: the Gnostics, the Cathars, and the Adamites, who believed that *coitus reservatus* was one of the constituents of Paradise. 'Male continence transforms the sexual act into a prolonged exchange of "social magnetism"; and this prolonged exchange [a Spanish Adamite had intercourse with a prophetess which lasted for 20 days] makes possible an ever-deepening knowledge of the mystery of human nature – the mystery which merges ultimately, and becomes one with the mystery of Life itself.' He called attention to the fact that near the end of *The Plumed Serpent* D. H. Lawrence has a passage 'that hints at what is revealed by physical tenderness, when it is prolonged by Male Continence into a quasi-mystical experience'. Huxley himself has a passage about it in *Antic Hay* where Gumbril spends the night with Edith. And as well as this psychological side *coitus reservatus* was shown by the Oneida Community to be a reasonably effective method of birth control. As practised at Oneida each 'exchange of social magnetism' lasted for anything up to an hour or an hour and a quarter.

The Judgement of London

The belief in the superiority of woman was not confined to the theories of Eliza Farnham. In the everyday business of going about the streets one could see plenty of American women who acted in the knowledge that they were the most important beings on earth. Anthony Trollope, visiting the United States thirty years after his mother to give his own account of the domestic manners of the Americans,[1] was infuriated by the behaviour of a certain class of woman in the New York street-cars. Even though he admitted that they were 'respectable, intelligent, and, as I believe, industrious' their manners were to him 'more odious than those of any other human beings' he had ever met anywhere else. America had its full share of ladies as bright, as beautiful, as graceful, as sweet as any other country; but it was not these natural 'female aristocrats' of whom he was speaking. 'Women, by the conventional laws of society, are allowed to exact much from men, but,' he argued, 'they are allowed to exact nothing for which they should not make some adequate return.'

Trollope epitomized the anger of men at the attitude of the woman's rights movement. They felt they were being cheated as well as insulted. Women's privileges had come to them from the spirit of chivalry which had taught men to endure hardship, lesser or greater, in order that women might be at their ease. Women in return had, in general, been taught to accept this ease with grace and thankfulness. But in America in the 1860s it appeared that both sides were not obeying the rules with equal rigour. Because of greater material well-being and wider education in the United States than in Britain, men had learnt to be more chivalrous, and their conduct to women throughout the States, as earlier travellers had always reported, was, so Trollope repeated, 'always gracious'. Women, on the other hand – or more particularly the class of women who had raised Trollope's ire – were always talking about their rights but seemed to have little idea of the duties that were the complement of those rights. 'They have no scruple at demanding from men everything that a man can be called on to relinquish on a woman's behalf, but they do so without any of that grace which turns the demand made into a favour conferred.' This was breaking the rules indeed. Americans themselves, he claimed,

[1] Anthony Trollope, *North America* (1862).

complained of such behaviour, 'swearing that they must change the whole tenor of their habits towards women'. And he had heard American ladies speak of this ill-mannered feminism 'with loathing and disgust' – not unnaturally, it may be added, for there were four groups in the sex war: the feminists, their male supporters, the majority of the male sex, and those women like the young married lady who told Hepworth Dixon that she would not dream of joining the Society for Promoting Equal Rights between the sexes because she was 'far too fond of being taken care of'.

In one respect, at least, American girls had the edge over their sisters in England. The efforts of the educational reformers had borne fruit. Trollope visited a number of girls' schools in New York and was impressed by the excellence of the free-place schools as compared with those in London. The girls at a London free school were either ragged paupers or charity girls, the sort who 'become our servants and the wives of our grooms and porters'. But the girl at a New York free school was neither a pauper nor a charity girl. She was clean, and in speaking to her you could not 'in any degree guess whether her father has a dollar a day or $3,000 a year'. As to the amount of knowledge she had, Trollope described it as 'terrific'.

Another English visitor at this period, Theresa Yelverton, was more concerned with the education of young ladies than of free-place schoolgirls. The former, she said, were not given time to complete a thorough education, however solidly it may have been begun. At about the age of thirteen, when English girls were still in short frocks and long trowsers, an American girl began 'to exercise her vocation as a young lady, to devote herself to dress, to look out for flirtations, to promenade with gentlemen and to read novels'. Because they married so young American ladies had no time for the cultivation of their minds with the result that their accomplishments were poor, although as singers they excelled. 'Their voices, which in speaking are shrill and loud, in singing are fine-toned, clear and powerful, though not sweet.'

Theresa Yelverton who was one of the very first of a redoubtable band of Victorian lady travellers who voyaged round the world writing and lecturing about their experiences, lived for more than two years in the United States after the final failure of her long-drawn case to prove that she was legally the wife of

William Charles Yelverton, later the 4th Viscount Avonmore.[1]
Her attitude to the States was coloured by what she considered
to be her rightful place in Society. As the wife of a future
Viscount she looked down her nose at the pretensions of American ladies, and having suffered the ostracism that resulted from
her equivocal position she was quick to pounce on hypocrisy
and false modesty. Prudery and mealy-mouthedness in any case
were quite abhorrent to her frank nature. Even more so was the
pose of American ladies who professed prudery and practised
what she considered to be almost licence. 'American ladies
scruple as little to display their legs as do the Boulogne mate-
lottes,' she wrote in *Teresina in America*,[2] 'but to mention them
greatly shocks their sensibilities. They are particular even to
straitlacedness in what they say, but not often in what they do.'

One of Theresa's many attractions was a deep vibrant voice
of which she made good use in giving elocution lessons, lectures
and readings. American prudery led her into trouble in her
recitations. 'There is scarcely a piece in my repertoire which in
some portions was not considered unfit for public utterance. I
was gravely asked if it was not to be supposed that Tennyson's
May Queen was talking from her bed, and, if so, the situation was objectionable. Longfellow's *Wreck of the Hesperus* was
demurred to on account of the word "bull", which I was
advised to omit, substituting the words "gentleman cow"! Let
my readers essay the purified edition –

> "She struck where the white and fleecy waves
> Looked soft as carded wool;
> But the cruel rocks they gored her side,
> Like the horns of a *gentleman cow*"!'

But while they objected to the bull these same ladies, 'would-be
Dianas' Theresa called them, revelled in an account of the
Byron scandal in Harriet Beecher Stowe's article in the Septem-
ber 1869 *Atlantic Monthly*.[3]

It was the blatancy, brashness and absence of genuine

[1] See Duncan Crow, *Theresa: The Story of the Yelverton Case* (Hart-
Davis, 1966).
[2] Thérèse Yelverton (Viscountess Avonmore), *Teresina in America*
(Bentley, 1875).
[3] On the basis of information given her by Lady Byron, she accused
Byron of incest with his half-sister Augusta.

delicacy that most upset Theresa, as indeed it upset other English ladies. ('An American woman . . . will start and tell you the whole family history and affairs before you have known her half an hour.') Nor was Theresa impressed by the looks of American women, who, she said, with the exception of the belles in Baltimore, had poor complexions and bad figures. Harriet Martineau, Mrs Houstoun and Anthony Trollope all agreed with her about the poor complexions, the result of the universal use of anthracite stoves for central heating. ('Hot air is the great destroyer of American beauty,' wrote Trollope.) But Hepworth Dixon took a far different view about the attractiveness of American ladies. Disagreeing with the other judges from London he wrote that 'among the higher classes in America the traditions of English beauty have not declined' and 'may be seen in all the best houses of Virginia and Massachusetts. The proudest London belle, the fairest Lancashire witch, would find in Boston and in Richmond rivals in grace and beauty whom she could not feign to despise. Birth is one cause, no doubt, though training and prosperity have come in aid of birth.'[1]

[1] *New America*, Vol. II, p. 35.

Chapter 12

THE GIRL OF THE PERIOD

One of the greatest obstacles the Woman's Rightists had to overcome was their own feeling of guilt. They had been brought up to put everything, especially their own personal happiness, second to the ideal of family life, and within that life to accept unquestioningly that the young must always and inevitably be sacrificed to the old. The constriction and monopoly of this filial obedience drove many of them beyond the edge of despair, but whenever they sought to escape from it in even the smallest way – as for instance by having a dog of their own – the sense of guilt overcame them and drove them back into the cocoon of the drawing-room. And even in those cases where the urge to freedom gave them the courage to ignore their inhibition, there remained a supreme practical difficulty: well-brought-up young ladies had no money to spend.

Despite these trammels there were growing numbers of women on both sides of the Atlantic whose intellectual ambition was too strong to allow them to accept the indignity of being relative creatures. Throughout the 1860s and onwards the woman's movement gained momentum as a result of the enthusiasm and social fearlessness of these women. Like an advancing column the movement probed forward in education, in employment opportunities, in changing the law, and in suffrage.

The leader in the attempt to get higher education for English girls was Emily Davies. She succeeded first in opening the Oxford and Cambridge Local Examination to girls, and then turned her attention to the Universities themselves. Unable to secure the entrance of young women to Oxford or Cambridge. which was her first target, she established a college herself at

Hitchin in Hertfordshire. This realization of Princess Ida's ideal received its first six students in October 1869. Later the college moved to Cambridge and became Girton. A rival plan for a woman's college was drawn up by Jemima Clough, sister of the poet, and became Newnham, also at Cambridge. Broadly speaking, the difference in intention between Girton and Newnham paralleled some of the differences between Queen's College and Bedford College. The point at issue was one which always dogged the progress of women's education. It was this: should women's education be conceived as an off-shoot of men's education or should it be something which was designed specially for women? Behind this difference of opinion lurked the different philosophies about woman. Was she a relative creature or was she a human being in her own right? If she was a human being in her own right then, as far as education was concerned, she should take the same degree examinations as a man. But if she was only a relative creature then examinations must be tempered to her lesser brain. Newnham was founded in this latter belief, Girton in the former.

In furthering employment opportunities for women, the most publicized steps were the endeavour to get women accepted for medical studies. The pioneer was Elizabeth Blackwell, whose brother Henry married Lucy Stone. Elizabeth was born in Bristol in 1821 and taken to America as a child. There, after many struggles, she qualified as a doctor in 1849. By virtue of her foreign degree she was accepted on the British Medical Register in 1859, but her acceptance awakened the medical profession to the existence of the loophole in its regulations, which did not specify that the Register was open to men only. On her visit to England to take advantage of this loophole she inspired the young Elizabeth Garrett to become a doctor. Garrett took advantage of another loophole: she got on to the Register through passing the exams of the Society of Apothecaries. These loopholes were abruptly closed. For a woman to become a doctor now seemed impossible. On the one hand she was debarred from obtaining the necessary qualifications because the hospitals and dissecting-rooms were closed to her by prejudice; and on the other she was prohibited by Act of Parliament from practising without them. But there were some who refused to accept defeat, among them Sophia Jex-Blake who eventually qualified as a doctor in Edinburgh.[1] By the mid-1870s women doctors, if still unusual, were at least accepted. Part of the problem they encountered during their studies – as indeed did women taking degrees in other subjects – was that because only exceptional women had any chance of surviving the indignities and struggles that their pioneering led them into, they so often beat most of the men in the examinations and came out top of the class lists.

The 1860s also saw the beginning in Britain of the long struggle to get women the vote. It began with the candidature of John Stuart Mill for the City of Westminster in 1865. Mill, whom we have already met as a distributor of birth control propaganda when he was a young man, only agreed to accept the invitation to stand for Parliament if he was allowed to include women's suffrage as one of the issues which he would bring forward. Unexpectedly, at least to some of his supporters, this condition was accepted and when he was returned to Parliament he moved an amendment to extend the vote to women.

Mill had been persuaded into supporting the cause of woman's rights by his wife, Harriet Taylor, and her daughter. In 1851 Harriet had written an article in the *Westminster Review* which ably reasoned the case for votes for women. Mill incorporated her ideas into *The Subjection of Women*, written with her help between 1851 and 1858 but not published until 1869, eleven years after her death. Although Mill's amendment was defeated by 196 to 73 in the House of Commons the prestige of his name and the persuasiveness of his words had a telling effect on educated opinion on both sides of the Atlantic, so that gradually it came to be accepted that the issue of woman's rights was not simply a 'wild disturbance of the female mind'

[1] The opposition to Sophia Jex-Blake caused one little nine-year-old Edinburgh girl to write a fierce defence which she presented to her four brothers and their tutor under the title of 'Fair Play, or a few words for the Lady Doctors'. Unable to make herself heard at table against the weight of male dissent this was the only way she could stand up for her sex. 'There needs to be one rather bold woman to fight against men,' she wrote. 'You say women are weak and inferior to men, and when men get lazy and loll about you call them effeminate. You say women do nothing hardly except to please themselves, and when women want to work you will not let them.' She finished with the prophetic words, 'The women are determined to get to the top of the hill and they shall.' She signed herself 'Keeper of Women's Rights', instead of by her real name, Elizabeth Haldane. (See Chapter 17.)

but was of fundamental importance. He argued that 'the principle which regulates the existing social relations between the two sexes – the legal subordination of one sex to the other – is wrong in itself, and is now one of the chief hindrances to human improvement; and that it ought to be replaced by a principle of perfect equality, admitting no power or privilege on the one side, nor disability on the other'.[1] Apart from the fact that half the nation was prevented from applying itself to the common good, the existing principle meant that women could never properly fulfil themselves as human beings because of 'the dull and hopeless life to which it [Society] so often condemns them, by forbidding them to exercise the practical abilities which many of them are conscious of, in any wider field than one which to some of them never was, and to others is no longer, open'.[2]

After the failure of his amendment Mill and his male supporters realized that success would be long delayed. But this was not the opinion of the women who felt that the size of the vote in favour of the amendment showed they were on the verge of gaining their suffrage, and that if they nagged and agitated sufficiently they would soon achieve success. In 1870 a Second Reading victory seemed to prove them right, but further progress was barred by the opposition of Gladstone, the Prime Minister. Second Reading defeats in 1875 and 1876 showed that the way would be long indeed.

The suffrage question split the ranks of the woman's rightists. In the September 1864 issue of the *Alexandra Magazine* Bessie Rayner Parkes explained the principles on which she had conducted the *Englishwoman's Journal*, which had just been merged with the *Alexandra*: 'The only subject which I steadily refused to discuss was the political one, believing it too impractical in the present constitution of the world to make it worth while to risk very vital and practical interests by the introduction of so unpopular an element.' The management of benevolent institutions, the entry of women into the medical profession, greater educational opportunities, the possibility of women going into business – all these were discussed in the *Englishwoman's Journal*, but not the question of the vote.

[1] John Stuart Mill, *The Subjection of Women* (Longmans, Green, Reader and Dyer, 1869), p. 1.
[2] ibid., p. 187.

Even among those dedicated to getting the vote there was dissension, fostered some might say by *agents provocateurs*. Both in England and America there were splits in the suffrage organizations. For six years from 1871 there were two bodies organizing the campaign for the vote in Britain. In the United States the split lasted for twenty-one years, from 1869 to 1890, with Elizabeth Stanton and Susan Anthony leading the National Woman Suffrage Association, and Lucy Stone the American Woman Suffrage Association. In the case of the English fission, the main cause was the reluctance of many of the suffragists to have their movement publicly connected with the movement to repeal the Contagious Diseases Act which gave legal countenance to prostitution in certain English towns.[1] In the American case personal animosity between Susan Anthony and Lucy Stone was a key factor, as well as the rivalry between Boston, which Susan Anthony mocked as Boss-town, and the Westerners.

To a large extent, too, the division was between radicalism and respectability. The Americans were the respectables concentrating solely on achieving suffrage for women, the Nationals were the radicals supporting all reforms. This division was accentuated by Elizabeth Stanton's infatuated support of the fabulous Victoria Woodhull, when Woodhull made an able speech before a Committee of Congress in January 1871 claiming the right to vote. In return Victoria championed the National's views of woman's rights in her paper, *Woodhull and Claflin's Weekly*, along with campaigning for free love and spiritualism. Victoria and her sister Tennessee Claflin were notoriously unconventional. They had started a brokerage business under the wing of the stupendous Commodore, Cornelius Vanderbilt, and had made a short-lived fortune. Tennessee was the Commodore's mistress having arrived in that estate at the suggestion of Victoria that it would be good for the priapian old man's health. Support from Victoria Woodhull was no recommendation for the National.

Victoria went too far when she tried to take over the National for her own political ends. Susan Anthony foiled the attempt, and Victoria set up her own 'party' which nominated her to run for President of the United States. Branded as 'a vain, immodest, unsexed woman' and a 'brazen snaky adventuress' in a Cleveland paper in her home state of Ohio, and castigated by Horace

[1] See Chapters 14 and 15.

Greeley in the New York *Tribune* for her private life, she got her own back in violent fashion by publishing the details of what came to be called the Beecher–Tilton scandal to show that 'many of my self-appointed judges and critics are deeply tainted with the vices they condemn'. She advocated free love 'in its highest, purest sense, as the only cure for the immorality, the deep damnation by which men corrupt and disfigure God's most holy institution of sexual relations. My judges preach against free love openly, practise it secretly.' She declined to stand up as the 'frightful example' when, for example, she knew of one man, 'a public teacher of eminence, who lives in concubinage with the wife of another public teacher, of almost equal eminence. All three concur in denouncing offences against morality. "Hypocrisy is the tribute paid by vice to virtue."'

The public teacher of eminence was the Reverend Henry Beecher, the most popular preacher in the country and the first president of the American wing of the suffragists. Between him and Mrs Elizabeth Tilton there had been a love affair lasting for many years. Elizabeth was the wife of Theodore Tilton, a reform editor 'of almost equal eminence', who was the friend of Elizabeth Stanton and Susan Anthony. In October 1872 Victoria named names in her paper. Tilton sued Beecher for misconduct. At the trial Stanton and Anthony were accused of compromising conduct with Tilton in order to discount their testimony against Beecher. Tilton was also accused of misconduct with Victoria Woodhull. Stanton and Anthony took every chance of pointing out that under the law Mrs Tilton had no right even to testify on her own behalf. In the end there was a hung jury.

The Beecher–Tilton case did the woman's cause no good. It enabled the feminists' enemies to point to the suffragist associations as mere covers for the propagation of immorality, although in this avalanche of obloquy the American wing, despite its connection with Beecher, suffered less than the National. Some have maintained that the Woodhull revelation set the cause of woman's suffrage back for twenty years because suffrage had become linked in the public mind with free love. But Eleanor Flexner disagreed that it had any such effect: 'it was no help, but there were far too many other forces pushing it forward for the case to have any lasting impact'.[1] Be that as it may, the

[1] Eleanor Flexner, op. cit., p. 154.

Beecher–Tilton case and the National's fleeting connection with the charismatic Victoria alienated Lucy Stone still further and prevented a rapprochement between the two wings of the movement for many years.

Mrs Lynn Linton Sees Her Mistake

The various agitations for an improvement in the status of women achieved sufficient success as the 1860s progressed for them to raise up a formidable opposition. Among women there were many who felt that the winning of rights would result in the loss of those privileges which themselves had been hardly earned in place of the uncertain favours of earlier days. And even some of those who had welcomed the early steps now felt that things were going too far. An important example was Mrs Lynn Linton. She explained her change of heart in a letter to an evening paper some years later:

'I belong to the generation when women of a certain class were absolutely secure from insult, because the education of our brothers, as of our fathers, included that kind of chivalrous respect for the weaker sex which was then regarded as inseparable from true gentlehood and real civilization. And old traditions and associations cling close. I belong, too, to the generation which made the first steps for the emancipation of women; and I was one of the most ardent and enthusiastic of the advanced guard. I thought that the lives of women should be as free as those of men, and that community of pursuits would bring about a fine fraternal condition of things, where all men would be like big brothers and no woman need fear. I have lived to see my mistake. Knowing in my own person all that women have to suffer when they fling themselves into the active fray, I would prevent with all my strength young girls from following my mistake and guard them with my own body from such insults as you and your kind have showered on me when differing from you in opinion.

'The whole thing seems to me more and more to be a gigantic mistake. The women advocates themselves and their male backers . . . ought to open the eyes of all sane people to the true character of a movement which makes women hard and men hysterical, which gives to each sex the vices of the other while destroying its own hitherto distinctive virtues.'

Elizabeth Lynn Linton was born in 1822 in Keswick, in her

father's parish. She was the twelfth child. Her mother, who was the daughter of a bishop, died a few months after she was born, and as Vicar Lynn took very little interest in his children's upbringing the younger ones grew up as the subjects of their elder brothers and sisters. Lynn, his daughter said, was a man 'with a heart of gold and a temper of fire'. He was 'fond like a woman of his children when infants, but unable to reconcile himself to the needs of their adolescence, and refusing to recognize the rights of their maturity'. He was the archetypal Victorian father, considering it 'derogatory to his parental dignity to discuss any matter whatsoever rationally with his sons'.

Eliza Lynn was self-educated, her father having a strong prejudice against intellectual pursuits for women. In the 'old wild days' of her youth she was a tomboy. More than once she said that when she was born, a boy was due in the family and it was 'only the top-coating that had miscarried'. Although she was described as attractive and good-looking as a young woman, this is not borne out to all eyes by her portraits which show her to have had a soft, squashy mouth – possibly because she may have lost her teeth. (She once told how, during a period when she was teaching herself to bear pain and discomfort as part of a religious mania, she dug out one of her teeth with a knife.) Her eyes were somewhat bulbous and she was shortsighted. This drove her in on herself, until at the age of fifteen she was given spectacles; it was as if she had been given a new life. She was the rebel of the family – solitary, studious, thoughtful, with a burning desire for knowledge that she tried to satisfy with voracious reading.

At the age of seventeen she was obsessed by religion and republicanism. The Sermon on the Mount became a call for action and a way of life. This was the period of her stoicism and for a whole year she lay on the floor at night, despising a bed as 'an unrighteous effeminacy'. The combination of devout Christianity and her ardent desire for knowledge ended in mental disaster. Like her acquaintance Marian Evans, who was to become George Eliot, she began to delve into the mysteries of philosophy, and these intellectual investigations undertaken for greater belief ended in bringing disbelief.

To the distress caused by the loss of her faith was soon added the distress caused by her adoration of an anonymous Mrs X who had come to live in the neighbourhood. Mrs X was 'an elegant, silken, clever woman of the world', who seemed to Eliza to be queen and goddess in one. As a result of the ecstasy of her feelings Eliza had an attack of brain fever. When she recovered the Xs had left the district, Mrs X to become a confirmed invalid, Mr X to give himself up to mesmerism, opium and poetry.

Despite the advent of the penny post and the railway, both of which slightly stirred the stagnancy of Keswick, life at home became intolerably monotonous. At twenty-three Eliza left. Choosing the magazine by numeromancy she sent a poem to *Ainsworth's Miscellany*, which accepted it. On the basis of this encouragement she went to London to become a writer. Her father put her under the protection of the family solicitor who found rooms for her in a small boarding-house near the British Museum. From here she set out to make her way in the world, a frighteningly difficult task for any young lady in 1845. She started by spending hours in the British Museum reading-room, researching material for a novel about ancient Egypt called *Azeth the Egyptian*, which was published at her own expense in 1846 and received a favourable review in *The Times*.

After a short period at home, where she had returned in fulfilment of a pact made with her father, she came back to London bringing with her her second novel, *Amymone*, which was published by Bentley in 1848. *Amymone* was important in her life: it roused the enthusiasm of Walter Savage Landor with whom she was to have a close relationship; and it helped her to get a job in journalism. She applied to J. D. Cook of the *Morning Chronicle* and after successfully passing a test piece which she had to write on the spot she was hired. 'Thus,' said her biographer G. S. Layard, 'she gained the distinction of being the first woman newspaper writer to draw a fixed salary. She was not, as has been erroneously stated, the first woman journalist'. Mrs Norton, for one, had preceded her.

Cook, whose origins were obscure and who was probably illegitimate, was a strange man. He was violent, rude, and swore continuously – but he was a great editor. He was in the habit of throwing ink-wells at his employees and then of making it up by giving them tips. Eliza put up with his tantrums without letting them worry her very much until, after a couple of years, there was an occasion on which he was too violent even for her self-control and she left the *Chronicle*.

At this period of her life she was still a rebel, a free thinker, and an emancipated woman. She was very close with the Philanstery, that communal home shared by the Thornton Hunts, the Gliddens and the Lawrences, in Queen's Road, Bayswater. It was here that she came to know G. H. Lewes well, and she always thereafter stood up for Hunt against the stories that it was he who had seduced Lewes's wife Agnes away from him. In Eliza's view, Lewes was happy to be rid of Agnes so that he could start living with Marian Evans, who had now become George Eliot, the novelist. Eliza was bitter in later life about the way in which the world condoned the Lewes–Evans liaison, whereas it was critical of her own much less eccentric marriage.

In 1858 Eliza married W. J. Linton, communist and talented engraver. Linton's first wife had died, nursed in her last illness by Eliza, and for a number of reasons, including perhaps pity, she married him and looked after his children. They moved from Brantwood in Cumberland (later Ruskin's house) to London. By this time Eliza Lynn, who now began to call herself Mrs Lynn Linton, was a well-established literary figure. As well as her work on the *Chronicle* she had for a couple of years been a correspondent in Paris, and had also published a number of novels. She wanted to make her London home into a literary salon. To some extent she achieved this, but the cost was more than her income and Linton's spendthrift habits could sustain. They began to drift apart for reasons which were never fully disclosed. Incompatibility was no doubt involved and Linton was disappointed to find that Eliza was not the fierce republican and anarchist he had thought she was. Eliza was moving away from the rebellious and emancipated woman attitude towards the position she was soon to disclose so effectively in her writings. There may also have been some sexual reason for their parting. They had no children and, when talking to a friend on one occasion, Linton hinted at 'reasons which cannot be discussed'. Nevertheless, they always remained extremely fond of each other and to the end of their long lives they corresponded in the most affectionate terms. Linton by that time had long since emigrated with his own family to the United States.

The Saturday Opposition

In 1866 Mrs Lynn Linton began once again to work for Cook, who was by now the editor of the well-established and influential *Saturday Review*.

The *Saturday* was one of the strongest opponents on either side of the Atlantic of any change in the status of women. Almost from its first weekly number on November 3, 1855 it castigated the faintest sign of insubordination, and as the women's movement gathered strength these signs increased rapidly. Whether it was in a book review, or an article on legal reform, or the report of a meeting of women's rightists, the *Saturday* mocked and sneered and occasionally, when derision seemed insufficient, stormed at any gesture of 'non-relativity'. An early example of its attitude was an article on July 9, 1859 in which 'Women's Mission' was defined. Instead of agitating for rights 'on both sides of the Atlantic' women should stick to the real, though undefined, power that they had. 'Many wives and some husbands are aware that authority may exist without being ostentatiously proclaimed.'

Nor were its attacks to be taken lightly, for the *Saturday* rapidly attained a position of authority, and with a circulation of about 10,000 it reached the most influential cadres of opinion in England. If Mill influenced opinion towards emancipation, the *Saturday* influenced it almost as strongly towards continued relativity.

The list of contributors, regular and occasional, to the *Saturday* is probably as distinguished as any newspaper or periodical has ever had. Its original staff of writers was George Stovin Venables, Henry Sumner Maine, Goldwin Smith, Vernon Harcourt, James Fitzjames Stephen, M. E. Grant Duff, Beresford Hope (the *Saturday*'s proprietor), the Reverend William Scott (editor of the *Christian Remembrancer* and a High Church friend of Beresford Hope's), Thomas Collett Sandars, George Wirman Hemming, and Marshall Hayman. Occasional contributors in the early months who became regulars later were Edward A. Freeman and Christopher K. Watson. Specialists included Viscount Strangford, who had written regularly for Cook on the *Chronicle* (the first member of the aristocracy who became a steady contributor to the press), Whitley Stokes, Max Muller, Mark Pattison, G. H. Lewes, Walter Bagehot, John Pyke Hullah, William Bodham Donne, R. W. Church,

Francis T. Palgrave (of the *Golden Treasury*), and Philip G. Hamerton.

As the *Saturday* prospered, additions to the staff included several more names which were to become famous: James Bryce, the Bowens, John Morley, Leslie Stephen, and John Richard Green. In 1857 Beresford Hope, who was married to Lady Mildred Cecil, introduced his brother-in-law Lord Robert Cecil to Cook, and from then on for the next eight years, Cecil was a regular contributor. Lord Robert Cecil became the third Marquess of Salisbury and was three times Prime Minister. He married Miss Georgina Alderson, whose brother Charles also became a *Saturday* contributor.

Nor were the staff all men. Its women writers included Mrs Bennett, Anne Mozley, and notably Mrs Lynn Linton who, among all this universe of talent, wrote the most famous article that the *Saturday* ever published. It was called 'The Girl of the Period' and appeared on March 14, 1868.[1]

'The Girl of the Period' was a vehement attack on the young woman of the later 1860s. Partly it was a reaction against Emily Davies and her other 'strong-minded' friends – 'drawing-room blights' the *Saturday* called them. But it also contained much of that unpleasant bitterness that the older generation is always ready to use in its descriptions of the failings of those with whom it can no longer compete – the young. The article aroused a public storm. It brought out into the open the seething hatred that was infecting the relationship between the sexes and which, for a mad moment, was to put the basis of social life in jeopardy. As Lysistrata depicted the consequences of a women's revolt in Ancient Greece so did 'The Girl of the Period' epitomize the questioning that was going on about the whole ethic of marriage.

---

[1] Others who wrote for the *Saturday* included George Eliot, J. A. Froude, Francis Galton, Richard Garnett, Abraham Hayward (who had been on the *Chronicle* with Cook and was the means of Beresford Hope's introduction to that paper), T. H. Huxley, Charles Kingsley, Coventry Patmore, Emilia Pattison (Mrs Mark Pattison, later Lady Dilke), and James Cotter Morrison. 'As memoirs are published,' wrote Leslie Stephen's biographer, F. W. Maitland, in 1906, 'it becomes always more evident that anyone who never wrote for the *Saturday* was no one.' And G. S. Layard in his biography of Mrs Lynn Linton wrote of the *Saturday* under Cook's editorship that 'to have been a Saturday Reviewer in those roaring days is even now [1901] one of the highest of literary credentials.'

Instead of the 'fair young English girl of the past', who was 'neither bold in bearing nor masculine in mind', a girl who, when she married, 'would be her husband's friend and companion but never his rival ... a tender mother, an industrious housekeeper, a judicious mistress', England now had 'a creature who dyes her hair and paints her face as the first articles of her personal religion – a creature whose sole idea of life is fun; whose sole aim is unbounded luxury'. This new Girl of the Period had 'done away with such moral muffishness as consideration for others' and 'purity of taste'. No one could say of the modern English girl that she was 'tender, loving, retiring or domestic'; love indeed was the last thing she thought about – 'the legal barter of herself for so much money, representing so much dash, so much luxury and pleasure', that was her idea of marriage. Not that she married easily. 'Men are afraid of her; and with reason. They may amuse themselves with her for an evening, but they do not readily take her for life. Besides, after all her efforts, she is only a poor copy of the real thing; and the real thing is far more amusing than the copy, because it is real. Men can get that whenever they like; and when they go into their mothers' drawing-rooms, with their sisters and their sisters' friends, they want something of quite a different flavour.' If there had to be only one sort 'let us have it genuine, and the queens of St John's Wood in their unblushing honesty rather than their imitators and make-believes in Bayswater and Belgravia'. It used to be the old time notion that 'the sexes were made for each other, and that it was only natural for them to please each other, and to set themselves out for that end. But the Girl of the Period does not please men. She pleases them as little as she elevates them; and how little she does that, the class of women she has taken as her models of itself testifies. .... She will not see that though men laugh with her they do not respect her, though they flirt with her they do not marry her; she will not believe that she is not the kind of thing they want, and that she is acting against nature and her own interests when she disregards their advice and offends their taste.'

'The Girl of the Period', like all articles in the *Saturday* was anonymous. The excitement about its author's identity was enormous. Many, including Thomas Hardy and Henry Vizetelly, were sure it had been written by a man. Hardman reported the rumours about its authorship to his friend in

Australia. He had heard that it was by Lady Salisbury. The fact that her brother was on the staff of the *Saturday* gave some colour to the rumour, and it was widely believed. Mrs Lynn Linton thus found herself between the Scylla of those of her friends who knew that she was the author, and consequently made her pay 'pretty smartly' for what they considered her libel, and the Charybdis of losing her just claim to fame by allowing others to pretend to the authorship. She was twice 'introduced to the writer of The Girl of the Period'. On the second occasion she was so stung that she disclosed her secret. One of the men present at a reception at which Lady Salisbury was sitting next to Mrs Linton said, 'We have to thank Lady Salisbury for that very able article'. Lady Salisbury smiled acquiescence, but Mrs Linton blurted out, 'Lady Salisbury may have written the article, but it was I who received the cheque.'

The phrase, the Girl of the Period, became the catchword of the day. It figured in cartoons, in farces, and in a host of articles. There were Girl of the Period waltzes, Girl of the Period galops, there was even a *G.P. Almanack* and a *G.P. Miscellany*.

'The Girl of the Period' was not an isolated attack. Week after week Mrs Linton poured her anonymous scorn on every type of English woman except the 'brown-haired girl of the past' who had been demure and lacking in every trace of sophistication. Modern mothers, fashionable women, nymphs, weak sisters, grim females, widows, dolls, sphinxes, *femmes passées*, and spoilt women were all ruthlessly and cold-bloodedly annihilated.

Nor had she changed her attitude when the articles were reprinted as a book in 1883. 'In re-reading these papers,' she wrote in the preface, 'I am more than ever convinced that I have struck the right chord of condemnation, and advocated the best virtues and most valuable characteristics of women. I neither soften nor retract a line of what I have said. One of the modern phases of womanhood – hard, unloving, mercenary, ambitious, without domestic faculty and devoid of healthy natural instincts – is still to me a pitiable mistake and a grave national disaster. And I think now, as I thought when I wrote these papers, that a public and professional life for women is incompatible with the discharge of their highest duties or the cultivation of their noblest qualities. I think now, as I thought then, that the sphere of human action is determined by the fact of sex, and that there does exist both natural limitation and natural direction.'

The women's rightists had no more bitter or able opponent than Mrs Lynn Linton. Rarely did she say a word in praise of her own sex. She excused herself by saying that women's virtues were well-known and it was more important for the friends of women to point out their follies. Bloomerism, in her opinion, was one of these. So too was the desire of some women to become doctors. Mrs Linton met Elizabeth Blackwell, Elizabeth Garrett, and Mary Walker. Of the last of these three young women who, in her words, 'had clanked into the dissecting-room', she wrote, 'The Bloomer costume which she wore, with that huge rose in her hair as a sign of her sex, did much to retard the Woman Question all round.'

Mrs Linton never changed her attitude, and until her death in 1898 she continued to write books and articles with obsessive vehemence against every aspect of woman's emancipation. Whether the popular name of the moment was the Girl of the Period, or the Shrieking Sisterhood, or the Girton Girl, or, in the 1890s, the Wild Women, Mrs Linton's pen never ceased to condemn them.[1]

The True Danger of True Colleges

The *Saturday Review* was not the only periodical that attacked the changing status of women in the years of high conflict at the end of the 1860s and the 1870s. A series of anonymous articles in the *Imperial Review*, a Conservative weekly which ran throughout 1867 and 1868, was re-published as *Essays in Defence of Women*. There were some who might doubt whether the substance justified the title. The *Essays* had in the main a slightly bantering tone and were imperturbable, except when they encountered any suggestion that woman's place in society

---

[1] In his capacity as reader, George Meredith rejected her books when they were offered to Chapman and Hall. He rejected them, he wrote in a letter, because of her 'abhorrence of the emancipation of young females from their ancient rules'. But although this was always his line of preaching, in practice with his own daughter Meredith never relaxed those ancient rules. It is easier to urge emancipation for other people's daughters than to suffer the jealousies and torments of giving dangerous freedom to one's own!

should in the slightest way be altered – as, for instance, by having a university education.

An essay on 'True Colleges for Women', arising out of an appeal to the public to subscribe for the foundation of a true college for women somewhere between Cambridge and London – an appeal that was to result in the College at Hitchin and its development at Girton – revealed the ferocity that underlay the banter. It began with sneers at this 'foolish project', suggesting that there would no doubt be an annual croquet match at Lord's and that the Boat Race, already threatening 'the night of the Derby Day to be considered, *par exellence*, the "Olympic Games" of the metropolis', would undoubtedly prove the more popular of the two when the crews were selected from 'the first and freshest young ladies in the land'.

But then, lest the sneers were not pointed enough, the author was more forthright in his condemnation: 'It is difficult to treat with gravity this preposterous proposal of a University career for the potential wives of Englishmen without being betrayed into an indignation such as, nowadays, is never effective and is not infrequently ridiculous.' It was a subject of the most serious importance. 'Home, and home only', was the 'True College' for girls. Away from home they would be the prey for immoral influences. 'We are treading on delicate ground and must needs pick our way daintily. Nevertheless, we need not shrink from saying that the congregating of young girls at a certain age, either in boarding-schools, true Colleges, or any other gregarious establishment . . . is a downright forcing of minds which ought, for the moment, to be kept as dormant as possible. By minds we do not mean intellects; we mean what everybody who is acquainted with human nature will understand. It is on this account, and on this alone, that female boarding-schools are so unspeakably pernicious.' 'True Colleges' would aggravate the mischiefs.

These mischiefs, of course, though the word was never mentioned in the essay, were connected with the dangerous subject of sex. While sex could be kept more or less dormant in the minds of young girls while they were safe within the citadel of home, what protection could there be against its insidious fingers when they were living outside the citadel? 'Contaminating influences do not disqualify a man from becoming a good husband and an excellent father. Could the same be said, without violating truth and nature, of those who are intended to become wives and mothers?' The essay ended with a quotation from Coventry Patmore, that popular poetic apostle of domestic bliss, in which he wished woman to be,

'So wise in all she ought to know,
So ignorant of all beside.'

'We very much doubt even if the wisdom of the first line would be attained in these "true Colleges"; but we are quite sure that they would not long protect the happy ignorance so delicately alluded to in the second.'

Ignorance of what was in store for them when they married was an essential part of the upbringing of Top Nation young ladies. Mrs Menzies who published her *Memories Discreet and Indiscreet* anonymously in 1917 as by A Woman of No Importance, was married in the early 1870s. Her husband was a subaltern in the Gordon Highlanders, home on leave from India, and he was in a desperate hurry to be married as his leave was nearly up. So one bright day in May she was married at the parish church 'while still nothing but a child'. She was taken to church by her rather tearful father, who was the squire, in a carriage drawn by four grey horses with postillions in grey and blue. The schoolchildren strewed flowers for her to walk on, the bells rang merrily, and the church was crammed with people.

'Thus I was shot out into the realities of life after the manner of those days, in a condition of absolute black ignorance of practically every fact of life that would be almost unbelievable to girls of that age today – happily for them. The fact that I had not the faintest idea of what I was doing was a matter of legitimate self-congratulation to my parents as a proof of the success of the upbringing they had bestowed on their child. It seems a little incongruous that a man who, say, for instance, murdered an aged aunt, should be regarded as such a naughty fellow and probably hanged, while the people who launched their daughters into life before they knew what they were about should be adjudged quite praiseworthy. The gentleman who murdered his aunt had only shortened an old life, while the others had done their best to ruin a young one.'

The congratulations Mrs Menzies received before her marriage from an old woman in the village still remained in her mind fifty years later. 'She had known me all my life and when I told her I was going to be married, with tears in her eyes she put her dear old hand on my shoulder and with shaking head said, "Poor dear". This was not inspiring. She had been through a good deal herself during her married life and presented her husband with eighteen children, so she may have had some excuse for the form her congratulations took.'[1]

For girls of the Lower Nation there was rarely 'black ignorance' before marriage. Apart from the incestuous conditions of cottage and slum bedrooms, there was the old rural habit that Mrs Lynn Linton remembered in Caldbeck, where pregnancy had to precede marriage. The custom was common in those parts of the country where children were wage-earners. It was considered unthrifty and unnecessary to marry a girl who had not given evidence of fertility. 'She who cannot at least show fair prospect of adding young piecers, tenters, or hurriers, as well as her own person to the common stock is no better than an unproductive incumbrance. "If thou houd'st, I wed thee; if thou doesn't, thou'rt none the waur," is a north country proverb, familiar enough to many southerners, and acted upon to an immense extent,' wrote William Acton in his study of *Prostitution*.[2] Marriage automatically wiped out any stigma. If the man refused to marry her a girl could sue him for seduction or breach of promise.

An article by the Reverend William Scott in the *Saturday* of August 2, 1856 discussed this accepted routine. Entitled 'Breach of Promise and Marriage Morals' it cited many examples taken from local newspapers which showed that these actions for breach of promise were usually successful – even in cases where the action was brought by a 'gay girl'. They would be settled for damages of £25, £50, or sometimes £100. Those who brought the actions – and who caused them – were generally of 'the farmer class'. Among the cases cited was one in which the plaintiff told the court that the young farmer had assured her that both his sisters had been incontinent before marriage and that 'it was all right'. Most of the cases mentioned were in Norfolk and Dorset.

The *Saturday* advocated a change in the law, although Scott admitted that it would be difficult to bring this about because

---

[1] [Mrs Menzies], *Memories Discreet and Indiscreet* (1917), pp. 45–6.
[2] William Acton, *Prostitution* (1870 edition), p. 47.

those concerned with the moral and religious education of the country were 'literally afraid to face, or even to acknowledge' the truth about the moral condition of the female population in rural districts. But if a change could be made then it would surely improve morals because a girl, if she found it more difficult to bring an action, would not give herself so readily. As it was, there was no restraint and the papers were full of these cases with their gross details and their evidence and pleadings. 'Female honour by no means holds its theoretical position in public esteem,' Acton assured his Top Nation readers.

Echoes from the Clubs
Another periodical which reflected the importance of the woman question at this time was *Echoes*, a weekly 'record of political topics and social amenities' that first appeared at the end of 1867 under the title of *Echoes from the Clubs*, and then in October 1869 changed its name again to *The Period*. It had begun publication under the title of *Echoes* some months after Mrs Linton's 'Girl of the Period' had become the talking-point of the day, and from its first number it turned again and again to this enchanting Miss. Indeed on its very first page it announced that a copy of 'The Girl of the Period Galop', expressly composed for the purpose, would be given free to every subscriber.

Echoes defended the 'fair and pure daughters of England' against the serious slander of the anonymous Mrs Linton's article. But this did not mean that *Echoes* was in favour of emancipation or that it approved of the women's movement in any way. Its position about women was made clear in an article on 'The Press Upon Women' (March 13, 1869). 'If the destiny of woman is to be the companion of man and a mother of children, there is no need that she should educate herself into a state of energetic acuteness which might fit her for being the attorney of the neighbouring village or the pushing secretary of a joint-stock company.' A man did not want to be reminded of his book-keeper or his clerk when he got home. Women had a right 'to be freed from hard, constant, energetic work of every kind. They have their home duties, their accomplishments and amusements, and by all means let these be duly attended to; but we insist and boldly affirm that ceaseless occupation of the above kind is utterly destructive of woman's true beauties.' It was woman's part to bring a little poetry and sweetness into the gruff hard world of man – very much what Mrs Ellis had been saying thirty years before!

The ridiculousness of women's employment in the professions was the subject of a two-page cartoon that appeared the following month. It showed a man coming into a Civil Service office occupied by some two dozen attractive young women clerks; they are smoking, building 'book castles', reading *Le Follet*, chatting, looking at bonnets, playing battledore, crocheting, looking out of the window with opera glasses, and generally passing the time without doing any work. On the floor are balls of wool, a Mudie's library book, spilt inkwells, and the Court Circular. These verses accompany the cartoon:

'Employment' For Women?

I

Throw open the Service to ladies –
  For capital clerks they'll be found
Though the chiefs of departments at Hades
  May wish them, when errors abound.
The Age has original features,
  And with novel ideas is crossed,
And we've got to employ the dear creatures,
  Whatever the trouble or cost.

II

To be fair wives and fortunate mothers
  Were happiest, as destiny runs;
But what shall we do with those others
  Who pine to be nurses or nuns?
Or with those whom we teach and examine,
  And put to all manner of pains,
Till at last we find out there's a famine,
  Of work for their dear little brains.

III

Well, give them their clerkships; else verily
  'Twill be absolute war to the knife.
Let them pass their time gaily and merrily –
  Reading *Le Follet*, *The Queen*, or *Belles' Life*;
Stick Government quills in a chignon
  While its wearer is quite in the dark;
And fill the official dominion
  With every species of lark.

IV

Let the shuttlecock fly to the ceiling –
    Only don't smash the Government glass;
There's a game too, shy beauties revealing,
    Which I fancy is known as *Les Graces*:
And if still four o'clock, coming slowly,
    Tires our poor little hardworking pets,
Why to tyrannize *would* be unholy . . .
    So they surely may smoke cigarettes.

It was easy enough to mock at the desire for employment, but sympathy, had it been part of the mental furniture of the day, would have been an apter sentiment. 'The position of a single woman of thirty in the middle classes is horrible,' confessed a spinster in 1868. 'Her cares are to be properly dressed, to drive or walk or pay calls with Mamma; to work miracles of embroidery – but for what? What we want is something to do, something to live for.' And at thirty a spinster had only one chance in sixteen of ever marrying.

Just what *Echoes* did envisage for women was shown in another cartoon called The Dovecot. This depicted a hyper-domestic scene – one daughter reading the paper to her father, while another (or is it the mother?) sews by his side. Another daughter ties the bow-tie of a young brother. Three more daughters admire the baby being held aloft by a fourth. A little girl hangs on the skirts of one of the admirers. Through the french window can be seen another daughter giving an arm to the old grandmother as they walk along the garden path.

The text for this family bliss was taken from the *Saturday Review*: 'In the midst of the reign of the Girl of the Period with her slang and her boldness we come every now and then upon a group of good girls of the real old English type – doves who are content with life as they have it in a dovecot.' The first of the verses accompanying the cartoon was:

Well, we have heard strange stories, doubted not,
    Of girlhood emptied of its girlishness
Envious it may be, of a manlier lot,
    Driven to wild freaks of dress:
Yet are there sweeter women, you may guess,
In multitudinous homes of this fair land –
Creatures whom critics cannot understand,
    Dwelling in loveliness.

This idyllic picture of family life was in stark contrast to another that had emerged some months earlier. Throughout the greater part of 1868 the *Englishwoman's Domestic Magazine*, now edited by Mrs Matilda Browne[1] though still under the literary control of S. O. Beeton, ran a protracted correspondence on the efficacy of whipping one's daughters. *Echoes* in its first issue had been appalled at the revelations in this correspondence:

'The letters have only too evidently been genuine. There have been a few objectors but the general voice of mothers – and fathers too – is in favour of the *Châtiment de l'enfance qui commence par alarmer la pudeur, qui met dans l'humiliation extrême* . . . This is to be applied to girls up to the age of sixteen or eighteen if they need it. One humane mother suggested a slipper as the instrument; but this was indignantly rejected by other mothers as not giving pain enough, and there was a loud outcry for birch. At last some contributors – one of them a father, and evidently a man of education – came forward to suggest that not even that ancient instrument gave sufficient pain. Nothing like leather! Cut a strap into strips; let your governess tie your daughter down upon an ottoman after evening prayers; the strap thus cut may be depended upon to inflict "acute suffering"; you then make her "kiss the rod" and let her go . . . All suggestions in favour of any kind of delicate reserve were scouted by the fathers and mothers who took part in this divine council; "shame" is an essential part of their treatment.'

This was a sentimental, sadistic age, and the whipping of daughters – or more particularly its discussion in print – was one expression of the surge of sadism which also revealed itself in other ways, including the revival of tight lacing which had been fashionable in the 1840s, had gone out of fashion, and had returned in the middle 1860s.

The whipping of girls was an especially satisfying subject for the Reverend Frank Kilvert, whose diary of life in the Welsh village of Clyro and the Wiltshire village of Hardenhuish in the 1870s is as graphic a record as exists of those years: the croquet and archery parties, the picnics, the dinners, the walks, and shoots – and also the account of his 'villaging' (his visits to the

---

[1] Mrs Browne, married to C. R. Browne of the Westminster Fire Office, was foster-mother to Beeton's two boys and the two families lived together in Greenhithe. She died in 1936 in her hundredth year.

poor people of his parish).[1] Kilvert, who had a keen perception and a great power of writing, was susceptible to a degree, the sweet eyes of young girls being particularly captivating to him. He was much taken with little girls and was an enthusiastic voyeur in a mild way. In his diary he always recorded any sights of bare female legs or girls dressing themselves on the beach or paddling 'with shoes, stockings and drawers off', their clothes held up 'nearly to their waists and naked from the waist downwards'. On one occasion the tables were turned. The habit had been for men to bathe in the nude, but in the early 1870s they were being encouraged to adopt what Kilvert called 'the disgusting habit' of wearing a costume. He would have none of it, and at Lyme Regis one day he stumbled up the beach in the nude to the great interest of a mother and her two daughters.

But naturally, in conformity with the temper of the times, Kilvert's predilection for bare limbs and the revelations made by the short petticoats of fourteen-year-old girls climbing up steep rocks on windy days did not prevent him from being severely critical of by-blows, concubinage and the old Welsh habit of bundling. He was fascinated by – indeed he had a fixation about–daughters being whipped. For example, there was the sad case of Annie, Phoebe, and Lizzie Corfield, who had lost their mother and whose father beat them outrageously. 'It seems that when he comes home late he makes the girls get out of bed and strip themselves naked and then he flogs them severely or else he pulls the bedclothes off them and whips them all three as they lie in bed together, writhing and screaming under the castigation. It is said that Corfield strips the poor girls naked, holds them face downwards across his knees on a bed or chair and whips their bottoms so cruelly that the blood runs down their legs. The neighbours fear there is little doubt that the girls are often flogged on their naked bodies till the blood comes.' It had been suggested that some woman neighbour should examine the children. 'We fear the soft tender flesh would be seen, if the poor thin ragged frocks were lifted, sorely cut and wealed by the cruel spikes of the whip.'[2]

It needs no psychiatrist to interpret the relish of the writing and the pleasure of the repetitions.

[1] William Plomer (ed.), *Kilvert's Diary*, in 3 vols. (Jonathan Cape, 1938–40).
[2] *Kilvert's Diary*, 1870–71, pp. 367–8.

The beating of the Corfield girls was only one of several such descriptions that Kilvert included. In the case of a poor girl called Fanny Strange who had apparently sinned against God as well as against her mother, her father being dead, Kilvert himself offered out of the goodness of his heart to thrash her severely for the good of her soul. And lest anyone might be artless enough to imagine that it was only the hard duty of punishing that demanded the baring of little girls' bottoms there is one revealing sentence in Frank Kilvert's diary which unequivocally discloses the strong sadistic element involved. One day he was watching a girl on a swing. She had no drawers on and as he watched her slipping forward on the seat Kilvert noted with pleasure that 'her flesh was plump and smooth and in excellent whipping condition'.

Another aspect of women which received attention from *Echoes* was stage morality. In January 1869 the Lord Chamberlain had woken from his sinecure to complain to theatre managers of 'the impropriety of costume of the ladies in the pantomimes, burlesques, etc., which are now being performed in some of the Metropolitan theatres'. *Echoes* commented that although a large number of actresses were undoubtedly virtuous, this did not prevent vice from flourishing to an alarming extent in the profession, and this being so there could be no surprise at the number of girls who regarded the stage as a means of arriving at 'infamous luxury'. Several theatres had become little better than 'a market for the display of female beauty', and pantomime, which was formerly intended for the amusement of children, had now become 'a mere pretext for the display of legs more or less padded, and bosoms more or less uncovered'.

But *Echoes*, having pontificated in the Lord Chamberlain's favour in that instance, subsequently proceeded to mock him. 'The Lord Chambermaid, is, we understand, indefatigable in the cause of delicacy. We understand that when Miss Charlotte Saunders was called upon to fill up a heading under Schedule B', giving her length from waistband to knee, to enable the Lord Chamberlain to prescribe the exact fullness of the trunk-hose she must wear, 'she flatly or roundly, refused, and none of the other ladies', *Echoes* continued archly, 'are expected to fall behind in adopting the same broad basis of action.' The puns were typical of the day.

Another issue contained a two-page cartoon on 'Stage

Morality'. The left-hand page showed the Lord Chambermaid at St James's – St James's Palace that is. An official in court dress is on one knee holding a tape-measure from a girl's waist to six inches above her ankles to demonstrate how long her stage trunks should be. She, in fact, is dressed in trunks to mid-thigh only and is looking disconsolately at him. Another official is noting details at a high desk. Behind the actress, hanging on pegs, are her ordinary clothes. Featured boldly are a pair of enormously full, long drawers with ribbon round the end of each leg leaving a frill below. On the right-hand page, captioned 'St James's Barbe-bleue', an evening-dressed audience is lapping up the scene on the stage with opera glasses and avid looks. One young lady, eyes agog, seems rather surprised; two others are looking from behind a fan and between fingers. A verse of the accompanying poem runs:

> Wicked and wild be the reckless dance
> That we get from the pleasant realm of France –
>   The memory never rankles:
> But the lovely nymphs of the English stage
> Immodest dreams in the mind enrage,
>   Unless they hide their ankles.

This 'reckless dance' at the St James's was the can-can. It was the first time it had been danced in England by women in women's clothing and it formed part of the exciting finale of Offenbach's 'Orpheus in the Underworld'. *The Times* had stigmatized the dance as the most outrageous can-can ever seen on any London stage, and warned the fastidious who were going to the theatre that they should leave at the end of the third tableau in order to avoid the spectacle – although in giving this warning it admitted that it realized it was in fact recommending many to stay to the rapturous end.

The dance took the theatre by storm night after night and the whole company danced it again and again, while the audience cheered and stamped its feet and abandoned itself to the maenadic paroxysms of the music. The following year when the can-can was danced in a ballet at the Alhambra there was great uproar as a result of which the theatre lost its licence. The can-can dancers went over to the Globe and there they were allowed to perform their dance in a burlesque without any further trouble from the authorities.

13. *Top left:* Jane Catherine Gamble, benefactress of Girton College, Cambridge, from a painting by A. E. Chalon, R.A., 1838. Emily Davies, (*right*) realized Princess Ida's ideal at Hitchin and then Girton. The Hitchin Students (*bottom*) at the first 'true college for women'.

14. VICTORIAN 'PIN-UPS'
'Skittles' (*above*) – 'A childish face, but wise with woman's wit.' Florence Bilton (*right*), of the 'Sisters Bilton'. Her sister became Fifth Countess of Clancarty.

From a stereoscopic daguerrotype c. 1842, *The Era of the Photograph*.

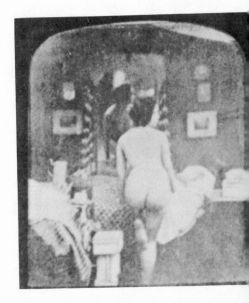

The higher education of women was another subject that *Echoes* had a dig at. It noted that the Chelsea and Kensington Committee which had been formed to promote this object had given notice of a course of lectures on Size and Shape as an introduction to Geometry. *Echoes* celebrated the news with some predictable verses about a Fellow Trin. Col. Cam. lecturing young ladies on size and shape.

Women's suffrage too was a potent source for ridicule. Under the headline 'Childhood Suffrage' a meeting was reported at which Frances Power Cobbe, who had been associated with Mary Carpenter in the ragged school movement, took the chair, supported by Emily Faithfull, the Marquis of Townshend, John Bright, M.P., Henry Fawcett, M.P., John Morley, M.P., and others, to consider the question of children's right to the vote. The cod report concluded with the precis of a pretty seventeen-year-old girl's speech in which she said that as she was not allowed to take an active part in political life she was forced to exercise her talents ('devastatingly, no doubt', *Echoes* commented) in the social sphere.

But there were also many items to remind readers of the normal relations between the sexes. One set of verses sang of the flirtatious joys of the croquet lawn. One couplet ran:

'And I'm sure that you ne'er saw a neater-turned ankle,
Than peeps from 'neath Jeanie's white fanciful frills'

and the verses ended:

'Ah! these maids of the mallet, they shake out their tresses
Whilst men gather round at their siren-like call –
As they artfully loop up diaphanous dresses
And break stalwart hearts as they croquet a ball!'

Chapter 13
PRETTY HORSE-BREAKERS AND OTHERS

In his biography of Charles Dickens John Forster asserted that there was scarcely a page of Dickens which could not safely be put into the hands of a child. This assertion made Wilkie Collins explode with wrath in the margin of his own copy of the book: 'If it is true, which it is not, it would imply the condemnation of Dickens's books as works of art, it would declare him to be guilty of deliberately presenting to his readers a false reflection of human life. If this wretched English claptrap means anything it means that the novelist is forbidden to touch on the sexual relations which literally swarm about him and influence the lives of millions of his fellow creatures [unless] those relations are licensed by the ceremony called marriage.'

Wilkie Collins might rail at Forster for approving of this 'claptrap', but the fact remained that novelists had to abide by it if they wanted the success that only the circulating libraries could assure. Meredith, for one, had experienced the truth of this when *The Ordeal of Richard Feverel*, which appeared in 1859, the same year as *The Origin of Species*, and which one of his biographers has described as the poetic counterpart of Darwin's book, was not put in Mudie's advertised catalogue because of 'the immoralities' it depicted, and this despite *The Times*' approval of the book. 'It was an age when nothing was thought so hideous as nakedness, and nothing so wicked as impassioned love.'[1]

Yet there was nakedness and passion abounding, and for this

[1] R. E. Sencourt, *The Life of George Meredith* (Chapman and Hall, 1929), p. 65.

reason Victorian novels as a whole give an adulterated picture of Victorian life. They were false by omission and euphemism.[1] Furthermore, because the nineteenth century was a heyday for the novelist and because books are the most easily available source of evidence for other writers and opinion-formers, this adulterated picture was spread wide and contributed importantly to the general Victorian image created in the minds of succeeding generations. A truer source, however, is to be found in the newspapers and periodicals of the time. Looking through these, reading the breach of promise cases, the murders, hangings, frauds and bankruptcies, the divorce trials, the articles on the lower depths, it is clear indeed that it was not human nature which had been eviscerated, but that the censorship exercised over the novelists by the circulating libraries on behalf of their readers had invalidated most novels as truthful sources of everyday Victorian life. The fact that captions to cartoons in general circulation no longer had the vulgarity of Hogarth's or Gillray's did not mean that coarseness had been abolished or that dirty jokes no longer swept the clubs and taverns and barbers shops. William Hardman's memoirs, for example, show that the Rabelaisian humour and coarse schoolboy fun which are a basic feature, especially of the human male, were not eradicated by the code of the Victorian 'moral civilizers'. And there was a whole world of publication – 'Holywell Street literature' it was called from the London street in which it was usually sold – which catered to the huge taste for pornography and near-pornography.[2] From time to time the *Saturday Review* and debates in Parliament would deplore the amount of Holywell Street literature available, but little could effectively be done about it and the *Saturday* on one such occasion (May 16, 1857) turned away and suggested that as 'wife-beating and indecent books, two of the old stock-grievances of society' were 'such palpable and undeniable abominations' 'if we cannot cure them, we had perhaps better not talk about them'.

[1] 'We are condemned to avoid half the life that passes us by,' Robert Louis Stevenson complained: 'What books Dickens would have written had he been permitted! Think of Thackeray as unfettered as Flaubert or Balzac. What books I might have written myself. But they give us a little box of toys and say to us, "You mustn't play with anything but these"!'

[2] There is an account of Holywell Street and its wares in Michael Sadleir's magnificent documentary novel of the London underworld in the 1870s *Forlorn Sunset* (Constable, 1947), pp. 410–22.

That sexual relations, however carefully excluded from novels, did indeed 'literally swarm about him' was obvious to any city-dweller. Street satyrs on the one hand, and prostitutes on the other thrust the subject to the fore. London was the worst city for vice in Britain, but it was apparently not the worst in the world. Hepworth Dixon was told by men who knew that 'in depth and darkness of iniquity, neither Paris in its private haunts, nor London in its open streets' could hold a candle to New York. 'Paris may be subtler, London may be grosser, in its vices; but for largeness of depravity, for domineering insolence of sin, for rowdy callousness to censure, they tell me the Atlantic city finds no rival on earth.'

The geography of vice in both London and New York was carefully charted in the 1860s. London's vice was described in detail by Bracebridge Hemyng in the fourth and concluding volume of Mayhew's *London Labour and the London Poor*; New York's by George Ellington Galtey in *The Women of New York*. The pattern is the same in both cities; only the street names are different.

'Men Can Get That Whenever They Like'

Exactly how many prostitutes there were in London nobody knew. Estimates varied enormously. Eighty thousand was the widely accepted figure and occurs repeatedly in arguments about prostitution at this period. It was mentioned, for example, in *Aurora Leigh* written in 1856 ('Eighty thousand women in one smile'). But although no more accurate figure can be calculated with precision, it does seem that 80,000 is a vastly inflated number. It appears to have been first quantified 'scientifically' in *The Lancet* in 1857 in an article which said that one house in every sixty in London was a brothel and one female in every sixteen of all ages a whore – 6,000 brothels, 80,000 prostitutes. In mid-Victorian times the male population of London of all ages was about 1,300,000. Simple division shows the unlikelihood of 80,000 prostitutes even allowing for a large number of male visitors to the city.

Other estimates of the number of prostitutes varied down to 8,000. Tait's *Edinburgh Magazine* in 1857 published figures for 1840 which gave 2,000 women in brothels in Liverpool, 1,800 in Glasgow, 1,500 in Manchester, 700 in Leeds, 300 in Hull, and 250 in Paisley. Princes Street, Edinburgh, was, it said, as bad as the Haymarket in London. William Acton in his book on the 'moral, social, and sanitary aspects' of *Prostitution* gave the number of prostitutes in London as 9,409 in 1841, 8,600 in 1857, and 6,515 in 1868, but these figures were only for those known to the police. In 1860 the *Saturday Review* disbelievingly mentioned a figure of 360,000 for Great Britain as a whole.

Whatever the exact number, however, it was sufficient to form what the *Saturday* early in 1862 called 'an army of occupation' which had 'seized upon the West End'. The lady of popular song who had her beat on the sunny side of Jermyn Street was following in the footsteps of her forebears who, in the 1860s, claimed the sunny side of Regent Street exclusively for their own, while 'the pavement of the Haymarket they rule with a sway no prudent passenger will care to challenge after the sun has fallen', and Portland Place was occupied 'by a French detachment of voluble habits and by no means backward manners'. There could be no doubt that Mrs Lynn Linton was right when she said that 'men can get that whenever they like'.

Bracebridge Hemyng divided prostitutes into three classes: first, those women who were kept by men of independent means; second, those women who lived in apartments and maintained themselves 'by the produce of their vagrant amours'; and third, those women who lived in brothels.

'The state of the first of these,' he wrote, 'is the nearest approximation to the holy state of marriage and finds numerous defenders and supporters. These have their suburban villas, their carriages, horses, and sometimes a box at the opera. Their equipages are to be seen in the park, and occasionally through the influence of their aristocratic friends they succeed in obtaining vouchers for the most exclusive patrician balls.'

The second class usually congregated in houses in which each had her own private apartment, in most cases with the connivance of the proprietor. 'These generally resort to night-houses where they have a greater chance of meeting with customers than they would have were they to perambulate the streets.'

The brothels in which the third class lived were defined by Hemyng as 'houses where speculators board, dress and feed women, living upon the farm of their persons. Under this head we must include introducing houses where the women do not reside but merely use the house as a place of resort in the

daytime. Married women, imitating the custom of Messalina...
not uncommonly make use of these places.'

The first class were of two types, kept mistresses, and 'prima
donnas or those who live in a superior style'. The kept mistresses Hemyng regarded as perhaps the most important division
of the entire profession. They were the queens of St John's Wood,
the pretty horse-breakers of the Grove of the Evangelist, the
genuine article in 'their unblushing honesty'. Some of them were
ladies of great influence – and great charm. Two of the most
famous were Laura Bell, who ended up as a social missionary,
and the enchanting Skittles.

Laura Bell

Laura Bell, 'the Queen of London Whoredom' during the
1850s as William Hardman called her, was born in Antrim,
Ireland, in 1829, the daughter of a bailiff on the estates of the
Marquis of Hertford. She started as a shop-girl in Belfast and
from there became a lady of pleasure in Dublin where she was
famous for her beauty and for her carriage drawn by a pair of
white horses. The next step was to London where she arrived
about the time of the Great Exhibition. Sir Francis Burnand
recalled seeing her when he was a young boy and she was
queening it in Hyde Park. She had 'a pretty, doll-like face' with
'big eyes and quick vivacious glances'. As she sat in an open
phaeton receiving the adulation of a group of swells, she was an
exciting object of interest for the young Burnand. She was
reputed to have had a liaison with the Nepalese Ambassador in
London and there is a story of how, after he had left London, he
sent Laura a magnificent ring telling her that if ever she needed
help she had only to send the ring back and he would do anything he could for her. When the Indian Mutiny broke out in
1857 Laura is supposed to have mentioned this pledge to a
friend who passed the information on to the India Office. The
ring was sent to India with a request from Laura that the
Government of Nepal should either join the British or stay
neutral during the Mutiny. The outcome of her request, so the
story goes, was that Nepal did not join the Mutiny and its
Ghurka regiments remained faithful to the British.

By the time of the Mutiny Laura was a respectable married
lady. In 1852 she married Captain Augustus Frederick Thistlethwayte who established her in Grosvenor Square, where she

lived so extravagant a life that on several occasions he advertised that he would not be responsible for her debts. Certainly she had to do something to take her mind off living with the gallant Captain, for he was not an easy man. One of his habits was to fire a pistol through the ceiling of his room whenever he wanted to summon a servant.

By the early 1860s Laura had adopted another career. She became a social missionary and an eloquent preacher. According to contemporary observers her performances on the platform were not greatly inferior to those of the spell-binding Spurgeon at the Metropolitan Tabernacle. She had a great intellectual capacity to which was added a poetical imagination, a combination that was irresistible to Victorian audiences, especially when the poetic flights of oratory came from one who signed herself as 'a sinner saved by Grace through faith in the Lamb of God'. The headquarters of her mission was her home in Grosvenor Square, and here she was visited by many notables including the Prime Minister, William Gladstone, and his wife. The Gladstones indeed were on confidential terms with Laura Thistlethwayte. Her husband, the Captain, died in 1887 – mysteriously, it might be said, although as he was found shot by the revolver he kept by his bed it is possible that he made a mistake when trying to summon a servant!

After his death Laura moved to a cottage in Hampstead where she continued her social missionary work and her friendship with the Gladstones until her own death in 1894. She was buried in the Thistlethwayte family vault in Paddington cemetery beside her mother-in-law who was the daughter of a Bishop of Norwich. Twenty years earlier when Sir Willoughby Maycock heard her preach at the Polytechnic he noted that 'the lustre of her beautiful eyes' was 'only surpassed by the sparkling of an array of large diamond rings which adorned her fingers as she raised them in eloquent exhortation to follow the path that alone leads to salvation'. In his chronicle of mid-Victorian morals, *The Girl with the Swansdown Seat*, Cyril Pearl permitted himself to wonder whether some of her more sceptical listeners may not have felt like asking by what path she had been led to those large diamond rings.

Skittles

The second of the great *demi-mondaine* queens was Skittles, whose real name was Catherine Walters. Born in 1839 in Liverpool where her father was a tide-waiter, she first came into prominence in London about 1860. In 1861 Alfred Austin, a later poet laureate of no great fame, wrote a satire on London Society called *The Season*. Of Hyde Park in the afternoon he said:

> 'Gone the broad glare, save where with borrowed bays
> Some female Phaeton sets the Drive a-blaze:
> Or, more defiant, spurning frown and foe,
> With slackened rein swift Skittles rules the Row.
> Though scowling matrons champing steeds restrain,
> She flaunts Propriety with flapping mane.'

In case there should be some of his readers who were unaware of the gossip of the town he added a footnote to explain that 'Skittles is as well-known and as much an object of interest as the last shape of Madame Elisa', and that speculation about her origin, her abode and her doings was one of the key talking points among fashionable ladies *à deux*.

The following year a second international exhibition was held in South Kensington at the science museum, nicknamed, because of its shape and location, the Brompton Boilers. Although it did not attract the tremendous crowds and arouse the widespread enthusiasm and lasting fame that the Great Exhibition of 1851 had done, partly because the Court was in deep mourning for Prince Albert's death, nevertheless it was popular and well-attended. A letter to *The Times* (in reality an article) by a wealthy man-about-town called James Matthew Higgins, who was a frequent correspondent to the papers, often under the pseudonym of Jacob Omnium, drew attention to another attraction which was causing traffic congestion in Hyde Park, at the approaches to the Exhibition.

Though the letter was entitled *Anonyma* it was in fact about Skittles. It made her famous. Under the guise of being concerned about traffic jams caused by the fashionable world swarming to see her as she drove in the park, Higgins broadcast her charm and created a mystery about her identity. At the end of the year she became even more famous by eloping to the United States with a married man, Aubrey de Vere Beauclerk, a kinsman of the Duke of St Albans. It was when her place was sold up after she had bolted that sightseers were fascinated to discover the swansdown-covered lavatory seat that gave Cyril Pearl the title for his book.

The elopement to the United States lasted only a few months, and in 1863 Skittles was in Paris under the wing of the Marquess of Hartington. It was here according to one legend that she got her nickname because of her proficiency in a skittles alley which was popular with the young attachés of the British Embassy. According to another and, in view of the date of Austin's poem, more likely story she got it by telling a crowd of noisy young guards officers that if they didn't shut up she'd knock them down 'like a row of bloody skittles'.

It was in Paris that she met Wilfred Scawen Blunt, then a young attaché of twenty-three who, although he had already seen a good deal of the world and was no novice with women, was still, according to his own description, 'a fair-faced, frightened boy with eyes of truth'. Blunt, later to become famous as a poet, traveller, rebel, and anti-imperialist, was in Margot Asquith's opinion one of the four handsomest men she ever met in her life – and the photographs of him in his young manhood suggest that she was in no way exaggerating.[1] This 'frightened boy' fell deeply in love with the twenty-four-year-old Skittles and remained her close friend for the rest of their long lives. Years after they first met, Blunt was said to have confessed that Skittles 'set his passion so full ablaze that it burnt out once for all' and no woman after her could do more than stir the embers. He celebrated his love for her in passionate poetry. She is the heroine of *Esther*, a sonnet sequence published in 1892, and she is Manon of his *Love Sonnets of Proteus* as well as being the subject of most of the early love lyrics in the *Sonnets and Songs by Proteus*. And in many of his later poems he returned again and again to that greatest love of his life which never paled. It was a love so great that 'as long as I was in love', he wrote, 'my love sufficed me, and I cannot say . . . that no human love ever satisfied the desires of the soul. I have, on more than one occasion, seemed for days together to be walking some cubits high above the ground'.

In *Esther*, against a background of imaginary scenes and events, Blunt tells the story of his love for Skittles. It was a love that had its agonies and penalties as well as the superlative ecstasy of walking with one's feet high above the ground. The poet arrives at Lyons after spending a summer wandering in the

[1] The others were the 13th Earl of Pembroke, the 10th Earl of Wemyss, who led the Adullamites, and Viscount D'Abernon.

Alps. There at the fair as he stands gazing at the 'two female monsters' in a sideshow a woman clutches his arm.

> 'She was a little woman dressed in black,
> Who stood on tiptoe with a childish air,
> Her face and figure hidden in a "saque",
> All but her eyes and forehead and dark hair,
> Her brow was pale, but it was lit with light,
> And mirth flashed out of it, it seemed in rays,
> A childish face, but wise with woman's wit,
> And something, too, pathetic in its gaze.'

The poet falls in love with her at first sight. Later in the evening he meets her again coming out of the theatre where she is playing the heroine in *Manon Lescaut*. They wander together throught the streets, his love for her increasing with every step. They go to a house where she is lodging and there make love:

> 'Life has given me much
> And pleasure much, and Heaven may yet have store
> Of nobler hopes to kindle and to touch,
> But never for all time, ah, never more,
> That delicate dawn of wonder when lips move
> First to the love of life and love of love.'

For three days the enchantment lasts – three days only and then they have to part:

> 'This was my term of glory. All who know
> Something of life will guess untold the end.'

Whether in Paris or in London, Skittles was surrounded by a group of men of fashion and wit who idolized her. Her Sunday parties in Chesterfield Street and then in South Street, off Park Lane, were frequented by the Prince of Wales and other leading members of London Society. In public she was always to be seen leading the fashion, whether by riding a horse in Rotten Row that no one else could ride, or by driving the ponies of her phaeton, or by roller-skating with inimitable grace on the new rinks of London and Tunbridge Wells that were opened in the 1880s when the sport arrived from the United States.

It was not only her physical attractions – her small head with its bright chestnut hair, her delicate features, large grey-blue eyes, slender figure and beautiful hands – that made her so

charming and exciting. She had a superabundant vitality and
zest for life that electrified all around her and made even the
slothful feel that they were in the presence of enchantment. And
with this vitality went a pride and waywardness that made her,
in Blunt's phrase, 'brave as a falcon and as merciless'. Her mood
would change from grave to gay, from laughter to tears, like
the wind chasing across a summer pond.

To this infinite variety of glorious womanhood was added a
sense of humour that was charmingly vulgar and racy:

> 'She went on talking like a running stream,
> Without more reason or more pause or stay
> Than to gather breath and then pursue her whim
> Just where it led her, tender, sad or gay.'

And her interests were wider than the latest dress or social
foible. She was interested in modern art, knew something of
music, liked serious reading. In everything she said and did she
was candid and entertaining. She may have been no paragon
of virtue in the eyes of the respectables but to her many friends
and lovers she was without equal. Perhaps the greatest testimony
to her charm is that even those like Blunt who ceased to be her
lovers remained her devoted friends.

Prima Donnas, White Satin, and Dollymops

According to Bracebridge Hemyng the kept mistresses, of whom
Laura Bell and Skittles were the stars, were usually uneducated
women, although, as he admitted, 'they undeniably have
ability'. Their accomplishments were in the main entirely
superficial and their disposition was to be mercurial and thoughtless 'which qualities are, of course, at variance with the existence of respectability'. They were recruited from a class where
education was not much in vogue. 'The fallacies about clergymen's daughters and girls from the middle classes forming the
majority of such woman are long ago exploded; there may be
some amongst them, but they are few and far between.' Most of
them were not ashamed of their way of living and looked forward to marriage and a 'certain state in society as their ultimate
lot'.

One of these 'seclusives' told Hemyng her life history. She
was the daughter of a Yarmouth tradesman. She was twenty-
three and had been seduced when she was nineteen. 'I tell you

candidly,' she said, 'I was as much to blame as my seducer; I wanted to escape from the drudgery of my father's shop.' She was partly educated, could 'cypher a little, and knew something about the globes', so she thought she was qualified for something better than minding the shop occasionally, or sewing or helping her mother in the kitchen. She was very fond of dress and at home could not gratify her love of display. Her parents, she said, were 'stupid, easy-going old people and extremely uninteresting'. Together these various causes induced her to encourage the addresses of 'the young gentleman of property in the neighbourhood and without much demur' she yielded to his desires. They went to London together but got tired of each other in six months. 'I was as eager to leave him as he was to get rid of me.' Since then she had lived with four different men. She occasionally sent money to her parents, who chose not to know what she was doing, although 'if they had any penetration they might very well guess'. She was not at all tired of what she was doing. On the contrary she rather liked it. 'I have all I want, and my friend loves me to excess.' When Hemyng asked her what she thought would become of her she answered, 'What an absurd question. I could marry tomorrow if I liked.'

The second sort of 'seclusives', the prima donnas, were not kept like the mistresses, although several of their admirers were in the habit of visiting them periodically. 'From these they derive a considerable revenue, but by no means rely entirely upon it for support. They are continually increasing the number of their friends, which is indeed imperatively necessary as absence and various causes thin their ranks considerably.' What these causes were Hemyng did not say, but they may well have included venereal disease, which was rampant.

The prima donnas were to be seen in the parks, in boxes at the theatres, at concerts, and almost everywhere where fashionable people congregated. 'At night their favourite rendezvous is in the neighbourhood of the Haymarket, where the hospitality of Mrs Kate Hamilton is extended to them after the fatigues of dancing at the Portland Rooms[1] or the excesses of a private party. Kate may be visited not only to dissipate ennui, but with a view to replenishing an exhausted exchequer, for as Kate is careful as to who she admits into her rooms – men who are able

[1] In Foley Street, north of Regent (now Oxford) Circus, also known as Mott's.

to spend, and come with the avowed intention of spending five or six pounds or perhaps more if necessary – these supper-rooms are frequented by a better set of men and women than perhaps any other in London.'

Although they were usually found at Kate Hamilton's, which was one of the most famous night-houses of the time, the prima donnas did not go into any of the cafés in the Haymarket or the neighbouring supper-rooms, nor would they go to any casino other than Mott's. Between three and five in the afternoon they would wander in the Burlington Arcade. If their signals were responded to they would glide into a friendly bonnet shop and mount the stairs to the upper rooms. The park was another favourite promenade for picking up clients. Some of them would do this on horseback, which was said to be frequently more successful than on foot. Hemyng found it difficult to define the social position from which these women came 'but generally their standing in Society has been inferior'. Probably they were tradesmen's daughters or girls who had been apprenticed in shops in fashionable localities and who had got tired of the endless drudgery and had exchanged it for the glitter of the dancing saloons. 'Loose women generally throw a veil over their early life,' wrote Hemyng, 'and you seldom, if ever, meet with a woman who is not either a seduced governess or a clergyman's daughter; not that there is a word of truth in such an allegation – but it is their peculiar whim to say so.'

The next category described by Hemyng were the 'convives' – those who lived in the same house as a number of others, but who were not under the control of the mistress of the house. The chief stamping-grounds of these women were in the vicinity of the Haymarket and they operated at night, after the theatres and casinos were shut. They were charged exorbitantly for the rooms they occupied and their landlords defended themselves for making these high charges by alleging that as their lodgers were not notably honest they were compelled to compensate themselves for moonlight flits in this way. 'A drawing-room floor in Queen Street, Windmill Street, which is a favourite part on account of its proximity to the Argyll Rooms, is worth three and sometimes four pounds a week.' The convives did not live together because of any gregarious instinct but simply from necessity, because their trade excluded them from respectable lodging-houses. One of their most remarkable characteristics,

Hemyng found, was their generosity towards each other. Sometimes they were employed by café-keepers in the Haymarket to sit gorgeously dressed behind the counters as bait.

One convive interviewed by Hemyng described the pattern of her life. 'If I have not letters to write or visits from any of my friends I get up about four o'clock, dress and dine. After that I may walk about the streets for an hour or two and pick up anyone I am fortunate enough to meet with, that is if I want money. Afterwards I go to Holborn, dance a little, and if anyone likes me I take him home with me, if not I go to the Haymarket and wander from one café to the other, from Sally's to the Carlton, from Barnes's to Sam's, and if I find no one there I go, if I feel inclined, to the Divans.'

The Argyll Rooms and the Holborn were the principal dancing-rooms of London. According to William Acton in the 1870 edition of his book on *Prostitution* there was formerly a striking difference between these two casinos, the one catering for the upper, the other for the under current of fast life. But by 1870 this distinction had disappeared. The Argyll, on a site at what a hundred years later was the Piccadilly Circus end of Shaftesbury Avenue,[1] and the Holborn, near High Holborn, were both spacious sets of rooms with brilliant gas illuminations reflected by numerous mirrors, which were open for music and dancing every evening except Sunday from half past eight to twelve. Although, according to Acton, all the women were prostitutes, 'for the most part pretty, and quietly, though expensively dressed', not all the men were there to indulge their 'vicious propensities'; the majority of those of the better class were simply there to while away an idle hour chatting with friends in a place where they could 'hear good music and see pretty faces'.

The third category of prostitute were the board lodgers. These were the women who gave a part of what they earned to the mistress of the brothel in return for board and lodging. In many cases they had to give not a part but the whole of their earnings for board, lodging and clothes.

In Lambeth there were great numbers of the lowest sort of

---

[1] A frequenter of the Argyll Rooms in the late 1860s, whose ghost visited the immediate district a hundred years later, might have been initially surprised at the fashions and the beat of the music but the rest of the entertainment would have been familiar.

brothel. Around the Waterloo Road area the villainy and horror of prostitution were appalling. However, the difficulties and expense of bringing legal action against the men and women who kept these brothels in the lower depths were such that only seldom did complaints come before the courts. The effect even of successful prosecutions was a mere drop in the ocean of crime and depravity. The disgusting rookeries in the back streets off the Waterloo Road were black labyrinths of mental and physical decomposition, the worst among the worst of London.

The higher sort of brothel was to be found in the streets round Langham Place, north of Regent (now Oxford) Circus. Hemyng reported an interview with a girl living in one.

Her life as she described it was one of absolute slavery. She was seldom if ever allowed to go out and then not without being watched in case she should try to 'cut it'. The house she was in was rather popular and they had lots of clients. She had some particular ones who always came to see her. They paid her well but she hardly ever got any of the money. 'But what's the odds,' she shrugged. 'I can't go out and spend it and what would I want with money except now and then for a drain of white satin?'

'What's white satin?' Hemyng asked.

'Where have you been all your life to ask such a question? Are you a dodger?' [a parson].

She was glad to hear he was not.

'Well, white satin, if you must know, is gin, and don't say I never taught you anything.'

She had been born in Stepney somewhere. What did it matter exactly where? She didn't care to say. She was 'ticed when she was young – that is, decoyed by the mistress of the house. She met the woman in the street who talked to her in a friendly way, asked her where she lived, who her father was (he was a journeyman carpenter), and extracted all the information she could about her and then asked her home to tea. The child, delighted at making the acquaintance of so kind and well-dressed a lady, went willingly as she never dreamt of anything wrong happening and had never been cautioned by her father. Her mother had been dead for some years. She had not been brought direct to the house where she was now. Oh no. There was a branch establishment over the water [across the Thames] where the girls were broken in. She'd been kept there for two or three months and then when her spirit was broken she was moved from the first house to a more aristocratic neighbourhood.

How had they tamed her and broken her spirit?

Oh, they'd made her drunk and then given her some papers to sign which she knew gave them great powers over her although she did not know exactly what. Then they clothed her and fed her and gradually inured her to the sort of life they wanted her to lead.

'And now,' she concluded, 'is there anything else you'd like to know particularly, because if there is you'd better look sharp about asking it as I'm getting tired of talking, I can tell you.'

'Do you expect to go on living this life till you die?'

'Well I never. If you ain't going to preachify. I can't stand that – anything but that.'

Hemyng apologized and assured her that he was not inquiring from the religious point of view or from any motive other than curiosity.

The girl thought him a very inquisitive old party. Still, as he was so polite she didn't mind answering his questions. Would she stick it till she was a stiff'un? She supposed she would. What else was there for her? Perhaps something might turn up. How was she to know? She lived in the present and never went blubbering about as some did. She tried to be as jolly as she could; where was the fun of being miserable?

Another woman Hemyng interviewed told a story that was much of a pattern. She was seduced, had a child, was given fifty pounds by her seducer and deserted by him. Unable to return to her friends she supported herself and the child after the money was gone by doing machine-work for a manufacturer. Bad times came, she was thrown out of work, and the child starved to death 'by inches before her face'. While he was alive she could not bring herself to go on the streets to save his life or her own. But when he died she became 'half mad and three parts drunk after the parish burying', and she went on the streets at last. Smiling sarcastically she said:

'Then I rose in the world and I've lived in this house for years, but I swear to God I haven't had a moment's happiness since the child died, except when I've been half drunk or maudlin.'

Hemyng's comment on this sad biography was that, although the woman did not look upon the death of her child as a crime committed by herself, nevertheless it undoubtedly was. 'She shunned the workhouse which might have done something for her and saved the life, at all events, of her child; but the repugnance evinced by every woman who has any proper feeling for a life in a workhouse or a hospital can hardly be imagined by those who think that, because people are poor, they must lose all feeling, all delicacy, all prejudice and all shame.' Those who did think so were in fact the vast majority of the respectables of Britain.

Even in the West End 'where vice is pampered and caressed' there were low lodging-houses in the small streets between Covent Garden and the Strand and in one or two streets running off Oxford Street. These were no better than the dens in Waterloo Road and Lambeth, or farther east in Whitechapel, Wapping and Ratcliff Highway.

Hemyng divided the low street-walkers into a number of categories. There were sailors' women, soldiers' women ('There is not much to be said about soldiers' women. They are simply low and cheap, often diseased, and as a class do infinite harm to the health of the service'), thieves' women, and park women.

The park women were 'those degraded creatures, utterly lost to all sense of shame, who wander about the paths most frequented after nightfall in the parks and consent to any species of humiliation for the sake of acquiring a few shillings . . . These women are well-known to give themselves up to disgusting practices that are alone gratifying to men of morbid and diseased imaginations. They are old, unsound, and by their appearance utterly incapacitated from practising their profession where the gas lamps would expose the defects in their personal appearance and the shabbiness of their ancient and dilapidated attire.' One park woman told of her husband being bedridden, so helpless that he 'can't do nothink but give the babies a dose of "Mother's Blessing" (that's laudanum, sir, or some sich stuff) to sleep 'em when they's squally'.

Sometimes the street-walkers came to a violent end. In 1888 the country, including the Queen herself, was shaken by the butchery of five prostitutes off the Commercial Road in the East End of London. Their murderer, Jack the Ripper, was never caught.

Another class that Hemyng distinguished was the clandestine prostitute or, what a later age has called, the enthusiastic amateur. These included female operatives, maidservants, more commonly known as 'dollymops', and ladies of intrigue 'who see men to gratify their passions'. This clandestine prostitution was, in Hemyng's opinion, the most serious side of prostitution. 'A thousand and one causes may lead to a woman's becoming a professional prostitute, but if a woman goes wrong without any cogent reason for doing so, there must be something radically wrong in her composition and inherently bad in her nature to lead her to abandon her person to the other sex, who are at all times ready to take advantage of a woman's witness and a woman's love.' Ignoring – unless he was ignorant of – the country custom which the *Saturday Review* had discussed, Hemyng continued, 'There is a tone of morality throughout the rural districts of England, which is unhappily wanting in the large towns and the centres of particular manufactures. Commerce is incontestably demoralizing. Its effects are to be seen more and more every day. Why it should be so it is not our province to discuss, but seduction and prostitution, in spite of the precepts of the Church, and the examples of her ministers, have made enormous strides in all our great towns within the last twenty years.'

Hemyng believed, along with many other Victorian respectables, that female operatives – in which definition he included almost all women working for a living from milliners to ballet girls – were by their nature unchaste and in the habit of prostituting themselves either for money 'or more frequently for their own gratification'. Female servants too were considered 'far from being a virtuous class'. They were badly educated and not at all well looked after by their mistresses as a rule, 'although every dereliction from the paths of propriety by them will be visited with the heaviest displeasure and most frequently be followed by dismissal of the most summary description'. Dereliction was always cropping up. 'In small families the servants often give themselves up to the sons, or to the policeman on the beat, or to soldiers in the parks, or else to shopmen whom they meet in the streets.'

The Sin Fighters and the Rescuers
In the preface to the fourth volume of Mayhew's *London Labour*

and the London Poor, the Reverend William Tuckniss listed the agencies in London concerned with the suppression of vice and crime. He divided them into four categories: curative; preventive; repressive and punitive; and reformative.

Religion occupied the foremost place in the curative category. The preventive agencies, which included the temperance associations, were those whose object it was to remove 'peculiar forms of temptation, or to abridge the power of special producing causes of vice'. Two sorts of working women stood in great need of the help of preventive agencies: servants and dressmakers. Of 100,000 female domestics in London 10,000 were continually in transition from one job to another, and were in need of temporary homes. The Female Servant's Home Society, founded in 1837, was one of the first to provide them. In 1861 it had four homes. A kindred institution was the Female Aid Society founded in 1836, and there were half a dozen other institutions for 'the accommodation, temporary relief and permanent benefit' of servants. All were habitually short of funds.

The dressmakers were still in as sore straits as they had been when the *Illuminated Magazine* published 'Death and the Drawing-Room': 'white slaves' who were 'shamefully underpaid and cruelly overworked'. Two agencies formed to help them were the Association for the Aid and Benefit of Dressmakers and Milliners, and the Needlewomen's Institution, which was established in 1850. The first of these, according to Tuckniss, was 'a noble breakwater against the inroads of oppression and a valuable counteracting agency to the force of temptation'.

Another institution then recently established was the Young Women's Christian Association and West London Home, which was concerned with the religious and social improvement of young women engaged in business houses. The Y.W.C.A.'s rooms were open every evening from seven until ten, during which time educational and religious classes were held. 'The better to appreciate the importance of this noble and truly womanly enterprise,' said a contemporary pamphlet on the origin and aim of the Y.W.C.A., 'only let the solemn and fearful fact be borne in mind that in London alone a thousand girls are yearly crushed out of life from overtoil and grinding oppression, while 15,000 are living in a state of semi-starvation. Ah, who can wonder that our streets swarm with the fallen and the lost when SIN OR STARVE is the dire alternative! We cannot track the *via doloroso* between the 15,000 starving and the thrice that number living by sin as a trade.' Tuckniss was among those who believed that an increasing opportunity for earning their living in the 'paths of honest industry' would help young women to resist the strong temptation 'to abandon themselves to a life of criminal ease and self-indulgence'.

In Tuckniss's third category of repressive and punitive agencies, as well as the Society for the Suppression of Vice established in 1802, there was the Associate Institution formed in 1844 to improve and enforce the laws for the protection of women. It maintained a strenuous crusade against houses of ill-fame, and in the first fifteen years of its existence brought 300 prosecutions against those who had committed criminal assaults on women and children or who had decoyed them away for immoral purposes. In most of these prosecutions it was successful. In 1861 two Bills prepared by the Associate Institution were submitted to Parliament – one for the protection of girls between the ages of twelve and thirteen; the second to simplify and facilitate the prosecutions of persons charged with keeping houses of ill-fame. Both Bills were lost, on technical grounds and for want of support.

The fourth category included twenty-one reformative agencies in London whose particular object was the 'rescue and reformation of fallen women or such as have been led astray from the paths of virtue'. Ten of them were in connection with the Church of England, the remainder were evangelical or unsectarian. Altogether the twenty-one could provide accommodation for about 1,200 women and girls. The Female Temporary Home, the Trinity Home, and the Home of Hope were three designed for the reception of 'the better educated and higher class of fallen women'. Another – the London Society for the Protection of Young Females – was limited to girls under fifteen years of age. And yet another, the Marylebone Female Protection Society, afforded 'shelter exclusively to those who have recently been led astray and whose previous good character will bear the strictest investigation'. The Marylebone Female Protection Society was run by three ladies, Miss Marsh, Mrs Wightman and Mrs Sheppard. Most of the reformative agencies, as indeed most of the agencies in the other categories, had a high percentage of women among their directing and operating staff, for this was one of the ways in which women's philanthropic work had developed.

The oldest reformatory institution in London for the reception of fallen women was the Magdalen Hospital, founded in 1758. But the rescue of fallen women was not a pursuit that recommended itself strongly to early Victorian or, for that matter, eighteenth-century sentiment. Over fifty years elapsed after the foundation of the Magdalen Hospital before any similar institution was established. In the 1850s, however, public attention, under the influence of evangelicalism and the strengthening of social feminism, became directed with increasing interest to the subject and efforts then began to be made to provide accommodation on a wider scale for those who wanted to escape from the misery that had befallen them. The London by Moonlight Mission which had been launched earlier in the century by Lieutenant Blackmore was followed in Tuckniss's day by the Reverend Baptist Noel's Midnight Meeting Movement, which operated in many other large towns as well as in London. Street meetings were held at which tracts were distributed and invitations handed out to a 'Morality Tea' where the evils of prostitution were denounced against a background of hymns, cakes and cups of tea. Tuckniss reported that at the time he was writing twenty-two of these meetings had been held in London attended by more than 4,000 women of whom about 600 had been rescued and either restored to their friends or placed in situations 'where they are giving satisfactory evidence of outward reformation and many of them of a thorough change of character'. But another report, quoted by Cyril Pearl,[1] said that 'after holding twenty meetings, preaching the gospel to 4,000 girls and circulating 23,000 scripture cards, tracts and sermons, the Mission was able to report that upwards of thirty girls have given evidence of a change of heart'.

As a nucleus of reformative operations and a centre of information and encouragement, the Reformatory and Refuge Union was established in 1856, and in conjunction with it was a Female Mission which maintained a staff of female missionaries whose business it was to distribute tracts among the 'fallen women of the metropolis', to talk to them in the streets, and to visit them in their houses, in the hospitals or in the workhouses. These

[1] Cyril Pearl, *The Girl With The Swansdown Seat*, p. 49.

missionaries 'as a rule', reported Tuckniss, 'leave their homes between eight and nine o'clock at night, remaining out till nearly twelve, and occasionally till one in the morning. They are located in different parts of London near to the nightly walks and haunts of those they desire to benefit. They have been the means of rescuing a large number who have been placed in the Homes or restored to their friends'. Rescue work and the provision of Homes for the fallen was not confined to the large towns, nor was it carried out only by organized societies. Some ladies saw it as their Christian duty to save local girls. Lady Sitwell, widow of Sir Reresby Sitwell and grandmother of Edith, Osbert and Sacheverell, started a Home in Scarborough. To keep the number of inmates up to full establishment a method somewhat similar to the Midnight Meeting Movement's was adopted. Lady Sitwell would drive round Scarborough with Archdeacon Blunt, cornering likely subjects and inviting them to tea at Wood End, her Scarborough house. Her sixteen-year-old daughter Florence recorded one such tea-party which she watched surreptitiously on August 24, 1874. Four 'bad girls', as she called them, turned up; one left immediately, while the others were talked to individually and earnestly by the frosty Archdeacon, one agreeing to enter the Home. Flo and her cousin Grace were in a great state of excitement peering at these 'bad girls' from behind curtains in the library as they walked in the garden with Lady Sitwell and the Archdeacon.[1]

---

[1] There is an *envoi* to the Home in Dame Edith Sitwell's autobiography *Taken Care Of* (Hutchinson, 1965), pp. 66–7, where she recounts that the first thing that happened to those young persons who agreed to enter the Home was that they were given a bath and then next morning dressed in the uniform of the Home, 'hideous navy-blue coats and skirts, and boots like those worn by policemen in years past'. With this they wore shapeless navy-blue felt hats. On one occasion one of the young persons who had what John Knox called 'a deplorable state of joyosity' was brought to the Home and steadfastly refused to have a bath. Nothing would persuade the young person to have a bath. Some time later it was discovered that every single inmate of the Home was pregnant. 'My grandmother, smoothing down her gloves, said that this phenomenon was no doubt due to the transit of Venus.' But in the presence of Lady Sitwell the matron caught, and succeeded in disrobing the non-bather, whereupon it was discovered that the pregnancies were not in any way due to the transit of Venus but were caused by the fact that the latest recruit was a flippant young man who had taken a dislike to the frost-bitten Archdeacon and had used this method of discomfiting him.

The largest association in London for the reformation of fallen women at the time Tuckniss was writing was the Society for the Rescue of Young Women and Children, of which he was chaplain. Started in 1853 the Society by 1861 had eleven homes in various parts of London and one at Dover. The choice of Dover as a location is evidence of the considerable white slave traffic that was going on at that time, and for another twenty-five years at least, to equip the brothels of Belgium with young girls. Nor was the traffic only one way. The Rev. T. Garnier, rector of Trinity Church, Marylebone, reported to the annual meeting of his mission in 1859 about the importation of prostitutes from across the Channel and described a room where the girls were auctioned. And there was a reciprocal traffic in young girls of about fifteen or sixteen between Liverpool and Hamburg through the port of Hull. It was this trade with the Continent which, as we shall see in a later chapter, Mrs Josephine Butler, with the help of W. T. Stead, editor of the *Pall Mall Gazette*, attacked so effectively in the 1880s.

As Wilkie Collins said, sex was swarming everywhere.

Chapter 14

MRS BUTLER'S CRUSADE

The prevalence of prostitution created a strong body of opinion in favour of regulation. It was felt that without an Act of Parliament to enforce medical inspection of prostitutes, venereal disease would continue to spread until it had infected large sectors of the nation. Those in favour of regulation, including William Acton, claimed that the evil effects of unregulated prostitution could be seen most strikingly in the army. Syphilis was particularly prevalent among soldiers. In his book on prostitution Acton gave statistics to demonstrate that syphilis was the British soldier's worst enemy. Reports on the sickness, mortality and invaliding of troops in the United Kingdom, the Mediterranean and British America presented to Parliament in 1839 had shown that over a seven-year period one soldier in five had been attacked by the disease. Figures for later years showed that between 1837 and 1847, out of every thousand cavalrymen 206 were infected, 250 per thousand footguards, and 277 per thousand infantrymen. And the incidence of the disease continued to mount. In the second edition of his book, published in 1870, Acton showed that contagious, that is venereal, disease was two-and-a-half times as common in the British army as it was in the French. The lowest rate in European armies was the Prussian with 62 per thousand infected as against 258 per thousand – over one quarter! – in the British.

These figures were the basis of the argument for legislation. A committee appointed by the Secretary of State for War and the Board of Admiralty in 1864 to report on the best means of protecting the army and navy from the ravages of venereal disease were convinced by Acton who later claimed 'without vanity' to have thus helped to pave the way for legislation. The

232

committee's recommendation resulted in the passage of a temporary Contagious Diseases Act that same year. Previous Acts of this nature had applied to animals only; now women were also liable to inspection if it was thought they were diseased. The Act applied to eleven garrison towns only. Any medical practitioner, superintendent or inspector of police could lay an information before a Justice of the Peace against any woman believed to be a common prostitute, whom he suspected of having a contagious disease. The Justice then served the woman with a notice requiring her to appear before him in order that the truth of the information might be inquired into. If the information was substantiated to the Justice's satisfaction the woman was ordered to submit to a medical examination at a hospital and if this examination proved the correctness of the information that she was diseased, she was ordered to be detained at the hospital until she was cured, although in no case was she to be detained for longer than three months. If she refused to be examined or to conform to the rules of the hospital, or if she left before she was discharged, she was liable to imprisonment for up to two months. Periodical examinations of all registered prostitutes were held in the various districts specified in the Act.

In 1866 a second Act was passed to extend and strengthen the original scheme, and on August 11, 1868 a third Contagious Diseases Act became law. In all, eighteen places in the United Kingdom were made subject to the C.D. Acts. They were: Aldershot, Canterbury, Chatham, Colchester, Dover, Gravesend, Maidstone, Plymouth and Devonport, Portsmouth, Sheerness, Shorncliffe, Southampton, Winchester, Windsor, and an area round Woolwich; in Ireland, the Curragh, Cork, and Queenstown. In all these places a list of registered prostitutes was kept. In Aldershot, for example, in June 1869 there were 243 on the list and 12,000 troops. Some of the women had twenty or more men in a night. The Acts also applied to places like Malta where there were British garrisons, and an Order in Council of 1866 authorized the regulation of prostitution in British cantonments in India.

The decision as to whether a woman was believed to be a common prostitute or not depended entirely on the opinion of the police officer making the arrest. The abuses that could result from this were obvious – especially as the Acts established a special police force, centrally appointed and not under the control of the local authority as were the ordinary police. These men, who did not wear uniform, made and kept the list of recognized prostitutes. If they had 'good cause to believe' a woman was a prostitute they could arrest her. But there was no liability on the police to prove 'good cause', nor was there any definition of prostitution. Even if a woman were found innocent after arrest, the arrest itself was enough to ruin her. The opponents of the Acts pointed out, exaggeratedly it is true, that no woman was safe from arrest as a common prostitute in any of the areas to which the Acts applied. The special police had immense power that could be exercised on mere whim, or more likely, for vicious spite.

Apart from possible corruption in administering the Acts, there were other reasons for antagonism. Firstly, the Acts were held to be a gross interference with the liberty of the subject; and secondly, and even more strongly felt, they were held to violate Christian moral principles, because their existence meant that prostitution was recognized by the State. Linked with this was the third and possibly the most implacable strand of antagonism: that the Contagious Diseases Acts were 'an outrage on the sacred rights of womanhood'. These were the words of Mrs Josephine Butler who led the crusade for the repeal of the Acts.

'... the Whole Question as One'

Josephine was born in 1828, the seventh child of John and Hannah Grey. The Greys were one of the great Border families. They had three branches: the Greys of Howick, the Greys of Fallodon, and the Greys of Milfield. From Howick came the Grey who carried the Reform Bill of 1832; from Fallodon came the Grey, born in 1862, who was to be Secretary of State for Foreign Affairs from 1905 to 1916; and from Milfield came the Grey whom many consider to have been the greatest of all those remarkable women – Nightingale, Garrett, Jex-Blake, Hill, Beale, Buss, Davies, Clough – whose work revolutionized the opportunities for women in the Victorian age. 'Of all the women engaged in fighting for the woman's cause,' says her biographer, 'she alone saw the whole question as one. She alone perceived that the various things for which women were asking could be comprised in the simple demand that a woman should be regarded as an individual with needs and rights like any other human being – the right to work, to be regarded as equal with men in the eyes of the law, to share with men the responsibility of making the conditions in which both must live.'[1]

Both Josephine's parents were passionate believers in the importance of freedom and the hatefulness of injustice. John Grey supported his kinsman over the Reform Bill, supported the repeal of the Corn Laws, the reform of the Poor Law, the movement for educating the people. Above all he supported the abolition of the slave trade, for which he had been fired with hatred by his mother. It was in this tradition of reform and liberty that Josephine was brought up. Added to it was an eclectic, informal education that derived from her parents encouraging her to take an interest in the things they themselves were doing and thinking about; not for her the rote of Mangnall's catechism. She was musical and played the piano with unusual skill. And she was deeply religious.

In 1851 Josephine and her younger sister Hattie went to London to see the Great Exhibition. For part of the time they stayed with their cousin Charles Grey, who was equerry to Prince Albert. Great was Josephine's joy when Charles Grey bought a Broadwood Grand at the Exhibition and, in January 1852, gave it to her as a wedding present, when she married George Butler in Corbridge Parish Church, Northumberland.

Josephine had met Butler in 1850 when he was a lecturer at Durham University. Like his wife's family he was a hater of injustice, and a Liberal. His own family was a scholastic one. His father had been headmaster of Harrow and he and his three brothers all became eminent in the same profession, one becoming headmaster of Harrow like his father, another becoming headmaster of Haileybury, and George himself becoming principal of Liverpool College. Between Durham and Liverpool, however, came appointments at Oxford and Cheltenham. Immediately after their marriage Josephine and George Butler moved to Oxford, where George had been appointed Examiner to the University. They stayed there until 1857 when the effect of the damp Oxford climate on Josephine's weak lungs made it essential for them to move. They went to Cheltenham where George Butler accepted the post of vice-principal of Cheltenham College. Here in 1864, the year of the first Contagious Diseases Act that applied to women, the

[1] E. Moberly Bell, *Josephine Butler, Flame of Fire* (Constable, 1962), p. 12.

Butlers suffered a traumatic experience. Their only daughter, aged five, fell to her death from a landing as she ran forward to greet them on their return home one evening.

A change of scene seemed all that could save Josephine's health from complete breakdown, especially as immediately after little Eva's death she had to nurse her second son, Stanley, through diphtheria. In 1865 Butler was offered the principalship of Liverpool College and gladly accepted it. Josephine, to her surprise, found that Liverpool did not offer the friendly community life she had been used to in Oxford and Cheltenham. When her husband and sons had left for school in the morning she found herself with the blankness of an empty day ahead of her; neither her piano, nor her books, nor her paintbox could fill the hours or still the gnawing sense of sorrow over Eva. To help herself she determined to help others.

The contrast between the two nations was as tragically marked in Liverpool as in any other city in the kingdom. A great seaport filled with immigrant Irish provided the environment for poverty and distress on a monstrous scale. This pullulating misery created dark feelings of guilt which the well-off endeavoured to exorcize by innumerable charities. So chaotic did the charitable effort become that William Rathbone, mayor of the city, conceived the idea of centralizing all the charitable funds and administering them by a joint committee. In London, too, in 1869, the London Charity Organization Society was founded to rationalize and put on a business basis the scattered efforts of innumerable private charities. Part of the Charity Organization Society's dogma was that it was wrong to make gifts in cash or kind to supplement the earnings of the poor, because this would lead to the undermining of self-reliance and the exacerbation of poverty, rather than to any improvement in social welfare. Every man, it was maintained, had a fair chance of making his way and looking after his family if he worked diligently and spent and saved responsibly. The Charity Organization Society's outlook was austere. Rehabilitation not relief was the key. And there must be discrimination between the deserving and the undeserving poor. The unregenerate must be cast aside; the rest disciplined into self-help. It was an approach that was much admired among those in America who were drawn to charity organization in the 1870s and 1880s, and it was a similar stern approach that had informed the

Sanitary Commission during the Civil War. Irresponsible benevolence, as the Sanitary Commission termed it, was the enemy of efficient welfare work. 'Neither humanity nor charity' was the Sanitary Commission's aim, but 'to economize for the National Service the life and strength of the National soldier'. In 1872 Louisa Lee Schuyler left the Sanitary Commission to start the New York State Charities Aid Association, which opposed public relief as 'undermining the self-respect of recipients, fostering a spirit of dependence opposed to self-support, and interfering with the laws governing wages and labour'. And ten years later Josephine Shaw, whose husband and brother were killed in the Civil War, helped to found the New York Charity Organization Society.

But the stern, unfeminine philosophy of the Charity Organization approach had no appeal for the other Josephine, for Josephine Butler. Nor indeed did it have appeal for some men, among them Charles Booth who, born and brought up in Liverpool, was, at the very time Josephine Butler was searching for a way to help others in the city, himself being robbed of his peace of mind by the extent of Liverpool's poverty, which he found impossible to reconcile with the wealth of its middle and upper classes. For Booth the answer proved to be a contribution of enormous importance to public life and to sociology. Unable to refute the argument of the Charity Organization approach by using its own language which had the 'common-sense' support of the time, he set out to refute it by demonstrating the facts, by analysing in the greatest detail what was for him the Problem of all Problems – poverty. For Josephine Butler the beginning of the answer proved to lie in the Brownlow Hill Workhouse, a grim prison-like building where the derelicts of society were kept alive in the most unpleasant and uncomfortable surroundings, so that none should choose State charity if they could avoid it. Here she joined some two hundred women and girls in the oakum sheds, becoming their friend and tearing her fingers as she untwisted the tarry ropes.

As well as visiting at the workhouse, she went to the Infirmary and moved about the quays and streets. Among the many women she met was one young girl who had gone on the streets after being seduced and deserted. The girl had got venereal disease and had drifted in and out of the workhouse. Unable to return home because her parents were 'too respectable' to receive her she was befriended by Josephine and taken into the Butlers' home, where she stayed until she died after being reconciled with her family through the Butlers' initiative. Mary was the first of many such guests whom the Butlers received over the years.

From Mary and the oakum sheds the road to the attack on the Contagious Diseases Acts took three years for Josephine Butler to travel. During this time she extended her rescue work and became actively concerned in improving employment opportunities and providing higher education for women. She filled the dry cellar and the attics of her house with sick prostitutes. She opened a Home of Rest for others near by. She established an Industrial Home where those who were not sick could live. She started a sewing workroom where she paid the girls 6d a day, and a small envelope factory to give employment to a few others. She was in touch with other rescue homes like those started in London by Mrs Gladstone. And in 1866 she met Jemima Clough who had come to Liverpool from Cambridge seeking support for the higher education of women. Josephine's attitude to this, somewhat surprisingly perhaps in view of her uncompromising approach to the repeal of the Contagious Diseases Acts, was the same as Miss Clough's and different from Emily Davies's 'all or nothing' principle. She did not demand that women be allowed to sit the same examinations as men and she was opposed to a frontal attack on the universities, which, she felt, would only make them determined to keep women out altogether. In the introduction to a volume of essays on *Woman's Work and Woman's Culture*, collected by her and published in 1869, she wrote that she wanted to lift the discussion of women's education from 'the flippant and heartless treatment, and from the exaggerated and too passionate advocacy, to which it may have been subjected on the one hand and the other'. She refused to accept that men and women were engaged in a never-ending struggle against each other. Their interests were supplementary, not antagonistic. Society could only benefit if they worked together and if women were allowed to contribute their own share to the common effort. Thus, for instance, the depressed masses of the population – and these were ever in her mind as she saw the misery of Liverpool – could only be dealt with satisfactorily by a joint effort of men and women. The 'poor-peopling' approach was out of date. 'We have had experience of what we may call the feminine form of philanthropy, the independent individual ministering, of too medieval a type to suit the present day. It has failed. We are now about to try the masculine form of philanthropy, large and comprehensive measures, organizations and systems planned by men and sanctioned by Parliament. This also will fail.'

Josephine became the President of the North of England Council for the Higher Education of Women, and Jemima Clough became its Secretary. It was through the Council that Newnham College was founded. But that was after Josephine's connection with it had ceased. In 1870 she reluctantly resigned from its presidency in order, on the one hand not to compromise it by the stigma attached to the work on which she was now engaged, and on the other to devote herself entirely to that crusade.

Reglementation

Government regulation of prostitution was not peculiar to Britain, nor had it been initiated there. There was regulation in ancient times among the Greeks and Romans to prevent the religious, social, and political consequences of prostitution, which would otherwise have jeopardized the integrity of the family, the clan, and the city-state. At the beginning of the Middle Ages the states of Western Europe pursued a strictly repressive policy, as the Hebrews had done. By the tenth century, however, prostitution came to be tolerated and a set of regulations was gradually evolved to achieve three main aims. The first aim was to satisfy the lecherous impulse of the floating population in a city, so that the wives and daughters of the burghers would be safe and the family kept inviolate. The brothel, therefore, was not only tolerated but was considered a necessary social service in city life. Prostitutes were required to live in a special quarter and to wear a distinguishing mark, usually a yellow or red ribbon on their sleeve. As an American investigator of vice in New York wrote in 1901, 'there was no trace of the modern feeling that vice should be quite hidden from respectability, ignored by decent society . . . The Middle Ages believed vice to be nothing evil, so long as it showed its true colors.'[1]

The second aim of medieval regulation was to prevent the

[1] Alvin S. Johnson, *The Social Evil* (Putnam's, 1902), pp. 19–20.

brothel from becoming a centre of disorder. And the third aim
was the regulation of prostitution for fiscal purposes. Prostitutes
had to contribute to the public treasury, and even the Church
accepted revenue from them. As in Greek and Roman regulation, there was no hygienic consideration involved. But in the
later Middle Ages an epidemic of syphilis of plague proportions
spread throughout Europe, carried from city to city and family
to family as a result of the general 'permissiveness' of the age.
For a large part of the fifteenth and sixteenth centuries the
licensed brothels were generally closed because of this disease.

Modern regulation of prostitution reflected the extension of
the unit of society from the city to the nation, and then from the
nation to the Western nations as a whole. Whereas in medieval
times the prostitute was an alien who was imported into the city
to safeguard the virtuous, this alien character of prostitution
now disappeared because, in the final analysis, these victims of
vice must necessarily be recruited from within the new unit of
society itself. Furthermore, there was no longer the unchallenged
belief that the existence of a vicious class was indeed a safeguard for the virtuous. The consequence was that every modern
system of regulation in the nineteenth century avowed the
purpose of preventing, as far as possible, 'the degradation of
those who are not yet depraved, and the rescue and restoration
to honorable life of fallen women who are still susceptible to
moral influences'.[1] The main distinguishing feature of modern
regulation, however, was its hygienic or, to use the word most
favoured in the second half of the nineteenth century, its
sanitary aspect. Regulation was aimed at controlling and if
possible reducing venereal disease. Indeed the term 'regulation'
was used generally to denote sanitary regulation alone.

Modern regulation began in Paris at the latter end of the
eighteenth century, although the very beginnings of French
sanitary control can be traced back to 1684. By the end of the
Napoleonic régime the Paris police had established the system
which, after reorganization in 1843, ran for the rest of the
century – and beyond. Prostitution was confined to licensed
brothels or houses of accommodation and prostitutes were
obliged to submit themselves to frequent medical examinations.
Those found to be diseased were sent to the hospital of St
Lazare prison and kept there until they were cured. A list of

[1] ibid., p. 23.

15. *Top left:* The Morning Gossip by George Cruikshank. Domestic service was the chief occupation for employed women in England. *Right:* 'Women had been spinning since time immemorial.' Elizabeth Haldane, aged thirty-three, spinning wool, home-grown and home-carded. *Bottom:* 'By the end of the century the female agricultural labourer had almost disappeared' – except at harvest-time. *Country Camera.*

16. Eight of the nine Miss Potters, 1894. Beatrice (Mrs Webb since 1892) is in the centre of the centre row.

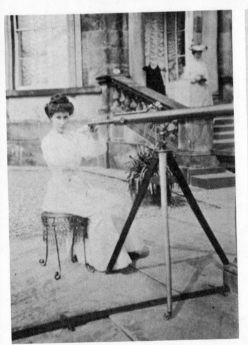

The astronomers were the first professional bodies to accept women members both in Britain and the United States. *Crow Collection. Right:* Theresa Yelverton (Viscountess Avonmore), one of the first of a redoubtable band of Victorian lady travellers.

prostitutes was kept by the Service des Moeurs, and the control of prostitution was carried out by a body of special agents who formed part of the general secret service. Clandestine prostitution was punished severely enough for it to be worthwhile for regular prostitutes to register themselves with the Service des Moeurs.

The Parisian system was the model for most of the systems in force in Europe. Practically all the cities and large towns of France had regulation, as did the cities of Belgium and Switzerland. German cities in the main followed the lead of Berlin, where there had been the modern type of regulation since 1700. In Berlin, unlike Paris, brothels were prohibited from January 1, 1846, but this difference was less significant than it appeared because less than one-tenth of Paris's 6,000 registered prostitutes lived in brothels.[1] Hungary had what was considered to be an efficient system; Austria one much less so. In Russian cities there were attempts to keep prostitution under sanitary control from about 1850 on. In Italy the larger cities had a system modelled on that of Brussels, itself taken from the Paris one, from the unification under Cavour until 1888. Only Norway, of the Scandinavian countries, did not regulate prostitution in their larger cities, and there was regulation in Spain and Portugal.

In Britain, as we have seen, the experiment of regulation began in 1864, when it had been quietly introduced under cover of the ambiguous description 'Contagious Diseases' which to many Members of Parliament seemed to imply just another regulation in the series about animals. The stealth with which the Bill was passed through Parliament was even abetted by those who suddenly woke up to its true purpose and were opposed to it. Prostitution existed – everyone knew that – every man at least; but it was not the sort of thing that should be discussed publicly, even in Parliament, in case a whisper of it sullied the innocence of wives and daughters. So in stealth the Bill was introduced, and in silence it was passed into law.

Not that the opposition to the introduction of the system had been entirely silent. In 1863 Harriet Martineau wrote four articles in the *Daily News* challenging those who favoured regulation, or reglementation as it was more generally called, to produce statistics showing that regulation did in fact lead to a diminution of venereal disease. None were forthcoming. She

[1] 6,000 was the 1897 figure.

also argued that regulation must have an evil effect on army morals because it gave recognition to vice as a necessity.

But the regulationists were no less sure of their ground despite their failure to publish convincing statistics. A British branch of the Continental Association for the Control of Prostitution by Government Regulation was started in 1866 with Dr Berkeley Hill as its Secretary. Within a short time his vigorous propaganda had resulted in forty-three branch associations throughout the country and from these branches came a succession of petitions to Parliament asking for the Contagious Diseases Acts to be extended to further districts. To demonstrate its aims its name was changed in May 1868 to the Association for Promoting the Extension of the Contagious Act of 1866 to the Civil Population of the United Kingdom. The timing of this change was determined by the report of a Select Committee of the House of Lords, which had been inquiring into the working of the Acts. Although the evidence put before the Committee could hardly be conclusive, nevertheless their Lordships were so impressed by the statistics presented to them about the improvement in the health of the armed forces and by 'proofs of the moral and religious effects upon the unfortunate young women themselves' that they recommended a cautious extension of the Acts. This was carried out in the third Contagious Diseases Act which became law on August 11, 1868.

As far as the Association for Promoting the Extension of the Act was concerned the new legislation fell far short of what was needed, for it merely brought some more garrison towns and naval stations and their surrounding areas into the sphere of reglementation. But when the Association's spokesmen continued their campaign they found that opposition to the Acts was mounting and was beginning to become organized. In Newcastle, the Reverend Dr Hooppell and in London Daniel Cooper, Secretary of the Rescue Society, and Professor Sheldon Amos, a jurist, were the leaders of this opposition, and by October 1869 they had achieved sufficient standing for *The Times*, a wholehearted supporter of the Acts, to report on the Social Science Congress at which three papers about the Acts had been read – two in favour and one against – that 'a large number of persons, many of them apparently clergymen, had come to the meeting with the express purpose of protesting against the Acts, and did so with the enthusiasm of those who fancied they saw in physical disease a Divine Judgment against moral transgression'. It was an agitation, suggested *The Times*, that would carry little weight with sober-minded men.

But in fact it did. The paper against the Acts had been read at the Social Science Congress by Dr Charles Bell Taylor of Nottingham, and he was not the only doctor who came out against regulation. This was important because up to then the medical profession as a whole, and very much including the newly qualified women doctors, were strongly in favour of the Acts. With the prestige of science at a high peak the yea or nay of the doctors was the word of the soothsayer.

The success of the opposition at the Social Science Congress made the organizers determine to start a National Association for the Abolition of the Acts. But who was to lead it? Among the abolitionists at the Congress was Miss Wolstenholme, prominent in the field of education and a north of England leader in the cause of women's rights. She knew Josephine Butler and it was she who proposed that Mrs Butler be invited to lead the campaign. Clearly she was the ideal person. She was married, and married to a man whose position was in itself a guarantee of probity. She was a rescue worker among the type of women who were subject to the Acts. She was a good speaker. And, most of all, she was a woman of great courage in whom there burnt the flame of the saint and the martyr.

Miss Wolstenholme sent a telegram to Josephine which was delivered to her at Dover as she returned from a holiday on the Continent. For days she was in torment. She felt compelled to accept the challenge that made the flame burn bright within her. It was God's work, for she believed without question that the Acts were inspired by the Devil. And yet . . . it was equally certain that the notoriety she would bring on her husband would ruin his career. But George Butler was no less heroic than his wife. When eventually she could bring herself to tell him of the torment in her mind, ending with the cry, 'I feel as if I must go out into the streets and cry aloud or my heart will break', he looked up at her as she stood near his study desk and said quietly, 'Go and God be with you'. Thus began what came to be called 'the revolt of women' but which to Josephine herself was 'the consecrated revolt'.

Chapter 15
'THE REVOLT OF WOMEN'

It was thirteen years before success was achieved. On December 31, 1869 the Ladies' National Association for Abolition published its Manifesto in the *Daily News* and the following day it was reprinted in the rest of the press. It listed eight objections to the Acts, primarily that they deprived women of their constitutional rights under Magna Carta and Habeas Corpus, the touchstones of the English rule of law. Also that everyone must be regarded as innocent until proved guilty, whereas under the Acts a woman was guilty unless she could prove herself innocent. Furthermore that it was manifestly unjust that only one person should be liable to punishment for an 'offence' which by its very nature involved two persons. These, as well as condemnation of 'official vice' because 'a moral restraint is withdrawn the moment the State recognizes, and provides convenience for, the practice of a vice which it thereby declares to be necessary and venial', were the arguments of the abolitionists. But their opponents, in order to discredit them, proclaimed that it was only sentimental pity for degraded women that inspired the 'shrieking sisterhood'. Those who were against the Contagious Diseases Acts, said the *Saturday Review* on January 1, 1870, were the sort of people who condemned lightning-conductors or safety-lamps on principle. And the following week it dismissed the whole idea of the Ladies' National Association by saying that those who had signed the Manifesto did not know what they were talking about. This at any rate was demonstrably untrue, for among the signatures was that of Florence Nightingale and if anyone knew about the ravages of venereal disease in the armed forces she did. Josephine Butler too was no stranger to the visible effects of syphilis and gonorrhoea; they were amply in

244

evidence in her Home of Rest. And she knew what the inside of a brothel was like, for as soon as she had accepted the leadership of the abolitionist campaign she went with Cooper of the Rescue Society to visit a Chatham brothel. What appalled her was the youth of many of the soldiers. They were there, they told her, 'because there was nowhere else to go and everyone went'. No doubt a deplorable situation, her opponents would have said, but at least one in which the soldiers were not likely to catch V.D., as they would undoubtedly have done without the Contagious Diseases Acts.

The first success of the campaign was the defeat of Sir Henry Storks at a by-election in Colchester in 1870. Storks was a General who had been Commanding Officer at Malta where the Acts, with his wholehearted approval, applied. His only dissatisfaction with them was that they did not include the soldiers' wives. This dissatisfaction he unwisely expressed during his candidature at Colchester, which was also a 'protected' town. Abolitionist opposition had already obliged him to withdraw from a by-election earlier in the year at Newark, and now followed him to Colchester. Colchester was a safe Liberal seat and Storks stood for the Liberals. But the Conservative candidate, pledged to a repeal of the Acts, won the seat. 'Bird shot dead' said the telegram that Josephine received announcing the result.

But just as the near-success of Mill's measure for women's suffrage had given false hopes in 1865, so the electoral defeat of Storks seemed to presage an early repeal of the Acts that was equally unwarranted. In 1871 a Royal Commission was appointed to inquire into their working. It reported after six months, having examined a number of witnesses including Mrs Butler. Its report was equivocal, recommending that certain features of the law be amended – that the hated periodical examination of prostitutes be discontinued, although medical witnesses had said that this was essential to the effectiveness of the regulations; and recommending instead that if a common prostitute was found to be diseased after an examination upon a voluntary submission or a magistrate's order she should be detained in a certified hospital until discharged by a magistrate's order or by the hospital authorities, providing that detention should in no case exceed three months. Recommending too that the special police should wear uniform and be responsible to the Home Office.

The following year, on February 13, 1872, the Home Secretary, Bruce, introduced a Government Bill to repeal the Contagious Diseases Acts. Instead of being a matter for excited satisfaction among the abolitionists, Bruce's Bill divided them, for although it proposed the repeal of the Acts it substituted other regulations which would permit police all over the country, and not only in special areas, to arrest women on suspicion. The principle of State regulation was not abandoned in the Bill, as Josephine Butler pointed out. Indeed it was unlikely that it would be in view of the fact that Bruce, a tall stout man with coat tightly buttoned over a 'proud stomach', was a confirmed Regulationist. In introducing the Bill he praised the Acts which, he said, had cleaned up the streets, reduced prostitution, and entirely stopped the appalling vice of juvenile prostitution. He was dismayed that the Acts could not be continued, but it was impossible to maintain laws 'which have not the sanction of public opinion', and the Royal Commission had shown the doubts in many minds. But although the Acts must go there was no need for despondency, he assured his supporters. 'I believe we shall have powers, with regard to the whole country, such as we never had before. The mesh may be somewhat larger, but the net will have a far larger sweep; and although many who are now taken will escape, many more will be taken than is now the case under the existing law.' Bruce found the abolitionists unwholesome and distasteful. The agitation they were making was 'extremely mischievous', and the Government, he said, had remarked with 'grief and sorrow how much that reserve and delicacy, for which our women were so distinguished, had been broken through'.[1] In saying this he was expressing the key to the animosity that had been brought violently to the surface by the campaign for the abolition of the Contagious Diseases Acts, and his words justified the description of that campaign as the 'revolt of women'. The split concept of woman as virgin and prostitute which was the fundamental tranquillizer of male apprehensions would be totally destroyed if the virgin and the

[1] The dislike was mutual. When a deputation from the National Association for Abolition saw the Home Secretary to make known its views about the Royal Commission's report, Mrs Butler recalled that she 'never disliked Mr Bruce until I saw him, but I was most unfavourably impressed, and so were others. Nothing could be more haughty, and he several times attempted to browbeat members of the deputation.'

prostitute made common cause, or, to put it in an even more disturbing way, if the virgin refused to play the part that had been written for her. What new concept could then be evolved which could contain man's eternal ambivalence towards woman?

Unfortunately for the peace of mind of the abolitionists Bruce's Bill contained other clauses which were entirely satisfactory to them. As well as considering the working of the Acts the Royal Commission had also perforce to look at 'the social evil' in all its causes and characteristics. Mrs Butler especially had used the occasion when giving evidence to point out that prostitution resulted from poverty, ignorance, and overcrowding more than from choice. She had also been questioned about the number of very young children found in brothels and on the streets. Girls under fourteen were on the police register of common prostitutes. 'Our law declares a girl of twelve a woman,' she said. 'On this Parliament could and should act, the age of consent must be raised.' The Commission took notice of what she said. Other witnesses were closely questioned on the business of children being driven or sold into prostitution. The law was lax on the matter of abduction, and the punishment for trafficking in girls was derisory. Little girls under eight were not allowed to give evidence against anyone who had outraged them on the grounds that the victims were too young to understand the nature of an oath.

At least on this point the Commission's Report was not equivocal. 'The traffic in children for infamous purposes is notoriously considerable in London and other large towns. We think that a child of twelve can hardly be deemed capable of giving consent and should not have the power of yielding up her person. We therefore recommend the absolute protection of female children to the age of fourteen years, making the age of consent to commence at fourteen instead of twelve as under the existing law.' This Bruce's Bill proposed to do. Other protective clauses for women and girls were that harbouring a girl under sixteen would be made a misdemeanour punishable by six months' imprisonment on summary conviction, and by up to two years on indictment, and obtaining possession of a woman of any age by false pretences would be a misdemeanour. Anyone keeping women in a disorderly house would be subject to a fine of twenty pounds or six months imprisonment. (As the law then stood only a landlord who kept women he suspected of being diseased was subject to those penalties. The new clause would apply to all women, diseased or not.)

At a conference of the National Association held on February 29, a resolution was proposed that Bruce's Bill should not be opposed. Most of the early speakers supported this resolution, but they were men. The women took a different view. Both Lydia Becker, a suffragist leader, and Josephine Butler spoke against it. 'Half a loaf is better than no bread,' her friends told her. 'Not if it's poisoned,' she answered. A compromise resolution was passed, which approved the clause repealing the Acts and hoped that the objectionable parts of the Bill would be removed or amended as it progressed through Parliament. This was the advice of those Members of Parliament who were abolitionists. But the women were not satisfied, and in the end they persuaded the majority of the Association's members to oppose the Bill. With the repealers against it as well as the regulationists, and the press strongly in favour of retaining the Acts, there was no hope for the Bill. In the summer it was withdrawn by Gladstone, the Prime Minister, with the excuse that it was too late in the session to continue with such a controversial issue. Everyone seemed to have forgotten the little girls in the brothels – or if they remembered them they felt that they must not be allowed to stand in the way of rejecting the 'half loaf' that was poisoned with State encroachment into individual liberty so dear to those who, like Josephine Butler, had been brought up on generations of radical belief. Indeed the struggle over the Contagious Diseases Acts was one of the many fronts in the long battle between State-Help and Self-Help which came to the fore at this period.

With the withdrawal of Bruce's Bill the age of consent remained at twelve and the little girls continued to be cajoled and sold into white slavery.[1]

Civil 'Life' For Women
Had the abolitionists realized how long it was to be before their case was carried to a successful conclusion, they might have been less amenable to Josephine Butler's rejection of 'half a loaf'. But they were confident that at the next general election

---

[1] See Sadleir, op. cit., for an account of an establishment that bought little girls and the methods used to 'break them in'.

the results of their propaganda, especially among the lately enfranchised artisans who had been the determining factor against Storks, would not only make the C.D. Acts a major issue but would ensure that when Gladstone's Liberal Government was returned to office it would have a mandate to repeal the Acts. They were disappointed on both counts. Moral issues which cut across party lines are not the stuff of general elections; the crusade against reglementation found no place on the parties' platforms. And the artisan electors, for reasons quite other than public morality, turned against Gladstone and voted Tory. The Conservatives took office under Disraeli and they, in general, were less sympathetic to the repeal of the Acts than the Liberals. The abolitionists were set back on their heels.

Two good results, however, came out of this disappointment. The first was that J. B. Stansfeld, who had been President of the Poor Law Board in Gladstone's Cabinet, now that he was out of office joined the National Association for the Repeal of the Acts as its Vice-President. His importance to the cause lay not only in his public standing but in his knowledge of parliamentary methods. Facts must be used as well as enthusiasm and flames of fire if the abolitionists were to succeed. This he taught them.

The second result of the 1874 election rebuff was that instead of the quick dagger thrust of success which would have achieved the abolitionists' aim but would have removed them from the public gaze after only a short period of campaigning, they had to conduct a long siege in which their arguments were continually repeated and developed until these arguments had an effect far beyond their immediate purpose. Mrs Butler's crusade may have been an embarrassment to the women's movement as a whole, because in the public's mind they were all part of the same struggle for reform, with the result that the women's rightists, who were concerned with improving opportunities for employment and getting the vote, were looked upon as part of the same indecent regiment of women who were openly discussing the unmentionable subject of prostitution and sending pamphlets and petitions about it into homes throughout the country, so that gentlemen became afraid of what their wives might find on the breakfast-table – nevertheless, the crusade kept the issue of women's emancipation fiercely alive and made it impossible for Parliament to ignore it. Thus whether they welcomed the crusade or not other branches of the movement benefited from it, even if it was a benefit they failed to recognize and would rather have done without.

To determine causation in the matter of the woman's rights movement as a whole and the crusade for the repeal of the Contagious Diseases Acts is impossible. The fact remains that from 1870 onwards women began to have a modicum of civil 'life'. Legislation was passed giving them certain political rights. They had the right to fill a number of public posts including overseer, guardian, churchwarden, sexton, governor of a workhouse, medical officer of a workhouse, surveyor of highways, inspector of factories, member of a school board, member of a parish council. From the late 1880s women were also entitled to vote in the majority of municipal elections. But they were still not allowed to become county councillors, to be returned as Members of Parliament, to perform the duties of a mayor or a juror, or to vote in parliamentary elections. This denial of certain rights as a citizen that continued well beyond the end of Victoria's reign appeared to be based on no particular principle. Why, for instance, should a woman be allowed to sit on a parish council but not on a county council? As Arthur Cleveland pointed out in 1896,[1] 'the law has given a single woman a vote upon the question of education and the internal government of the County of London. Both the County Council and the School Board have the disposal annually of vast sums of money and exercise powers affecting numerous trades and all classes of people. For candidates for both these offices the law allows women to vote. But upon questions of imperial interest womankind must be silent. Why? Not because she is liable to be influenced in the exercise of her vote, because, were that the argument, she should never have been allowed to vote in municipal elections. Because she is incapable of forming a correct opinion upon imperial matters? Surely not, for the same argument would apply in those cases in which she now has a vote, if it apply at all. . . . That the law should have given woman a vote on municipal matters. and denied her a vote in the election of Members of Parliament, appears to us slightly inconsistent to say the least of it.'

It was indeed a most curious inconsistency, and one may think perhaps that the denial of the parliamentary vote to women was occasioned not by any belief in women's ability or

[1] Arthur Cleveland, *Woman Under the English Law*, p. 254.

lack of ability or because of the upset to the electoral see-saw which it was presumed it would make, but more fundamentally because 'Votes for Women' had become symbolic of the whole contentious change in the status of women. It achieved this significance because of the time at which it first came to the fore, a time when working-men of the towns were being given the vote. If the artisan who came to the house to carry out the mistress's orders was considered a fit person to vote then surely the mistress herself was too! And once the barricades were up, once the mistress of the house was refused the vote because she was a woman, even though she was superior in the social hier-archy to the little shopkeeper round the corner who was a fully-fledged member of the great imperial democracy, women's suffrage could be neither abandoned nor granted without conceding a moral victory over a wide front. Not that the vote is not a crucial issue in democratic government, but votes for women became an obsession with both the attackers and the defenders, an obsession in which the practical issue was overlaid with dark psychotic clouds, so much so that even when there had been major concessions on other fronts – when, for instance, married women were allowed control of their own property, when women were allowed to become doctors, when they had achieved 'civil life' in a number of important ways – still the parliamentary vote was refused.

In the matter of property, which the law still held to be almost more important than life, there were important changes. Three Married Women's Property Acts of 1870, 1882, and 1893 successively granted the rights for which Barbara Leigh Smith had started agitating in 1855. First, married women were given full rights over their own earnings made subsequent to their marriage, and then finally over all their own property, so that by the time Cleveland was writing in 1896 he could say that a married woman 'can now acquire, hold, and dispose of any property, real or personal, as her separate property, as if she were a single woman, without the intervention of any trustee. In fact, at the present day', he wrote, 'the law gives the husband no rights whatever over the property of his wife.' And not only did the law now allow married women to possess property – if they were lucky enough to have any – but it also removed many of the disabilities under which they had formerly lain, as, for instance, in the matter of suing and making contracts.

Even with these enormous male concessions in the sacrosanct realm of property the parliamentary vote was still refused, which demonstrates the psychological symbolism it had attained with an importance far beyond its practical value.

Social Purity
The effect of Josephine Butler's crusade on the social climate was not confined to Britain. In March 1875 the British and Continental Federation for the Abolition of Government Regulation of Prostitution was formally constituted at an international conference in Liverpool, held after Mrs Butler had returned from a three-month winter tour of the Continent in which she had examined at first-hand the working of reglementation in Paris, Lyons, Marseilles, Naples, Rome, Florence, Milan, Geneva, and Neuchâtel. In 1876 two representatives of the British National Association went to New York to help organize resistance to the introduction of reglementation. From 1870 to 1873 there had been regulation of prostitution in St Louis, Missouri, and although this experiment had not been repeated either in St Louis or in any other American city there were powerful forces at work urging the necessity of putting prostitution on a rational, scientific basis. Brothels, it was argued, released sexual tensions that would otherwise lead to sexual crimes. Furthermore, regulated prostitution was the only way to control 'contagious disease' and save women from being infected by their husbands. The majority of women were protected from sexual evils at the expense of a tiny minority. The prostitute herself benefited. Regular inspection safeguarded her own health as well as her customers'. Reglementation, it was maintained, also reduced police corruption, which was inseparable from the vice trade. To such a pitch indeed did this corruption come by the end of the century that in New York a number of influential citizens calling themselves the Committee of Fifteen organized an inquiry into the causes 'of the present alarming increase of gambling and the Social Evil in this city', and published the results of their investigations so that legislation might be promoted which would 'render it less difficult to reach offenders'.[1]

[1] The Committee's work showed, among other things, how the Raines Law, which permitted only hotels to sell alcohol on Sundays, gave rise to the so-called 'Raines Law hotels'; these were in effect houses of assignation

'The Revolt of Women'

The representatives from Mrs Butler's Association were sponsored in Boston by William Lloyd Garrison, and their public meeting was chaired by Garrison's fellow reformer and abolitionist Wendell Phillips. Although the American women's suffrage movement was split at that period – as indeed the English one was, largely over Mrs Butler's crusade – women from both the National Woman Suffrage Association and the American Woman Suffrage Association supported the campaign against reglementation and against prostitution. Lucy Stone spoke at the Boston meeting, Elizabeth Cady Stanton and Susan B. Anthony spoke on behalf of social purity (as vice suppression was called in America) in New York. The meetings gave the impetus, sporadic at first, to the formation of vigilance committees in many communities. In 1883 the Women's Christian Temperance Union, which was the most powerful women's organization in the country, opened its own social purity department. Social Purity Congresses began to be held, at which national action was concerted. In 1895 these resulted in the formation of the American Purity Alliance. The work of the reformers was more difficult, in one respect, than Josephine Butler's campaign because there was no central legislation to symbolize the enemy that must be destroyed. Regulation was a matter for local decision. However, the anti-regulationists succeeded in altering the climate of opinion even without the help

---

or, as a later generation would have called them, 'clip joints'. It also exposed the notorious 'cadet' system. The 'cadet' was a young man of from eighteen to twenty-five who, having served an apprenticeship as a 'lighthouse' or lookout to warn tenement house brothels of approaching danger, went into business on his own account as a pimp. He would get his staff by courting a young girl of foreign birth who knew little or nothing of the conditions of American life, offering marriage, taking her out – often with her parents' blessing for they were flattered by the attention being paid to their daughter by such a prosperous-appearing young man – visiting a Raines Law hotel, and drugging her. The girl was seduced and forced by fear and promises to become an inmate of a brothel. For each client the girl received a brass or pasteboard check from the cashier of the brothel entitling her to twenty-five cents. The 'cadet' returned at frequent intervals, collected the checks from his victim, and cashed them with the cashier. A girl would bring him in forty to fifty dollars a week, and each 'cadet' would have several girls.

The Committee of Fifteen recommended that reglementation was no answer to the evils connected with prostitution – 'even in their merely physical aspect'.

of such a rallying-point as the Contagious Diseases Acts, and whereas when Mrs Butler's representatives had arrived in New York in 1876 there seemed every likelihood of St Louis' example being followed in many other parts of the United States, in 1902 when the Committee of Fifteen came out strongly against regulation, even in the conditions then obtaining in New York, it was reflecting the firm belief of public opinion that commercial vice should not be officially tolerated.

Mrs Percy's Purgatory

By this time Josephine Butler's crusade had long since achieved success. After the set-back in 1874 there was renewed support for the abolitionists in March 1875 when Mrs Percy, an actress who appeared in small music-halls and who had just been performing at the Queen's Tap in Aldershot for an audience composed mainly of private soldiers, was found drowned in the Basing-stoke Canal. A fortnight before her death she had written to the *Daily Telegraph* in order to bring to the notice of those who were agitating for the repeal of the C.D. Act, 'a proceeding which I cannot but stigmatize as a shameful and high-handed use of power given to the police under its provisions'.

She was, she wrote, a professional singer and actress who had lived in Aldershot for twenty years. Her husband, also on the stage, had died a year ago leaving her with three children, the eldest a girl of sixteen who had been brought up to be an actress and who had never been out of an engagement since she first appeared in public.

'Anyone at all conversant with the habits of soldiers,' she continued, 'is perfectly well aware that they are, as a rule, very indulgent and gracious with those who contribute to their amusement. My Pauline is very much in their company; but would you believe it, Sir? My every action has been watched by the Police, my outgoings and incomings; in fact I have been placed under a system of surveillance which had I known of it in time, I might have taken some steps to put a stop to it, but I was going about my usual business in blissful ignorance. But I was destined to a rude awakening! One morning I was visited by a representative of the Commissioner in the form of a member of the Metropolitan Police who quietly warned me to attend the Lock Hospital [for venereal disease] next day, accompanied by my eldest daughter! Do you believe it, Sir? I must confess I could hardly believe my ears. And when I indignantly refused to entertain any such warning, I was calmly told I would be summoned before the Commissioner. On asking the reason for this arbitrary proceeding, I was informed that I and my daughter had been seen in the company of different soldiers for some time and that two of them had stayed in my house till twelve o'clock one night. This was the excuse for ordering me to take steps which had the result of completely disgracing me in the eyes of all my acquaintances; consequently I at once gave up my engagements and those of my daughter and left the town, knowing full well that I was unable to cope with the Police in their high-handed work.

'The above is precisely what has occurred; without any comments however I leave it to your numerous readers to judge the workings of this obnoxious Act from this solitary specimen.'

She signed the letter 'Professional'.

The *Telegraph* did not print the letter until after Mrs Percy's body had been found in the canal on Sunday, March 28. There was then a tremendous uproar. At the inquest it was suggested that the letter showed Mrs Percy had been driven to commit suicide by the persecution of the police. Witnesses said that the music-hall proprietor had been warned not to continue her engagement. The local superintendent of police denied any knowledge of the matter – and rightly, because the uniformed police were not involved. But the special plain-clothes police were not called to give evidence and they said nothing to confirm or deny the allegations. The coroner declined to hear evidence from the music-hall proprietor or from Pauline Percy. But he did hear the evidence of two soldiers, one of whom said he had seen Mrs Percy part of the way home on Saturday night and that both she and he were tipsy, and the other who said that he had seen her hanging about the tow-path early on Sunday morning. An open verdict was returned.

The National Association was not satisfied. There were a number of inconsistencies in the story. This was just the sort of case it had been on the look-out for. Had Mrs Percy in fact been driven to suicide by the persecution of the special police? And could this be proved?

The abolitionists held a meeting of protest at the City Terminus, Cannon Street, London, on May 4. The chair was taken by William Shaen, chairman of the National Association. Shaen was a solicitor, and Mrs Percy's case had been investigated under his direction with Mrs Butler's enthusiastic support. The facts were as Mrs Percy had stated them in her letter. She and her daughter were popular entertainers and every night after the performance they would be seen home by one or two of the men from the audience, who would be given a glass of beer. There was no evidence to show that they got anything more. The music-hall proprietor admitted that he had been warned not to employ Mrs Percy or her daughter. The special police had ordered Mrs Percy and her daughter to attend voluntarily for a medical examination, or to appear before the magistrate as persons whom the police had good reason to suppose were common prostitutes, if they would not go to the Lock Hospital voluntarily. Mrs Percy and her daughter had refused to do either. They left Aldershot and went to Windsor – which, incidentally, was another 'protected' town. How, then, had her body come to be found in the Basingstoke Canal near Aldershot if she had gone to Windsor?

Unfortunately for Mrs Percy she had been followed to Windsor by an old friend and admirer, Mr Ritson, who was also on the stage. Ritson persuaded her that if she returned to Aldershot, where after all she had lived for twenty years and where her home was – if she returned there as his wife the police would not be able to touch her. He was booked to appear at the Queen's Tap; let Pauline and her appear with him. She decided to risk it. She went back to Aldershot calling herself Mrs Ritson – there was no marriage certificate as Ritson was already married, though living apart from his wife. After a week at the Queen's Tap the manager, warned by the special police that his licence would be in danger otherwise, sacked her. Whether the police also ordered her once again to appear before the magistrate was not known. Nevertheless, it was clear that Mrs Percy had been driven to take her own life by the despair she felt at the unjust persecution she was suffering. Her daughter testified to that despair.

Indignation reached a new peak. The protest meeting

reaffirmed continued agitation to have the C.D. Acts repealed. Stansfeld spoke denouncing the Acts as 'having for their end to make smooth and easy the path of vice for men and to make it appear to be safe, and all this at the cost of woman alone'. Sir Harcourt Johnston, who the following month was to move the second reading of another Bill to repeal the Acts, said: 'We scarcely know the depths of degradation to which the daughters of the lower classes of this country have been subjected by these Acts.' It was stated that the Baptist Union had petitioned against the Acts and that the Congregational Union was to hold a meeting of protest.

Officialdom, however, was not prepared to admit error. In answer to a question in Parliament in June, the Under-Secretary for War ignored the facts revealed by Shaen, and said that Mrs Percy had lived an immoral life for years and had trained her daughter to immorality. She had been turned out of her lodgings twice for immoral behaviour – a statement which Shaen was later to prove as utterly false – and that as she lived opposite the special police they could see for themselves without any special surveillance that by bringing home men at night she could reasonably be supposed to be a common prostitute. When she returned to Aldershot to live with Ritson as his wife she had in no way been molested by the police.

Public opinion veered against Mrs Percy. Her profession was against her. She had been 'living in sin'. The official answer was accepted. As for Pauline Percy, she had no redress. She had been named as a common prostitute and there was no way of restoring her good name. That it was good Josephine Butler had no doubt; she and her husband took Pauline into their own home for some time and thought very highly of her.

Nevertheless, Mrs Percy's purgatory was not in vain. The circumstances of her death revived the flagging spirits of the main body of the crusaders against the Acts. Though Harcourt Johnston's Bill was defeated, the tenor of the debate was different from that during Bruce's Bill in 1872. Derision and abuse had given way to serious argument. Even so there were still some years to go before Mrs Butler's 'revolt of women' succeeded. In 1879 a Select Committee of the House of Commons was appointed to inquire, yet again, into the working of the Acts. Its majority report of 1882 still favoured their retention. But Stansfeld produced a minority report which had a more telling effect. Although each year a Bill to repeal the Acts was introduced and each year it was defeated, the continual pressure of the abolitionists was wearing away the opposition, not least by that most telling of weapons – boredom. On April 20, 1883, by astute parliamentary tactics Stansfeld succeeded in effectively killing the Acts. Instead of trying to have them repealed he got compulsory examination abolished and the special police disbanded. Three years later to the day, on April 20, 1886 while she was travelling on the Continent, Josephine Butler heard by telegram that after sixteen years the flame of fire had consumed its enemy. The Contagious Diseases Acts had been repealed.

The Maiden Tribute

The efforts to raise the age of consent and protect little girls from the white slave traffic also succeeded in the end. The Royal Commission of 1871 had unanimously recommended that the age of consent be raised to fourteen. This, Bruce's Bill of 1872, the 'poisoned half loaf', had proposed to do. When the Bill was withdrawn the age of consent remained at twelve until in the summer of 1875, as a result of a parliamentary compromise, it was raised to thirteen, the age at which the Factory Acts and the Education Act defined childhood as ending.[1] But the change hardly affected the traffic in young girls.

Some details of this trade were first hinted at publicly that same year by Josephine Butler in a book called *The New Abolitionists*, in which she recounted what she had seen and heard on her Continental tour at the beginning of the year. The following year on the way back from a holiday in Switzerland she actually encountered the white slave traffic herself for the first time at Liége. 'Poor girls,' she wrote, 'are being sought from everywhere to be enslaved in this diabolic service, waggons full of them arrive by train from other countries under the care of the police, crowded *comme la bétaille.*' The horror of it haunted her, but for the moment she could not see what could be done to kill the trade.

The publishers of *The New Abolitionists* were the small Quaker firm of Dyer Brothers in the City of London. At the beginning of 1880 Alfred Dyer wrote to the *Daily News* about a young English girl who had been duped into going to Brussels on a promise of marriage, had found herself in a brothel, and

[1] Ann Stafford, *The Age of Consent* (Hodder & Stoughton), p. 77.

had eventually been rescued and returned to England. The purpose of his letter, he said, was to put parents on their guard and to get 'sympathy for the effort which is about to be set on foot by a few gentlemen to recover other victims of this diabolical slave traffic'.

Dyer's letter also appeared in the *Standard*, and it attracted a good deal of attention. Many of the letters in answer to it told Dyer that he had been duped himself. 'The houses in Brussels are inspected nightly by the Police,' wrote one correspondent who hid behind the initials A.R.D. 'Girls are often willing victims; when they are awakened to the horrors of their work, they concoct a pretty little story to enlist public sympathy.' And the honorary secretary of the British Charitable Fund in Brussels, whatever that was, said that the Fund was doing all that was needed and there was no need for another; chaplains constantly visited the 'houses' and girls who were rescued were looked after. Possibly the British Charitable Fund was a 'front' for some of the white slave traffickers, or perhaps it was a way of paying conscience money.

The British consular officials also slated Dyer for his inaccuracies and on January 17, fifteen days after Dyer's letter had been published, the Commissioner in Chief to the Brussels Police des Moeurs had a letter in the *Standard* in which he held up his hands in astonishment at the wildness of Mr Dyer's allegations.

But Dyer and his friends held on their way. They formed a Committee for the Exposure and Suppression of the Traffic in English Girls for the Purposes of Continental Prostitution. The chairman was Benjamin Scott, the Chamberlain of the City of London and an active supporter of Mrs Butler's crusade for the abolition of the C.D. Acts. Alfred Dyer was the honorary secretary. And despite the Brussels Commissioner's warning to the *Standard*'s readers 'against the call for money on behalf of the girls in question, which looks very like a new kind of speculation' the Committee raised a fund.

Dyer himself went to Brussels to visit the brothels and investigate the methods by which the girls were trapped. Having been got into the brothel on the specious excuse that it was a hotel or the place where she was to work, she would first be examined to make sure she was a virgin. Then she would be interviewed by the police – as indeed she had to be by law because she was not allowed to work in a brothel except of her own free will. But the reason why the police were actually interviewing her and the reason she thought they were interviewing her were not the same. The madame of the brothel would tell her that she had to have a permit before she could work there. She would also have to have a birth certificate. She hadn't got one? What a pity! Wait a minute. The madame happened to have a birth certificate handy. Admittedly it had the wrong name and the age on it was twenty-one, but it was only a formality after all and all the girl had to do was to sign the police register in the name on the birth certificate.

The only thing the girl would really understand in the police interview was the question, Did she want to work here of her own free will? Of course she did because she still did not know what the work really was, and while a more sophisticated girl might have had forebodings long before this, ignorant young girls from English country villages regarded it as all part of the strange, incomprehensible, exciting habits of the city, so remote from her own rural experience that it was another existence altogether.

So the girl, prompted by the brothel-keeper's representative who accompanied her to the police interview, said that she wanted to work here of her own free will. Then she signed the register with the false name on the birth certificate, had another medical examination – which must have made her wonder even more about the strange habits of the city – and was taken back to the brothel. And then she discovered what it was really all about. But it was too late. The doors could only be opened from the outside. There was no way out of the brothel without the brothel-keeper's keys. And even supposing that a miracle happened and she did escape, she was wearing clothes provided by the brothel; her own had been removed. She could be arrested for stealing. Why then did she not complain to the Police des Moeurs at the regular medical inspections? Because she had signed a false name and used false papers. She was liable to prosecution for breaking the law.

There were refinements to this basic routine. Sometimes the girls arrived with their false birth certificates showing them to be twenty-one even if they were eleven or twelve. It was perfectly simple to get copies of suitably aged girls' birth certificates from Somerset House in London. The girl who, for whatever enticement had been held out to her, had agreed to go to this new life, was told that she must, for reasons that were too difficult to explain but which were really only a formality, sign the register in Brussels with the name on this new birth certificate.

Dyer's discoveries forced the Belgian authorities into the bold step of inviting Scotland Yard to send representatives to see for themselves that Dyer was mistaken. Two Inspectors called on the brothels in various towns but the results of their tour, not unnaturally for it was easy to hide under-age girls, were inconclusive. Later Mrs Butler heard from a Belgian detective that the Commissioner of the Police des Moeurs had rushed round Brussels in a carriage removing young girls and sending them across the frontier, so that the invitation to Scotland Yard could be issued without fear of the investigation disclosing any unfortunate evidence.

As a result of Dyer's failure to get any publicity in the British press for what he had discovered in Brussels, Mrs Butler wrote a letter in *The Shield*, the organ of the National Association for the Repeal of the Contagious Diseases Acts, about the 'sacrifice of the innocents'. There were no repercussions to the letter in England but on the Continent it stirred things up. A Juge d'Instruction in Brussels communicated with the British Home Secretary asking that under the extradition laws Mrs Butler either withdraw her charges, or make a deposition on oath before a magistrate, or face the legal penalty of being sent to prison.

Josephine Butler's friends were frightened on her behalf, her enemies were delighted. To substantiate the truth of the stories she had published was almost impossible. Better for her to be a martyr and go to prison. But Josephine Butler was the only one not dismayed. She was delighted at the opportunity of making public what she had said and a great deal more. On November 8 she made a deposition on oath, naming names and quoting cases. 'There is reason to believe,' she said, 'that the conduct of the chief of police encourages the keepers not only to receive minors, but in some cases ... to provide children for the gratification of their fastidious clients.' She made a further statement which the magistrate would not let her swear to, but which was attached to the deposition. In this statement she described how the girls were prevented from escaping. And then to cap it all she wrote a personal letter to the Home Secretary telling him how the children had been moved by the Police Commissioner, and how that same Commissioner under the trade name of his son was making a huge profit out of selling wine to the brothels.

The Home Secretary sent the whole lot – including a copy of the personal letter – to Brussels. He also sent a barrister, S. W. Snagge, to conduct an independent inquiry. The outcome was that in Brussels there was a series of prosecutions against brothel-keepers and procurers, as a result of which several brothels were closed, including that of a Madame Hortense who, in her very costly establishment, had specialized in English girls of ten, eleven, and twelve. Fifteen people were accused and all were found guilty. A Treasury Solicitor appeared for the English girls involved. In London, after some agitation from Mrs Butler, and Mr Dyer's Committee, a Select Committee of the House of Lords was set up 'to inquire into the law relating to the protection of young girls from artifices inducing them to lead a corrupt life and into the means of amending the same'.

In 1882, at the same time as the House of Commons Select Committee was writing its report on the working of the Contagious Diseases Acts, the House of Lords Select Committee reported on what was happening to young girls. Their Lordships pointed out that, whereas in other European countries girls were protected absolutely to the age of twenty-one, in England protection ceased at thirteen. The Committee was not particularly concerned with the foreign trade in girls. The extent of that trade, the report felt, was not as large as had been suggested, and although it was true that a certain number of girls had been induced to go to the Continent and that the agent had received on average between £8 and £12 a girl, most of those girls in their Lordships' opinion knew what they were going for, and were bad lots before they went. What the girls had not realized in advance, and what had upset them was that they were kept under restraint in the brothels.

But although the white slaves for the Continent had not stirred their Lordships unduly they were appalled at what happened to little girls in England. There was no doubt at all, they said, that juvenile prostitution 'from an incredibly early age is increasing to an appalling extent in England and especially in London'. They made some strong recommendations which would effectively limit, if not kill, the white slave traffic.

The first recommendation was that it should be made a serious misdemeanour to solicit or endeavour to procure any woman to leave the United Kingdom for the purpose of entering a brothel, whether she were aware of her destination or not. Secondly the Committee recommended that all birth certificates at Somerset House of women between the ages of twenty and thirty should be stamped in red with the advice, written in French, that foreign police should check on the holder of it. Thirdly, it was recommended that the age of consent be raised to sixteen, and the age of unlawful abduction for immoral purposes be raised from sixteen to twenty-one. Finally, it was recommended that search warrants should be issued upon application of a police inspector who had reason to believe that some girl had been received into any premises for immoral purposes.

The recommendations were all that the reformers wanted. But would Parliament enact them? It seemed at first that it would. A Bill, the Criminal Law Amendment Bill, was introduced into the House of Lords in 1883. It passed the Lords but was lost in the Commons. The following year it was re-introduced in the Lords, passed again, but once again was rejected in the Commons, this time because the Liberal Government was at daggers drawn with the Lords over the latter's rejection of a Bill which would have the effect of enfranchising a large number of agricultural labourers, and on which the Government set great store. For a third time the Bill was passed by the Lords and sent to the Commons in the spring of 1885. In an endeavour to rouse public opinion, which was already beginning to stir itself as a result of the formation of the Society for the Prevention of Cruelty to Children, Alfred Dyer and his Committee, supported by Mrs Butler and the British and Continental Federation for the Abolition of the State Regulation of Vice, brought a case against a well-known brothel in Chelsea run by Mrs Jeffries, whose clients included many wealthy and eminent gentlemen. In a modern phrase it might be said that she ran a brothel for the Establishment. Mrs Jeffries was well advised. She pleaded guilty, was fined two hundred pounds, which was a very substantial sum, but one which the wealth of some of her clients made it easy for her to pay, and was then driven away in her carriage escorted by Guards officers. From the reformers' point of view the case was a fiasco. By pleading guilty Mrs Jeffries had ensured that no evidence was called. She went back to business as usual and Mrs Butler's disgust at the licentiousness of the upper classes was made even greater. 'If the corruption of our aristocracy were fully known,' she wrote, 'I think it would hasten republicanism among us.'

The Criminal Law Amendment Bill continued to languish. Benjamin Scott decided on another attempt to revivify it by publicity. He went to W. T. Stead, the thirty-six-year-old editor of the *Pall Mall Gazette*, and asked for his help. Mrs Butler added her plea. Stead decided to act – and to act, as was his nature, in the most dramatic way possible. He realized that no ordinary means could overcome the obstacles presented by the politicians' lethargy. And the subject itself made the task almost impossible. 'The very horror of the crime was the chief secret of its persistence,' he wrote in his *Reminiscences*. 'The subject was tabooed by the press.' On the other hand, it was a story that must be told, and to tell it could be the journalistic sensation of the age, whatever obloquy it brought.

Stead embarked on a personal investigation of child prostitution in London with the help of the Salvation Army, which had been formed eight years before by William Booth and which had quickly established itself as among the foremost of the 'rescuers'. 'With the aid of a few faithful friends,' he wrote, 'I went disguised into the lowest haunts of criminal vice and obtained only too ample proof of the reality and extent of the evils complained of. I then published the Report of the Secret Commission of Enquiry into the Criminal Vice of London under the title of "The Maiden Tribute of Modern Babylon", in the *Pall Mall Gazette*, beginning on the sixth of July and closing its publication on the twelfth. The sensation which these articles produced was instantaneous and world-wide.'

Stead was not exaggerating. The articles were direct and specific in their details. They told of padded rooms in West End brothels, of unwilling girls strapped down in Half Moon Street, of a child of thirteen bought for £5, of the purchaser coming into the bedroom, locking the door behind him, and hearing the child's cry, like 'the bleat of a helpless lamb'. They told of decoy methods, of agreements that Stead himself had got from seven girls between the ages of fourteen and eighteen who were prepared to be seduced for various sums up to £5. All were

virgins, certified as such by a Harley Street doctor. The articles
disclosed the economics of this type of transaction and the
method of obtaining the girls.

'The Maiden Tribute of Modern Babylon' was reprinted in
the *New York Sun* and the *Chicago Tribune*, and in many other
papers throughout the English-speaking world as well as in
France and Belgium. The *Pall Mall Gazette* not only sold out all
its editions but exhausted its stock of newsprint. Copies sold at
a premium. On the fifth day the Criminal Law Amendment
Bill was rushed through its second reading in the House of
Commons. A month later it became law. The age of consent was
raised to sixteen, and procuring or attempting to procure any
woman under the age of twenty-one was made a criminal
offence punishable by two years' imprisonment.[1]

[1] Stead's reward for what was one of the greatest demonstrations of the
power of the press, apart that is from the satisfaction of fame and of having
achieved a noble reform, was a three-month term in prison. The ostensible
reason for this was that he had made an illegal contract; the real reason
was that his enemies – and he had added greatly to them by the publication
of 'The Maiden Tribute' – were determined to humiliate him on whatever pretext they could find. In the course of his investigations, in order to
prove how easy it was to procure a young girl, he had, with the help of
the Salvation Army, actually bought a thirteen-year-old girl from her
mother for £5. Unlike the 'helpless lamb' described in the article this
girl, Eliza Armstrong, had been kept, suitably protected, in a London
brothel overnight, with medical examinations to prove that she was a
virgin both before and after her sojourn, and had then been taken under
care to Paris and lodged in a Salvation Army hostel. When Stead's
enemies later raised a hue and cry in rival newspapers, the mother claimed
that she had only let Eliza go to be a servant. Stead could not prove
otherwise for he had omitted to get a proper receipt. That was his first
mistake. His second, and the one on which he was arraigned, was that he
should have made the contract with Eliza's father, as her mother had no
legal right to make such a contract. Only after Stead had served his
sentence was it discovered that Eliza was illegitimate and, therefore, the
father had no rights over her.

Stead himself was delighted that this was not discovered until too late
to rob him of his martyrdom. For the rest of his life, which ended in the
Titanic disaster, he always wore his prison uniform on the anniversary of
his conviction and committal to Coldbath-in-the-Fields Prison, a costume
that attracted much attention as he travelled to his office in the suburban
train from Wimbledon, and walked across Waterloo Bridge. This gesture,
as Roy Jenkins pointed out in his biography of Sir Charles Dilke (Collins,
1958, footnote to p. 241), would have been more justified if Stead had not
been transferred to Holloway Prison as a first-class misdemeanant and
allowed to wear ordinary clothes after the first two days of his sentence.

The Sex War

And so at last something had been done for the little girls, and the hated Contagious Diseases Acts were gone. There still remained another struggle to get the Government of India not to evade repeal by use of the Cantonment Acts, and it was not until 1895 that brothels in cantonments were abolished. But reglementation remained on the Continent. So too did the Contagious Diseases. So too did prostitution.

This is not to suggest that the whole long struggle was without avail. Quite apart from its declared object the crusade was undoubtedly, for many of its supporters, consciously or unconsciously, a veritable revolt. It was an attack against male supremacy. It was a release for that rankling frustration at woman's relative status. The prostitute became the symbol of that status and of a husband's right, until 1884, to possess his wife by force – 'Prostitution within the marriage bond' the extreme feminists called it, reglementation seemed an insulting insistence by men that that status was some sort of natural law and could never be changed. Furthermore in the dark turmoil of some women's minds was an anti-phallic complex that found an outlet in Josephine Butler's crusade. 'The opposite of sympathy for the prostitute was hostility to the masculine world that created and abused her. In saving the prostitute,' an American historian of feminism has suggested, 'one also struck a blow at the men she pleasured. If visiting a prostitute profaned the sanctities of womanhood, the denial of her services had an opposite meaning. Symbolic rape was met with symbolic castration. Extreme feminists expressed this by forgetting the help social purity everywhere got from sympathetic men.'[1]

Most men, however, were not sympathetic. They reacted, first banteringly, then harshly, to the revolt which they had to some extent brought on themselves by creating for middle-class women the role of the virgin in the drawing-room. This doctrine of purity and gentility reinforced a natural desire on the women's part to escape from the brutality and animalism of a more primitive society. Carried to its extreme, as it was by some, it meant that women were superior beings whose only fit associates were each other and who must band together to protect themselves against the coarse lusts of their moral inferiors –

[1] William L. O'Neill, op. cit., p. 40.

men. This was what Eliza Farnham had had revealed to her in the Truth of Woman and had proclaimed to the world in 1864 in *Woman and Her Era*. This was what Eliza Gamble expounded in *The Evolution of Woman* in 1894.[1] As *The Queen* magazine commented in 1873, underneath the conventional surface of politeness was a deep undercurrent of enmity between the sexes. For some women the crusade against the C.D. Acts and the campaign for social purity was the vehicle by which that enmity could be expressed.

Other motives too were involved: missionary zeal, religious belief, and humanitarian feeling, although the last was somewhat at a discount as a motive. Nothing had aroused the contempt of Georgiana Sitwell, later Mrs Campbell Swinton of Kimmerghame, more than the lack of religious feeling among the German nobles at Wiesbaden. To be kind to one's fellow human beings as a natural instinct was almost despicable. These nobles, she wrote, 'were charitable to the poor, kindly to children and to the sick, hospitable to all, industrious, devoted to their domestic duties, but for all this a naturally amiable character seemed the only mainspring. A religious motive for any good action seemed never to suggest itself.'[2]

And there was no doubt in some cases a motive apart from any of these. In later years it became fashionable for opponents of women's rights to sneer at all feminists as being actuated by a lesbian impulse. While this was a gross exaggeration it was undoubtedly true that some women who had a natural predilection for their own sex were active feminists. As Andrew Sinclair has pointed out, 'the history of women's rights in the United States is a history of *personal* contacts. The movement grew by the laying on of hands'.[2] Antoinette Brown, who was the first woman to become an ordained Protestant minister and later married Samuel Blackwell of the famous Blackwell family and became the mother of six children, fell in love with Lucy Stone at Oberlin, 'with all the passion and sentimental licence possible between women of the time, before they learned to question their subconscious motives'.[3] And Susan Anthony, who berated Antoinette at the birth of her second child and wrote

<hr>

[1] See Chapter Eleven, 'Eliza's Truth of Woman'.
[2] *Two Generations*, with a preface and edited by Osbert Sitwell (Macmillan, 1940), p. 140. Mrs Campbell Swinton was Florence Sitwell's aunt.
[3] Andrew Sinclair, op. cit., p. 155.

'not another baby is my *peremptory command, two* will solve the *problem* whether a *woman can* be anything *more* than a *wife* and *mother* better than half a dozen or *ten* even' – Susan Anthony was passionately in love with Anna Dickinson, the young 'Joan of Arc' of the feminists in the 1870s. Her letters to the younger woman plead with her 'not to *marry* a *man*', tell her that at her apartment in New York she has a double bed, 'big enough and good enough to take you *in*', and are continually saying that she wants to give her 'one awful long squeeze'. 'Yet, throughout her letters,' Sinclair noted, 'Anthony never asserted that her desperate love was more than a maternal feeling. She could not think in other terms, nor give her passion a modern name.'[1]

Across the Atlantic, too, there were passions without a modern name which seem to have reached their heights after the turn of the century when the militant suffragettes brought the revolt of women to its climax.[2]

[1] ibid., p. 76.
[2] See, for example, George Dangerfield, *The Strange Death of Liberal England* (MacGibbon & Kee, 1968).

Chapter 16

THE GREAT DEPRESSION AND 'THE BABY QUESTION'

On May 1, 1876, exactly twenty-five years to the day after she had opened that Great Exhibition which was to become the shining symbol of British self-complacency, Queen Victoria was proclaimed Empress of India. This time she was not reflecting the inarticulate aspirations and romanticism of her subjects. The idea was her own.

In 1876 the Queen's popularity was at a low ebb. Since the death of her husband in 1861 she had become almost a recluse, rarely appearing in public and doing few of a monarch's visible duties. Among these was the duty to spend money freely and thus encourage extravagance throughout the Top Nation, especially that part of it in close touch with the Court. The drabness and parsimony of life at Court was hurting the tradesmen and creating a bad impression everywhere. There was nothing the nation loathed more than a mean monarch. Gone were the days when the Queen could write to her uncle, 'They say no Sovereign was ever more loved than I am'. A powerful republican movement had sprung up, led by Sir Charles Dilke, radical M.P. for Chelsea and advocate of a Greater Britain.[1]

The Queen did not regain her early popularity until her

[1] Ten years later, in the summer of 1886, the Queen had an adventitious revenge on Dilke when his brilliant career, which seemed to be taking him to the premiership, was ruined by the most mysterious of all divorce cases, in which he figured according to some, as villain, according to others, as the victim of an ingenious conspiracy of women.

Golden Jubilee in 1887 released the same flood of sentimental herd emotions that the Great Exhibition had done, although this time with more material justification. From 1887, through her Diamond Jubilee in 1897, until her death on January 22, 1901 she became a legend like the gods of old, so enduring and immovable in most people's minds that when in fact she did die it seemed for a moment as if the earth had halted on its axis.

The years from 1876 to 1901 were the high noon of the British Empire. During that quarter of a century its size increased by almost one-third to a total of 13,000 million square miles of territory, and its population increased by a quarter to 370 million of whom nearly 300 million lived in India. And Britain's own population increased by over 40 per cent from 26·1 million in 1871 to 37 million in 1901. It had doubled once between 1801 and 1851, and now it doubled again in the sixty years to 1911.

Overseas trade continued to expand enormously. Between 1876 and the end of the reign the quantity of exports increased by about two-thirds, although in money value they rarely exceeded the amount reached in the boom years of 1872–3. Imports more than doubled in volume and rose by over one-fifth in value. The adverse balance of imports over exports created no problem because of high 'invisible' earnings by British shipping and the income from overseas investment which, even when they had met the visible deficit, still left a large annual surplus for further investment.

But despite the growth of empire, the expanding volume of overseas trade, and a continued rapid advance in industrial production, the last quarter of the nineteenth century came to be known in Britain as the Great Depression. To a large extent this was a misnomer economically, although there were two sectors of the national life where it accurately expressed the state of affairs. One was the unorganized, exploited mass of sweated workers, many of them women in the garment trades, who lived in dreadful conditions of virtual slavery on starvation wages. The other was agriculture.

Forced out of grain production by cheap wheat imported from the vast American prairies, the British farmer turned from arable to pasture. But this too failed. It was not only cheap wheat he had to compete against. The development of refrigeration, part of the technological progress that was infiltrating into everyday existence, allowed dairy products and frozen meat to be brought from Australia and the Argentine. Britain could now largely be fed from abroad. Four-fifths of the wheat was imported as well as three-fifths of the butter and four-fifths of the cheese. For the rest of Victoria's reign and beyond, British agriculture was in decline. Nor did the majority of the population care, for over half the population now lived in towns, and until 1884 the agricultural labourer had no vote. Even when he had, the weight of urban numbers made cheap food a more powerful political cry than prosperous farming. During the late Victorian decades Britain ceased to be primarily an agricultural nation. The rural setting in which it had been created and matured was broken to pieces and the social ecology of the past was finally destroyed. A new ecology had to be painfully evolved.

Looked at historically the Great Depression can be seen as a slowing-down in the rate of Britain's economic progress, and not as a cessation of progress altogether, nor as an absolute decline. But for those who lived through it, this interpretation was not at all evident. Some, like the skilled workers in full employment and the lower middle class, experienced a rise in their standard of living greater than ever before. Others, like the farmers and landowners without urban estates who were dependent on the rents from farming, experienced a harsh drop in their incomes, so much so, in some cases, that it needed marriage to the rich daughters of the new American millionaires to keep the family estates together.

Those whose economic situation most accurately reflected the real nature of the Great Depression were the better-off sections of society. From the mid-1870s onwards they found it harder to maintain, let alone increase, the differential standard between themselves and those immediately below them in the ordered ranks of the nation. The skilled workers and lower middle class were leaving the poor farther and farther behind and were catching up with those ahead of them. The 'Middle Three' of Bessie Parkes's calculation were becoming the Middle Five or the Middle Six. Like a worm in motion, the middle part of society was thickening as it closed up towards the front part and drew away from the tail. During the previous twenty years the front of the worm had quested rapidly ahead; now, apart from the very tip, it was hardly moving.

271

The main effect of the Great Depression on those in the middle and upper range of incomes was psychological. Even by their own standards they could not be said to have suffered any great economic hardship, although in the bad years, it is true, their incomes had a setback, and throughout the period there was the servant problem to contend with. Female domestic servants' wages rose by a third between 1871 and 1900 (compared with a rise of one-fifth for women's wages in general) as a result of servants becoming harder to get, partly because of the growing number of middle-class households who wanted them, and partly because girls had adopted the attitude long prevalent in America and were no longer prepared to become domestic servants if they could possibly avoid it.

For the pessimists there were other things to cause despondency as well as servants. There were the reverses in Afghanistan in 1880, defeat by the Boers at Majuba Hill the following year, and Gordon's death in the Sudan in 1885. There was Ireland – as there would be Ireland for many years to come, there were the riots of the unemployed, dangerously evocative of the terror of the Paris Commune in 1871 when the dissatisfied masses had swept away the established order of Society, there was the growth of powerful industrial rivals in the United States and Germany. There were indeed reasons enough for pessimism.

But why be pessimistic? The police had set the rioters back on their heels, the English workman had shown that he had too much sense for red revolution, coercion would tame Ireland, property was still sacrosanct – (more so almost than human life), village people still showed a proper respect for the squire, doffing their caps or curtseying as he rode by or as his wife and daughters passed in their carriage, the religious backbone of the country was as firm as ever, the Empire was expanding, England was still cock of the walk.

One thing, however, the Great Depression undoubtedly did to all alike in the better-off sections of Society. It shook that unconscious assumption of inevitable progress which had been strong in the previous generation. This linear idea of progress, of climbing forward up the century from the '50s to the '60s, from the '60s to the '70s, up into the golden haze of the future was a secularized version of the Judaeo-Christian interpretation of history which assumed an advance towards a goal ordained by God. It was confirmed by the rapidly rising standard of

Country Girl. 'No unsuitable frippery'. *Country Camera.*

17. The Girl at the Gate by George Clausen, R.A. It was from the country cottages that the servants came 'to black the grates and carry the coals and fill the baths of the Top Nation'.

Girl members of the Matchmakers' Union in the East End of London, 1888. Annie Besant, 'Socialist Labour Agitator', organized a strike of these girls.

18. Five little girls of Kirklees Hall, the Yorkshire home of the Armytage family, in the 1890s. Second from the left is Edith Armytage who is seen as one of the first woman motorists in a later picture. In 1905 she became Mrs M. K. North; in 1971 she celebrated her ninetieth birthday. *Crow Collection.*

living that had ballooned up during the twenty years after the Great Exhibition. Provided one obeyed the rules, subscribed at least outwardly to the ritual of righteousness, kept one's nose clean and one's peccadilloes out of sight, one would inevitably progress year by year to that preordained goal that shimmered over the horizon.

But from 1876 on, who could be so sure? Progress was clearly not inevitable after all. For years it had seemed that England was on a moving stairway which was taking it ever upward and onward. Now, all at once, it appeared that the moving stairway was in fact a switchback. There were downs as well as ups and who could say whether at the end of it all the downs might not more than cancel out the ups. Perhaps there was no progress. Perhaps the Greeks were right and there was only recurrence, perpetual movement, displacement which was circular, spiral, endlessly recurrent.

If one no longer believed unquestioningly in inevitable progress it followed that to keep one's position in society and improve on it – for nothing is ever kept by standing still – one must limit one's inelastic commitments. Bulking large among these were children, because one of the implications of a linear idea of progress was that one's children's future chances must be no less bright than one's own had been. Children must be given as good, or even better, an education than one had had oneself. They must start their own married lives at the standard of living they had been used to at home. This was the law of Society. 'The son must not marry until he can maintain an establishment on much the same footing as his father's.' If he broke the law 'his family lose caste, and he and his wife are quietly dropt out of the circle in which they have hitherto moved'.[1]

Thus it happened that the Great Depression contributed significantly to the fall in the birth rate which began during the years of the Empress.

The Unwanted Quiverful

When applied to families the adjective Victorian is invariably synonymous with large. That the Victorians had large families is true; but the commonly held belief that this was something especially Victorian is not true. Large families were a

[1] Letter in *The Times*, signed 'Theophrastus', May 7, 1857.

characteristic that the Victorians inherited from an earlier age. The eighteenth century, particularly the latter part of it, went in for enormous families – fifteen or more children from the same mother, or more often from different mothers, because the death rate in childbirth was high and one man would marry several times. Many of the children survived at least until adolescence, despite the swathe-cutting epidemics which took a heavy toll of young life.[1]

But although the Victorians did not 'invent' large families they brought the trend to its highest point and then, in the later decades of the reign, began the decline towards much smaller families which was to characterize the half-century from 1911 to 1961. The birth rate in England and Wales fell from 35·5 per thousand of the population in 1871–5 to 14·4 per thousand on the eve of World War I.

The years between 1871 and 1875 saw the highest point in the recorded birth rate of Britain. But some time before this statistical peak was reached the basis of a high birth rate had already been undermined. Top Nation women were showing a marked disinclination to produce those endless arrays of children they had done in earlier decades. The evidence for this is to be found, not so much in statistics as in the tone and content of articles in contemporary periodicals. In several of her thin-lipped essays in the *Saturday Review* in 1868 Mrs Lynn Linton anonymously noted the trend towards limited motherhood. There was, she wrote, 'an increasing disinclination of married women to be mothers at all';[2] and 'the unnatural feeling against maternity existing among fashionable women is one of the worst mental signs of their state, as their frequent inability to be mothers is one of the worst physical results'.[3]

The short-lived *Imperial Review* printed several essays on the same subject. Criticizing the current tendency to small families it said that 'if it is still considered rather undignified to have no children at all, it is looked upon as supremely ridiculous to have a great many'.[4] Unlike Mrs Lynn Linton the *Imperial* did not

[1] The infant death rate for England and Wales in 1875 was 158 per 1,000 births. It was half this among the upper and professional classes.
[2] Mrs Lynn Linton, 'Modern Mothers' in the *Saturday Review*, February 29, 1868.
[3] 'The Fashionable Woman', August 8, 1868.
[4] 'Large Families' in *Essays in Defence of Women*.

suggest that the reason for this new trend was women's reluctance to bear children. It surrounded the subject in more
evasive terms and if it can be said to have assigned any specific
reason at all, this reason was the postponement of marriage
'until the couple could afford it', for age at marriage is critical
in determining family size when there is no birth control
practised within that marriage. Since fecundity begins to fall
sharply in the later thirties the average family of women
marrying at, say, twenty-three could well be twice as large as
that produced by women marrying at thirty.

The trend towards smaller families was not peculiar to
Britain. At the third annual convention of the American
Spiritualists held in Providence, Rhode Island, in August 1866,
one of the movement's leaders, Brother Wright, declared that
'the baby question is the great question of the world'.[1] Nor was
it only Noyes's Perfectionists at Oneida Creek who did not
multiply beyond their wishes, according to Hepworth Dixon's
researches. There was, he discovered, 'a very strange and rather
wide conspiracy on the part of women in the upper ranks – a
conspiracy which has no chiefs, no secretaries, no headquarters;
which holds no meetings, puts forth no platform, undergoes no
vote, and yet is a real conspiracy on the part of many leaders of
fashion among women; the end of which – if the end should
ever be accomplished – would be this rather puzzling fact:
there would be no more baby-shows in this country, since there
would be no longer any Americans in America'. Only in the
new states out West was there 'a high and healthy rate of
natural increase'. In Massachusetts 'the young women marry;
but they seldom become mothers'.[2]

Dixon's discovery of this widespread 'conspiracy' can be
confirmed from American sources. *Fruits of Philosophy* had been
circulating extensively since its first publication in 1832, and

[1] The Spiritualists were a cult which claimed, exaggeratedly no doubt,
to have three million members at this period. They believed that the old
religious gospels were exhausted, that the churches founded on them were
dead and that new revelations were required by man. Like other cults
Spiritualism crossed the Atlantic looking for converts, but unlike many of
them it caught on in London and there was a tremendous Spiritualist
vogue. Mrs Lynn Linton was one of those who was greatly taken with
Spiritualism for a time. It appealed strongly to the inquiring, confident
mood of the day.
[2] Hepworth Dixon, op. cit., p. 269.

275

other literature describing contraceptive methods was frequently advertised. The Reverend John Todd complained in *Serpents in the Doves' Nest*, published in 1867, that whenever a marriage was announced in New England – 'and probably it is so throughout the land' – the new wife was 'insulted within a week by receiving through the mail a printed circular, offering information and instrumentalities, and all needed facilities, by which the laws of heaven in regard to the increase of the human family may be thwarted'.[1] In its issue of October 17, 1867, *The Nation* carried an article which commented, in much the same terms and at much the same time as the *Imperial Review*, that a large family was no longer considered to be a cause for congratulation but rather a demonstration of recklessness or barbarism. And *Echoes* on March 6, 1869, reported with cries of outrage that it had heard that a 'taste for infanticide' had sprung up 'among "the first circles" in New York. There is not one in ten of the married women who have children.'

The desire for relief from excessive child-bearing was at least latent in the first half of the nineteenth century. There are letters by Jane Austen which show that the subject was discussed, and the twenty-one-year-old Queen Victoria wrote to her uncle, King Leopold of the Belgians, on January 5, 1841, a few weeks after the birth of her first child, 'I think, dearest Uncle, you cannot *really* wish me to be *"Mamma d'une nombreuse famille"*, for I think you will see with me the great inconvenience a *large* family would be to us all, and particularly to the country, independent of the hardship and inconvenience to myself; men never think, at least seldom think, what a hard task it is for us women to go through this *very often*.' But she, like so many others, was fatalistic. 'God's will be done,' she added. Child-bearing for the Queen was the 'shadow-side' of marriage, *die Schattenseite* as she more often called it since the indelicacy sounded less offensive in a foreign language.

Later in the century the latent desire turned into positive action. At a meeting of the Manchester Statistical Society in 1863 a lecturer said there was undoubtedly some foundation in the stories about married ladies in good society inducing miscarriages by excessive exercise on foot or horseback. Nor was it

[1] As quoted by Arthur W. Calhoun in *A Social History of the American Family from Colonial Times to the Present* (Cleveland, 1919), Vol. III, p. 239.

only ladies in good society who terminated their pregnancies, though the methods used by Lower Nation women were not as discreetly elegant as excessive exercise. In an article on 'Sweet Auburn' in the *Saturday Review* of March 14, 1857 the method of inducing miscarriages was described in a horrified survey of what went on among the lowest classes. 'It seems to be a recognized practice among the women of the place to take a drug known by a familiar name *hicra-picra* for this infamous object.' 'Sweet Auburn' was the town of Chesham in Buckinghamshire. The occasion for the article was the trial of a married man named White who had brought a woman to live with him and had connived with her, first to procure an abortion on his daughter to prevent her bearing a child by him, and then to poison his wife. 'Fornication and adultery, incest and murder, abortion and poisoning – all are tangled together in one hideous web of sin and horror,' wrote the *Saturday*.

There is no way of determining what the abortion rate was in Victorian times. Occasionally, apart from such cases as White of Chesham, there were trials of abortionists reported in the papers and fleeting references to the various abortifacients like Dialehyn pills, supposed to contain lead and hicra-picra (which was the common pronunciation of hiera-picra, derived from the Greek for sacred bitterness). Hicra-picra, also called hickery-pickery, was a purgative composed of aloes and canella bark. There is little doubt that its use was widespread.

A second way of limiting family size was infanticide, which was also extensively practised. The *Saturday Review* of August 9, 1856 contained a long article on the subject written by the Reverend William Scott in which he pointed out the extreme reluctance of juries to find mothers guilty of this crime. 'The fact is in too many instances that young people "keep company" on the understanding that marriage is to be postponed till it becomes necessary. The girl generally selects this view of life as a safe investment and makes up her mind to all chances. The road to matrimony in too many rural districts lies through antenuptial incontinence. In the farmer class the girl, if the man repents of his bargain, has the action for seduction and breach of promise to fall back upon – in the labouring classes it seems to be the rule that infanticide should clear off the score. . . . A conviction for infanticide is all but impossible.'

Scott cited a dozen recent cases to show that juries would not convict even in the most flagrant instances – and medical evidence always tended to support the juries' bias: confinements alone in the dark might lead a young mother to cut an infant's throat in mistake for its umbilical cord; there was nothing to show whether a child had had two fingers thrust down its throat or had failed to start breathing; if a child was found drowned at the bottom of a well, there was no indisputable proof that it had been born of the young woman in question; if the child died for any of half a dozen reasons who was to say that it was murder and not inadvertence or manslaughter? When a girl of the labouring class found herself pregnant, he wrote, she did not fly to the law or make a fuss, but did her best to conceal her condition so that she could kill the child undetected. Indignant denials of pregnancy were occasioned not by affronted dignity but by the desire to dispose of the infant.

According to Scott, the rot had set in with the trial of a girl called Celestine Sumner 'a few years ago at Dorchester'. The country girls made common cause with the infanticide mother. When she was acquitted they clapped in court and 'left the town boasting that "now they might do what they liked"'. The recent trials for infanticide were a national disgrace, he concluded. But Queen Victoria was one of those who supported the abolition of capital punishment for this crime.

Not only did infanticide purposely limit the number of children, but death from natural causes and border-line cases in which death was not prevented also kept down the size of families. Mortality among infants in their first year was about 10 per cent and, as we have seen in Chapter 6, to such a pass did things come when children were left with inefficient nurses while their mothers were out at work that a Select Committee was appointed in 1871 to report on the Best Measures of Protecting Infants put out to Nurse. The Committee's recommendations had little effect, but their revelations were gruesome to those who were unused to them as a normal part of Lower Nation life.

Nor was it only working mothers whose children's lives were in jeopardy. Epidemics would sweep through families; medical ignorance and prejudice affected all social classes. When so eminent an authority as Miss Nightingale could fiercely deny that disease could be transmitted by bacteria it is not surprising that scarlet fever could decimate family after family. Archbishop Tait of Canterbury, when he was Dean of Carlisle in 1856, lost six of his seven daughters in four weeks from scarlet fever.

The Harlot's Habit

As well as abortion and infanticide the third way in which the natural size of families was limited was by contraception. The public attitude to this in the 1870s was no less vehemently disapproving than it had been when Francis Place and John Stuart Mill were distributing the Diabolical Handbills fifty years earlier. The violence of this disapproval was felt by Lord Amberley, Bertrand Russell's father, when he stood as Liberal candidate for South Devon in November 1868. Some months previously he had taken the chair at a meeting of the London Dialectical Society – a philosophical body 'founded on the principle of absolute liberty of thought and speech' – at which Malthusianism and family limitation had been discussed. Among those who had spoken at the meeting was Charles Bradlaugh, secularist, freethinker and reformer, who in the early 1860s started a Malthusian League to teach the benefits and practices of limiting the population. Charles Knowlton's *Fruits of Philosophy* and Robert Dale Owen's *Moral Physiology* were still in circulation, and to these had now been added a third guide, 'the most important account of contraception published in Britain during the "quiet infiltration" period', according to Peter Fryer.[1] This was the work of George Drysdale, an Edinburgh doctor. It was first published pseudonymously in 1854 as *Physical, Sexual, and Natural Religion*, but in later editions – and the book went through thirty-four English editions, to say nothing of the editions in ten other European languages, before the thirty-fifth and last English edition appeared in 1905 – the main title was changed to *The Elements of Social Science*. It was this book, read on the recommendation of his tutor, that had interested Amberley in family limitation as 'an outlet for the great social difficulty' raised in the Malthusian question. Also at the meeting of the London Dialectical Society was George Drysdale's younger brother, Dr Charles Robert Drysdale.

[1] Peter Fryer, op. cit., p. 110.

After Bradlaugh, Drysdale, and one or two others had spoken, Amberley himself, then aged twenty-six, had made what seemed to him to be a perfectly innocuous speech in which he approved the principle of family limitation in order to prevent over-population, and hoped that the medical men present would tell the meeting how best this might be achieved. He had heard, he said, that American women, especially in the big cities, had methods of holding back pregnancies but that these were, he believed, harmful to health. Hence his desire to hear a discussion by the medical men present as to whether some harmless method might not be possible.

The meeting was supposed to be private, but a full report was leaked to the medical journals. The *British Medical Journal* was disgusted that the medical profession should have such a function assigned to it and approvingly reported that one of the doctors at the meeting 'wishes us to intimate that he would not by any means be a party to assigning to the profession any such anti-genetic functions', while another had told them he had resigned from the Society because it had discussed 'the propriety of assigning to medical men the intimated function of teaching females how to indulge their passions and limit their families'.

When the election campaign began Vice-Count A–B Lie, as his Tory opponents called him, found that the discussions in the press about the meeting, together with the known presence at it of the atheist Bradlaugh and one of the contraceptionist Drysdales, had raised a violent and vulgar opposition which hounded him until the results of the poll were declared. He was not elected.

The opposition to contraception as a filthy, disgusting, degrading practice is to be found in many periodicals of the time. *Fraser's Magazine*, for instance, in its issues of April and May 1871 had two long articles condemning contraception as a harlot's habit, something that no decent woman would even allow to be mentioned in her hearing. While *The Lancet* two years earlier, after ruminating on the Amberley affair, had announced that 'a legitimate check to population is to be found only in prudence in contracting marriage; and all other checks entail evils that are far worse than the disease'. The evils, said this organ of the medical anxiety-makers, were both moral and physiological. 'A woman on whom her husband practises what is euphemistically called "preventive copulation"' was 'necessarily brought into the condition of mind of a prostitute', while, from the health point of view, she had only one chance, 'depending on an entire absence of orgasm, of escaping uterine disease'. From the man's side, 'the practice, in its actual character and in its remote effects, is in no way distinguishable from masturbation'.

Nevertheless this anxiety-making was less effective and the violent opposition more of a surface reaction than the anti-contraceptionists would have liked to believe. Throughout the 1860s the quiet infiltration of birth-control propaganda had begun to have real effect, and although it is impossible to give any statistical evidence to bear this out there can be no doubt that in the private recesses of middle-class society the determination was taking root to use birth control as the most acceptable – indeed the only acceptable – method of keeping down the size of families. But there was no general economic pressure to spur this quiet infiltration; it was being adopted for other reasons, for convenience among them, so that what Mrs Lynn Linton excitedly called 'the mad race after pleasure' could be indulged in. Then came the Great Depression which made it increasingly difficult for the middle classes to preserve the differential standards they had achieved. Thus economic considerations began to exert an influence on the birth-control question.

The influence of economic considerations is itself a phrase standing for a variety of causes that make up what may be called 'the complex of civilization'. To determine the relative importance of the various factors in the complex web of cause and effect and to decide which were the most important in bringing about a decline in family size is a problem which even the 1949 Royal Commission on Population considered insoluble. The complex is compounded of lack of confidence in continuing prosperity; rising living standards; the growth of competitive individualism; changes in the long-term cost of rearing children and the limitations on their economic value by compulsory education and employment restrictions; the decline of agriculture and the rising importance of industry and commerce with the concomitant shift of population from rural dispersal to urban crowds, from the family domestic system to the factory; the growth of a scientific outlook in however embryonic a fashion and the tentative rejection of traditional beliefs, even if lip-service was still emphatically paid to them; the slow growth of humanitarianism; the emancipation of women; and also – far from unimportant in any society, especially one in which improved communications were bringing it ever closer together – the contagious effect of the idea that it had become, in the *Imperial Review*'s phrase, 'supremely ridiculous' to have a great many children. The complex of civilization in fact is an amalgam of physical, psychological, social, and legal conditions which gives a society the mental muscle that enables it to brave the wrath of its ancient gods and the taboos of its anxiety-makers. In the case of birth control, the various trends taken together made 'individual control over the size of the family seem desirable or necessary', while the improvement in contraceptive methods made this control more possible. 'The widespread adoption of family limitation in the 1870s, in our view,' the Royal Commission's Report continued, 'was due to the cumulative effect of these circumstances and to the special jolts which the depression of 1875 onwards and the Bradlaugh–Besant trials of 1877/8 gave to public opinion.'

Bradlaugh–Besant

Nine lives Annie Besant had. Her biographer, Arthur H. Nethercot, listed them[1] as the Christian Wife; the Atheist Mother; the Martyr of Science; the Socialist Labour Agitator; the Chela of the Mahatmas; the Indian Educator, Propagandist and Mystic; President of the Indian National Congress; the Deserted Leader; and finally, Life in Death. Before she was forty she was 'known all over the English-speaking world, and by many people on the Continent, as one of the most remarkable women of her day. She was a freethinker; a consorter with materialists like Charles Bradlaugh; an agitator in Radical political circles, again like Bradlaugh; a feminist; an early convert to Fabian Socialism, through the agency of Bernard Shaw; a teacher of science; an author-editor-publisher; the first prominent woman to dare to fight openly for what is now called birth control; a social and educational reformer; and an orator whose power was so compelling and whose charm was so potent that Shaw was only one among thousands who extolled

[1] Arthur H. Nethercot, *The First Five Lives of Annie Besant* and *The Last Four Lives of Annie Besant* (Hart-Davis, 1961 and 1963).

her as the greatest speaker of the century.'[1] All this was by 1885. Soon afterwards she increased her fame and notoriety still further by becoming a militant strike leader and trade union organizer. And within the next ten years she caused yet another sensation by rejecting her social feminist past and turning to theosophy, which led in turn to India and the struggle for Indian independence. In 1933 she returned into the 'everywhere' at the age of eighty-five.

Annie Besant reached her many peaks of fame from an unlikely starting point. She was born in London in 1847, the middle one of William and Emily Wood's three children, and the only girl. Despite her birth-place, she was three-quarters Irish – 'three-quarters of my blood and all my heart are Irish', she said. Her father was a qualified doctor who never practised, but who worked in a relative's City business house. In 1852 he died of consumption. His death turned his wife's hair white overnight. Soon afterwards the younger boy died, confirming his mother's clairvoyant knowledge that his father wanted him.

The sudden death of William Wood left his family almost destitute. After much persuasion Emily Wood allowed Annie to go and live with Miss Ellen Marryat, the youngest sister of that famous novelist Captain Marryat who had seen the four piano limbs dressed in modest little trousers. Her maternal instincts unsatisfied by spinsterhood and her ability as a teacher undoubted, Ellen Marryat had a number of protégés, all poor 'but gently born and gently trained', whom she brought up. With Miss Marryat Annie lived in Bonn and Paris as well as on Miss Marryat's estate near Charmouth in Dorset, and in London. At sixteen she went back to her mother. By now she had the makings of a precocious blue-stocking and she was a passionate reader of theology. In 1866 she met the newly ordained Frank Besant, who was seven years her senior. The following year she married him.

It was a disastrous marriage. And the disaster, which was exacerbated by Frank's authoritative attitude to a girl who had never been ordered about or reprimanded, stemmed from Annie's sexual ignorance. She was, she wrote, 'so scared and outraged at heart' at what happened from the first night of her marriage that she could never expunge its humiliation. Two

[1] Arthur H. Nethercot, op. cit., p. 13.

children, nevertheless, were born to her: a son, Digby, in 1869, and a daughter, Mabel, the following year. The arguments with her husband were endless and sometimes ended in blows. To add to the unhappiness her passionate religious questing toppled over into atheism. It was the breaking point of the marriage. He demanded that she take Holy Communion. She refused. She left him and returned to London from Sibsey, Lincolnshire, where Frank had been given a living by the Lord Chancellor, Lord Hatherley, who was a cousin of Annie's.

In London Annie was drawn to the freethinkers. She listened to the Rev. Charles Voysey, one of the latest members of the Established Church to become a dissenter, preaching in St George's Hall, Langham Place. She was consoled and delighted by what he said. She met him and his wife in the vestibule afterwards, returned to St George's Hall again and again, and soon became a close friend of the Voyseys. Through them she met Thomas Scott, the great freethinker of his day and the correspondent of all the liberal thinkers in the country. She helped Scott with his pamphlets, wrote some of her own, and widened her circle of freethinking friends, among them an American Moncure D. Conway and his wife. Conway was born in Virginia, educated at Harvard, and had come to England in 1863 to further the abolitionist cause. In 1864 he had started to preach at the South Place Chapel in Finsbury, London, first as a Methodist, then as a Unitarian, and by the time Annie Besant met him, as a theist and rationalist. It was at the suggestion of Mrs Conway that Annie went one evening in 1874 to hear Charles Bradlaugh lecture in the Hall of Science in Old Street, London.

Charles Bradlaugh was a secularist, a reformer, an ex-Dragoon Guard, and a 'barrack-room lawyer' of professional ability who could argue and win his own case in a court of law, as he did on many occasions; his was a litigious vocation. He had stood for Parliament in the two-seated constituency of Northampton on a platform of compulsory national education, land reform, separation of Church and State, representation of minorities in Parliament, abolition of hereditary peerages, and legal equality of employers and employees. He was defeated; but he stood again, unsuccessfully, in 1874; and in 1880 he was to be elected, although it was another six years before he was to be allowed to take his seat on account of the fact that as a secularist, he refused to take the oath and demanded that he be allowed to affirm.[1]

Annie Besant made a deep impression on Bradlaugh. He gave her a staff position on his *National Reformer*. Soon they became close colleagues and had a joint establishment in St John's Wood, where they lived with Bradlaugh's daughters Alice and Hypatia, and Annie's daughter Mabel. (Her son had been kept by Frank Besant under the deed of separation that ended their marriage.) Despite this domestic proximity, however, no evidence of the slightest impropriety between them was ever found, though Frank Besant's detectives did their best. Indeed 'although there were to be many more men, some of them quite famous, in Annie Besant's life, and with some of these she was undoubtedly in love', Annie's biographer believed it 'very unlikely that she ever took a lover', and in the particular case of Charles Bradlaugh 'there was little time for love, idyllic or otherwise, in the Besant–Bradlaugh schedule'.[2]

The beginnings of the case that were to make Annie Besant nationally known for the first time occurred in 1876, when a Bristol bookseller, Henry Cook, was sentenced to two years' hard labour for selling an obscene publication. The prosecution was brought under the Campbell Act, the 1857 Obscene Publications Act, which had been passed to check 'Holywell Street literature'. The wide terms of the Act had caused concern when it was passing through Parliament, and the Lord Chief Justice, John Campbell, who sponsored it, had assured members that its purpose was only to apply to works 'written with the single purpose of corrupting the morals of youth and of a nature calculated to shock the feeling of decency in any well-regulated mind'. But in 1868 a new Lord Chief Justice, Alexander Cockburn, had redefined the word 'obscenity' so that literary and even scientific works might fall foul of the Act. The obscene publication that Cook had been convicted of selling was none

---

[1] The other member for Northampton was Henry Labouchere, 'Labby', who had many objects of his scorn, including the Established Church. Bradlaugh's idealism, his humility, honesty, and benevolence in his everyday behaviour were in such contrast to the urbane, Church-scorning Labby that when he corrected a fellow member in the House of Commons who referred to him as 'the member for Northampton' by saying 'the *Christian* member', the House roared with laughter at the irony.

[2] Arthur H. Nethercot, op. cit., pp. 115 and 116.

other than *The Fruits of Philosophy* which, as we saw in Chapter 6, had been circulating in Britain without let since 1834. It is true that Cook had inserted some illustrations of his own – probably of the genital organs – into the copies that he was selling. Nevertheless the pamphlet was otherwise the same as it had been for forty years.

The actual publisher of *The Fruits of Philosophy* was Charles Watts, who had bought the plates from the widow of the first English publisher, James Watson. Having made a start at Bristol, the authorities now decided to prosecute Watts himself. Watts pleaded guilty and was let off with a suspended sentence and costs. Bradlaugh and Besant were aghast. Watts was employed by Bradlaugh as sub-editor of the weekly *National Reformer* and was also its publisher. His admittance of guilt was an act of treachery to the cause of freethought. Bitter words were spoken. Bradlaugh withdrew all the printing business of the National Secular Society from Watts, including the *National Reformer*, and dismissed him as sub-editor of the weekly.

Bradlaugh and Besant now formed the Freethought Publishing Company and Annie was appointed sub-editor of the *National Reformer*. They decided to provoke a test case. They re-published *The Fruits of Philosophy* with medical notes by Dr George Drysdale and announced when they would be in their shop behind Fleet Street to sell it in person. For forty years *The Fruits of Philosophy* had been selling about seven hundred copies a year. In the first twenty minutes at the shop in Stonecutter Street five hundred copies were sold. That was on March 23, 1877. But it was not until the middle of April that the law obliged and Charles Bradlaugh and Annie Besant were arrested. They were tried at the Guildhall on June 18 before a special jury, with the Lord Chief Justice, Sir Alexander Cockburn, hearing the case himself. The verdict was ambiguous. It amounted, as Annie put it, to, 'Not guilty, but don't do it again'. However, the court held that the verdict must be interpreted as meaning 'Guilty'.[1] The following week the defendants came up for judgement. The Lord Chief Justice did his best to save them by asking if they would submit to the

[1] The jury's decision was: 'We are unanimously of opinion that the book in question is calculated to deprave public morals, but at the same time we entirely exonerate the defendants from any corrupt motive in publishing it.'

jury's verdict and promise not to sell the book again. They refused, and were sentenced to six months' imprisonment and fines and recognizances amounting to £1,400. Using his knowledge of the law Bradlaugh kept the case open by applying for a writ of error on a technical point, execution of the sentences being stayed in the meantime. In February 1878 the appeal was heard. Bradlaugh won his technical point and the verdict of the Guildhall trial was reversed. Charles Bradlaugh and Annie Besant were not guilty. They were free 'to do it again' if they wanted.

The importance of the Bradlaugh–Besant trials was the tremendous publicity given to the whole question of contraception and to the merits of the different methods of contraception available. The trials were fully reported in the newspapers, especially in *The Times*, and although press opinion was on the whole hostile[1] it nevertheless brought the subject firmly into people's minds from the subliminal corners where it had been lurking. Once it was in the light of day, contraception was automatically stripped of some of its taboo. The effect of the extensive press coverage can be gauged from what Bradlaugh himself told an audience on August 26, 1877: in the four months since his prosecution, sales of *The Fruits of Philosophy* had amounted to 130,000 copies.

Nor was *The Fruits of Philosophy* the only printed source of information available. In 1877 Annie Besant wrote *The Law of Population* 'in the hope that it may point out a path from poverty, and may make easier the life of British mothers'. She wrote it because both she and Bradlaugh thought that Knowlton's book was largely out of date and could be much improved on. In it she listed all the 'prudential checks' that were available – the 'safe period', *coitus interruptus*, syringing, the *baudruche*, and the sponge (which seemed preferable) – and she answered the anxiety-makers' and moralists' objections. *The Law of Population* had a vast circulation before it was withdrawn by its author, when she became a theosophist.

[1] The *Saturday Review* in an article called 'A Nasty Case' discussed the trial at length without mentioning either it or the defendants by name or giving the faintest idea what it was about. But to those who knew what the Nasty Case was, the article was a vinegary denunciation of contraception and those newspapers which spread the 'evil seeds' by their reports. It was one of the most adroit pieces of allusive journalism to be found anywhere.

The Victorian Woman

For Charles Bradlaugh *The Fruits of Philosophy* trials were another phase in his long duel with Church and State. For Annie Besant they were more than that. It took supreme courage, as her biographer says, 'to become the first woman to dare to advocate publicly a cause which most men of the time feared to support'. She paid the penalty by losing the custody of her daughter.[1] But the result of her courage was that in 1882 the first birth-control clinic in the world was opened in Holland by Dr Aletta Jacobs, and Annie herself received letters from 'thousands of poor married women – many from the wives of country clergymen and poor curates – thanking and blessing me for shewing them how to escape from the veritable hell in which they had lived'.

An immediate result of the Guildhall trial was that Bradlaugh's Malthusian League, which he had started in the 1860s to spread contraceptive knowledge and which had since fallen into desuetude, was now revived. It began its work again in July 1877 with Dr C. R. Drysdale as president and Annie Besant, for a time, as secretary. Drysdale's wife, Dr Alice Vickery, was a leading member and succeeded her husband as president when he died in 1907.

The Malthusian League had to work with a measure of circumspection. Bradlaugh–Besant's successful appeal in February 1878 did not restrain the opposition, except in so far as neither of these leading birth-controllers were brought to trial on a similar charge again. But the 1857 Obscene Publications Act was still there, to be used against other Malthusians when suitable occasions offered. Furthermore the Post Office Act gave the Post Office authority to open and impound packets of obscene prosecutions and to prosecute the sender. The Society for the Suppression of Vice – which Annie Besant sarcastically called the Society for the Promotion of Vice – was an ever-watchful enemy of the Malthusians, and it started several successful actions against members of the League, the first of

[1] She also became the subject of dirty stories and rhymes. One of these, printed in full in Peter Fryer's *The Birth Controllers*, pp. 167 and 306–7 begins:

Said good Mrs Besant,
To make things all pleasant,
If of childeren [*sic*] you wish to be rid,
Just after coition, Prevent all fruition.
And corpse the incipient kid.

them in 1878, resulting in fines and imprisonment and, in the case of doctors, removal from the Medical Register. Birth-control trials took place sporadically until the early '90s.

Nevertheless, knowledge and practice spread. While the community's lip-service continued to be paid to the 'disgusting-ness' of contraception by the societies for the suppression of vice and crime, whose targets were society's scapegoats, these actions became more and more a pasteboard façade behind which general opinion gradually turned to the feeling that discussion of contraceptive methods, if conducted discreetly, was not dis-gusting but was in fact timely advice. Articles in magazines and handbooks on marriage did not openly advocate birth control, but they assumed that everyone agreed that smaller families were desirable. By 1895 the *Saturday Review* was acknowledging that the only woman who was willing 'to be regarded as a mere breeding machine' was the one who lacked 'the wit to adopt any other role'.[1] The warnings of doctors and the disapproval of the Church continued vehemently. But even here there were soft patches where the waters of public opinion, swept on by the propaganda of the Malthusians and their allies, began to seep through. The Church indeed found itself in an uncomfortable dilemma. If it persisted in condemning contraception as the practice of harlots and the work of the devil, then it must accept that if people wanted to limit the size of their families – as they clearly did – the only acceptable method of doing this was to postpone the time of marriage. This still seemed to be the common practice in the '80s, for in 1888 the marriage rate was the lowest on record and the age at which people married was still rising. But postponement of marriage made the other horn of the dilemma. It meant that prostitution would continue to be rife. It was all very well for intellectually adjusted priests to preach continence and control, but the passions of the ordinary man would find an outlet and create a demand. Thus the Church, in effect, had to decide whether as a matter of practical policy, even if not of theoretical approval, it would support birth control or prostitution. Gradually it followed the changing opinion of the Top Nation that birth control was 'the proper thing to do', and though the Roman Catholic Church for one condemned the prevention of conception as a sin, and continued

[1] 'The Maternal Instinct' in the *Saturday Review*, June 8, 1895, quoted in J. A. Banks, op. cit., p. 167.

to disallow the use of contraceptives until the present day, yet the tacit admittance of the 'safe period' by the Lambeth Conference of Church of England Bishops in 1908 showed that, despite earnest calls 'upon all Christian people to discountenance the use of all artificial means of restriction as demoralizing to character and hostile to national welfare', they were accepting family limitation as inevitable. It was to be fully another half-century, however, before contraception was a subject that could be freely discussed in all media of communication in Britain.

Comstockery

Bitter as it was, the opposition of the anti-vice societies, and especially the Society for the Suppression of Vice, in Britain was as nothing compared with the relentless campaign conducted in the United States by the New York Society for the Suppression of Vice, under its secretary Anthony Comstock. The Society was founded in 1873 and for the forty-two years until his death in 1915 Comstock ran it with fanatical hatred of all advocates of contraception, whom he believed to be doing the devil's work in the most literal sense. 'He could not imagine anyone sincerely proposing birth control as a solution to the social and medical problems of over-large families. His hatred of the physicians who tried to give evidence on family limitation, and of the radicals who championed their right to do so, was not lessened by the close links which existed, in America as in Britain, between the birth-control and freethought movements. Infidelity (i.e. atheism) and obscenity occupied the same bed, he declared in a characteristic metaphor. As for dealers in contraceptives, he called them "abortionists". And for abortionists he had no pity whatever.'[1]

Not content with bringing charges against actual 'offenders', Comstock framed others by decoy letters and incited people to commit offences so that he could arrest them. As well as being Secretary of the New York Vice Society, Comstock was special inspector for the Post Office Department so that his writ ran well beyond New York City. He proudly announced that he had travelled 190,000 miles outside the City between 1873 and the end of 1882 in his relentless search for indictable vice. For it was not only the birth-controllers he was after. He once admitted

[1] Peter Fryer, op. cit., p. 193.

blatantly in court that he and four other vice-hunters had hired three young women in a brothel to parade naked in front of them so that he might arrest them for indecent exposure. Among his victims was Madame Restell, New York's best-known professional abortionist, who cut her throat the night before she was due to appear in court. In his book *Traps for the Young* published in 1883 Comstock gave the New York Vice Society's bag for the first nine years. The Society had been responsible for 700 arrests, 333 sentences totalling 155 years and 13 days of imprisonment, fines totalling 65,256 dollars, and the seizure of 27,856 lbs of 'obscene' books and 64,836 'articles for immoral use, of rubber, etc.'.

For most of his reign Comstock was supported by the American medical profession, either from conviction or discretion. But despite the fact that, as Peter Fryer put it, 'for forty-two years Anthony Comstock's violent and unshakeable prejudices stood between the American people and the free dissemination of contraceptive knowledge'[1] that knowledge nevertheless spread and was acted upon so that there was no reversal of the trend that Hepworth Dixon had discovered: large families among native-born Americans became increasingly rare.

[1] Peter Fryer, op. cit., p. 193.

Chapter 17

'AN IDEAL OF SERVICE'

In his six studies of *Victorian People* Asa Briggs regretted that he had not had space to include at least one woman in his gallery, 'for women – often "maiden aunts" – played a leading part not only in family welfare but in the making of Victorian social quality and the practical application of an ideal of service. A community devoted to getting on, and limited at its edges by masculine codes of inherited authority of formalized professionalism, had little to offer women of spirit and ability. Exceptional women like Florence Nightingale, who rejected marriage for service – because marriage did not provide for the promptings of "a moral, an active nature, which requires satisfaction" – played a really prominent part in the foreground of national life.'[1] And, as we have seen, exceptional women like Josephine Butler, who embraced both marriage and service, also played a prominent part in the making of Victorian social quality on a national scale. 'Many other women, including married women who reacted against the formality and superficiality of subordinate status, were central figures in local life.'[1] The *Handbook for Women Engaged in Social and Political Work*, edited by Helen Blackburn a leading feminist, which came out in 1881 and had a second, expanded edition in 1895, listed some of those women.

The opportunities for service were more numerous informally than formally, but in the last decades of Victoria's reign the formal opportunities increased, as the *Handbooks* show. Especially was this the case in education and Poor Law administration. The 1870 Education Act, which made elementary education obligatory for all children was administered by school boards,

[1] Asa Briggs, *Victorian People* (Pelican Edition, 1965), p. 21.

on which women were permitted to serve. The first woman was elected to a school board in 1872 and by the end of 1880 there were seventy women members of school boards in England and Wales. Among the first to be elected was Mrs Creyke of Raw-cliffe, Yorkshire, who was widowed young and who for many years, on the school board and other committees, was the central figure in local life round Goole, near which Rawcliffe lies. In 1873 Mrs Nassau Senior, sister of Thomas Hughes, the author of *Tom Brown's Schooldays*, was appointed the first woman Poor Law Inspector. In 1875 the first woman Poor Law Guardian was elected – by 1894 there were two hundred women Poor Law Guardians. Although the struggle for the parliamentary vote was unsuccessful, in 1888 women were included in the franchise for the newly-created county councils. In the 1890s women served on the Royal Commission on Labour and on the Royal Commission on Secondary Education.

Less formally, too, women regulated the mores of local and national life. Augustus Hare's Grandma Leycester was found all over the country, all variations on the same theme; disapproving of village girls who appeared at the annual school feast in a bonnet trimmed with artificial flowers because such frippery was 'quite unsuitable for schoolgirls or servants', sending imperative orders to the local school that the children's hair should be shortened 'to the back of their necks' and at the same time sending a barber to carry it out, seeing that a poor girl who came to the school feast in stolen boots was marched off by the constable.[1]

'The Keeper of Women's Rights'

One maiden aunt who played a part in national life, and who was certainly a central figure in the local life of Edinburgh and Perthshire, was Elizabeth Haldane, that 'Keeper of Women's Rights' at the age of nine. Elizabeth was one of five children, the others all boys. One of these, Richard became Viscount Haldane, lawyer and cabinet minister, another became Professor J. S. Haldane, the father of Professor J. B. S. Haldane and Naomi Mitchison, whose maiden aunt Elizabeth was. The third brother was Sir William Haldane, and the fourth, George, died as a boy.

Elizabeth Haldane was a talented woman, who translated

[1] These examples come from *Two Generations*.

several books of German philosophy and had wide intellectual
interests. But her chief activity was in various fields of social
reform and organization. Thus, for instance, on the one hand
she organized a public library for the people of her Perthshire
neighbourhood, and on the other she assisted in setting up
benefit societies for women and became an expert in hospital
and nursing management. It was in the last of these fields that
she became best known, but her social work was unobtrusively
important in many ways. Her brother Richard's political
connections brought her in close touch with the leading politicians of the day, and she was in a strong position to implement
the reforms that seemed so necessary to her. In 1920, at the age
of fifty-eight, she became the first woman justice of the peace in
Scotland.

The Haldanes' father was a clergyman and their mother was
the daughter of a clergyman. 'Religion,' wrote Elizabeth in her
autobiography,[1] 'permeated our lives and the sense of sin and
its consequences seemed to dog our footsteps when we remembered what it meant. But strangely enough the churches did not
influence us as did the influence of home. Church in the country
had a pleasant aroma of outside life and outside people, and the
oppressive theology that was apt to overshadow our lives was
blown aside by the fresh country breezes. In town, church, as a
rule, just meant nothing to us but weariness of spirit.'

The Haldanes spent part of the year in Edinburgh and part –
the wonderful part that Elizabeth preferred – in the country at
Cloan near Auchterarder in Perthshire. Like the young Lynns
of an earlier generation they led a simple life with few parties
and plain food. 'Porridge and bread and butter for breakfast,
mutton and plain puddings for dinner, and toast and butter for
tea – no supper and therefore no cuddling up in warm dressing-
gowns and bedroom slippers for the evening meal as happens
nowadays.'

The first part of Elizabeth's education took place in the
country. She remembered being dragged to the schoolroom to
have lessons from the tutor, 'in tears, because the boys had
teased me about the horrors of the "lessons" that were in
prospect. I was consoled, however, by bread and butter
sprinkled with sugar given us as luncheon. In those days tea

[1] Elizabeth Haldane, *From One Century To Another* (Maclehose, 1937),
p. 43.

and sugar were given out weekly to the servants as well as beer or beer money, and they were very kind in giving some of the former to the children. But there was also a luncheon for the scholars at eleven o'clock.'[1] In due course she loved lessons whether they were given by the tutor or by the village school-master who rewarded the children with jujubes. Elizabeth was also sent to attend special classes for girls, because she was thought to be much too boyish by some of her elderly relatives and was consequently in need of training in the technique of young ladyhood. She broke her dolls to see what was inside them, played cricket and climbed trees, 'and altogether was conscious of the impossibility of ever attaining social success'.

Exams for Girls

Elizabeth's lessons came at a time when girls' education was slowly passing from one stage to another. The school boards, instituted by the 1870 Education Act, meant inspection of schools, and inspection meant examination: 'all the poor little mites of the next decade were going to have individual "passes", and the schoolteachers were to tremble when the inspector came round and pray for fine weather so that he might be in a good temper. It is just possible that Her Majesty's Inspector might himself have had a faint heart, though he dared not show it!'[2] There were examinations too in the new collegiate schools initiated by Miss Buss and Miss Beale, and extended by the Girls' Public Day School Company. This had sprung from the Women's Education Union which was formed in 1872 in order to bring people engaged in promoting the education of women into co-operation with each other and to promote the establishment of good schools. The Girls' Public Day School Company opened schools where girls would receive as thorough and sound an education as grammar schools provided for boys. The first school was opened in Chelsea, London, in November 1873 and by the middle of 1880 there were twenty-two schools open.

At the next level of education university courses for women were now available at Girton and Newnham in Cambridge, and at Somerville and Lady Margaret Hall at Oxford. Birmingham, Bristol, Newcastle and London also gave university instruction

[1] ibid., p. 167.
[2] ibid., p. 19.

to women, as did Dublin, Belfast, Cork and Edinburgh. From 1878 London University had a new charter which empowered it to open all its degrees and prizes to women. The first examinations under this charter were held in January 1879. The only other universities where women could obtain degrees were at St Andrews, in Scotland, which had instituted special degrees in arts for women in 1877, and at the new university in Ireland, which was given its legal existence in August 1879. At Oxford and Cambridge instruction did not lead to a degree. The University of Cambridge had opened its local examinations to girls in 1865, and by 1880 these examinations were being held in eighty-four centres. In 1869 it had started examinations for women over eighteen. That same year Oxford University established local examinations for girls, and in 1875 established other local examinations for women.

In Elizabeth Haldane's case, when it was quite evident to any outsider that the girls attending the special classes were learning practically nothing, it was suggested by one bold mother that they should be entered for a local examination. 'The idea was most exciting, and we, who had never even had an examination of any sort but just learned our day's lesson as it came, regardless of what preceded or succeeded, were delighted at the idea. A tutor was brought in to prepare us for this great ordeal and he did his work admirably, since he knew just the sort of questions that we were likely to be asked. But then came a snag, for it was discovered that we could not have an examination in our own classroom but should have to go to the University of Edinburgh. Such a wild step could not be thought of for "young ladies", though the original mother who desired the examination kept to it for her daughter. We were examined by I forget whom, but by someone who did not know anything of our preparation, and consequently, while the brave candidate produced her parchment triumphantly, we had done none too well and had nothing to show.'[1]

Despite these problems created by propriety, university instruction, the new Public Day Schools, the Proprietary Schools (of which there were twenty-eight at the end of 1880) and the creation of a large number of endowed schools for girls as a result of the Schools Inquiry Commission of 1868, all helped to make girls' education at last a little more worthy of the name.

[1] ibid., p. 20.

This did not mean that the schools of 'accomplishments' had altogether disappeared; but into the inanity of this sort of so-called education there was now injected a cadre of proper learning.

Every Lady Must Take Her Maid

Young girls in those days were much over-dressed by later standards. From the top of their heads to their toes their bodies were protected from everything including fresh air. Both sun and rain had to be kept off – 'sun-stroke and, for girls, sunburn (almost as bad) would result from one and colds from the other ... It was no use saying that all this induced colds and even phthisis, for no one would believe it'.[1] Both boys and girls wore stays, though the boys were released from their imprisonment at about the age of seven, while the girls were sentenced for life – each year their cage becoming stronger and more bony.

When a girl reached her later 'teens she entered a new life. Her clothes became a carapace. She was laced into stays which moulded her waist to as near twenty-one inches as possible – less, if that could be achieved; but certainly not over twenty-five. She was arrayed in the elaborate long dresses of maturity – often to her great satisfaction, but sometimes, as Gwen Raverat recalled in her own case, to her deep discomfort and misery.[2] She was furnished with a small trousseau to take on her formal visits to country houses. These visits, like the new uniform, were part of the new life. They were solemn occasions, as Elizabeth Haldane recalled. Her own initiation began towards the end of the 1870s when 'the great still preserved their place in Society almost unimpaired'.

Elizabeth often stayed with family connections in a large house in Warwickshire. The ritual was inflexible. 'Footmen,

[1] ibid., p. 21.

[2] 'The thought of the discomfort, restraint and pain, which we had to endure from our clothes, makes me even angrier now than it did then,' she wrote in 1952 (*Period Piece*, p. 258). 'Except for the most small-waisted, naturally dumb-bell-shaped females, the ladies never seemed at ease, or even quite as if they were wearing their own clothes. For the dresses were always made too tight, and the bodices wrinkled laterally from the strain.' She and her sister rebelled against stays, but to no avail. 'They were real instruments of torture; they prevented me from breathing, and dug deep holes into my softer parts on every side.' And 'after the torture of stays came the torture of hats, the enormous over-trimmed hats'.

none under six feet high, abounded; and they marshalled the guests to carriages, while maids and luggage were provided for in omnibuses. Luggage was portentous, for the voluminous skirts of satin or moiré required much room, and no one thought of the unfortunate porters who had to carry the boxes. The fitted dressing-case, without which no lady travelled, was a constant care, for it seemed always on the eve of being lost. Then morning prayers were something to be remembered. There was the row of chairs set out for the gentry to which they advanced while an enormous array of servants stood to attention. Immediately everyone turned round as at a signal, and knelt. The guests had walked into the room in order of precedence, and so had the servants: there was the regular and well-understood precedence of the house-party and possibly the more intricate order of precedence of the maids and valets, which depended on that of their masters and mistresses. No under-servant was allowed to speak at table till the upper-servants departed for the house-keeper's room, there to complete their meals. Young servants had to be up betimes and get their work done before there was a chance of their meeting the gentry in the house, and they had to be ready for morning prayers. All the servants were marshalled to church on Sundays – the men in livery and the women in black frocks and bonnets.' One girl told Elizabeth that some-times she hid under the bed to escape the ceremony!

No lady could go to a house-party without taking her maid. If she did she would have been lost, for she could have got no attention from any other servant on her own. The ritual con-tinued throughout the day. And at eleven o'clock exactly every-one rose and went to bed. 'The butler and footman stood by the door and the gentlemen handed lighted candles in old-fashioned silver candlesticks to the ladies. So armed, all wended their way through dark passages to their candle-lit rooms. A fixed bath was unknown, but the housemaids brought up great cans of water from downstairs, hot and cold, and there were bright fires burning so that it was quite cheerful. Coals were cheap.'[1]

Elizabeth used to visit the cottages and schools round the great house with her Warwickshire hostess. What she saw shocked her democratic Scottish mind. Schoolteachers and schoolchildren alike were subservient to the last degree. She hated visiting the schools, nor did she find any pleasure in the

[1] Elizabeth Haldane, op. cit., pp. 79–80.

visits to the labourers' cottages ('armed with soup, or giving promises of soup'), for she felt that if only labourers were given proper wages and decent houses this would be the real cure for their worries. The labourers were receiving ten or twelve shillings a week and it was explained to her that although her hosts were financially quite able to pay higher wages, it would be unfair on the neighbouring landlords if they did so.

English agriculture was on the verge of collapse. The catastrophe began in 1875 with a series of bad harvests, and came to a head in 1879 with the wettest summer ever known, which blackened the harvest in the fields and left three million sheep dead of rot. The bad weather obscured the trend that had already started some years before and was soon to prove totally inimical to any long-term recovery: the opening-up of the limitless Middle West cornlands under the new reaping-machines and combine-harvesters, as a gigantic grain-basket within reach of the British market. For the agricultural labourer 1879 was the nadir. Thereafter Joseph Arch and his agricultural trade union slowly began to free him from his slavery. It was in south Warwickshire that Arch's movement began.

West End

Country-house visiting was one part of an upper-class young lady's new life; the London Season was the other – as it had been in Adeline de Horsey's day. One of those who first experienced it in the 1870s was Beatrice Potter, then in her early 'teens, who wrote in her diary on August 3, 1874, 'I enjoyed it immensely. It is seldom I have had so much pleasure in so small a space of time.'

This happy excitement did not last, however. Beatrice felt a revulsion and determined that she would not 'come out'. But before the moment arrived this decision was overborne and at the conventional age of eighteen she joined her sisters 'in the customary pursuits of girls of our class, riding, dancing, flirting and dressing-up, an existence without settled occupation or personal responsibility, having for its end nothing more remote than elaborately expensive opportunities for getting married'.[1]

In retrospect she pitilessly examined these customary pursuits. The annual London Season she identified as the

[1] Beatrice Webb, op. cit., p. 81.

complement for women of the masculine world of big enterprise, with its passion for adventure and power. 'In the '70s and '80s the London Season, together with its derivative country-house visiting, was regarded by wealthy parents as the equivalent for their daughters of the university education and professional training afforded for their sons, the adequate reason being that marriage to a man of their own or a higher social grade was the only recognized vocation for women not compelled to earn their own livelihood. It was this society life which absorbed nearly half the time and more than half the vital energy of the daughters of the upper and upper-middle class; it fixed their standards of personal expenditure; it formed their manners and, either by attraction or repulsion, it determined their social ideals.'[1]

The chief characteristic of the London Season and country-house life, and the one which, in Beatrice's estimation, distinguished it from 'the recreation and social intercourse of the rest of the community, was the fact that some of the men and practically all the women made the pursuit of pleasure their main occupation in life'.[2] As confirmation of this fact she cited the autobiography of Margot Asquith, second wife of H. H. Asquith, Liberal Prime Minister from 1908 to 1916, and later Earl of Oxford and Asquith. In this book Lady Oxford and Asquith unflinchingly disclosed the intimate life of herself and her friends. Understandably the autobiography created a great stir on its publication in 1920. But the very frankness and unapologetic attitude which upset so many people on its appearance made it, in Beatrice's opinion, a document of great value to the sociologist. 'Riding, dancing, flirting and dressing-up – in short, entertaining and being entertained – all occupations which imply the consumption and not the production of commodities and services, were the very substance of [Lady Asquith's] life before marriage and a large and important part of it after marriage. And my own experience as an unmarried woman was similar . . . the presentation at Court, the riding in the Row, the calls, the lunches and dinners, the dances and crushes, Hurlingham and Ascot, not to mention amateur theatricals and other sham philanthropic excrescences.' Naturally there was a purpose behind all this activity, apart from the

[1] ibid., p. 45.
[2] ibid., pp. 47–8.

pursuit of pleasure, so that its futility had a ravening base. This purpose was the business of getting married, 'a business carried on by parents and other promoters, sometimes with gentile surreptitiousness, sometimes with cynical effrontery'. By the end of the Season reaction had set in, at any rate for those who had not the new excitement of a splendid marriage to look forward to. 'Indigestion and insomnia had undermined physical health; a distressing mental nausea, taking the form of cynicism about one's own and other people's character, had destroyed faith in and capacity for steady work.'[1]

After her girlhood was over and she had become her father's housekeeper and hostess, Beatrice discovered that for women the pursuit of pleasure imposed its own hard work of a kind that she had not realized before. It was work that she herself found tiresome, involving as it did innumerable decisions on what she considered to be insignificant matters. 'There was the London house to be selected and occupied; there was the stable of horses and carriages to be transported; there was the elaborate

[1] ibid., pp. 48–9. The hard round of Society had not changed much since Mrs Stevenson found it 'laborious beyond anything' in 1838, or since 1861 when a letter appeared in *The Times* of July 1 describing the modern girls' way of passing the Season. Although signed 'Grandmamma' there is something about it which suggests a male author: 'In London they ride in the crowded park from 12 to 2, then home to luncheon: probably some friends drop in at that hour; then a short drive – a visit or two; then the five o'clock tea, the sort of little assembly so happily called "kettle drum"; then home to dress for dinner or the opera, to be followed perhaps by a rout. The "whole to conclude", as the playbill says, with a ball and perhaps a cotillion at three o'clock in the morning. Why, sir, it puts me out of breath even to write it. Their life in the country is nearly as hard. They're always going from one country house to another, where they dress four times a day. Rustling silks for breakfasts, a habit or linsey petticoat and Balmorals for the mid-day ride or walk, a pretty dressing-gown for the five o'clock tea, a London ball dress for dinner and the subsequent romp of "whip up Smouchy" on "Pont".' But there was always the criticism that manners were getting too lax. 'Grandmamma' said that in her day when she was in London, she never was 'at home' in the morning. 'Mothers now tell me that young men are running in and out of the house all day, as long as the girls are home. And then the conversation; when people talk for fifteen hours a day there must be much folly, if not worse, spoken. Spirits must flag when there is so much straining, and topics more exciting than proper will be introduced.'

Beatrice, too, found that the Season involved 'a mania for reckless talking' which, together with 'the experimental display of one's own personality, ousted all else from consciousness'.

stock of prescribed garments to be bought; there was all the commissariat and paraphernalia for dinners, dances, picnics and week-end parties to be provided. Among the wealthier of one's relatives and acquaintances there were the deer forests and the shooting-boxes all entailing more machinery, the organization of which frequently devolved on the women of the household.'[1] Many of these women, in contradistinction to Beatrice Potter, found such responsibility satisfying and even enthralling. It was the scope they were given for wielding power and exercising their organizing ability that they enjoyed. Whether the matters on which they had to give decisions were insignificant or not was a question of personal opinion. For some they did not seem insignificant. Furthermore the crucial point was the decision-taking itself. It was that which gave the satisfaction and feeling of importance.

Looking back on her Seasons in London Society Beatrice Webb may have found them a personal bore and a social disease, but there were hundreds of women who lived for them and relished them, and many thousands more who would have liked to be in her place.

Gracedieu
When she was twenty-one Beatrice's cousin Mary Booth wrote of her that she was 'as odd as ever she can be but a good sort of girl. She is dreadfully bothered with the "weltschmerz"; the uselessness of life, etc. etc., and fancies that no one ever went through the like before. I sympathized and comforted as well as I could.' In due course the sympathy and comfort bore fruit, but not perhaps in the way that Mary Booth might have expected. The Booths too had been troubled, but not by the troubles that were bringing the anguish of uselessness to Beatrice. Social problems, and above all the Problem of all Problems, as Charles Booth called it, were the source of their disquiet. Booth, born and brought up in Liverpool, was tormented by the poverty around him and could neither ignore it nor reconcile it with the wealth and comfort of the Top Nation to which he himself belonged. In 1871 he married Mary Macaulay, daughter of the historian's youngest brother Charles, and together they 'argufied' for hours about the crippled nature of Society and what could be done to cure it. By 1882 Charles Booth was

[1] ibid., p. 49.

approaching the moment when he was about to move from discussion of theories to their translation into practice. Beatrice by this time had arrived at a decision about her own life. Her main interest, she had discovered, lay in analysing social problems rather than in practical philanthropy. She had been led to this discovery by listening to the Booths' discussions and, as she grew older, taking part in them herself. But there still remained some years of doubt before she refused Joseph Chamberlain's offer of marriage and followed the bent of her intellect. She joined Charles Booth in the new craft of social investigation which he began to carry out in the East End of London, and which eventually led to his monumental seventeen-volume survey of *Life and Labour of the People of London* published between 1891 and 1901. During her years of mental turmoil Beatrice relied greatly on Charles and Mary Booth. 'They and their family are the bright spot in my life,' she wrote in her diary, 'a continual source of strength – an everlasting, up-springing interest.'

The Booths had seven children. One died in infancy, but the other six, three boys and three girls, inherited the longevity genes of their mother. Mary was taken to see the Great Exhibition in Hyde Park when she was a small girl of four, and she lived to see the outbreak of the Second World War in 1939. All her six surviving children passed the age of eighty and several passed the age of ninety. The young Booths were brought up partly in London and partly in Leicestershire where Charles Booth had rented Gracedieu Manor in Charnwood Forest. He chose this particular part of the country because it stood almost midway between Liverpool, where he had his shipping business, and London where he had part of his tanning business and where he was also engaged in his social research. Gracedieu was a huge house with thirty bedrooms, 700 acres of wood, and a trout stream.

In an unpublished memoir, *Six-to-Sixteen at Gracedieu*, the second daughter, Margaret, who later married W. T. D. Ritchie only son of Thackeray's eldest daughter, has preserved a delightful picture of the Booths' life there. 'The morning after our arrival at Gracedieu my baby sister and I were turned out on a big lawn. It was white with daisies and seemed to stretch for miles. There was a line of ilex trees on one side and a row of stately cedars on the other. Beneath the cedars sweet williams grew in neglected profusion.' While the children were outside their mother was battling with problems indoors. The roof leaked and buckets had to be set in every corner to collect the drops. 'It was a marvel she kept smiling for a baby was on the way. But her spirit was indomitable.'

While Mary Booth was putting Gracedieu in order, her husband came and went continually. The children had no idea where he was when he was away. Even their mother could not always follow every detail of his many journeys. But she knew to the full what he was doing and thinking, for he would write to her sometimes twice a day and depended upon her for everything, from the special food which he needed because of his poor digestion to his stockings which had to be knitted in closest fashion so as to fit tightly round his thin legs. And beyond these material aids he depended on her too for help with his sociological works. Not a page of his manuscripts was passed until she had read it, and her disapproval was sufficient reason for him to amend or delete as she suggested. But Mary Booth was no flouter of convention. Because polite society assumed that she could not like the social work her husband was doing she presented a front of dutiful tolerance. The fact that she actually helped him was a closely-guarded family secret, and it is possible that even his staff had no idea that she actually rewrote sections of their work. 'They must never know,' she told her husband firmly, but sometimes the Macaulay style must have made the perspicacious wonder. 'She proved to be an active and fertile contributor to the conception and gestation of the whole great scheme,' wrote Charles Booth's biographer, 'her wide cultural background and critical approach providing an essential frame of reference for the narrower specialisms of her husband and cousin,'[1] Beatrice Potter.

The Booths' summers were spent at Gracedieu, their winters in London – until 1889 at a house in Grenville Place, Kensington, and thereafter at 24 Great Cumberland Place, which the children nicknamed 'Cumbersome'. The London to which they returned from the country was the London of four-wheelers, horse buses, hansom cabs. 'Ladies armed with card-cases paid calls,' recalled Margaret in her memoir. 'Children took walks

[1] T. S. Simey and M. B. Simey, *Charles Booth, Social Scientist* (Oxford University Press, 1960), p. 74. See also Duncan Crow, *A Man of Push and Go, the Life of George Macaulay Booth* (Hart-Davis, 1965).

19. By the end of the century women's fashions allowed them to run races at the village fête ... *Country Camera*.

Or go upstairs on buses. Leeds c. 1895. *Crow Collection*.

But one still had to 'dress with decency' – even in the heat of Khartoum. The lady is one of Mary Booth's daughters-in-law.

20. THE NEW CENTURY

Edith Armytage (*above*) driving a Baby Peugeot at Kirklees, Yorkshire – before registration numbers were introduced in 1903. The photographs on this page were taken by Edith's brother, Jack Armytage, the author's father-in-law. *Crow Collection.* 'Two out of three played tennis all summer'. The lady (*above right*) is the sister of the astronomer on an earlier page. *Crow Collection.* Miss North (*centre*), who became Edith's sister-in-law, was a relative of Marianne North, a famous lady traveller and flower painter. *Crow Collection.* Miss Littledale (*below*), like Jack Armytage, a crack shot. *Crow Collection.*

with governesses; there were Monday pops;[1] and there were dinner-parties. The gentlemen and ladies walked arm-in-arm down the stairs and small girls in white frocks watched their descent and then listened for the buzz of conversation which rose like steam from the dining-room to the upper floor. If you were awake later, you could hear the whistling for cabs when the guests were on the move.' There were muffin-men with trays on their heads who rang a bell as they walked. 'It was thrilling to watch from our window the nurserymaid run out to stop him and buy his wares. Nor must we leave out the organ-grinders. How cheerfully they ground out tunes such as "Will you be mine?"' On Sundays their father would come to the nursery and help to colour the Kate Greenaway and Walter Crane pictures in their books. 'Then everything must be cleared away and tea laid, and if Maria, our nurserymaid, were in a good temper, she would make Fizzledick, that is toast our slices of bread and butter by the fire. After tea there was my mother to read aloud and show picture-books.' On other days there were lessons, and dancing and singing classes.

While his children were growing up in a cheerful, busy atmosphere surrounded by a rich supply of friends and relations, Charles Booth was engrossed in his Inquiry into the conditions of the London poor – as well, that is, as running his diverse and successful business. 'Often after dinner,' his daughter Margaret relates, 'he would change his clothes and go off to see what was happening in humble streets. Once my mother heard that a coachman whom she had dismissed and who was angry on that account had observed in an interview, "Do you know what Mr B. is really? He is a burglar!" Indeed it must have seemed the most probable explanation. But of all this we knew nothing at the time. When we came down to eight o'clock breakfast he was always there reading his paper and he would be gone to his office by nine.'

After some months of this London life it would be time to go to Gracedieu again, 'to long summer days and cotton frocks and lessons in an upstairs schoolroom'. The schoolroom was only for the little girls, as Margaret and her younger sister Imogen were called, although the eldest of the family, Antonia, did join them for drawing. Antonia's education was 'as original as it was successful. Constance Garnett, later the translator of Tolstoy,

[1] Popular concerts.

taught her the classics, sometimes by correspondence, and sometimes she came to stay for the purpose.'

A large number of people came to stay with the Booths at Gracedieu, but the family knew very few neighbours. 'Distance was the main cause,' Margaret's memoir continues. 'The pair of horses . . . hired for the summer did not carry my mother very far. Added to this my father never did anything in the shooting or hunting line and had no leisure for county sociabilities. He regarded Gracedieu as a working box. So that my mother turned her energies to friends who stayed in the house; to village doings; and to one or two families who lived within reach.' Sewing bees, school treats, and the cricket club were all included in the village doings.

In the early years at Gracedieu the guests were often the people who were working with Charles Booth – people like Arthur Baxter, Hubert Llewellyn Smith, and Clara Collet. 'The fact that she wore ankle-length skirts not only in daytime, but of an evening, showed that she was a worker. She had not time to brush trailing petticoats, she said. It was a labour of the age,' Margaret remembered. Others who came were, of course, Beatrice Potter, 'brilliantly handsome and somewhat alarming', Canon and Mrs Barnett of Toynbee Hall, Whitechapel, who caused much mirth among the young Booths because the Canon was so very bald and his wife always alluded to him as 'my holy man'. And on one occasion, Octavia Hill came with her sister Miranda. 'They were tiny women possessed of great dignity.' Octavia Hill, grand-daughter of Southwood Smith who had been one of the explorers of the 'newly-discovered regions' in the 1830s and '40s, made vital contributions to social reform in housing, open spaces, cadet-training, and Poor Law Reform. Other close friends of the Booths were the Holman Hunts, who often came to stay, and among their vast cousinhood the Llewellyn Davieses, the family of Emily Davies, were frequent visitors.

East End

It was from the world of Gracedieu and 'Cumbersome' that Charles Booth and Beatrice Potter went to the East End of London to live the life of the poor and examine the conditions under which the Lower Nation existed. Beatrice worked as a 'plain trouser hand' in several East End sweat-shops. In this way she obtained material for what she called her one and only literary success – an article published in *The Nineteenth Century* in October 1888 called 'The Pages of a Work Girl's Diary'.

This article was, in fact, little more than a transcript of her diary with a few of the facts disguised to avoid possible libel actions and some of the experiences expurgated to be 'suited to a female pen!' These expurgations referred chiefly to the prevalence of incest in one-room tenements. 'The fact that some of my workmates – young girls, who were in no way mentally defected, who were, on the contrary, just as keen-witted and generous-hearted as my own circle of friends – could chaff each other about having babies by their fathers and brothers was a gruesome example of the effect of debased social environment on personal character and family life, and therefore on racial progress. The violation of little children was another not infrequent result. To put it bluntly, sexual promiscuity, and even sexual perversion, are almost unavoidable among men and women of average character and intelligence crowded into the one-room tenements of slum areas, and it is the realization of the moral deterioration involved, more than any physical discomfort, that lends the note of exasperated bitterness characteristic of the working class representative of these chronically destitute urban districts.'[1]

Charles Booth himself – perhaps with the aid of Mary Booth – described a street of those one-room tenements in a slum area in London. It was typical of the sort of place where Beatrice Potter's workmates lived. It was called Shelton Street.

'It was just wide enough for a vehicle to pass either way, with room between curbstone and houses for one foot passenger to walk; but vehicles would pass seldom, and foot passengers would prefer the roadway to the risk of tearing their clothes against projecting nails. The houses, about forty in number, contained cellars, parlours, and first, second, and third floors, mostly two rooms on a floor, and few of the two hundred families who lived here occupied more than one room. In little rooms no more than eight feet square would be found living father, mother, and several children. Some of the rooms, from the peculiar build of the houses (shallow houses with double frontage) would be fairly large and have a recess six feet wide for the bed, which in rare instances would be curtained off. If

[1] Beatrice Webb, *My Apprenticeship*, footnote to p. 231.

there was no curtain, anyone lying on the bed would perhaps be covered up and hidden head and all, when a visitor was admitted, or perhaps no shyness would be felt.'

On every hand in Shelton Street were drunkenness, dirt, and bad language; violence was common, amounting at times to murder. Three-quarters of the rooms, with only sticks of worthless furniture, were filthy to the last degree. 'Not a room would be free from vermin, and in many life at night was unbearable. Several occupants have said that in hot weather they don't go to bed, but sit in their clothes in the least infested part of the room. What good is it, they said, to go to bed when you can't get a wink of sleep for bugs and fleas?'

Most of the doors stood open all the time and the passage from the street to the back door, which was scarcely ever swept, let alone scrubbed, gave shelter to some who were altogether homeless. 'Here the mother would stand with her baby, or sit with it on the stairs, or companions would huddle together in cold weather. The little yard at the back was only sufficient for dustbin and closet and water-tap, serving six or seven families. The water would be drawn from cisterns which were receptacles for refuse, and perhaps occasionally a dead cat.' It is not surprising that at times the street was fever-stricken.

The main amusement of Shelton Street was gambling. 'Sunday afternoon and evening was the heyday time for this street. Every doorstep would be crowded by those who sat and stood with pipe and jug of beer, while lads lounged about, and the gutters would find amusement for not a few children with bare feet, their faces and hands besmeared, while the mud oozed through between their toes. Add to this a group of fifteen to twenty young men gambling in the middle of the street and you complete the general picture.'[1]

Not all the inhabitants of the mean streets were addicted to gambling and drink, but just as it was difficult for a young girl to avoid incest in a one-room tenement, so it was difficult to be a respectable citizen in the poverty and filth of places like Shelton Street.

Housing was one of the fundamental issues in the bitter political struggle that lasted throughout most of the Great Depression. Under the economic doctrine of *laissez-faire* which had flourished from about the middle of the eighteenth century

[1] Abridged from Charles Booth, *Poverty*, Vol. II, pp. 46–8.

onwards, the free action of the individual in commerce and industry was held to be inviolable. Economic behaviour was judged solely by the standard of enlightened self-interest, in the belief that public and private interests were ultimately identical and that consequently if each man did what was best for himself the result would benefit all. *Laissez-faire* had allowed individual enterprise to thrust ahead after the restrictiveness of obsolete paternal legislation that had been carried over from earlier centuries. Now it had gone too far, and its social defects were too blatant in a sophisticated industrial economy. The reports of the Employment Commissioners and factory inspectors had disclosed the misery and exploitation that resulted from the free play of enlightened self-interest – as did the investigation of Charles Booth and his helpers. Even so the concept of *laissez-faire* was too deeply embedded for the state to assume even the most minimal obligations without great reluctance and against violent opposition.

There were a number of factors responsible for this reaction against *laissez-faire* at this period. There was the continued pressure and influence of the humanitarians, there was the political enfranchisement of the working class, and there was the snowball effect of the minimal obligations, undertaken though they were in piecemeal fashion and without any overriding social philosophy through successive Factory Acts. These obligations gradually created a new concept which suggested that everyone, whatever their industrial status, had a right to a minimum standard of welfare in their working conditions. In effect this new concept of a 'national minimum' was a return in a new setting to the philosophy that had preceded *laissez-faire* and which included an ethical standard in its judgement of economic behaviour, a standard that took account of social effects.

Once having been undertaken these minimal obligations could lead only to further commitment, provided that there was no reversal in the underlying trend towards making the state rather than the individual supreme. Nor was there any reversal. On the contrary, the supremacy of the individual was under attack from two opposed quarters. Both imperialists and socialists – an unnatural alliance it might seem – deified the state, the imperialists because it was the vehicle for their romantic paternalism and sublimated aggression, the socialists because they regarded it as the only instrument for creating egalitarian conditions and ensuring social justice. Between them they spread the gospel of state supremacy.

There may also possibly have been another factor exerting a subtle influence against *laissez-faire*. This was the reaction to the theory of evolution expounded in Darwin's *Origin of Species*, published in 1859. The theory had first been put forward fifteen years earlier by Robert Chambers in his *Vestiges of the Natural History of Creation* and by Darwin himself. It was an adaptation into biology of *laissez-faire* economics, for both Darwinian biology and classical economics had in common the idea of progress through free competition and the survival of the fittest. The outrage felt by religious orthodoxy at the theory of evolution – even though it was in due course generally accepted – may well have had the side-effect of casting doubts on the economic theory with which it shared its basic assumptions.

Those who favoured the demise of *laissez-faire* defended the new concept of a national minimum from more than one point of view. Its value could be argued on economic as well as on humanitarian grounds. 'Never will I believe,' Macaulay declared, 'that what makes a population stronger and healthier and wiser and better can ultimately make it poorer.' But there were others who disagreed. The increasing compass of the national minimum was strongly resisted. The belief in self-help as glorified by Samuel Smiles was still widespread. So too was the belief in free choice. The poor were still considered to be poor because they were paying the penalty for their moral failings – lack of riches resulted from lack of righteousness. Slum-dwellers chose to be slum-dwellers because they were an immoral, shiftless lot who preferred drinking and gambling to spending their money on improving their homes and who would only keep coals in the bath if they were provided with one.

Those who opposed the involvement of the state in housing problems through the Torrens and Cross Acts of 1868, 1875 and 1879 believed, with Herbert Spencer, that legislation could not combat social evils of any kind. Housing, like other social problems, was a matter for private charity. To think otherwise was to threaten the basis of democracy. In 1882 the powerful Liberty and Property Defence League was founded to thwart the growth of collective responsibility for housing. 'Self-Help versus State-Help' was its slogan. The following year an anonymous penny pamphlet called *The Bitter Cry of Outcast London* showed that for the social residue in the slums there was no help – nor hope – at all. *The Bitter Cry*, written by a slum missionary, the Reverend Andrew Mearns, became a household word and immediately created a public conscience on housing. The Queen was much distressed by its revelations and was far from satisfied at Gladstone's coolness on the subject, or by Cross's assurance, quite unjustified as Charles Booth's surveys were soon to prove, that the *Cry* was exaggerated. Despite the humanitarian clamour, however, the opposition to state-help remained powerful in council chambers and in Parliament.

While the widening ambit of state involvement was too much for some, who had nightmares of being collectivized up to the neck, it was far too little for others. The 1880s saw the rise of socialism out of the Radical movement. To begin with it was dominated by the Social Democratic Federation led by H. M. Hyndman, who was Marx's most eminent English pupil. The conditions seemed ripe for the success of the social revolution that Marx had predicted. After a brief revival in 1882, the Great Depression plunged ever downward. *The Bitter Cry* and a Royal Commission on the Housing of the Working Classes which was set up in 1884 and reported the following year showed the horrors of the lower depths. Production declined, unemployment rose. Hyndman and his colleagues, including John Burns, who was later to be the first former manual worker to become a cabinet minister, drilled the unemployed, led them in shattering the windows of the Pall Mall clubs and in battling with the police in Trafalgar Square. On November 9, 1886 London was virtually in a state of siege as it waited for the S.D.F.'s mass demonstration. Shops were boarded up, transport stopped, streets blocked, troops and police massed at strategic points. But although it was the greatest working-class demonstration ever seen in London it passed off without much violence. A year later, on Sunday November 13, 1887, after the Government had closed Trafalgar Square to all meetings, Burns and Cunninghame Graham led columns of unemployed against the police guarding the Square. Among those who marched were George Bernard Shaw and Annie Besant, who had by then embarked on her fourth life as a socialist labour agitator. The police charged the columns, the Life Guards and the Scots Guards helped the police. The day became known as Bloody Sunday.

Others besides the S.D.F. preached violence. Some went even further in their use of it. There were bomb outrages in London, mostly by the Fenians but sometimes by Anarchists. The Fenians were using dynamite solely for the freedom of Ireland, but the Anarchists operated on a wider front. Anarchist bombs were exploding in most countries of Europe and also in the United States, where labour unrest was as widespread as in England and even more violent. The first Anarchist bomb thrown in the United States exploded among a phalanx of Chicago police who were arresting a speaker at a labour 'public indignation' meeting in Haymarket Square on May 4, 1886. The aftermath made even Bloody Sunday look like a peaceable demonstration by comparison.

When trade revived in 1889 the influence of the S.D.F. declined and was replaced by Fabianism and the Independent Labour Party. Under Sidney and Beatrice Webb (as Beatrice Potter had by then become) and George Bernard Shaw the Fabian Society evolved a type of socialism that was more distinctively British than the international revolutionary Marxism of the S.D.F. Instead of full-blooded socialism they aimed for social changes tending towards socialism. They preached 'Gas and Water Socialism' – and 'Electricity Socialism' too, although electricity supply was still in its early stages. By this they meant that there should be public ownership of utilities through municipalities, public ownership which was initiated at Birmingham by Joseph Chamberlain in 1874 and was approved by many others far beyond the ranks of the Fabian Society. Socialism when it arrived by Fabian methods would simply be the logical consummation of progressive social reform.

In all this social and political turmoil there was opportunity for women to play an important part in the practical application of an ideal of service. From 'poor-peopling' they had in a generation progressed to being active participants in social reform.

Chapter 18

WOMEN'S WORK

A few miles from the great house in Warwickshire that Elizabeth Haldane visited was the hamlet of Juniper Hill on the Oxfordshire–Northamptonshire border. Here in 1877 was born Flora Timms, the daughter of a stonemason and a nursemaid. Many years later, under her married name of Flora Thompson, she celebrated the annals of her hamlet in a masterpiece called *Lark Rise*, in which she told the quiet story of life in an English village in the 1880s and '90s. It was from the cottages of Juniper Hill and thousands of other villages and hamlets that the servants came to black the grates and carry the coals and fill the baths of the Top Nation.

'Gentleman's Service'
In Juniper Hill in the '80s and '90s there was not a girl of over twelve or thirteen living permanently at home. By that age, and sometimes even younger, they had been sent out to their first places as servants. For a year or so after they left school at ten or eleven they were kept at home to help with the younger children. Then they were found a 'petty place', as it was called, in some local household of a tradesman or schoolmaster or farm bailiff. The wages were small, often only a shilling a week, but the girls were usually well fed and given little odds and ends of material and sometimes the Christmas gift of a frock or a coat. After a year – for she had to stay in the 'petty place' for a year at least – the girl would be big enough to go into 'gentleman's service'. This would take her away from home, and all she would see of it from then on would be during the brief fortnight's annual holiday when she would return to the hamlet in her town clothes, complete with gloves and veil, which her

mother would insist on her wearing when she went out in order to impress the neighbours.

It was not only to earn their weekly shillings that the girls were sent out to service as soon as they were thirteen. There was also the sleeping problem. None of the cottages had more than two bedrooms and the alternative to going away into service was the cramped and potentially incestuous sleeping arrangements which the *Saturday Review* called 'the first step to the Haymarket'.[1] When the summer holidays came round father slept downstairs and the girl shared her mother's bed. Fifty years later Flora Thompson said that it was 'common now to hear people say when looking at some little old cottage, "and they brought up ten children there. Where on earth did they sleep?" And the answer is, or should be, that they did not all sleep there at the same time. Obviously they could not. By the time the youngest of such a family was born, the eldest would probably be twenty and have been out in the world for years, as would those who came immediately after in age. The overcrowding was bad enough; but not quite as bad as people imagine.'[2] A generation earlier it had been worse.

When the time came for a girl to leave her petty place the *Morning Post* or the *Church Times* would be scanned to see what situations were vacant; or the clergyman's daughter would be consulted; or sisters or friends already in employment would be asked. 'When the place was found, the girl set out alone on what was usually her first train journey, with her yellow tin trunk tied up with thick cord, her bunch of flowers and brown-paper parcel bursting with left-overs. The tin trunk would be sent on to the railway station by the carrier and the mother would walk the three miles to the station with her daughter. They would leave Lark Rise, perhaps before it was quite light on a winter morning, the girl in her best, would-be fashionable clothes and the mother carrying the baby of the family, rolled in its shawl. Neighbours would come to their garden gates to see them off and call after them "pleasant journey! Hope you'll have a good place!" Or, "Mind you be a good gal, now, an' does just as you be told!" Or, more comfortingly, "You'll be back for y'r holidays before you knows where you are and then there won't

[1] 'Cottage Reform' in the *Saturday Review*, April 3, 1858.
[2] Flora Thompson, *Lark Rise to Candleford*, A Trilogy (Oxford University Press, 1954), p. 164.

be no holdin' you, you'll have got that London proud!" And the two would go off in good spirit, turning and waving repeatedly.'[1]

The good spirit would not last, however. Flora once saw the departure of such a couple, the girl dressed in a bright blue poplin frock which had come from a second-hand clothes shop and was three years out of fashion, the mother proud of her daughter and the frock. Some hours later the mother returned alone. 'She was limping, for the sole of one of her old boots had parted company with the upper, and the eighteen-months-old child must have hung heavily on her arm. When asked if Aggie had gone off all right, she nodded, but could not answer; her heart was too full. After all, she was just a mother who had sent her young daughter into the unknown and was tormented with doubts and fears for her.'[2]

When the girl arrived at her situation she would either go into the kitchen, where she would begin as a scullery-maid washing stacks of dishes, cleaning saucepans, preparing vegetables, and scrubbing, scrubbing, scrubbing. Or she would do housework and take part in the endless fetching and carrying that went on, up and down the flights of stairs of the tall, tall houses – carrying coals, carrying cans of hot water, black-leading, dusting, cleaning, polishing. Architects put the coal store as far as possible from the kitchen in order to induce economy in the use of fuel – and they also put the dining-room as far as possible from the kitchen, and the bathroom from the hot water, though what this induced except fatigue for the servants is difficult to surmise.

For all this labour the girl would be paid about seven pounds a year, apart, of course, from her board and lodging and her uniform. But out of this seven pounds she would always spare something to send home to 'our mum'. Some of the girls would stint themselves and send more than half their wages home. From what was left something would be saved for the bottom drawer. 'A few of the girls were engaged to youths at home, and, after several years of courtship, mostly conducted by letter, for they seldom met except during the girl's summer holiday, they would marry and settle in or near the hamlet. Others married and settled away. Butchers and milkmen were favoured as

[1] ibid., p. 171.
[2] ibid., p. 172.

husbands, perhaps because these were frequent callers at the houses where the girls were employed. ... The girls who had married away remained faithful to the old custom of spending a summer fortnight with their parents, and the outward and visible signs of their prosperity must have been trying to those who had married farm labourers and returned to the old style of living.'[1]

One great change in this style, since a generation earlier, was that the wives of the labourers were no longer field labourers themselves. The number of women employed in agriculture in England and Wales shrank considerably during the latter half of the nineteenth century. From 169,300 of all ages in 1851, the number dropped to 115,500 in 1861, to 85,400 in 1871, and to 64,600 in 1881. And within these totals there were two outstanding constituents: the number of girls under fifteen who were employed, virtually all of them as labourers, dropped from 13,300 to 6,100 between 1851 and 1861 and then to 4,300 in 1871 and 2,200 in 1881; and the number of women over fifteen employed as labourers fell from 130,300 in 1851, to 84,500 in 1861, to 53,900 in 1871, and to 38,200 in 1881. By the end of the century the female agricultural labourer had almost disappeared. The cause of this decline, which had first become noticeable during the 1867 Inquiry, was the combined effect of the raising of the men's wages (itself partly the result of the formation of an agricultural trade union by Arch), which reduced the need for women's contribution to the family wages, and also the introduction of mechanization in agriculture, which lessened the need for labour. As in industry machines took the place of women, but unlike industry the machine-minders in agriculture were men.[2]

It was the girls who left the Lark Rises with their yellow tin trunks and bursting brown-paper parcels who formed part of

[1] ibid., p. 176.
[2] The picture was different in Scotland and in Ireland. The number of women of all ages employed in agriculture in Scotland was 60,700 in 1851, 47,700 in 1861, 50,900 in 1871, and 51,700 in 1881 – a decrease of only 9,000 in thirty years. Nor was there any significant change in numbers under fifteen years of age: 3,600 in 1851 and 2,200 in 1881. The change in the total reflected the change in the number employed as labourers: 51,100 in 1851 and 42,000 in 1881.

In Ireland the figures were: 167,300 in 1851 and 95,800 in 1881, the main fall coming between 1851 and 1861 when the figure was 100,600.

the chief occupation for employed women, and this despite the swelling opposition to going into domestic service which, together with the growing number of households demanding servants, created the faint beginnings of a check in the adequate supply of servants.[1] Of the three-and-a-half million women and girls employed in England and Wales in 1881, just over one-third were indoor domestic servants. Although there was an increase in the number of servants between 1871 and 1901, there was a decrease in those aged twenty and under. The lack of supply may have been the result of a falling rural population, for the bulk of servants had previously come from the families of agricultural labourers.

So, despite the thousands of tin trunks and the sad farewells at railway stations all over the country, by the end of the century there was a servant problem as well as a woman question. This had its effect on the birth rate. There was an argument current 'that the middle-class mother must perforce be provided with domestic assistance, not that she might indulge in indolence, but that she might be freed to devote all her energies to the proper upbringing of her children. This view of motherhood, held in both religious and purely secular circles, persisted at least until the end of the century, and for that reason', in J. A. Banks's opinion,[2] 'it is likely that the impact of the servant problem was quite considerable. Once it had become established that birth control was not immoral, the fact of not being able to obtain domestic assistance would itself become a salient factor in the fall of family size. If more children implied more domestic

---

[1] Flora Timms did not follow the normal path to a 'petty place' and then, a year later, into 'gentleman's service'. Her mother wanted something better for her than that – just as she wanted something better for her son than that he should go on the land as a labourer. She helped Flora with her lessons so that when she left the little village school at fourteen she had acquired a good grounding for the education she was to give herself later. Six months after leaving school Flora went to work as a learner in the Post Office at 'Candleford Green', eight miles from Lark Rise. She became a letter-carrier for the postmistress, who also kept the local smithy. Then she married, and her husband later became a postmaster. From the public library she borrowed the classics in translation; she read Ibsen, and Shaw, and Yeats. She became a writer herself and in 1939 published *Lark Rise*, her own enchanting classic. She died in 1947. Her brother defied his mother and went on the land, until he joined the army in 1914 and was killed in Flanders.

[2] J. A. Banks, op. cit., p. 138.

assistance, less domestic assistance implied either more domestic appliances or less children.' Mrs Timms's resolve to keep her daughter from 'gentleman's service' was part of a trend with important consequences.

Unwelcome Protection

In 1871 the percentage of women and girls in employment in Great Britain had declined slightly compared with ten years earlier, and was 28·7 as against 29·5. The total female population had gone up from 11,449,600 to 13,410,300, and the number in employment from 3,386,800 to 3,851,200. This trend continued. In 1881 the total female population was 15,270,600 and the number of women and girls in employment was 4,121,400 – 27 per cent. The main occupations remained the same as earlier in the reign, though their relative positions were now changed and they employed a slightly smaller percentage of the female labour force. Domestic service was now first in importance, and together with textiles and dress manufacture employed 2,927,400, or 76 per cent of the total female working population in 1871, and 3,064,300, or 74·4 per cent, in 1881. In Ireland the total population had decreased only slightly compared with earlier decades, and in 1871 it was 5,412,300 of which 2,772,600 were females – of whom 869,700 were employed (31·4 per cent). In 1881 the number of females in a total population of 5,174,800 was 2,641,500 of whom 30 per cent, 792,400, were employed.

Although in Ireland textile manufacture as an occupation for women shrank drastically, in Great Britain it continued to be the main manufacturing source of employment. The textile trades as a whole employed nearly 700,000 women and girls, of whom about one-half were in the cotton-mills. As in an earlier generation this aggregation in large factories and special localities gave to the 325,000 in the mills an undue amount of attention, so that their occupation seemed to be the chief occupation for women, and their history seemed to be the history of all working women, whereas what happened in Lancashire could hardly have been less typical.

Nevertheless, in the long term the factories had a great importance quite apart from the crucial value of their products to the nation's economy. As was pointed out in the previous chapter it was through successive Factory Acts that the new concept of a 'national minimum' was created.

Apart from the 1842 Act which prohibited women and girls from working below ground in coal-mines, the various Factory Acts up till 1864 applied only to textile factories. The incidence of regulation had been: first cotton-mills only, then textile factories except silk-mills, then all textile factories. In 1850 the intention of the 1847 Act for a 'Ten Hour Day' had been secured, and a weekly half-holiday had been added. In fact, of course, the 'Ten Hour Day' was a misnomer; the working week was actually sixty hours with a normal day of ten-and-a-half hours.

In 1860 bleaching and dyeing works were brought under the regulations. In 1861 lace works were included. In 1863–4 calendering and finishing works became subject to regulation. None of these new Acts improved the conditions of the workers, whose employment was already under control. Nor did the Act of 1864. But it was an important departure because for the first time, apart from women in mines, a number of non-textile trades were made subject to regulation. Pottery works were among these trades. In 1867 the regulative system was at last made applicable to all factories employing more than fifty workers. In the same year a Workshops Act – a workshop being a place where manufacture was carried on with fewer than fifty employees – made workshops subject to the supervision of local authorities. This sounded better on paper than it proved to be in practice, because local authorities on the whole were not prepared to carry out their duties seriously. But it was a start, and it was the first legislative result to show from the facts about domestic industrial conditions presented by the Children's Employment Commission twenty-five years earlier. That the result was long in coming and initially ineffective was partly the result of the climate of opinion and partly of the nature of the problem. 'The irregularity of certain trades, the impossibility of restricting the work done in homes, and the superhuman task of reaching thousands of small shops hiring only a few workers, explain immediately why the efforts of the Commission counted for almost nothing . . . Here in a class of labour little affected, in many cases, by the Industrial Revolution, one has an extensive view of what working conditions were for all women before machinery changed the making of cloth into a factory enter-prise.'[1] In fact the Factory Act of 1864 and the Workshops Act

[1] Wanda Neff, op. cit., p. 89.

of 1867 were the outcome of another Commission, appointed in 1862 on the recommendation of Lord Shaftesbury (as Lord Ashley had by then become), which confirmed the findings of the earlier Commission and aroused the will to action.

In 1874 the textile operatives achieved the actual Ten Hour Day at last, the standard weekly hours being reduced to fifty-six-and-a-half – that is, ten hours a day except on Saturdays. Four years later the dual system of factory and workshop was combined under a single system of state inspection by the Consolidated Factory Act. It included regulations for the industrial labour of women, which fixed the limits of the hours beyond which women were not to work, ordered the times to be allowed for meals, the places where they must not be eaten, and the holidays that must be taken. The Act's policy, said the 1881 edition of Helen Blackburn's *Handbook*, was 'to secure that women shall not work beyond an average of ten hours a day – and to secure this end it limits the freedom of contract both of employers and of women operatives – leaving the freedom of the men untouched'. The feminists, in fact, did not see legislation of this sort as an amelioration of women's position at all; they saw it as another grapple being used to hold women down in the hated status of a 'relative creature'.

When the next Factory and Workshops Bill was being debated in 1891 the Government, continuing to expand the growing concept of a minimum standard of welfare in working conditions, included a clause to make it illegal for any employer of labour at a factory or workshop 'knowingly to employ a woman within four weeks of her confinement'. There was only one speech in opposition to this clause throughout the whole debate in both Houses of Parliament. It came from Lord Wemyss, one of Margot Asquith's four handsomest men, who was acting as spokesman for the women's rights party. He quoted the party's leaders. Dr Garrett Anderson, for example, urged that 'many women who work hard all their lives are quite able to work in less than a month after their confinement, and whether they are or not, they ought to be left entirely to decide for themselves'.[1] The Secretary of the Women's Employment Association, Miss Ada Heather Bigg, regarded the clause as another step in the campaign by male trade unionists to oust women from the labour market. Miss Lipton, the Secretary of

[1] Quoted in Margaret Hewitt, op. cit., pp. 177–8.

the Laundry Women's Co-operative Association, wanted to known what was to become of 'these women, who are mostly breadwinners, if they are prevented from working for a month; God alone knows, I don't'. And Mrs Fawcett prophesied that a month's exclusion from work would drive widows, deserted wives, and unmarried mothers to the Poor Law if not worse. The only reply given to this point was that factory legislation had long been based on the inability of women to look after their own best interests, and that the evil effects of employment too soon after confinement could no longer be tolerated. The clause remained in the Act, which received the Royal Assent that same year.

The last Factory Act of the reign to affect the employment conditions of adult women was passed in 1895. Its provisions reflected trade union endeavour to concentrate wage-earning work in large factories where labour could be more easily organized and where regulations could be more easily enforced. As far as women were concerned the Act had the object of discouraging homework and trying to do away with overtime. Commenting on the new Act in the 1895 edition of her *Handbook* Helen Blackburn wrote: 'In considering these clauses it should be borne in mind that they are based on the endeavour to bring the inferior and ill-managed workshops and factories up to the level of the best. The question to cause anxiety is, whether the end can be adequately reached by legislative restriction.' The continuation of 'sweating' showed, in fact, that it could not, and the feminists maintained that under the guise of protecting the welfare of working women what was actually happening was that the screw was being tightened on their relative status as wage-earners. Protection to starve was the way they saw the growing restrictions of successive Factory Acts.

The Professions

With the exception of mining all other trades were legally open to women, even if in practice many of them did not employ women; but this was not the case with all the professions. By the end of Victoria's reign an Englishwoman could still not be a minister, although she was allowed to be a deaconess in the Church of England, fulfilling something of the role of a nun in the Roman Catholic Church. This was also largely true of the United States, except that certain Protestant churches – not

he Lutheran, the Presbyterian, the Protestant
nd the Reformed churches – allowed women to be
the end of the century a few hundred had made
ir career. The army and the navy were closed to
...ough within less than twenty years there were to be
women in both. Nor could a woman be a barrister or a solicitor.
Women in England were not admitted to the legal profession
until 1919, and the first woman was called to the Bar in 1922.
There were, on the other hand, a few women who qualified to
become engineers in the late 1890s, and the first woman was
admitted to membership of the Institute of Electrical Engineers
in 1899.[1] The profession of medicine too, thanks to the efforts of
Elizabeth Blackwell, Sophia Jex-Blake and others, was now
open to women, and the 1895 edition of the *Handbook for Women*
mentioned that *Medical Women*, edited by Dr Jex-Blake, listed
264 women who had been registered as doctors, a considerable
increase since the first edition of the *Handbook* in 1881 when only
twenty-one had been registered.

The two professions which employed more educated women
than any others were teaching and nursing, both of which had
made great advances since the days of Mrs Gamp and *Mangnall's
Questions.* Other professions open to women of talent were
journalism and authorship. In some cases it was even an
advantage to be a woman. Thus Beatrice Potter found that
instead of being pushed by 'self-respect, family pressure and the
public opinion' of her class into a money-making profession as
she would have been had she been a man, 'as a mere woman I
could carve out a career of disinterested research. Moreover, in
the craft I had chosen a woman was privileged. As an investigator [of social conditions] she aroused less suspicion than a man,
and, through making the proceedings more agreeable to the
persons concerned, she gained better information. Further, in
those days, a competent female writer on economic questions,
had, to an enterprising editor, actually a scarcity value. Thus
she secured immediate publication, and, to judge by my own
experience was paid a higher rate than that obtained by male
competitors of equal standing.'[2] Because she herself had never
suffered the disabilities that arose from her sex, Beatrice was at

[1] The first professional bodies to accept women members both in
Britain and the United States were the astronomers.

[2] Beatrice Webb, *My Apprenticeship*, p. 355.

this period of her life strongly anti-feminist, an attitude founded on her conservative temperament, her social environment, and her reaction against her father's 'over valuation of women relatively to men'. This reaction was intensified by what she considered to be 'the narrow outlook and exasperated tone of some of the pioneers of woman's suffrage', and at a luncheon given by an American lady to American suffragists, where she had not been given a cigarette, which might have soothed her distaste for the perpetual reiteration of the rights of women, Beatrice gave vent to this irritation by declaring that she had never met a man, however inferior, whom she did not consider to be her superior!

But there were few Beatrice Potters, and many thousands with merely average ability. The professional openings, not only in economic journalism and medicine, but in teaching and nursing, were only for women who were above average in ability. For the 'merely average' opportunities were still limited. 'The merely average girl,' wrote Clara Collet in November 1900 – and Clara Collet was far above average herself, being a Fellow of University College, London – 'the merely average girl must turn to some occupation in which more people are wanted, but for which less exceptional skill is required. Generally she looks for it in one or two directions: she either becomes a clerk or some kind of domestic help. Failing marriage, the latter occupation offers chances, but not certainties, of making warm friends and having abiding human interests. But clerical work in the case of the average woman can rarely be in itself satisfying; it is a means not an end.'[1] Unsatisfying as it might be, clerical work was occupying an increasing number of women. As against no female clerks and secretaries in the 1861 and 1871 censuses, there were 5,989 in 1881 and 17,859 in 1891.

The millennium had not arrived, but there had been limited progress in making it possible for middle-class women to earn a living other than as a governess or, as the *Saturday Review* had delicately put it, as *id quod dicere nolo*. Jane Eyre's situation, against which Charlotte Brontë had railed again in *Shirley* (1849), was no longer so typical by the end of the century. For some middle-class girls existence was no doubt still 'that useless, blank, pale, slow-trailing thing' that Caroline Helstone lamented when she asked that 'single women should have more to do –

[1] Clara Collet, *Educated Working Women* (P. S. King, 1902), pp. 139–40.

better chances of interesting and profitable occupations than they possess now'. But for others the plea of Charlotte Brontë's lifelong friend Mary Taylor – who appears as Rose Yorke in *Shirley* – seemed to have been answered as it never could have been answered at the time it was made. 'Make us efficient workers able to earn our living in order that we may be good, useful, healthy, self-respecting women,' she asked.

How far had Mary Taylor's ideal in fact been realized by the end of Victoria's reign? How far was it still accepted as the right one? And was it any longer considered a sufficiently ambitious one? These were the questions Clara Collet discussed in an essay on the economic progress of women that had taken place in the fifty years since *Shirley* was published. In her opinion there was no doubt that women had travelled much nearer to the ideal than anyone in 1849 would have foreseen, and farther than many pioneers of that period would have desired. 'We may safely assert that no middle-class women of average intelligence, educated in the high schools established during the last twenty-five years, is unable to earn a living if she chooses to do so.' And there had been one very important change in the outlook of the middle-class family. Whereas thirty years before it had been the rule for many parents, 'although with little hope of bequeathing an income to their daughters, to support them at home in expectation of their marriage, this lack of foresight' was becoming rare. 'Our schools,' wrote Miss Collet, over-sanguinely some would have said, 'are no longer staffed by women who have begun their work in life driven to it by necessity or disappointment. More and more it is being recognized by parents that girls should be fitted to be self-supporting; and the tendency among the girls themselves is to concentrate their energies on the profession they take up, and to regard marriage as a possibility which may some day call them away from the path they are pursuing, but which should not be allowed to interfere with their plans in the meantime. At the period of life, then, when there is the most opportunity of marriage there is now the least excuse for the woman who marries merely to obtain a livelihood. The economic advance has at least proved to be sufficient to enable women to preserve their self-respect.'[1]

But while great strides had been made in the right direction there were still some serious truths to be faced. In particular,

[1] ibid., pp. 138–9.

what was going to happen to the duller girls? The necessity for economic independence was greater than ever, but the glamour had worn off. There was no longer the excitement that had attended the eager young ladies from Langham Place forty years before, when they knocked on doors and clamoured for dull jobs that were made interesting by the difficulty of getting them.

Chapter 19
THE NEW DAUGHTERS
OF PROPRIETY

The middle-class girl who went out to work was one type of British Top Nation young woman in the 1880s and '90s. A second type, with whom in some cases she overlapped, was the cultured, intellectual type who had emerged as a result of the improved facilities for girls' education that had started with the foundation of Queen's College in 1848 and had progressed through the schools of the Girls' Public Day School Company and the growing availability of university education.

Girton Girls
Compared with the United States, where in 1880 there were 40,000 women, over a third of the entire student body, enrolled in institutions of higher learning – many of them it is true with standards so low that they were not worthy of the name – there were only a few hundreds in British universities and a mere handful, less than 200 in 1882, in the four women's colleges at Oxford and Cambridge. But despite their small numbers university women in Britain attracted considerable popular derision, and none more than the Girton girls who became fixed in the public imagination as the ghastly epitome of university women. Mrs Lynn Linton saw in them the lineaments of her perennial enemy, the New Woman, whom she had first attacked as the Girl of the Period, and then as the Shrieking Sisterhood, and whom now in a novel called *The One Too Many*, published in 1893, she castigated as the Girton Girl. By this time it had become an obsession with her that the feminine character taken collectively was in a state of galloping deterioration, and

326

she loaded her Girton characters with all the symptoms of this moral disintegration. An old Girton girl wrote to the editor of the *Lady's Pictorial* in which *The One Too Many* appeared as a serial, complaining of the caricature. 'Many foolish and ridiculous attacks on women university students are published from time to time, but I believe that this story, *The One Too Many*, stands alone for its offensive pictures of the so-called results of Girton training and education. To justify the language I have used, I have only to remind you that of the "Girton B.A.s" in the story, one marries a policeman, having first nursed him through an illness and then proposed to him; one flirts outrageously with a married man in the presence of his wife, the intimate friend of her "pal" who marries the policeman; the third constantly advocates suicide, and is consequently the indirect cause of the heroine's death by her own hand. All drink, smoke, swear, use vulgar language, and are represented as knowing and talking about unfitting subjects.' Mrs Linton's defence, though aggressive, was weak, and she came out of the skirmish without much credit.

Another critic of university women was Stopford Brooke, a man of letters and a clergyman who had seceded from the Church of England in 1880 and preached as a Unitarian at Bedford Chapel, Bloomsbury, until 1895. In a book on Tennyson[1] published some fifty years after *The Princess* came out, though still of course within Victoria's reign, Stopford Brooke wrote that Ida had made two fundamental mistakes. The first was to isolate woman from man; the second was that she thought knowledge alone was enough to lift woman into equality with man, to rescue her from her relative position as a doll to be played with or a slave to be exploited. 'Knowledge, of course, is good,' Brooke agreed, 'the more knowledge women get the better. It is an absolute necessity. But *alone* it injures more than assists their cause.' Brooke, who had for some years been a professor at Queen's College, was as critical of the New Woman as Mrs Linton. 'Many women in the present day,' he wrote, 'seem to look with a certain contempt on sentiment, on imagination, on beauty and art, on the affections, on the high passions of the ideal or of the religious life. It is a fatal pride, and a folly for which they will sorely suffer. Women do not want less

[1] Stopford Brooke, *Tennyson, His Art and Relation to Modern Life* (1894), p. 174.

emotion but larger emotion, nobler and less personal direction of emotion; more of love and not less, more true passion and not less; more sense of beauty and not less; more imagination, more of the energy of faith working by love, more sacrifice of self, that is, more universal, less particular sacrifice. Education in these they want above all, and they want it at present more than men.'[1] It was an indictment of woman's nature in the state to which it had been conditioned by her 'looking-glass' status.

Ten years before Brooke's criticism *The Princess* and all it advocated had been pilloried in Gilbert and Sullivan's *Princess Ida* which was based on Tennyson's poem. In 1884, the year in which *Princess Ida* was first produced, Girton's future was far from assured. Academically, after a shaky start, it had established itself against strong opposition from dons and from the families of some of the students, who regarded membership of the College for Women as a life 'merely of self-indulgence and self-satisfaction', distracting the girl 'from the plain duties that lay before her'.[2] Financially and physically it was still in difficulties; there was not nearly enough money and far too little space. The following year it received its first substantial gift, and although this did not answer all the financial problems, for Emily Davies insisted on an expansion programme so far beyond the college's resources that she left Girton £40,000 in debt, the gift, amounting to about £19,000, was of great importance, making possible a large extension of the buildings and the purchase of seventeen acres of additional land.

The gift to Girton came from a maiden lady called Jane Catherine Gamble who, having made various bequests to her god-daughters and to two of her companions with the condition attached to them that 'all legacies given by me to females shall be for their sole and separate use, and free from marital control', left her residuary estate to the college. This feminist action was the result of baleful experience. Jane Gamble came from a Virginian family, and is variously reported to have been born in

[1] ibid., pp. 175–6.
[2] This was the opinion of Anna Lloyd's family. She was one of the first Girtonians, going there when the college opened in 1874 after moving from Hitchin. Girton started to administer some academic shocks when Charlotte Scott was equal to the Eighth Wrangler in 1880, and Agnata Ramsay was head of the Classical Tripos in 1887. Newnham joined in with éclat in 1890 when Philippa Fawcett came out above the Senior Wrangler.

her father's home in Virginia in 1808 or in Tunbridge Wells in 1810. Her mother died when she was still a baby; her father married again; and when she was three years old she was adopted by her uncle and aunt, Mr and Mrs James Dunlop, of Russell Square, London. James Dunlop was a Scot who had lived for years in Chesterfield County, Virginia, and had made a considerable fortune in the tobacco trade before returning to London. It was in fact tobacco that financed Girton's first large gift. Dunlop himself died in 1841, his wife a few years later, and the Dunlops' only child, a son, in 1850. Jane found herself a considerable heiress, worth about £30,000. Promptly she was courted by a fellow-American, a Philadelphian of about her own age who had first met her on his first visit to London in 1835, but who had been too concerned with various journalistic, diplomatic, and theatrical excitements, including being the impresario for the delectable Fanny Elssler during her 1840–2 American tour, to keep up his friendship with her since. But in 1850, when on a visit to London to collect his quarterly cheque from the Foreign Office for whom he was then working as an unusual kind of press agent in Paris, he called on her again, fortuitously, or so he claimed, the day after she had buried her cousin and three days after she had become a lady of property. The courtship which followed took a bizarre course and ended in Genoa in November 1851, leaving the Philadelphian, Henry Wikoff by name, there in San Andrea prison until February 1853 for abducting Jane Gamble, and leaving Jane Gamble with an enduring hatred of men which resulted in the gift to Girton. The college commemorated her in 1888 by the foundation of the Gamble Prize, which is a prize of £20 offered annually for an original dissertation by a graduate member of the college. In all fairness it should really be re-named the Wikoff Gamble, for it was Harry Wikoff's character and compulsive actions that gave rise to its foundation![1]

Cyclists, Chums, and Doves

C. Willett Cunnington in his *Feminine Attitudes in the Nineteenth Century* distinguished four types of upper- and middle-class young woman in the 1880s. The first was the intellectual type, whom we have met in the previous section. The second was the athletic type.

[1] See Duncan Crow, *Henry Wikoff, The American Chevalier* (1963).

During the 1870s people had slowly been awakening to the fact that physical exercise was as beneficial for women as for men. Young ladies played croquet, they began to take long walks, they developed a passionate interest in archery. Later there came tricycles. Elizabeth Haldane wrote home from London in 1879 describing 'an extraordinary sight, a lady attired in a sort of riding habit tricycling, unconcerned, down Oxford Street'. Then in the late 1880s the bicycle appeared, not the penny-farthing, which was already in existence but which was unmanageable for a woman because of her dress and the demands of propriety, but the new safety bicycle. Even this raised problems and aroused male antagonism, but the women braved the men and overcame the problems.

The bicycle is idolized in many memoirs as the greatest emancipator of women in the nineteenth century. To Elizabeth Haldane it was 'the liberator of young womankind', and Flora Thompson in the third book of *Lark Rise to Candleford* described how the bicycle transformed life for young, and not so young, women living in country districts. 'Oh! the joy of the new means of progression. To cleave the air as though on wings, defying time and space by putting what had been a day's journey on foot behind one in a couple of hours! Of passing garrulous acquaintances who had formerly held one in one-sided conversation by the roadside for an hour, with a light *ting, ting* of the bell and a casual wave of recognition. At first only comparatively well-to-do women rode bicycles; but soon almost everyone under forty was awheel, for those who could not afford to buy a bicycle could hire one for sixpence an hour. The men's shocked criticism petered out before the *fait accompli.*'[1]

Across the Western world from St Petersburg to San Francisco the bicycle opened the way to freedom for the young. The radius of their world suddenly became permanently enlarged. Instead of being confined like a prisoner to the surrounds of her home, or to the journeys of the family carriage, a young woman could now jump on her bike and go off to see her friends or go for a ride in the country or pop into the nearest town whenever she felt like it. Furthermore the bicycle was a powerful instrument in relaxing the social formality between young men and young women. A woman on a bicycle could no longer be under the close vigilance of a chaperon, and although the practice of

[1] Flora Thompson, op. cit., pp. 545–6.

young men and women bicycling together was not thought to be quite proper, nevertheless it came to be tacitly permitted.

One of the great problems of bicycling in its early days was the encumbrance of full skirts and petticoats. Soon, however, most of the petticoats were left behind in the bedroom and the new vogue for coats and skirts with sailor hats – a vogue perhaps incited into popularity by cycling itself – made the activity a little easier, although there remained the necessity of fastening the skirts so that they neither entangled themselves in the back wheel, nor, even worse, blew about to reveal their wearer's legs in public, which was a heinous offence. In general, however, the trend towards athleticism did not remove from women the trammels of excessive impedimenta. Thus, for a walking-tour, a young lady was advised to take 'two cotton dresses, one cashmere dress, one ulster, one alpaca dustcloak, one parasol, one umbrella, one walking-stick, one pair of shoes, one pair of button boots, six pairs of stockings, two straw hats, one green veil, and a small flask of brandy in case of faintness'.

To croquet, archery and walking the 1870s brought another long-lasting craze which began under the name of sphairistike and soon acquired its permanent name of lawn tennis – 'two out of three played tennis all summer', said a magazine of the time. And in the 1890s they were playing golf, not 'two out of three' but certainly in sufficient numbers to adapt Kitson Clark's epigram and say that Victoria's reign 'starts with gentlemen fighting duels and end with ladies playing golf'. The first Ladies Championship in England, and New Zealand, was held in 1893; in America in 1895.

The third type of young woman was the 'society girl' whom one might also call 'the chum'. She was described in 1885 as knowing everything, reading everything 'from French novels to the evening papers', and 'for a wager she will dive head first off a boat or run you a race round Belgrave Square in the middle of the night' – hardly the sort of thing her mother or grandmother would have done, though her great-grandmother might have! This slightly fast young lady, the sort against whom Mrs Lynn Linton invariably blew her barbs, first made her appearance at the very end of the 1850s, when there was the beginning of that reaction against the simpering young woman who had made a habit of having vapours on the drawing-room sofa. She talked of 'the men' and preferred to sit with them when they were smoking, a habit which she herself soon took up. She had a blasé look and a free tongue and liked playing billiards. She was scornful of the undue femininity of her own sex. She wore gilets and favoured bonnets that had so contracted in size that her face was frankly visible. She adopted masculine tastes in slang as well as in cigarettes and gilets. In sum, she owed her characteristics to a large extent to the habits of the pretty horse-breakers who were the men's favourites.

One important result of 'the chum's' existence was the growing tone of familiarity between young men and women, which for many decades had been almost entirely absent. Together with the bicycle, growing opportunities for education, and the general leavening action of the woman's movement, 'the chum' was an instrument in changing the attitudes of the sexes towards each other, however impermanently and however slightly. And the chum herself was impermanent, except in odd instances. The mannish phase began to disappear towards the end of the 1880s, when the exhibitionist attitude which had inspired it was once more submerged under chronic, Gothic attitudes and principles; the swing of the pendulum, caused perhaps by the pessimism that was growing stronger in the collective subconscious as a result of the never-ending Great Depression. The chum type of young lady henceforward combined in herself the remnants of exhibitionism and the normal Gothic femininity. This ambivalence, which, one might hazard, is the natural state of women, was characterized thus in a magazine of the day: 'The modern girl who speaks in a loud and strident voice, sticks her arms akimbo, is rich in slang and goes in for women's rights, yet has a waist of eighteen inches and wears a hat that would make up into two, with a small barrowload of flowers piled upon it in front'.

The fourth type of young woman to be distinguished in the 1880s was the old-fashioned home-bird – the occupant of the dovecot, one of 'a group of good girls of the real old English type – doves who are content with life as they have it in a dovecot', as the *Saturday Review* had apostrophized her. Perhaps she was the only one among the four types who was not exactly duplicated in the United States – duplicated, that is, in terms of the conventions which bound her life. Certainly the intellectual and athletic types were well represented, and the Northern cities also had their own variety of the 'chum'. But in the case of the Top Nation home-bird, the differences from American characteristics were sufficiently noticeable to suggest a separate species.

There is a revealing example of the difference between American and English rules of propriety as they affected the average Top Nation young lady in Gwen Raverat's *Period Piece* which describes her life as a child in Cambridge, England, during the last fifteen years of Victoria's reign. Gwen's mother was an American, Maud du Puy, who had been introduced to Cambridge by her aunt, Caroline Jebb, widow of an American army officer and subsequently, in 1874, married to an Englishman, Richard Jebb, who became Professor of Greek at Cambridge. Gwen's father was George Darwin, the second of Charles Darwin's five sons. The George Darwins lived opposite the Jebbs, so that Gwen was brought up in an ambiance with strong American overtones, for Caroline Jebb was as forceful as she was attractive. Gwen's mother, soon after she settled in England, wrote home about the 'hard time' that 'the poor English girls' had, 'excepting in Alice Balfour's class, where they are more like American girls'. Those who were not 'gold lace hats' like Alice Balfour were under rigorous surveillance, 'but the upper middle class', wrote Maud Darwin, 'think they are acting rightly by over-protecting their daughters'. If the girls had been allowed to be as independent as they were at home, she said, they would have been thought fast. Maud was indignant about the etiquette of chaperonage which prevented a girl going to a dance in two undergraduates' rooms, even though the girl was to be chaperoned by two most correct Cambridge ladies, because the girl's mother was not also asked on account of the smallness of the rooms. 'It seems unutterably vulgar to me that girls, who are well brought up, and sons who are well brought up, should not be allowed to associate, without every girl having her mother at her elbow, to see that no indecency is committed. The real truth,' she asserted, 'is that the chaperons want the power in their own hands, and I believe, though they protest against it, they really enjoy the dances.'[1]

Mrs Darwin clearly considered herself to be, 'and really was' her daughter affirmed, more unconventional and broad-minded than the English ladies; 'and yet, later on, we young ones

[1] Quoted in Gwen Raverat, *Period Piece, A Cambridge Childhood* (Faber and Faber, 1952), pp. 99 and 100.

thought her distinctly more proper than they were. Perhaps the truth was that she was more puritanical, in an old-fashioned early-American way, while they were more concerned with gentility and appearances. The English ladies would not have been as shocked as she was, when she heard Spurgeon preach, and wrote: "Some of his sentences were hardly refined, as, 'We need the Lord to back us'.'" Presumably the phrase offended her because it was a betting one. On the other hand it is doubtful whether any of the English ladies would have bicycled, as Maud Darwin once did, from one end of Cambridge to the other, dressed as Santa Claus, beard and all. 'But I think', wrote her daughter, 'she was more particular than they were about such matters as bathing and undressing; and though parties were all right, she would never allow friendly couples to go anywhere alone together, no matter how old or respectable they might be.'[1]

Dressed with Decency

Propriety involved dress as much as behaviour. Writing from Weybridge to her friend Miss Senior on a sweltering day in June 1862, Mrs Sarah Austin said that it was so hot she felt she ought rather to make her will than attempt a visit. 'One difficulty is the necessity of being dressed with *decency*. The costume I wish to adopt is that in which I found the Princess Villafranca [in Malta] – a shift (of the simplest and most primitive cut), a large black lace shawl, a pair of silk slippers (feet bare), and a huge fan (N.B. she was fatter than I am). This I call a reasonable dress for this weather; but ... as Lady W. Russell said, the English conclude if your dress is loose, that your morals are also. In that case I am thoroughly dissolute.'

For the rest of Victoria's reign and beyond – up until the dress revolution caused by the First World War – there was no relaxation. Hot weather or a quick errand was no excuse for casual dress. As late as 1916 or 1917 when the author's mother, by then an Honours graduate of Glasgow University, a schoolmistress, and a married woman, was staying with an uncle in Leith she was violently berated by him for bringing shame to his house because she had gone out to post a letter to her husband in France without putting on her hat and her gloves. The pillarbox was five paces from the front door!

[1] ibid.

334

Nor did the fashions of the second half of the reign tend much towards comfort. With the passing of crinoline and the revival of tight lacing in the mid-1860s, the brief years of freedom from constriction and clutter were over. Not until the 1920s was there a return to that classical under-dressed form of fashion that had flourished in the Napoleonic wars a hundred years earlier. Crinoline, it is true, had imposed its own sort of clutter, but it had kept petticoats away from women's legs and made walking 'so light and easy', as Gwen Raverat's Aunt Etty told her. What followed it was enclosure and elaboration, with curves dominating the essential shape.

From 1863 crinoline changed gradually into crinolette with an enormous bustle at the back and the hitched-up skirt becoming a short overskirt. The colours were loud and clashing, implying, it would seem, a psychological disharmony that was also evident in those other contemporary 'wild disturbances of the female mind'. Underclothing was heavily embroidered, to the extent that one magazine called the amount of embroidery 'sinful' and added, with no great understanding of the female instinct, that such embroidering was wasteful on a garment 'which it was scarcely possible that any other human being except her laundress would ever see'. There was also a great surge of hair-mindedness. A woman's hair was her crowning glory – as indeed a man's exuberant hair and beard was his. Towards the end of the 1860s chignons became fashionable and sold at from thirty to sixty shillings each. *Echoes*, for example, reported continuously about chignons. 'Frisettes' too had an extensive sale. One firm was turning out two tons of them a week; they were small clusters of curls worn on the forehead. Although *Echoes* printed a note from Paris in February 1869 that chignons were 'to be abolished and false hair repudiated altogether' it was 1873 before chignons went out in Britain. Painting the face also became common among the fastest sort of fashionable lady about this time. 'Mind the Paint' was the punning caption of an *Echoes* cartoon. Powder and rouge, however, were not the emblems of respectability.

Elaborate trimmings were fashionable – looped-up skirts, aprons and tunics draped with large bows. One fashion magazine of the day described the latest trend thus: 'The tournure, of white horse hair, arranged in a number of puffs, is worn over a scanty jupon which has only a few steel circles round the bottom; two skirts, one plain, the other flounced, are worn over it. Flounces by themselves are not sufficient trimmings and must be completed by fluted trimmings.' The trend continued and reached such a pitch in 1875 that an article in the *Saturday Review* entitled 'Fashions Run Mad' talked about senseless frills, bows which tied nothing, buttons which had no use. 'A dress is considered a perfect fit when a lady can neither raise her arms nor use her legs; the fashions of the last six or seven years are certainly more picturesque than those of the crinoline days. From the way in which the female form is made up, from the false hair streaming over the shoulder, to the toes pinched in high-heeled boots throwing the weight of the body with its enormous humps and hoops on to the toes, the seeming giantess must surely prove a terrible dwarf to her husband when divested of her garnishing.'

The foot had now become a feature of sex attraction. High heels produced no calves and thin ankles. A woman who wanted to attract a man's attention would play with her feet, although in making a circular movement with her foot she could always plead that she was only carrying out an exercise to keep her ankles slim. In 1873 the points needed for a good figure were a well-developed bust, a tapering waist and large hips. The tapering waist, of course, was achieved by tight-laced corsets which Dr C. Willett Cunnington, the doyen of women's fashion historians, described as 'a happy contrivance . . . to inflame the passions of one sex while restraining those of the other'.[1]

The hobble skirt of 1875 was achieved by tying the back of it with interior tapes so that the main portion became close fitting and the rest trailed behind in a short mud-collecting train. This Princess shape necessitated the wearing of combinations, which by 1878 were 'universally worn' – or so the fashion magazines said. There were also cuirasse bodices which were like over-stays. For the evening nothing was worn under the bodice. This was the Aesthetic period, the time of Oscar Wilde and greenery-yallery that was so mercilessly satirized in Gilbert and Sullivan's *Patience*, first produced in 1881. 'The apostles of the new cult,' wrote Cunnington, 'were Greek in their looks, Pagan in their emotions, Cinquecento in intellect, Queen Anne in their curtains and Japanese in their pots – in effect, super orna-mental.'

[1] C. W. Cunnington, op. cit., p. 218.

Throughout the '80s until about 1887 there was a second bustle era, differing radically in shape from the first bustle of the early '70s. 'Then it had formed, as it were, an integral curve in the opulent undulations of the dress, and expressed an exaggeration of the sexual features of the wearer. It was therefore a part of the armour of sex attraction. But the Bustle of the '80s projected not in an alluring curve but as a bold promontory jutting out at right angles from the trunk.'[1] The front of the skirt was draped to give the impression of semi-pregnancy, for the bustle in the '80s was, in Cunnington's opinion, essentially an unconscious expression of a maternal craving, whereas the bustle of the '70s had been inspired by the mating instinct. 'As the old century passes onwards towards the new, this differentiation of woman's sexual instinct into its two component parts becomes more and more marked. She was beginning, at least subconsciously, to distinguish between them and to search for means of satisfying, often only by sublimation, their respective needs.' The dominance of curves indicated an unsatisfied sex instinct. Formerly, although the sexes had been in the main segregated, early marriage had supplied a solution. But the rising age of marriage caused by the social need to keep up with the rising standard of living delayed the solution, if it did not remove it altogether; instinct protested and found expression for its protest in an unconscious burlesque of the forbidden subject in dress.

The mating instinct symbols were sadistic forms (for instance, dead animals and insects as ornaments), as well as draping and painting, and ornaments with male significance. The maternal instinct symbols on the other hand were the bustle, the kitten-in-the-basket type of decoration, and the ornamental, cuddly, small animal. When Margot Tennant, aged twenty-one, went down to Aldworth, near Haslemere, in 1885 to be introduced to Tennyson by his second son Lionel, who was one of the Souls, she wore a scarlet cloak trimmed with cock's feathers and a black, three-cornered hat. It was clearly not the maternal instinct of the future Lady Oxford and Asquith that was dominant that day. The cruelty of bird slaughter for ornaments to hats became enormous at this period, and no attention was paid to the many articles in periodicals condemning it. Cunnington suggests that 'the cruelty merely stimulated the sadistic

[1] ibid., pp. 252 and 254.

craving, for it seemed to take the place of those flagellations and funeral orgies of the past'. In 1884 there were fashion notes of 'red silk stockings covered with black swallows', and the newest thing for the shoulder of a bold dress was 'velvet loops with a few white mice seemingly playing about them'. Women would also wear dog collars round their necks and have model railway engines as earrings.

Drape, drape, drape – that was the compulsion of the 1880s. The fireplace had to be hidden behind trellises, the walls behind draperies. Bulrushes had to be varnished to stand in draped drainpipes. The dinner bell must be draped to look like a statuette. The matchbox had to look like a castle.

This sort of thing, it is true, had been evident earlier in the reign. As we have seen in Chapter 7 an article on 'Recent Decorative Art' at the time of the Great Exhibition had called that the 'age of shams' in which everything had to be 'something else'. But the heights to which the disguising of realism attained at the end of the '70s and in the '80s was in a different class altogether.

By the end of the decade the Aesthetic craze had reached over towards romanticism and there was even a tendency towards crinoline again, although this was baulked by the growing democratic spirit which would never have countenanced the selfish pretentiousness of full crinoline. Dresses were on the whole ugly. The bustle shrank, ribbons and bows flourished, large wide hats appeared. Underclothing was romantic and fashionable ladies began to wear what Dr Spooner might have called gownless evening-straps. As the 1890s came in 'the fashions in dress, obeying the impulse which had started towards the end of the previous decade, developed', in Cunnington's view, 'a curious resemblance to the sequence seen in the '20s; a growing elaboration of the upper half, with expansion of the shoulder line and upper half of the sleeve, until in 1893 a full-grown "leg-of-mutton" provided a feast for the eye. At the same time vandyking above the hem, pointed waists and angular sloping lines from the shoulders carried out the superficial resemblance – but with a fundamental difference. The emotional impulse was restrained by Fear, and Prudery aped Romance. The huge sleeve, instead of suggesting a rapturous exuberance, was hard and formal, and the habit of making it of different material from the rest of the bodice, with a heavier tone, served to distract the eye from more intimate regions . . . The skirt underwent important changes. Modern conditions required a less hampering structure, but propriety necessitated that there should be no revelations. These requirements were beautifully met by a gored skirt.'[1]

Before the end of the century, however, this belligerent fashion was replaced by a return to femininity. The huge sleeve disappeared and the muscular symbolism of the 'leg-of-mutton' gave way to tight, long sleeves that emphasized the elegance and weakness of the wearer. And the rest of the ensemble followed this thought. The figure returned. The tightly swathed bodice displayed what art or nature had provided. Longer-waisted rigid stays and soft, unstarched petticoats under a skirt, tightly fitting round the hips and made on the circular form, made the woman of fashion 'a miracle of curves and grace', to use the words of a lady's magazine of 1899. The return of curves showed that woman, even the New Woman, had not rejected her womanhood after all.

'If You Compete with Us We Shan't Marry You'

It was only to be expected that the pressure for greater oppor-tunities for women should arouse enmity and awaken old fears in men. Men had no wish to see women as equals. The main lines of the argument were clearly stated in a discussion that Beatrice Potter had with Professor Alfred Marshall of Cam-bridge, England, in March 1889, three years before her marriage to Sidney Webb. It was a chaffing sort of argument but it had those serious undertones which exemplified entrenched positions. Marshall's line was that woman was a subordinate being, 'and that, if she ceased to be subordinate, there would be no object for a man to marry. That marriage was a sacrifice of masculine freedom and would only be tolerated by the male creatures so long as it meant the devotion, body and soul, of the female to the male. Hence the woman must not develop her faculties in a way unpleasant to the man: that strength, courage, indepen-dence were not attractive in women; that rivalry in men's pursuits was positively unpleasant. Hence masculine strength and masculine ability in women must be firmly trampled on and boycotted by men. *Contrast* was the essence of the matrimonial relation: feminine weakness contrasted with masculine strength:

[1] ibid., pp. 286–7.

masculine egotism with feminine self-devotion. "If you compete with us we shan't marry you," he summed up with a laugh. The laugh may have removed the sting, but the threat covered a genuine ultimatum.

Beatrice maintained a different argument, 'that what you needed was not different qualities and different defects' in men and women 'but the same virtues working in different directions, and dedicated to the service of the community in different ways'.[1] It was the same argument as Josephine Butler had advanced.

Beatrice at that time was no feminist. Indeed, in the spring of 1889 she joined with others in signing a manifesto, very notorious at the time, which was drafted by Mrs Humphry Ward, the novelist and niece of Matthew Arnold, and by some other distinguished ladies, setting forth their case against the political enfranchisement of women. By signing it Beatrice, to some extent, undermined her reputation as an impartial investigator of women's questions. The manifesto was indignantly refuted by Mrs Fawcett and Mrs Ashton Dilke, wife of Sir Charles Dilke's younger brother and sister of Mrs Virginia Crawford, who caused Dilke's downfall. James Knowles, editor of *The Nineteenth Century*, and Frederick Harrison pressed Beatrice to write an answer to the retorts of Mrs Fawcett and Mrs Dilke. But she was unwilling to do so because she found herself out of sympathy with them. In her diary she noted that she was not sure whether her strong prejudice against political life and political methods as a whole was not the real influence on her judgement over the question of enfranchising women. Despite her doubts it was nearly twenty years before she made a public recantation.

Beatrice never suffered the restrictions normally placed on women. This, more than anything else, made her anti-feminist in her earlier years, and her frank avowal that this was the case shows that the woman question was not always argued on strict philosophical grounds, but that during the course of woman's emancipation in Victoria's reign personal experience had most to do with the attitudes adopted. Furthermore, it shows yet again how important was the behaviour and attitude of the individual Victorian father towards his daughters in determining their adult approach to the true position of women in life.

[1] Beatrice Webb, *My Apprenticeship*, p. 351.

Most, it seems fair to say, had no need to worry about Professor Marshall's threat. They were either, like the young married lady of Hepworth Dixon's acquaintance in New York, 'very fond of being taken care of', or, like Mary Booth, they were busy with their homes and their families. Indeed if one had to choose a single individual to represent the Victorian woman the choice could fall on none better than Mary Booth, putting buckets under the drips, bringing up a large family, knitting her husband's stockings, arranging sewing bees, and with rigorous anonymity contributing to the work that was to help the world progress.

Index

343

Index

Index

Midnight Meeting Movement 229, 230
Mill, John Stuart 101, 107, 186, 187, 194, 245, 279
Mills, textile 74, 76–8. 96, 98–100, 106–10, 318, 319
Milliners 83, 85–7, 99
Mines, women and children in 78–82, 94–6, 321
Mines Act (1842) 80–2, 109, 319
Mitchell, Dr 80
Mitchison, Mrs Naomi 293
Montagu, Lady Mary Wortley 146, 167
Moral Physiology 102, 103, 170, 279
More, Hannah 144
Mormons 172, 173
Morning Chronicle 192–5
Morning Post 314
Mothers of England 48, 133
Mott, Mrs Lucretia (*née* Coffin) 164, 165, 171
Mott's (Portland Rooms) 220, 221
Mount Holyoke 168, 169
Mourning 83, 84, 338
Mozley, Anne 195
Mudie's Library 26, 203, 210
Murray, Miss 152
Murray, Mrs Judith Sargent 167

Napoleon III 116, 121
Nation, The 276
National Association for the Promotion of Social Science 160
'National minimum' 309, 310, 318, 320
National Reformer 285, 286
National Secular Society 287
National Woman Suffrage Association 188–90, 253
Needlewomen's Institution, The 227
Needlework 61, 62, 72
Neff, Wanda F. 82, 104, 106, 110, 319
Nethercot, A. H. 282, 283, 285
Nevill, Lady Dorothy 32, 34–6, 125
Neville-Grenville, Lady C. 39
Newnham College 185, 239, 295, 328
New Woman, the 326, 327, 339
Night-houses 213, 220, 221
Nightingale, Mrs Fanny 41, 42, 154, 156
Nightingale, Florence 13, 22, 41–4, 62, 67, 125 151, 154–6, 234, 244, 278, 292
Noel, Rev. Baptist 229
Nineteenth Century 307, 340
North London Collegiate School 153
Norton, Hon. Mrs C. 41, 156, 157, 192

Noyes, J. H. 177–9, 275
Nursing 42, 154, 156, 203, 294, 322, 323

Oberlin College 168, 169, 267
Obscene Publications Act (1857) 285, 288
Oneida Creek, N.Y. 177–9, 275
O'Neill, W. L. 170, 266
Origin of Species, The 210, 310
Ordeal of Richard Feverel, The 33, 210
Owen, Robert 170
Owen, Robert Dale 102, 170, 179, 279
Oxford and Cambridge Local Exams. 184, 296
Oxford University 184, 235, 295, 296, 326

Pall Mall Gazette 231, 264, 265
Paper patterns 131, 132
Parkes, Bessie Rayner (later Mme Belloc) 48, 67, 68, 105, 148, 149, 153, 158, 159, 187, 271
Paris Commune 30, 272
Patience 336
Patmore, Coventry 195, 200
Paxton, Sir Joseph 113, 116
Pearl, Cyril 215, 216, 229
Pembroke, 13th Earl of 217
Penny Post 62, 192
Percival, Alicia 149, 150
Percy, Mrs 254–7
Perfectionists 172, 173, 176–9, 275
Perry, Sir Erskine 156, 157
Philanstery, the 193
Philanthropy 153–5, 229, 239, 300, 303
Phillips, Wendell 253
Phossy-jaw 94
Pinchbeck, Dr Ivy 46, 76, 80, 89, 96, 98
Pittsburgh Visiter 166
Place, Francis 100, 103, 108, 279
Plomer, Wm 206
Poor Law Act (1834) 32, 88
Poor law administration 292, 293
'Poor-peopling' (*see also* Philanthropy) 42, 62, 63, 238, 299, 312
Population of Great Britain 45, 46, 56, 71, 72, 111, 137, 140, 158, 270, 274, 318. P. of Ireland 71, 72, 158, 318. P. of the U.S.A. 162
Population, Royal Commission on 281, 282
Pornography 211, 285

348

Index

Index

Smiles, Samuel 310
Smith, Barbara Leigh (later Mme Bodichon) 13, 154–9, 251
Smith, Benjamin 155
Smith College 169
Smith, Joseph 173
Smith, Dr Southwood 78, 306
Smoking 204, 323, 327, 329, 332
Snow, Dr John 51
Social Democratic Federation 311, 312
Society for Promoting the Due Observance of the Lord's Day 55, 56
Society for Promoting the Employment of Women 159
Society for the Prevention of Cruelty to Children 263
Somerville College 295
'Song of the Shirt' 85, 87
Speenhamland Act (1795) 88
Spencer, Herbert 310
Spenlow, Dora 13, 63
Spiritualism 174, 188, 275
Spurgeon, C. H. 215, 334
Stafford, Ann 258
Stansfeld, J. B. 249, 257, 258
Stanton, Mrs Elizabeth (née Cady) 13, 164–6, 168, 169, 171, 173, 188, 189, 253
Stead, W. T. 231, 264, 265
Stephen, Sir Leslie 195
Stevenson, Mrs Sallie (née Coles) 33–5, 64, 301
Stockham, Dr Alice Bunker 179
Stone, Lucy (later Mrs H. B. Blackwell) 165, 166, 173, 176, 185, 188, 190, 253, 267
Storks, Sir H. 245, 249
Stowe, Harriet Beecher 182
Strachey, Lytton 11
Strachey, Ray 161
Strangford, Viscount 194
Straw-plaiting 72, 74
Subjection of Women, The 186, 187
Sumner, Celestine 278
Sunday school 21, 58, 144, 149
Surplus men 162, 163
Surplus women 66, 162
Swedenborg, Emanuel 174
Swisshelm, Jane 166
Sybil 42, 99

Taine, Hippolyte 54, 55, 69, 86, 96, 163
Tait, Archbishop 279

Taylor, Dr C. Bell 243
Taylor, Harriet 186
Taylor, Mary 324
Taylor, R. W. Cooke 97
Telegraphy 12, 72
Temperance movement 117, 166, 171, 227, 253
Tennis 331
Tennyson, Alfred (Lord) 141, 145, 146, 182, 327, 328, 337
Tennyson, Lionel 337
Textile and dress manufacture 71–3, 158, 270, 318
Textile industries 73, 76, 77, 108–10, 114, 318–20
Thackeray, W. M. 61, 150, 303
Thistlethwayte, Mrs (née Bell, Laura) 13, 214, 215, 219
Thompson, Mrs Flora (née Timms) 313–17, 330
Tight lacing 120, 205, 297, 332, 335, 336, 339
Tilt, Dr E. J. 120, 121, 126, 127, 138, 139, 150
Tilton, Mrs Elizabeth 189
Times, The 68, 122, 123, 208, 210, 216, 242, 243, 273, 287, 301
Timms, Flora, *see* Thompson, Mrs Flora
Timms, Mrs 313, 317, 318
Todd, Rev. John 276
Tooke, Thomas 78
'Toy trade' 72, 92–4, 96
Trade, increase in British 111, 270
Trade unions 33, 108, 299, 316, 320, 321
Transport revolution 12
Travelling 12, 35, 36, 181
Tricycles 330
Trollope, Anthony 28, 180, 181, 183
Trollope, Mrs Frances 27, 28, 58, 76, 170
Troy Female Seminary 168
Truth of Woman 173–5, 267
Tuckniss, Rev. Wm. 227–31
Tufnell, Mr 78
Tunkers 172, 173
Two Generations 267, 293

Una, The 166
University College, London 153, 323
University education for women, *see* Education, higher, for women
U.K. Alliance 117